# MILITARY ANALYSIS
# OF THE REVOLUTIONARY WAR

## An Anthology by the Editors of
## Military Affairs

Introduction by
DON HIGGINBOTHAM

kto press

A U.S. Division of Kraus-Thomson Organization Limited
Millwood, N.Y.

*Reprinted with permission of the American Military Institute.*

**Library of Congress Cataloging in Publication Data**

Main entry under title:

Military analysis of the Revolutionary War.

   1. United States—History—Revolution, 1775-1783—Campaigns and battles—Addresses, essays, lectures. I. Military affairs.
E230.M47       973.3       76-41551
ISBN 0-527-63580-4

Printed in the United States of America

# Table of Contents

# INTRODUCTION

The essays from *Military Affairs* included in this volume appear at a time when interest in the bicentennial is still strong, although we are now beyond 1976. Antiquarianism and chauvinism are among the reasons for this interest, not the best motives for serious historical study. There are, however, better incentives for continuing to examine the American Revolution, and I hope that they also play some part.

Ours was the first of the modern revolutions carried out in the name of freedom, and it involved a protracted, painful military struggle with Great Britain that lasted over eight years—our longest war prior to the Vietnam conflict. We are now in the midst of what Richard B. Morris has termed a "Neo-Revolutionary Era." New nations, the products of revolution and war, blanket the maps of Africa and Asia. Wars by their nature often shape the course of revolutions, as do the previous experiences of revolutionists with military force and other forms of violence. Also significant is the extent to which insurgents are assisted in securing their objectives —usually paramount is control of the state— by outsiders. The relationship between war and revolution, particularly in the American Revolution, is dealt with in a variety of ways in the literary offerings found in *Military Analysis of the Revolutionary War*. As in all such collections, they vary in quality; but as a whole they represent some of the best Revolutionary War scholarship available, and deserve re-publication. Since the articles initially reached print during a period of approximately forty years, they shed light on the field of military history in general and the place of the Revolutionary War in military history in particular.

Few of the articles were penned by professional soldiers; however, during much of our past, at least until the end of World War II, military men dominated as writers of military history. In fact, from the late nineteenth century they had almost a complete monopoly on the study of battles and campaigns.

Why did soldiers-scholars neglect the formative period of our military development? The answer in part is that from General Emory Upton onward, our own warriors found negative rather than positive lessons in the American Revolution. The chief weakness of the Revolution, they felt, was the absence of a large, well-trained army enlisted for a long period of time or for the duration of the conflict. Washington and the other American generals were bedeviled by inexperienced, poorly trained regulars and by the militia. Owing partly to these negative factors, the war was primarily a defensive struggle for Americans. We gained our independence in spite of ourselves, thanks to a generous portion of foreign assistance and British miscalculation. For the professional military historian, therefore, the annals of the Revolution were a nightmare.

A second reason soldier-intellectuals have neglected our Revolutionary past is well stated by Russell Weigley in his provocative book, *The American Way of War: A History of United States Military Strategy and Policy* (New York: Macmillan, 1973). Washington was a defensive strategist; military planners in later years, however, were inspired by Napoleon, who ushered in an offensive style, the strategy of annihilation. In America, too, the preferred strategy became the offensive, not a surprising development in light of America's growth in manpower and material resources in the nineteenth century. From the Mexican War onward, Americans have sought quick, decisive victories. Even with the lack of a sizable regular army during an outbreak of hostilities, America was always able to mobilize somewhat quickly because of her overall internal strength and managed to implement the strategy of annihilation. Yet, as Weigley notes, such an approach to war has been less valid in the post-1945 era than it was for the Lincoln administration in the Civil War or for the Franklin Roosevelt administration in the Second World War. But if Weigley is urging a careful reconsideration of our Revolutionary military history, it must be preceded by a look at the attitudes and practices toward the military that evolved during the colonial decades.

Actually, this scholarly inquiry has been in progress for some time, and several contributors to *Military Affairs* have helped to chart its course. Clarence C. Clendenen's brief appeal for significant research in the field of colonial history, "A Little Known Period of American Military History," was followed three years later by a lengthy article by Louis Morton. A Duke University Ph.D., then with the Office of Military History, Department of the Army, and later a professor at Dartmouth College, Morton was one of the historians influential in causing military history to become a respectable field of study in colleges and universities following World War II. Military concerns, Morton reminds us, have always figured prominently in our history. That the colonists were expected to provide for their own defense is seen in the 1628 charter of the Massachusetts Bay Colony, which placed the responsibility upon the settlers "to incounter, expulse, repell and resist by forces of armes, as well as by sea and by lands" any and all invaders. Up and down the Atlantic seaboard Anglo-Americans established a militia system, and in so doing, dusted off and refurbished a military institution that the mother country had rejected in favor of a long-service professional army. Hence, the American tradition of the citizen-soldier as opposed to the military professional—a tradition that has been hotly debated throughout our history—dates from our earliest beginnings.

The militia laws provided for virtually all free, white men to become part of the military structure, to possess their own firearms, and to train a set number of days yearly. By the end of the seventeenth century, concludes Morton, "the militia system was firmly established . . . in one form or another, it remained an integral part of the nation's military policy for almost two more centuries." Further, "the obligation of universal service on which it was based, though often ignored, has never been abandoned. It con-

stitutes yet today the basis of our military organization." Sidney Forman points out in his essay, "Thomas Jefferson on Universal Military Training," that even such a confirmed anti-militarist as Jefferson had no quarrel with the concept of universal military training, since such a system for the militia would strengthen that defensive arm and make the country less dependent upon a regular army.

The militia, however, like all human institutions, was far more complex than our generalizations indicate. In those colonies where warfare was a frequent occurrence, it tended to be more efficient and effective, as in Massachusetts, whose early militia organization is surveyed by Jack S. Radabaugh. Massachusetts was aided defensively by the cohesive pattern of settlement, the clustering of its population in towns, and could more easily find men for distant service while leaving the community relatively secure than could colonists in the rural south.

It was in Massachusetts, of course, that the militia first challenged Britain's military might in the opening rounds of the American Revolution. How the militia in one Massachusetts town prepared itself for the task is explored in Ronald L. Boucher's examination of the local regiment in Salem. "The dramatic changes in the militia after 1774," Boucher asserts, "stemmed partly from the sudden demand that it become militarily more effective, but the colonists also sought to make the militia conform with patriotic attitudes." This latter objective was accomplished in Salem and other towns by a combination of peaceful persuasion and violence; officers of loyalist inclinations either resigned when asked to do so or were physically intimidated. So it was with Colonel Peter Frye and Major William Browne, both of whom witnessed the destruction of their property and consequently fled for protection to General Gage's British army in Boston.

Gage himself as commander-in-chief is the subject of an essay by Henry P. Beers; the Massachusetts militia's showdown with that general is the theme of Allen French's article, "The British Expedition to Concord, Massachusetts, in 1775." French, a native of Concord and a fine patrician historian in the New England tradition of Parkman and Prescott, probably knew more about the events of 1775 in the Bay colony than anyone has or perhaps ever will. Much of the rich distillation of his scholarship from such books as *The Day of Concord and Lexington: Nineteenth of April, 1775* (Spartanburg, S.C.: Reprint, 1975), *General Gage's Informers* (Westport, Conn.: Greenwood, 1968), and *First Year of the American Revolution* (New York: Octagon, 1967), may be found in his important contribution to *Military Affairs* included in this volume. Gage's inability to keep his plan to seize the Concord munitions a secret, Captain Parker's symbolic stand on Lexington green, the success of the citizens of Concord at removing most of the military stores before the enemy arrived, all helped touch off, in the words of the *Newport Mercury*, "the American Revolutionary War, which will hereafter fill an important page in History."[1]

Why were raw American militiamen not intimidated by Britain's veteran army? And more importantly, why did they so deeply resent the presence of scarlet regiments in their midst in Massachusetts? One gets some insight into these questions from J. Alan Roger's article "Colonial Opposition to the Quartering of Troops During the French and Indian War." Even when royal forces had been present in America in the 1750s during the last of the imperial wars, the colonists had viewed their presence as at best a mixed blessing. European armies, and Britain's was not an exception, invariably drew their rank and file from the lowest sectors of society— ignorant country boys beguiled by liquor and false promises, the poor, the unemployed, vagabonds, criminals pardoned on condition they shoulder royal muskets. During the French and Indian War, British commanders had insisted on billeting services from Americans. Provincial assemblies usually rendered succor, albeit not to the full extent sought by British officers. Americans complained because there were in the colonies exceedingly

[1]*Newport Mercury*, 24 April 1775.

few unoccupied public buildings and unoccupied houses. Several colonies were especially hard hit—Pennsylvania, New York, and Massachusetts—because they were staging areas for British campaigns against Canada.

Somehow these controversies were resolved, but they left a bad taste in the mouths of Americans, who for the first time in their history had experienced "a standing army" in their presence; and history—especially seventeenth century English history—taught that professional armies composed of the flotsam and jetsam of society always posed a threat to morality and liberty. But if the threat, on reflection, was relatively minor in the 1750s, it was much greater when British forces returned to New England to compel obedience to obnoxious Parliamentary laws, including quartering legislation aimed specifically at the colonists. When Gage's troops set out to seize the stores at Concord, they were opposed by farmer-militiamen who considered themselves morally superior and more highly motivated than the Redcoats who fought for pay instead of for rights and liberties.

The patriots were not the only ones to idealize the concept of citizen-soldier, especially the militia, in the War of Independence. The French, whose government gave the rebels secret support from the outset (and later in 1778 when they entered the conflict on the American side formally), believed it as well. Three essays included herein by Orville T. Murphy—one of them co-authored by Durand Echeverria—explore Bourbon attitudes. French writers romanticized the American militia as being conformers to the laws of nature. The use of productive citizens, not hirelings, to fight in a contest for freedom seemed only reasonable in an Age of Reason; it seemed the natural way to make war. Totally fearless American militiamen, according to the French press, surged forward by the thousands to repel the invading mercenaries. "All the Anglo-Americans," boasted the *Gazette de Leyde*, "breathed the same courage, the same desire of defending their rights and their liberties . . . to the last individual."[2] Even "old men disputed with the young for the glory of defending their homes and serving under the standard of liberty."[3]

Murphy rightly underscores the parallel between the French popular image of the militia and the subsequent French notion of the *levée en masse*, the harnessing of hordes of citizens rather than establishing a small professional army, in the conflicts of the French Revolution and the Napoleonic Era. Although the French concept did not originate with their observations about America, Murphy points out that the "idea of a nation in arms to preserve its liberties had already become an integral part . . . of late eighteenth century thought. It represented the corollary of force, or the military consequence, of ideals which characterized this period of military consequence, of ideals which characterized this period of intellectual history." The American Revolutionary experience seemingly gave meaning "to a set of abstractions already prevalent."

There is much to be said for the view of the American Revolution as a people's war—the theme of John Shy's recent *A People Numerous and Armed: Reflections on the Military Struggle for American Independence* (New York: Oxford University Press, 1976). Nevertheless, Shy and other scholars advance such an interpretation only with significant qualifications. Not all Americans were insurgents. Estimates vary, but current research suggests that at least twenty percent of the free, white population sided with the crown; and the British endeavored to raise military units from their own followers, as one sees from reading John R. Cuneo's account, "The Early Days of the Queen's Rangers." As months and years dragged by, apathy and war-weariness increased. Thomas Paine's *The Crisis* all too accurately depicted great numbers of his countrymen as sunshine patriots and summer soldiers. And the militia, even when it turned out in force, proved to be far less effective than the philosophes in the Paris saloons thought it to be.

French officers on the scene in America, observes Murphy, often expressed a much more unflattering opinion of the militia. Layfayette, for one, recognized the frailties of American irregulars, but he felt it desirable to hide their weaknesses from foreign eyes. Thus, on one occasion, he advised Washington against a massive call-up of the militia, for it would likely bring a disappointing response and would consequently tarnish the Old World view of American military prowess. "Europe has a great idea of our being able to raise when we please an immense army of militia," he cautioned. It was crucial to maintain this "phantom," for "the American interest has always been . . . to let the world believe that we are stronger than we ever expect to be."[4]

Did the militia, then, make any contribution at all in the American Revolution? And if so, what was its role in relation to that of American regulars—that is, to the Continental army under General Washington? The answer to the first question is decidedly affirmative. The accomplishments of the militia were impressive, and they occurred in the very sectors where the Continental army could exert minimal influence at times. To be sure, the militia was always poorly outfitted —as we learn from Hugh Jameson's article, "Equipment for the Militia of the Middle States, 1775-1781," and complex operations were invariably their undoing—as Henry I. Shaw, Jr. indicates in his examination of Massachusett's ill-fated Penobscot Assault on the coast of British-held Maine in 1779. Nor can one ignore the contemporary complaints that the state constabularies were ill-disciplined, wasteful, and distasteful to many patriots because of their tendency to tar-and-feather or even to shoot first and ask questions later.

Nevertheless, the militia at the outset of the Revolution helped the patriots gain or solidify their control of the machinery of

[2]*Gazette de Leyde*, "Supplement" 4 July 1775.

[3]Hilliard d'Auberteuil, *Essais historiques et politiques sur les Anglo-Americains* (Bruxelles, 1782), volume 1, pt. 2, p. 185; *see also* the *Gazette de France*, 25 August 1775.

[4]Marie Joseph Lafayette, *The Letters of Lafayette to Washington: 1777-1779*, ed. Louis Gottshalk (New York: Priv. print. by Helen F. Hubbard, 1944), p. 12.

government in the colonies. Everywhere they had a hand in toppling royal authority. Consequently, unlike most revolutionaries at other times and places, the Americans in 1775 began their insurgency in control of a vast (if far from perfect) military organization: the militia. As an anonymous French officer expressed it, "When the Royalists were driven out, the Americans seized the forts, arsenals, and all the military stores which the British has been forced to abandon." In military terms, the months immediately preceding and following the outbreak of fighting in Massachusetts were quite likely the most significant of all. The loyalists were to remain permanently on the defensive, and wherever British legions disembarked, they were met with resistance. Repeatedly the militia bludgeoned the Tories, beat back Indian raids, and harassed enemy foraging and reconnaissance parties. Nowhere were they more effective in partisan or guerilla operations than in the South. (Jac Weller's discussion of partisan weapons tactics focuses on the special talents of local militia chieftains such as Francis Marion and Thomas Sumter.) In short, the labors of the irregulars on the home front were indispensable.

Washington recognized as early as 1775 that the Continentals and militia should perform different but complimentary duties in the war. His army could not do all things, could not be in all places, could not contend with both Redcoats and Tories on all occasions. While the militia took on the Revolution's internal foes, the Tories, the American regulars would adhere to the military principle of concentration or mass. Hence, throughout the conflict Washington remained near the main British army.

There were, of course, numerous other aspects of the War of Independence. Washington spent endless hours in military administration, trying to hold together an army that always threatened to come apart because of desertions, bureaucratic snarls, and squabbles between his senior officers in distant departments. Desertion always plagued Washington; he lost more than twenty percent of his army from unauthorized departures. For this and other reasons, the Virginian was a stern disciplinarian, as Maurer Maurer concludes in "Military Justice Under General Washington," although on the whole desertion and other offenses brought less severe punishment than in the British army.

The medical administrators of the revolutionary army added to Washington's headaches, according to Howard L. Applegate's investigation of that subject. There were jurisdictional rivalries between regimental hospitals and general army hospitals, and a succession of directors of the Continental Medical Service came under fire for mismanagement, although no new controversies erupted in the final two years of the war while Dr. John Cochran occupied the top post. Some problems, to Washington's way of thinking, were better left to the Continental Congress. Certainly one was the appointment and removal of commanders in the area outside the Middle States region where his own army spent most of the war. Even so, he anguished over the quarrel that tore the Northern Department and seriously weakened for a time the effectiveness of the American army endeavoring to halt the southward stab from Canada in 1777 of General John Burgoyne's Anglo-German forces. In a most judicious essay, Paul David Nelson suggests that Gates, Schuyler, and Arnold all deserve substantial credit for defeating Burgoyne at Saratoga, and were thus responsible for halting the last British attempt to cut the American states in half along the Hudson-Lake Champlain waterway.

Given the manifold difficulties of the Americans, it may seem amazing that they prevailed over Britain, the most powerful planet in the European solar system, the mistress of the seas, the most industralized nation in the world, and the possessor of a winning tradition in warfare stretching over two centuries. The colonies had no viable central government. The Continental Congress, which endeavored to direct the fighting, was an extralegal body, existing only with the consent of the states until the ratification of the first national constitution in 1781, the Articles of Confederation. Congress could not tax and impose tariffs; it could not draft men except with the cooperation of the states; it could not secure substantial quantities of military equipment.

Withal, the patriots hung on, partly for some of the reasons explored in this volume —and especially because of the effectiveness of the militia when they were not thrust into major battles against enemy regulars, and Washington's diplomatic skills in dealing with political leaders and his ability to make the most of his inadequate resources. Increasingly the war became an endurance contest, with neither side showing signs of gaining and sustaining the upper hand. In a seemingly interminable struggle, which of the opponents would have the greater staying power? In the last analysis, it became a question of psychology, for Britain quite obviously had incomparably superior material advantages, by no means eliminated by the entry of France in 1778 and Spain in 1779. Indeed, it has been persuasively argued that Britain had a greater incentive than ever to win after her hated enemies challenged her in Europe and the New World. Also, the initial two years of the Franco-American alliance was a tale of a dreary succession of bungled joint operations until Yorktown, where Franco-American teamwork—the first and last significant instance of it in the war—brought a tremendous victory.

All the same, Britain militarily was scarcely a defeated power. After all, Burgoyne had surrendered an expedition to Gates in 1777 that was almost as big as the one Cornwallis lost. Another British army remained in New York City; smaller royal contingents continued to occupy the two principal cities of the South, Charleston, and Savannah; and the king's Indian friends remained troublesome on the frontiers.

Even so, after seven years Britain was ready for peace. The Americans, on the other hand, retained their will to resist, notwithstanding growing strains on a society plagued by physical destruction, rampant inflation, and civil-military tensions. (We are mindful from painful recent experiences of the divisions and frustrations that can result from an extended war, even though the Vietnam travail, unlike the Revolution, was not waged on American soil. Nor, of course, did we experience devas-

tation at home in a much more popular endeavor—the Second War War, about which General George C. Marshall nevertheless wrote that democracies are incapable of sustaining military efforts and sacrifices that are seemingly endless.)

From our vantage point of witnessing so-called total wars, we can say that in the Revolution neither side mobilized to the fullest—the Americans because they lacked the machinery and the resources; the British because they were unwilling to disrupt the domestic sector to the extent of imposing heavy taxes, regimenting the economy, and conscripting productive citizens into the army and navy. But certainly Americans came closer to full mobilization, and her citizens felt the impact of the struggle in ways unknown to most Britons.

Could Britain have crushed the rebellion had she pulled out all the stops? No one can say with assurance, but victory would have required total exertion in a contest three-thousand miles from Europe in a day of slow-moving transportation and communication against "a people numerous and armed," who were scattered over half a continent, in terrain nearly impenetrable, rough, mountainous, forested, and interlaced with myriad waterways. Awareness of the price of victory finally was realized by the English in 1781 and 1782. Any very few, least of all the king and his ministers, were willing to pay it. They would not risk derailing their mercantile economy; they would not risk arming citizens who might in turn demand a greater part in the political system in exchange for their service. No European monarchy in the period before the French Revolution would take that chance.

As for Americans, they did not win the war; but more importantly, nor did they lose it. The Americans had the greater tenacity or staying power, the greater incentive. As a result, they won their independence if not the war, and that was victory enough.

DON HIGGINBOTHAM

University of North Carolina at Chapel Hill
January 1977

# BACKGROUND

# THE ORIGINS OF AMERICAN MILITARY POLICY

By Louis Morton*

All too often, those who write about the American military tradition start with the Revolution, or with the beginning of the Federal government. They would have us believe that the founders of our nation created and formulated out of thin air a military policy at once complete and perfect.

To represent the origins of American military policy in this way is of course a distortion. The roots of our military policy, like the beginnings of our representative government and political democracy, are to be found in the early settlements at Jamestown, Plymouth, and elsewhere—in the arrangements the settlers made for their defense. The seeds of our policy go back even further in time—to the experience of the English people.

In this 350th anniversary year of the founding of Jamestown, it is perhaps not out of place to review some of the origins of our national defense establishment. Not only will we understand better why certain things are as they are today. We will also be struck by the fact that many of the problems and solutions of those earlier days are still with us in different form.

Before the new world settlers left their homes in the old world, they provided for their defense on the unknown continent of America. The businessmen who financed the colonizing ventures had invested too much money to risk the destruction of their property. The religious leaders were practical men, not visionaries, and their hope of attaining freedom from persecution was too strong to allow them to be negligent of their military strength. The British crown, which authorized the expeditions and granted lands, but which took no risks, empowered the colonists to take whatever measures were required (in the words of the Massachusetts Charter of 1628) "to incounter, expulse, repell and resist by force of armes, as well by sea as by lands" any effort to destroy or invade the settlement.

Weapons and military stores were therefore included in the cargo of the ships that came to Virginia and Massachusetts. Among the settlers were experienced soldiers, men specifically engaged to train the colonists in the use of arms, organize them into military formations, and direct them in battle if necessary. Such a man was Captain John Smith, an adventurer and veteran of the religious

*Dr. Louis Morton is Chairman, Department of History, Dartmouth College.

1Although there is an extensive bibliography containing material bearing on colonial military institutions, there is no single work on the subject. The records of the colonial legislatures constitute the basic primary source, a portion of which has been reproduced in Arthur Vollmer, *Background of Selective Service*, Mon. No. 1, Vol. II; *Military Obligations: The American Tradition* (1947). The best general treatment is in Herbert L. Osgood, *American Colonies in the Seventeenth Century*, I, Chap. XIII, II, Chap. XV. Works dealing with conditions in specific colonies or areas include: P. A. Bruce, *Institutional History of Virginia in the Seventeenth Century*, Vol. II, Part 4; W. P. Clarke, *Official History of Militia and National Guard in Pennsylvania*, (Phila, 1909), 3 vols; David W. Cole, "Organization and Administration of the South Carolina Militia System" (M.A. Thesis, University of South Carolina); Wesley Frank Craven, *Southern Colonies in the Seventeenth Century* (Louisiana State U. Press, 1949); Allen

French, "Arms and Military Training of our Colonizing Ancestors," *Massachusetts Historical Society Proceeding*, LXVII; A. Hanna, "New England Military Institutions of the Seventeenth Century," (Ph.D. Dissertation, Yale); Dallas Irvine, "First British Regulars in North America," *Military Affairs*, IX, 1945; Douglas E. Leach, "The Military System of Plymouth Colony," *The New England Quarterly*, XXIV (September 1951); H. Telfer Mook, "Training Days in New England," *The New England Quarterly*, XI (December 1938); S. P. Mead, "The First American Soldiers," *Journal of American History*, I (1907); H. L. Peterson, "Military Equipment of Plymouth and Massachusetts Bay," *New England Quarterly*, XX; J. S. Radabaugh, "The Militia of Colonial Massachusetts," *Military Affairs*, Spring 1954; L. D. Scisco, "Evolution of Militia in Maryland," *Maryland Historical Society*, XXXV (1940); Morison Sharp, "Leadership and Democracy in Early New England Defense," *American Historical Review*, XL (January 1945).

wars on the Continent. Such a man was Captain Myles Standish, hired by the Pilgrims to accompany them to Plymouth.

Not even a John Smith or a Myles Standish could fight off an Indian attack by himself. The settlers had to do that together, and every able-bodied man became in times of military emergency a front-line soldier. There was never any question about this. The obligation of every male who could carry arms to perform military service in the defense of his community was an ancient English tradition dating back to Saxon times. Such documents as the Assize of Arms (1181), the Statute of Westminster (1285), and the Instructions for General Musters (1572) rooted the obligation of military service firmly in English law. As late as 1588, when the Grand Armada threatened invasion, "the rugged miners poured to war from Mendip's sunless caves . . . and the broad streams of pikes and flags rushed down each roaring street" of London to defend the nation against the approaching Spanish fleet.

According to this tradition, which became organized into the militia system, every able-bodied man was considered a potential soldier. He had to train and drill in military formation at stated intervals. By law, he was required to possess arms and equipment and to have them ready for immediate use.

The system was local in character and organized on a geographical basis. It was administered by county and town officials who had full authority to impose punishment and collect fines. Yet English law also restricted the use of the militia to inhibit the crown from using it as an instrument of despotism and from employing it outside the kingdom. The militia, thus, was a military system for emergencies of short duration in defensive situations.

Since this was the military tradition of the colonists, this was the basis of the military system they employed in the New World. It was admirably suited to their needs. But there was an important difference. In England there had been but a single militia organization; in America there were as many militias as there were colonies. No man would serve in any but his own. "Let the New Yorkers defend themselves," said a North Carolinian of a later day. "Why should I fight the Indians for them?"

Arrived in the New World, the colonists were as much concerned with preparations for defense as with food and shelter. Acting in accordance with instructions from home, the original settlers of Jamestown—100 men and 4 boys—split into three groups upon landing. One group provided fortifications for defense, another furnished a guard and planted a crop, the third explored the nearby area. Within a month after their arrival, they had built a primitive fort, a triangular stockade of "Planckes and strong Posts, foure foot deepe in the ground."

The Puritans, similarly instructed in England, were also militant in defense of their property. As one of their number remarked, "they knew right well" that their church "was surrounded with walls and bulworks, and the people of God, in re-edifying the same did prepare to resist their enemies with weapons of war, even while they continued building."

Probably the first military legislation in the English colonies was the code of laws proclaimed in Jamestown by Sir Thomas Dale in 1612. On military leave from his post in the Netherlands, Dale assumed the governorship of Virginia at a time when the colony was in danger of extinction, its inhabitants on the verge of starvation. The strict regime he imposed, based on existing military regulations and on "the laws governing the Armye in the Low Countreys," was even more severe than the English laws of the period. But it accomplished its purpose.

Order was restored, crops were planted, and peace was made with the Indians. "Our people," wrote John Rolfe, "yearly plant and reape quietly, and travell in the woods a-fowling and a-hunting as freely and securely from danger or treacherie as in England."

Martial law soon outlived its usefulness. As soon as the colony ceased to be a military outpost, the Virginians wrote into civil law the requirements for military service. The Massacre of 1622, which almost destroyed the colony, was still fresh in mind when the General Assembly in 1623 required all inhabitants "to go under arms." Three years later, Governor Yeardley specified that all males between 17 and 60 years of age were to serve when necessary and perform military duty when required. Changes were afterwards made in the law, but the obligation of universal service was never abandoned. Failure to comply subjected the offender to punishment and fine, as one John Bickley discovered when, for refusing to take up arms, he was sentenced to be "laid neck and heels" for 12 hours and pay a fine of 100 pounds of tobacco.

A local official known as the Commander controlled the militia in each district. He was charged with responsibility for seeing that his men were properly armed and supplied with powder and shot. Later, as the population grew and his duties increased, a lieutenant commander was appointed to assist him. The commander's duties were so varied and extensive as to make him the most important person in the community, its chief civilian as well as military official. Not only did he supervise the construction of defenses, drill his units, and have custody of the public gunpowder, but he also saw to it that everyone attended church services and observed the laws relating to the tobacco trade. Though the commissioning of officers remained in the hands of the governor, the commander appointed his own subordinates.

Once a man acquired a military title he retained it. So numerous were the officers produced by this system and so fond were the Virginians of their titles that a visitor in a later period, struck by the abundance of military rank, remarked that the colony seemed to be "a retreat of heroes."

The Pilgrims too lost no time in organizing their defenses. Captain Standish was designated military commander of the colony. Under him were formed four companies, each with its own commander and designated area of responsibility. A visitor at Plymouth in 1627 noted approvingly the defensive works and the careful preparations to meet an attack. "They assemble by beat of drum," he explained, "each with his musket or firelock in front of the captain's door; they have their cloakes on and place themselves in order, three abreast, and are led by a sergeant without beat of drum. Behind comes the governor in a long robe; beside him, on the right hand, comes the preacher with his cloak on, and on the left hand the captain with his side-arms and cloak, and with a small cane in his hand; and so they march in good order, and each sets his arms down near him. Thus they are constantly on their guard night and day."

By the middle of the seventeenth century Plymouth had established a military system based on universal service. Each colonist was required to own and maintain his own weapons, and the governor was authorized by law to prescribe military training. As new towns grew up along the frontier, they were brought into the defensive organization by the requirement to maintain their own companies under the central control of the government at Plymouth. The local companies elected their own officers, subject to approval of the government, and the officers appointed subordinates, selected training days, and drilled their units. Regulations were enforced by fines, collected by the clerk of the company or the local constable, and these fines often supported the military activities of the community. If the General Court (the legislature) required it, each town provided a quota of men for military expeditions.

The military system of the Puritans was much like that of Plymouth and Jamestown. According to a law of 1631, all males between 16 and 60, whether freemen or servants, were to provide themselves with weapons and to form into units for training. A council was established for the specific purpose of supervising military matters, for, declared the General Court, "the well ordering of the militia is a matter of great concernment to the safety and welfare of this commonwealth." Additional regulations were issued from time to time and in 1643, after the Pequot War, the entire militia system was overhauled. One of the results was the selection of 30 soldiers within each company "who shall be ready at halfe an hour's warning upon any service they shall be put upon." Here in essence are the Minutemen of the Revolution, more than a century later.

As in the other colonies, provision was made in the law to excuse from military service those with "natural or personal impediment" such as "defect of mind, failing of sences, or impotence of Limbes." Certain professions were also exempted—public officials, clergymen, school teachers, and doctors —as were those who practiced critical trades.

The companies established in Massachusetts numbered from 65 to 200 men, two-thirds of whom were musketeers and one-third pikemen. When the number exceeded 200, a new unit was formed; when it was less than 65, several towns combined to form a single unit. The officers elected by the men consisted of the captain, a lieutenant as his principal assistant, an ensign, sergeants, and corporals. The company clerk kept the roster of men liable for military service, checked attendance at drills, and collected the fines.

At an earlier date than any other colony, Massachusetts formed the militia into regiments. The Act of 1636 divided the military companies then in existence into three regiments and required regimental training at first once a year and then every three years. Commanded by a sergeant major, who was assisted by a muster master, the regiment came ultimately to comprise all the units in a county and its strength consequently varied. Plymouth adopted the regimental organization in 1658 when Josiah Winslow was given the rank of major and designated "chief officer over the military companies of this jurisdiction," "All Captains, inferior officers and soldiers," read his orders, "are hereby required to be in ready subjection to you during your continuance in the said office."

Training was the primary activity of the militia, and regular training periods were an integral part of the system. The first drills at Jamestown were held shortly after the colony was founded. Captain Smith, when he became President of the Council, held drills and target practice on a level stretch of ground within plain view of the Indians, who could see for themselves the effect of cannon shot on the trunk of a tree.

Training exercises in Virginia were initially held, by custom, on holy days. In 1639, when a muster master-general was appointed to enforce the militia regulations, even though the captain remained immediately responsible for training their men, no specific time was set by law for drills. In some districts they were held monthly, in others every three months. Failure to attend brought a fine, but absence was apparently so common that the the General Assembly finally set a stiff penalty of 100 pounds of tobacco, declaring that the offenders were bringing about the "ruin of all military discipline." By the end of the seventeenth century the militia regulations in Virginia required an annual drill for the entire regiment and quarterly exercises for companies and troops.

Training in New England was put on a regular basis earlier than in Virginia. In Plymouth drills were held six times a year to assure, in the words of the General Court, "that all postures of pike and muskett, motions, ranks and files . . . skirmishes, sieges, batteries, watches, sentinells, bee always performed according to true military discipline." The first military law of the Puritans called for weekly training periods, held every Saturday. In 1637, when conditions had become more settled, the number of training days per year was fixed at eight, and this number remained in effect for the next forty years.

From the weekly training of the first settlers to the monthly sessions a few decades later can be measured the decreasing threat of Indian attack. Before the century was out, the number of drills per year had dropped to four, with provisions for two extra days if the unit commander thought them necessary. Regimental drills, when held, were deductible from the total. But during times of emergency, interest in military matters revived phenomenally; during King Philip's War drills were held as often as twice a week.

The military code of the day enforced a strict discipline. A militiaman in Virginia guilty of three offenses of drunkenness had to ride the "wooden horse," an ingeniously uncomfortable and ignominious seat; if drunk on post he was liable to the death sentence. Drunk or sober, if he lifted his hand against an officer, he lost the hand; if he raised a weapon, the penalty was death. Should he express discontent with his lot during a march, complain about the ration, or sell his gun, he was treated as a mutineer.

Imposed freely, fines provided one of the sources for defraying militia expenses. All the colonies had laws fining those who failed to supply themselves with arms or to maintain them properly. Failure to attend drill as well as quarreling, and drunkenness during the drill were also punishable by fines.

The drill was usually held in a public place, such as the commons in Boston, and began early in the day. After roll call and prayer, the men practiced close order drill, the manual of arms, and other formations to the accompaniment of drums. Then followed a review and inspection by higher officers and public officials. After that, the units might form into smaller groups for target practice and extended order drill. Training closed with a sham battle and final prayers. By now it was early in the afternoon and the militiamen retired for food and other refreshment. The rest of the day was spent in visits, games, and social events.

The manuals provided for a remarkably complicated series of motions for forming troops, marching, fixing the pike, and firing the musket. These were standard in European armies, where the perfection of mechanical motions governed warfare, but they bore no relation to Indian fighting in the forests of North America. Nevertheless, the militiamen in the New World had to go solemnly through the prescribed movements on each training day. Fifty-six separate motions were required to load and fire the matchlock musket; only eleven for the pike, a fact which may account in part for its retention as a weapon and its popularity among troops. It was also a case, not altogether unusual in a more recent day, of the failure of training to keep pace with changing conditions.

The militia was not limited to foot soldiers; horsemen too were included. From the start, cavalry was the favored arm, and cavalrymen acquired special privileges that gave them higher status. Few men could afford to supply the horse and equipment required, a fact that limited membership to the well-to-do. Massachusetts, for example, restricted service in the cavalry to those with property valued at 100 pounds sterling.

Many advantages accrued to members of a horse unit. The trooper was exempted from training with the foot companies and from guard duty. He enjoyed special tax privileges; he could not be impressed into another service; he did not have to pay the customary fees for pasturage on common grounds.

The number as well as the quality of militia units varied widely in different periods and among the various colonies. Governor Berkeley of Virginia estimated in 1671 that he could put 8,000 horse in the field if needed, and the following year the militia of the colony consisted of 20 foot regiments and 20 horse, a proportion marking clearly the southerner's preference for cavalry.

Second only to Virginia was Massachusetts, which in 1680 had about the same number of foot companies but fewer companies of horse. Since the number of men in the companies varied so widely, exact comparisons are impossible. For Connecticut exact figures appear in the report made by the governor in 1650. "For the present," he wrote, "we have but one troope settled, which consist of about sixty horse, yet we are upon raysing three troopes more. . . . Our other forces are Trained Bands. . . . The whole amount to 2,507."

Though the militia was organized into units, it rarely fought that way. It was not intended to. The system was designed to arm and train men, not to produce military units for combat. Thus, it provided a trained and equipped citizen-soldiery in time of crisis. In this sense it was a local training center and a replacement pool, a county selective service system and a law enforcing agency, an induction camp and a primitive supply depot.

The forces required for active operations against the Indians came usually from the militia. The legislature assigned quotas to the local districts. Volunteers usually filled them. But if they did not, local authorities had the power to impress or draft men, together with their arms and equipment (including horses), into service. The law on this point was specific. The Virginia Assembly in 1629 gave the commanders power to levy parties of men and employ them against the Indians. In Plymouth during the Pequot War, when each town was required to furnish a quota, some of the men volunteered only on the understanding that if they did not, they would be conscripted.

Service was usually limited to expeditions within the colony, but there were numerous occasions when militiamen were employed outside. This right was specifically recognized in the law. Thus, in 1645, the Massachusetts General Court empowered the governor and council "to raise and transport such part of the militia as they shall find needful" outside the Commonwealth "without their free and voluntary consent" for a period of six months. When the term of service was over, the forces thus raised were dissolved and the men returned to their homes where they resumed their place in the militia.

There was no central command for the militia of all the colonies; each had its own organization and its own commander. Supreme authority within each colony rested usually with the legislative body and was based on the charter. In practice, however, the legislature left the administration of the militia system to other groups, sometimes the Upper House and at other times to various committees or commissions on military affairs or martial discipline.

The utmost care was exercised to maintain civilian supremacy. The General Court of Massachusetts repeatedly asserted its authority over military officials and representatives of the crown. The establishment of the Artillery Company of Boston in 1638 caused some suspicious officials to liken it to the Praetorian Guard in Roman times and to the Knights Templar; care was taken to make certain that the Artillery Company would not become "a standing authority of military men, which might easily in time overthrow the civil power."

The actual management of war was delegated to the governor and a small group of advisers usually, but the legislature in almost every case retained control of the funds and watched expenditures with a suspicious eye. When an expedition was formed, it was the legislature that gave approval, furnished the money—and later appointed a committee to look carefully into the conduct of operations.

The principal officer of the militia and the only single individual who could be considered to exercise supreme command was, in Massachusetts, the sergeant major-general; in Virginia, the governor. When New Hampshire, New York, and Massachusets came under royal authority late in the century, command of the militia there passed to the governor also.

The office of sergeant major-general—later shortened to major general—was an elective post and carried with it extensive powers and excellent opportunities for personal profit. In addition to general supervision of the militia, the sergeant major-general mobilized the militia, moved units to threatened areas, and procured arms and supplies. He commanded one of the regiments and had the unique privilege of training his own family. In wartime he commanded the colonial forces in the field, which, on occasion, he himself had raised and equipped.

To overcome the absence of a single unifying military authority in the New World, the colonies of New England formed a confederation in 1643. Representatives of Massachusetts, Connecticut, New Haven, and Plymouth came together in Boston and agreed that "inasmuch as the Natives have formerly committed sundry insolencies and outrages upon several Plantations of the English, and have of late combined themselves against us . . . we therefore doe conceive it our bounden duty to enter into a present Confederation among ourselves, for mutuall help and strength." Two commissioners from each colony met as a body, which had authority to declare war, call on the member colonies for funds and troops, select commanders, and unify in other ways the military efforts of the colonies in time of emergency.

Though it lasted 42 years, the Confederation ran into trouble immediately and foundered finally on the rocks of jealousy and conflicting interest. From the outset, Massachusetts contested the right of the Confederation to declare war or draft Massachusetts troops. The dispute came to a head in 1653 when Massachusetts refused to obey a Confederation ruling. There was considerable feeling also about the choice of commander, for no colony was agreeable to placing its troops under an outsider. Like sovereign powers of a later day, each colony was jealous of its prerogatives and quick to object to seeming encroachment on its authority.

In no colony was there a group that resembled a military staff. The need did not exist. In peacetime the various officials of the militia system sufficed; in war the Assembly and the Council of War exercised control over military operations and procured the equipment and supplies needed by the troops. The commander was always adjured to take counsel of his assistants, and he was expected to abide by their advice. In this sense the various councils were policy-making bodies rather than staffs.

Supplying the military forces of the colonies was a comparatively simple matter. The first procurement agencies were the joint stock companies that had financed the original settlements, but by the middle of the century responsibility had devolved upon the colonists. The procurement of individual arms and equipment was, in general, the responsibility of each militiaman. Every colony required each householder to provide for himself and his family weapons and equipment, and specified the type and condition of both. The community itself provided for the poor who served out the cost of their arms in labor. In addition, most colonies required the local authorities to keep on hand a supply of weapons and powder for emergencies, to be paid for by the town or county.

Normally there was no need for commissary or quartermaster in Indian warfare. Operations were of brief duration and the militiaman provided his own weapons, ammunition, clothing, and provisions, for which he was usually recompensed.

Extended operations, though uncommon, could hardly be supported in so informal a manner and there were in each colony various regulations and officials to provide the materials of war. In Massachusetts there was from earliest time an officer — variously known as surveyor of ordnance, overseer of the arms, or surveyor general — who had charge of weapons and ammunition. The officer was responsible for making certain that the towns had a supply of powder and ammunition; he also kept records and made purchases for the colony. Commissaries were appointed when required and were given authority to collect provisions. Two such officers designated for a force numbering 200 men sent against the Indians in 1645 were directed to procure bread, salted beef, fish, flour, butter, oil, cereals, sugar, rum, and beer. Only occasionally were such officials required to purchase arms.

When the colony needed funds for an expedition, it could fix quotas for the counties, borrow from private individuals, or impose special taxes. All methods were followed. The General Assembly in Virginia customarily set levies on the counties and imposed taxes payable in tobacco. In 1645 the expense of an expedition of 80 men to Roanoke was met by a levy of 38,000 pounds of tobacco to pay for the hire of boats, the purchase of provisions, powder, and shot, and the payment of surgeons' salaries. The pay of the men alone amounted to 8,000 pounds of tobacco. Those suffering injuries received special compensation. The levy was made against three counties, each tithable person paying about 30 pounds of tobacco.

Even in that era war was a costly business and a fearful drain on the economy. In the greatest Indian war of the century — against King Philip — Massachusetts spent 100,000 pounds sterling, an enormous sum for that day. And though the legislature fixed prices and dealt harshly with profiteers, the war debt at the close of hostilities was larger than the aggregate value of all the personal property in the colony.

By the end of the seventeenth century, the militia system was firmly established in the American colonies. Though the training it afforded was less than adequate and the number of training days had steadily declined as the frontier moved westward, the system had become deeply imbedded in the traditions and laws of the colonists. Under this system they had defended their settlements, driven back the Indians, and preempted the most desirable lands along the Atlantic seaboard. A century of military experience had made little impression on the method of instruction, but it had demonstrated to the colonists that a military system based upon the obligation of every able-bodied citizen to bear arms provided a practical solution to their defense needs. Other problems would arise later that could not be solved by this method alone, but the militia system, in one form or another, remained an integral part of the nation's military policy for almost two more centuries. The obligation of universal service on which it was based, though often ignored, has never been abandoned. It constitutes yet today the basis of our military organization.

# A LITTLE KNOWN PERIOD OF AMERICAN MILITARY HISTORY

By Clarence C. Clendenen*

Can anybody give a logical answer to the question, "Why do most writers on American military history assume that it started with the assembly of the New England militia before Boston, in the spring of 1775?" The long period during which the American colonies were an integral part of the British Empire is usually overlooked entirely by writers on the subject of military history. If it is mentioned at all, it is treated briefly, as "background."

Yet the fact remains that the colonial force which assembled after Lexington and Concord was the product of a century and a half of development and evolution, and was the result of a definitely established military tradition and practice. The spring of 1775 did not mark the first time that colonial military forces had assembled independently of any stimulus from the Mother Country, nor was George Washington the first American to command in battle an American force. Every war fought in Europe during the hundred and fifty odd years since the establishment of the first English settlements on the Atlantic seaboard had had repercussions in America. And not only were the American colonies at war each time that Great Britain was at war, they fought numerous savage little wars against the Indians on their own authority. The years of the colonial era were years of almost ceaseless war, in some part or another, of North America.

Probably few present day readers of American military history are familiar with the names of Phineas Lyman or Sir William Pepperrell, but both of them commanded American forces as large, or nearly as large, as the forces under Washington. Phineas

Lyman was in command of the provincial forces in New York, during the later years of the French and Indian War, and made herculean efforts to wield his colonials into effective soldiers. William Pepperrell commanded, successfully, the amphibious expedition organized by the New England colonies for the capture of the French stronghold of Louisburg. It was an enterprise that could not possibly be successful, but the French surrendered!

Lyman and Pepperrell, as well as a score of other colonial soldiers, made the army that assembled after Lexington and Concord possible. If Washington is the father of the American military tradition, they are certainly entitled to be considered as its grandfathers.

As early as 1636, forces separate and distinct from the local militia were raised in New England for the war against the Pequods. In 1690 a Massachusetts-Connecticut force commanded by Sir William Phips (the first American-born Royal Governor, and the first American to be knighted), captured Port Royal, and made a determined, and unsuccessful attack on Quebec itself. It was not until eighty years later that British forces next sighted Quebec. In 1704 a Massachusetts force under Major Benjamin Church ravaged the coasts of Nova Scotia. (Church had previously commanded four Massachusetts expeditions against the French and Indians in what is now Maine.) In 1702 a South Carolina force invaded Florida and captured St. Augustine, but were unable to reduce the fort because of the lack of artillery. Exactly forty years later the new colony of Georgia signalled its entrance into the colonial military scene by another invasion of Florida, commanded by James Oglethorpe himself.

*Dr. Clarence Clendenen is Curator Emeritus, Military Collections, Hoover Institute.

These instances could be multiplied a hundred times. The army that assembled after the Battle of Lexington was a replica of the colonial forces that had been assembling almost annually for many years. It had all of their weaknesses, and it had all of their elements of strength. The American army and the American military tradition had existed a long time before 1775.

# THE MILITIA OF COLONIAL MASSACHUSETTS

By Jack S. Radabaugh*

THE Godly, grave men of Massachusetts took pains, even while still thousands of miles from the American shore, to provide in principle for the contingencies which might arise to challenge their existence in the New World. When considering the problem of defense, the founding fathers, in the Charter of 1628, took note of chief commanders, captains, and governors, and their power to rule and punish.[1] After the Puritans had arrived in New England the General Court of Massachusetts was even more specific when it said, "as piety cannot be maintained without church ordinances and officers, nor justice without laws and magistracy, no more can our safety and peace be preserved without military orders and officers."[2]

The flowering of the militia was not all just a matter of thought.[3] Immediate and practical requirements for public safety in 1631 moved the General Court temporarily to forbid unarmed persons to travel between Plymouth and Massachusetts.[4] Guns were a requirement for all travelers except those in and around Boston,[5] and colonial law called for arms in every home.[6] Indeed, the colony's legislative body observed that, "the well ordering of the militia is a matter of great concernment to the safety and welfare of this commonwealth. . . ."[7]

The Indians living in and adjacent to Massachusetts very frequently played havoc with the white man's peace, though in the revolt against Edmund Andros, the enemy of the militia was the governor himself. The Pequot Nation in eastern Connecticut was the first tribe to feel the ire of the citizen-soldiers, and after its destruction, it was replaced by the Narragansetts, the allies of King Philip and his Wampanoags, as the ranking antagonists. However, the Rhode Island tribes were never to match the fury of the Abenakis and the Penobscots to the north. These Canadian tribes, the allies of the French, at the conclusion of King Philips War, became the principal enemies of the Massachusetts militia.

The shifting string of frontier villages served as the battle front for these Indian wars.[8] All along the frontier the rocky and heavily forested terrain weighed in favor of the tribesmen. Nor did the dense swamps of Connecticut make easier the task of the soldier. The bitterness of winter cold increased the militiaman's suffering in the field, but since it was Indian custom to cease hostilities during cold weather and go into winter

---

*Dr. Jack Radabaugh is Associate Professor of Social Science, Los Angeles Harbor College.

[1] Nathaniel B. Shurtleff (ed.), *Records of the Governor and Company of the Massachusetts Bay in New England*, I, 17. Hereafter cited as *Mass. Colony Records.*

[2] *Ibid.*

[3] The pedigree of the militia in America is contained in the history of the English militia from the time of the Anglo-Saxon fyrd through the Norman Conquest up to the Interregnum. *Encyclopedia Britannica,* "County," VI, 597; "Lieutanant," XIV, 42; "Militia," XV, 483-487. J. W. Fortescue, *A History of the British Army,* I, 12, 123, 194; II, 39, 294-295, 305, 307, 530; IV, 639-641, 888; V, 201, 229, 230, 239; VI, 38, 40, 180-183; VII, 34-35, 422-423. Of these references the article in the *Encyclopedia Britannica* on the "Militia" presents the most concise picture of pre-colonial militia history.

[4] *Mass. Colony Records* I, 85.

[5] *Mass. Colony Record,* I, 85.

[6] *Ibid.,* II, 119.

[7] *The Charters and General Laws of the Colony and Province of Massachusetts Bay,* p. 157. Hereafter cited as *Colony Records of Mass.* This collection is a codification of the *Mass. Colony Records.*

[8] Albert B. Hart (ed.), *Commonwealth History of*

quarters, the long marches through the snow provided the militia with some of its most spectacular victories.

Cultural differences lay between the two peoples. The Calvinistic convictions of the settlers caused them to view the Indians as heathens, even demons, if some of the Puritan divines were to be believed. The principles of common law so prized by the English mind made little impression on the tribes, and were regarded with bitter hostility when translated into hangings for murder. The Puritan attempts to enforce Indian allegiance to the English sovereign also met with scant enthusiasm. The unmilitary manner of the colonials caused the Indian, raised according to a warrior code, to regard the white people with little respect. And the ever expanding line of villages built by the new people menaced the Indian's land.

In view of their differences with the natives, the planters adopted the mode of military organization most proximate to their experience and resources. This was the company or trained band centered in the town. The company, usually bearing the town's name, was commanded by a captain who was assisted by a lieutenant, an ensign, three sergeants and three corporals. At first a company at full strength had sixty-four men,[9] but later the figure was raised.[10] The privates in a company were divided into two groups in which two-thirds bore muskets, and the rest carried pikes.[11]

It was of importance to these privates that their company be maintained at full strength. Only when he company was fully manned could the soldiers choose their commissioned officers. Otherwise the sergeant-major, the commander of the regiment, supervised the company, and company personnel could choose only their sergeants and corporals.[12]

For the older settlements at least, the matter of holding lists at full strength was no problem, since as early as 1635 the division of a company was felt to be necessary at Watertown and Charlestown.[13] Later the General Court decreed that the company should be divided every time there were enough men to form a group of one hundred.[14]

Naturally this division of units raised disputes as to priority when several companies met at a regimental drill. In Boston the General Court appointed senior officers,[15] but later it resorted to the unsatisfactory expedient of allowing priority in command to rotate.[16] A more satisfactory solution to the problem was found in determining precedence according to priority of the commandant's commission.[17]

But fast blossoming trained bands were only one side of the coin. In the newly established villages on the frontier the opposite was true. It was necessary to combine the company at Rowley Village with Rowley, and Piscataqua with Kittery, in order to attain sufficient unit strength.[18]

Like any military institution the company needed money to operate. The common way to finance military needs at the town level was by fines. The coin collected by the company clerk went for a variety of items which included anything from wood for the guard to powder for the poor.[19] In addition, rum

*Massachusetts Colony, Province and State*, I, 533; II, 74-75. Hereafter cited as A. B. Hart, *Commonwealth History*. Hart gives an excellent sketch of frontier conditions, and the type of people defending the more advanced regions. See also *Mass Colony Records*, III, 310; V, 48, 51, 79.

[9]*Mass. Colony Records*, III, 267; *Colony Records of Mass.*, p. 158; Great Britain, Public Record Office, *Calendar State Papers, Colonial Series, America anl the West Indies*, 1677-1680, 138. Hereafter cited as *Cal. State Papers*.

[10]*Mass. Colony Records*, III, 268; V, 16.

[11]*Ibid.*, I, 328; II, 119.

[12]*Ibid.*, III, 267-268.
[13]*Ibid.*, I, 160.
[14]*Ibid.*, III, 268; V, 16.
[15]*Ibid.*, III, 285.
[16]*Ibid.*, IV, Pt. I, 246.
[17]*Mass. Colony Records*, III, 284-285.
[18]*Ibid.*, II, 42; IV, Pt. II, 554; V, 16.
[19]*Ibid.*, II, 119.

and tobacco appeared along with the other staples needed to operate a frictionless war machine.[20]

Though the musketeers constituted a majority of each company, the pikemen, numbering about one-third of company strength,[21] and occupying position on the flank,[22] were the more colorful. The General Court saw the pikeman gallantly clad in corselet, head piece, sword and knapsack, but since corselets and helmets were rare, a more practical quilt or bluff coat came to be recognized.[23]

Service as a pikeman was very popular in the militia. This fact can be accounted for in part by the simplified manual of arms for the pike . There were only eleven operations required of the pikeman at drill while the musketeer was required to know fifty-six different motions.[24] But an even more cogent reason for the thrifty Puritan to appreciate the pikeman's art was the fact that it was inexpensive when compared to the cost of providing and maintaining a musket. Furthermore, the father of a large family was responsible for arming his sons till they were twenty-one.[25] For a really honest and soul-searching analysis of the wish to bear the pike one must lend ear to John Dunton.

I thought a pike was best for a young soldier, and so I carried a pike, and between you and I reader, there was another reason for it too, and that was, I knew not how to shoot off a musket. But t'was the first time I ever was in arms; which tho' I tell thee, Reader, I had no need to tell my fellow soldiers, for they knew it well enough by my awkward handling of them.[26]

The General Court did what it could to encourage service as a pikeman,[27] but with the evolution of warfare into a shooting affair even the pikemen were required to carry guns and ammunition.[28]. Within a year after the outbreak of King Philips War the pikeman disappeared from the militia scene.[29]

In contrast to the disappearing pikeman the horse company, because of its capacity for rapid movement, developed into one of the most effective fighting organizations in the militia. The horse company developed out of horse units which operated as scouts with the foot companies.[30] At first the horse units were limited to thirty men,[31] but later the number was increased to seventy.[32] Often the cavalry units were organized by officers who wished to continue their activities while their regiments were not due for drill.[33]

The troopers were under the command of the sergeant-majors and the general of the militia.[34] However, a company having forty horsemen could nominate its officers,[35] who were then subject to the approval of the County Court.[36] Later on, its own approval of cavalry personnel was required by the General Court, which was not bashful about using its power to prevent those not free men and those not taking the oath of fidelity from serving in the horse units.[37]

To be a member of the cavalry several qualifications had to be met. First, a man or his parents must own a £100 estate.[38] Only the fluency of his command officer could dispense a man from this law.[39] The rider pro-

[20]*Ibid.*, V, 73.
[21]*Cal. State Papers*, 1677-1680, 138.
[22]Ebenezer W. Peirce, *Indian History, Biography, and Genealogy Pertaining to the Good Sachem Massasoit of the Wampanoag Tribe and His Descendants*, p. 76. Hereafter cited as E. W. Peirce, *Indian History*.
[23]*Mass. Colony Records*, IV, Pt. II, 319; *Colony Records of Mass.*, pp. 167-168. Corselet—A Small cuirass, or armor to cover and protect the body.
[24]E. W. Peirce, *Indian History*, pp. 77-80.
[25]*Ibid.*, p. 76.
[26]*Letters Written From New England A. D. 1681 by John Dunton*, p. 140. Hereafter cited as *Dunton Correspondence*.

[27]*Mass. Colony Records*, II, 43.
[28]*Ibid.*, V, 47.
[29]*Cal. State Papers*, 1675-1676, 465.
[30]*Mass. Colony Records*, IV, Pt. I, 379.
[31]*Ibid.*, III, 265.
[32]*Ibid.*, III, 398.
[33]*Collections of the Massachusetts Historical Society*, 2nd Ser., VII, 56. Hereafter cite das *Coll. MHS.*
[34]*Mass. Colony Records*, III, 344.
[35]*Colony Records of Mass.*, p. 164.
[36]*Ibid.*, p. 158.
[37]*Mass. Colony Records*, III, 264.
[38]*Ibid.*, IV, Pt. II, 97.
[39]*Ibid.*, V, 438.

vided horse, saddle, bridle, holster, pistol or carbine, and sword; and the rider was to be fined 10s when he failed to supply himself with any one of these items.[40] However, in practice the horseman was more recognizable in his buff coat with a pistol, hanger, and corslet.[41] He was required to drill six days a year, and ocasionally was ordered to garrison duty.[42]

There were soem advantages to serving in the cavalry. The horseman could not be drafted,[43] nor was he subject to head-rates on houses.[44] He did not have to pay for ferry service,[45] and for a time he enjoyed free pasturing on the common lands.[46] The Court, in time, rescinded some of these privileges,[47] but while in force they helped to build up the colony's cavalry.

After the horse units had been built up in the various counties it became popular for the towns to organize their own cavalry. The frontier towns of Concord, Chelmsford, Billirrikey, Lancaster, and Groton were especially encouraged.[48] However, the most effective cavalry continued to come from the groups in Middlesex, Essex, and Suffolk, and the unattached Three County Troop.

The growth of the cavalry was rapid, but not without its hour of crisis. In the war with King Philip the General Court found the cavalry quite as useless as the pikeman and ordered a draft for most riders.[49] However, subsequent performances by cavalry forced the Court to reverse this hasty decision.[50]

Both trained bands and horse troops combined in a geographical unit called a regiment under the command of a sergeant-major. The regiment corresponded to the county in its area of jurisdiction. The men in a regiment could not be ordered out of the county,[51] except in time of war.[52]

Within the regiment, the sergeant-major and his chief company officers determined policy, but command decisions, such as orders for mobilization, were made by the General Court.[53] The Court also determined quotas of men in the counties in time of stress.[54]

In peace time the regiments were supposed to meet once in three years for drill, and for services received the county was to pay the sergeant-major £20.[55] Later a schedule was definitely fixed for meetings from 1649 to 1641,[56] and another schedule was established for the period 1671 to 1676 when new counties were added to the colony.[57]

Requests from the county to drop training were answered by the Court with explicit instructions to drill.[58] Still some of the counties managed to avoid the meetings in one way or another. Sometimes the period set aside for regimental drills was devoted to some other activity.[59]

By 1680 even the regiments had grown to the point where a division was necessary. In Essex nine towns with horse units combined to form one regiment, and the remaining eight towns formed another. A similar division took place in Middlesex County.[60]

As in any organization, the efficient functioning of the militia depended on the officers. From the sergeant-major-general, the chain

[40]Mass. Colony Records, III, 265; Colony Records of Mass., pp. 164-165. Carbine—A short musket used more particularly by cavalry.

[41]Cal. State Papers, 1675-1676, 221. Hanger—The girdle or belt from which the sword was suspended at the side.

[42]Mass. Colony Records, V, 75.

[43]Ibid., V, 70-71.

[44]Ibid., V, 49.

[45]Ibid., IV, Pt. I, 323.

[46]Ibid., III, 398.

[47]Colony Records of Mass., p. 164.

[48]Mass. Colony Records, III, 419; IV, Pt. II, 439; V, 254, 409-410.

[49]Mass. Colony Records, V, 47.

[50]Ibid., V, 70-71.

[51]Colony Records of Mass., p. 157.

[52]Mass. Colony Records, V, 70.

[53]Ibid., V, 53.

[54]Ibid., V, 85.

[55]Colony Records of Mass., p. 158.

[56]Mass. Colony Records, II, 256.

[57]Ibid., IV, Pt. II, 486.

[58]Mass. Colony Records, IV, Pt. II, 73.

[59]Ibid., IV, Pt. II, 276, 333.

[60]Ibid., V, 295.

of command rattled down through the echelons of sergeant-majors in the regiments to captains, lieutenants, ensigns, sergeants and corporals in the company. The horse unit also sported a cornet and a quartermaster, while regiments sometimes carried surgeons, commissary officers, and chaplains.

All the commissioned officers were nominated by their men and approved by their representatives in the County[61] and General Courts. Those having the power to nominate included freemen and persons taking the oath of residents. Later this group was expanded to include householders and those taking the oath of fidelity. But this constituted not even a majority of the militiamen, for in 1672, of the 15,000 militiamen, only 6,000 could vote.[62]

In the early days the regiments elected their commanding officers, and the town deputies presented them to the General Court. Towns nominated two or three men for the office of captain and lieutenant, and the Provincial Council then settled on one of them.[63] But in 1645 a sergeant-major was selected by votes which were sealed and delivered to the county seat. Here the votes were counted before the deputies and the winner was presented to the general for installation.[64]

From 1641 to 1664 the General Court allowed the County Court to approve company nominees,[65] but after this date the General Court exercised directly its power to "nominate, choose and appoint" all commissioned officers except the general and admiral. And this passing of elected militia officers was felt in all ranks, for now the non-commissioned officers were appointed by the company commanders.[66] However, this situation was somewhat altered when the committee of militia sat as a recommending body when the need for officers arose.[67]

Once elected or approved the protocol faced by the prospective officer was somewhat complex. To obtain for the officer a commission from the General Court, a freeman obtained a certificate of nomination from the county recorder. This was presented to the secretary of the General Court who drew up a commission. Then the eldest sergeant of the company involved delivered the commission to the governor for his seal. This accomplished, the sergeant then delivered the sealed document to the general, who gave it to the appropriate sergeant-major, who in turn gave it to the waiting winner.[68]

Though the clergyman Edward Johnson claimed that the Massachusetts colonial was one who labored to avoid high titles,[69] a spectacular exception to this statement was the title of the highest officer in the militia, the sergeant-major-general. This elective position[70] was described by another contemporary, Edward Randolph, as being one of good profit and no danger because the general remained at home and shared the spoils while younger men commanded in the field.[71] The office carried extensive powers. Among other things, the general could impress materiél of war. With the Council of War at Boston he could replace slain officers, and make rules for the death penalty. In war he had command of all forces in the field,[72] and in peacetime he could call out his own regiment once a year without the Court's

[61]*Ibid.*, II, 222; *Colony Records of Mass.*, p. 168.

[62]*Cal. State Papers*, 1669-1674, 332.

[63]*Mass. Colony Records*, I, 187.

[64]*Ibid.*, II, 117; *Colony Records of Mass.*, pp. 157-158.

[65]A. B. Hart, *Commonwealth History*, I, 116.

[66]*Mass. Colony Records*, IV, Pt. II, 368; *Colony Records of Mass.*, p. 168. *Cal. State Papers*, 1677-1680, 138.

[67]*Mass. Colony Records*, V, 30.

[68]*Mass. Colony Records*, III, 285-286.

[69]*Coll. MHS*, 2nd Ser., VII, 53.

[70]*Mass. Colony Records*, II, 49.

[71]*Cal. State Papers*, 1675-1676, 465.

[72]*Mass. Colony Records*, II, 42, 76-78.

approval.[73] He also had the privilege of training his family,[74] which meant they were exempt from drill.

The other general officer rank in the militia was developed by gradual steps. In 1634 the Court provided for two men to check on existing supplies.[75] Two years later one of these men, John Samford, was appointed surveyor of arms.[76] In 1641, one John Johnson acted in the same capacity, and a year later was officially dubbed General Surveyor of Arms.[77] His principal duty was to account for arms and ammunition,[78] and he also could buy and sell arms.[79]

The interests of the sergeant-major were more localized. At regimental drills he was cared for by £ 20 from the commonwealth treasury,[80] but later this entertainment bill was passed back to the county.[81] His principal duty was to see to company drills and attend to matters of delinquency.[82] In time of attack he was to attend to the relief of a distressed town,[83] and could impress goods.[84]

The captain was the top commander in a town. Here, he looked after arms, and saw to it that people carried guns when they attended church.[85] At times the captain was paid by the General Court, but often his pay came from company fines.[86]

In some cases it was not the captain, but the sergeant who commanded the town militia.[87] The sergeants were usually appointed to their positions,[88] though occasionally the commissioned officers allowed the men to choose their sergeants.[89] Sometimes a sergeant would jump to the rank of lieutenant.[90]

To collect money for the trained band the Court saw the need for a "discreet able man." Its understanding of the word discreet was made somewhat clearer by the 40s fine which accompanied a refusal to accept the elective honor of being company clerk. The office was not one which offered much promise of forming lasting friendships. It was the clerk who called roll at drill, and noted defects. It was the clerk who seized property in payment for overdue fines. And it was the clerk who added to the fine his traveling expenses for those who would flee his just assessments.[91] But all was not gloom in a clerk's life, for he was permitted to keep for himself one-fourth of all fines collected.[92] And on purchases made to equip those delinquent in providing themselves with knapsacks the clerk could retain any portion of the fine left over after buying the needed equipment.[93]

Though not military officers, the selectmen held the crucial task of assessing taxes for the purpose of providing the companies with artillery,[94] powder, match and shot. To be indolent about their duty cost these civil officers £ 5 per missing item.[95]

To examine the militia's officer personnel without mentioning their schooling would be to do an injustice to their best traditions. The organization for schooling officers most encrusted with tradition was the Ancient and Honorable Artillery Company. This honorary group was best known for the sermons presented to it by outstanding Puritan clergymen on "Anniversary Day." The ancient and honorable group had some difficulty ob-

[73]Ibid., III, 236.
[74]Ibid., II, 222.
[75]Mass. Colony Records, I, 120.
[76]Ibid., I, 183.
[77]Ibid., II, 26.
[78]Ibid., III, 398; Colony Records of Mass., p. 164.
[79]Mass. Colony Records, II, 31, 124, 222.
[80]Ibid., II, 256.
[81]Colony Records of Mass., p. 168.
[82]Ibid., p. 158; Mass. Colony Records, II, 118.
[83]Colony Records of Mass., p. 162.
[84]Mass. Colony Records, IV, Pt. II, 28.
[85]Ibid., II, 38, 223.
[86]Mass. Colony Records, I, 99, 138, 160.
[87]E. W. Peirce, Indian History, p. 74.
[88]Mass. Colony Records, I, 120; IV, Pt. 1, 322.

[89]E. W. Peirce, Indian History, p. 118.
[90]Mass. Colony Records, IV, Pt. II, 575-576; V, 75.
[91]Ibid., III, 398.
[92]Ibid., II, 118-119; Colony Records of Mass., p. 160.
[93]Mass. Colony Records, II, 122.
[94]Colony Records of Mass., pp. 162-163.
[95]Ibid., p. 164.

taining a charater in 1638 because some of its proposed members, such as John Underhill, were suspected of heretical religious beliefs. There was also the fear that a military clique might seize control of the colony.

Aside from instructional and social activities of the Artillery Company the training of officers placed them in one of two groups, American trained or European. John Mason had served under Sir Thomas Fairfax in the Netherlands, and under Cromwell.[96] Lion Gardiner, an engineer, was also a Fairfax graduate, and had served the Prince of Orange.[97] Major Robert Sedgwick had been a member of the London Military Gardens, but he also had fifteen years experience in New England operations.[98] Outstanding American trained officers included Edward Gibbons,[99] Josiah Winslow and William Bradford II.

Often the duties of these militia officers were of a diplomatic nature rather than strictly military. The range of activities varied from petty meddling in local Indian affairs[100] to bargaining for the release of white captives.[101] Visiting Indian dignitaries were sometimes dispatched from Boston with a noisy salute from militia musketeers,[102] and in pressing negotiations one officer was reputed to have seized a haggling chief by the locks and threatened him with a pistol as a means of pressing an argument.[103] Militia diplomacy was successful as long as it had force behind it, and troops were sent to keep the Indians quiet.[104] But in time, over-familiarity with the Indians finally broke down this respect based on fear.[105]

Nor was the diplomacy of Massachusetts officers limited strictly to Indian affairs. Intercolonial relations were handled by militia officers as in mutual aid discussions between Plymouth and Massachusetts, ammunition deliveries to Connecticut,[106] and the recommendations of Massachusetts officers to the New England Confederation.[107]

The well-being of the militia depended primarily on the corps of officers; but these military leaders had three jealous masters. Within the colony, two sources of authority were discernible. The first was the General Court with its subordinate commissions, councils, and committees operating on a colony wide basis, and the committees of militia which functioned in the towns. A second important group which had limited authority to call on the Massachusetts militia was the Inter-Colonial New England Confederation. And the third group consisted of the representatives of the Crown with their directives from England.

The principal master of the militia, the General Court, seemed never to tire of issuing statements of supremacy. And those statements were given concrete form as regards new appointments,[108] determination of duties,[109] and orders for supplies.[110] In some respects this was like giving orders to itself, for approximately one-third of all administrative officers and legislators held commissions. In spite of continuous attempts to legislate the details necessary to operate a militia the General Court sometimes left actual administration of certain aspects of the militia

96Coll. MHS, 2nd Ser., VIII, 124.

97Ibid., 3rd Ser., III, 132. 136-137.

98Coll. MHS, 2nd Ser., VII, 54.

99Ibid.

100Mass. Colony Records, II, 24.

101Edward Randolph: Including His Letters and Official Papers From the New England, Middle and Southern Colonies in America, with other Documents Relating Chiefly to the Vacating of the Royal Charter of the Colony of Massachusetts Bay, VI, 279. Hereafter cited as the Randolph Correspondence.

102Coll. MHS, 2nd Ser., V, 253-254.

103Ibid., 464-465.

104Cal. State Papers, 1675-1676, 318.

105Coll. MHS, 2nd Ser., V. 465.

106Mass. Colony Records, I, 160.

107Ibid., II, 268.

108Ibid., II, 124; V, 74.

109Ibid., I, 117.

110Ibid., V, 69.

to commissions, councils and committees.

As early as 1634 the General Court granted authority to the governor and three other men to manage any war which might befall the colony.[111] In other circumstances, and with a slightly larger membership, the men in this group were referred to as the commissioners for military affairs,[112] the committee on military affairs,[113] and finally the commissioners for martial discipline.[114] It is likely that the latter of these titles is the most accurate for the men were commissioned for a definite period of time, usually till the meeting of the next General Court, and they were required to take an oath before they could execute their commissions.[115]

This commission continued to manage militia affairs until 1636.[116] At that time it was committed to the Provincial Council, the upper house of the General Court.[117] Now for a short time the Provincial Council was in charge of militia affairs,[118] but it was not long before military matters were again in the hands of a small group of three men referred to simply as the Council.[119]

The close of the Pequot War marked the end of the General Court's experiments with commissions. In 1643 an advisory group of six men, mostly militia captains, was appointed to advise the General Court on preparations for war.[120] That year, while reaffirming its authority to command military forces, the General Court mentioned that a council should be set up to act in emergencies.[121] The General Court also mentioned the desirability of yearly meetings by the governor, council, lieutenants of shires, and sergeant-

majors for planning a system of defense.[122] In a more definite vein was the General Court's pronouncement in 1645 that in emergencies an assembly of assistants, regardless of number, could call out troops and seize supplies.[123]

After this date the General Court kept the power of regulating the militia to itself. But in 1661 it did grant extensive powers to the officers in the field who composed a battlefield Council of War.[124] Two years later a special committee was set up to codify militia law,[125] and in 1676 a committee was established to hear petitions of wounded soldiers.[126]

If the upper levels of military government tended to be unstable and confused this situation was balanced somewhat by the genuine effectiveness of the operation of the committees of militia in the towns. Here any three of the own's civil magistrates and the chief militia officers had authority to deal with a variety of problems.[127] Committees of soldiers and civilians could order the militia companies into action during an emergency until some higher authority intervened.[128] They executed the Court's warrants for drafts,[129] and discharges.[130] Financially they could assess estates in time of war.[131] They also made recommendations to the General Court for new officers.[132]

Another jealous but less successful contender for militia obedience during the seventeenth century was the New England Confederation. As an advisory body the confederation recommended storing of arms

111Mass. Colony Records, I, 135.
112Ibid., I, 129.
113Ibid., I, 138.
114Ibid., I, 143.
115Ibid., I, 143, 146-147.
116Ibid., I, 161, 165, 168.
117Ibid., I, 183, 192.
118Ibid., I, 187, 192.
119Ibid., I, 192, 197.
120Mass. Colony Records, II, 39.
121Ibid., II, 42.

122Ibid., II, 43.
123Ibid., II, 125.
124Ibid., IV, Pt. II, 28.
125Ibid., IV, Pt. II, 74.
126Ibid., V, 80.
127Mass. Colony Records, III, 268-269; IV, Pt. II, 120:Colony Records of Mass., pp. 161-163.
128Mass. Colony Records, III, 320.
129Colony Records of Mass., p. 162.
130Mass. Colony Records, III, 359.
131Ibid., V, 48-49.
132Colony Records of Mass., p. 170.

both by individuals and by towns.[133] As a command-giving body it claimed authority to declare war.[134] It dealt with repair and sale of arms, endeavoring to control these activities by demanding that the various legislature recall the licenses of those who dealt in arms with the Indians.[135] It also picked sides among the Indians in an effort to prevent inter-tribal outbreaks.[136]

But the military relations between Massachusetts and the Confederation were at best only politely frigid. The differences between the two grew out of Confederation demands from 1645 to 1650 for troops from Massachusetts to fight the Narragansetts.[137] The matter came to a head in 1653 when Massachusetts challenged the right of the Confederation to wage offensive war on the basis of the articles of confederation.[138] In this particular case the Bay Colony refused to act,[139] but subsequently, in 1675, when Massachusetts felt the Narragansett wrath, the proud colony struck a more humble pose as militiamen from Essex, Norfolk, Suffolk, and Middlesex[140] scurried to a rendezvous at Rehoboth at the command of the Confederation.[141] Massachusetts also accepted Josiah Winslow of Plymouth as commander of all forces.[142] But the commission issued to Winslow usurped practically all the powers which Massachusetts lawyers had been blustering about for years.[143]

The third, and to the colonials perhaps

the most ominous contender for military control was mother England. That the home country was at times quite conscious of the military events in America is evident in the Lord Protector's order from Whitehall in 1655 directed to John Leveret, the occupation commander at newly conquered St. Johns, to write reports to England on the condition of the fort so that new instructions could be sent to him by Cromwell's government.[144] Later, after the return of Charles II to the throne, there were complaints that Leveret was subjugating the eastern parts of New England without any power from England.[145] And in 1664, in secret instructions to Crown Commissioners the King's choice for major-general of militia was indicated as being a Colonel Cartwright.[146]

But along with this undercurrent of contention there was a veneer of flattery which in most cases involved sentiments of loyalty. His Majesty was pleased by New England military supplies sent to Barbados.[147] Nor were the colonials incapable of honeyed words. In 1677, Josiah Winslow, after writing an extremely obsequious letter to the king, accompanied the message with the gangling war trophies taken from the dead King Philip by Benjamin Church.[148]

However, during the period of difficulties with the Dutch in 1673 Sir John Knight wanted commanders sent to America to raise colonial armies in Massachusetts.[149] And while the colonials were not happy to hear of English commanders, they were ready to urge aid from England at all times.[150] The hand of foreign advisors was felt more heavily in Massachusetts with the arrival of Edward Randolph, vitriolic agent for the Crown.

---

133David Pulsifer (ed.), *Records of the Colony of New Plymouth in New England. Acts of the Commissioners of the United Colonies of New England*, IX, 12. Hereafter cited as *Ply. Colony Records.*
134*Coll. MHS*, 2nd Ser., VI, 473; *Ply. Colony Records*, IX, 22.
135*Ibid.*, IX, 105.
136*Ply. Colony Records*, IX, 12, 45.
137*Ibid.*, IX, 168; *Mass Colony Records*, III, 39.
138*Ibid.*, III, 311; *Ply. Colony Records*, V, 74-76.
139*Ibid.*, X, 101.
140*Mass. Colony Records*, V, 73.
141*Ply. Colony Records*, X, 357-358.
142*Mass. Colony Records*, V, 69.
143*Coll. MHS*, 3rd Ser., I, 66-68.

144*Coll. MHS*, 3rd Ser., VII, 122.
145*Cal. State Papers*, 1661-1668, 18.
146*Ibid.*, 1661-1668, 200-201.
147*Ibid.*, 1669-1674, 20.
148*Ibid.*, 1677-1680, 109.
149*Ibid.*, 1669-1674, 530.
150*Ibid.*, 1675-1676, 319.

Randolph recommended that Josiah Winslow be placed in command of the Plantation's militia in 1679, and that a board consisting of Randolph nominees be set up to administer the militia and issue commissions.[151] Later he recommended that the magistrates temporarily fulfill this office.[152]

Randolph's recommendations commenced to be realities in 1685 when Joseph Dudley received his commission from James II to appoint officers and take charge of defense.[153] Sir Edmund Andros' commission gave him the additional powers of moving troops out of the colony, drafting needed personnel, and execution of martial law. This commission also had an unpleasant reference to the apprehension of "Rebells both at land and sea."[154] And in 1691 William Phips was pompously styled by William and Mary as "Our Lieutenant and Commander in Chief of the Militia."[155] Through the charter of this same year the power to appoint officers, to train and govern the militia, and to defend the colony passed from the General Court to the King's governor. However, to send troops out of the province the governor had to have Assembly approval,[156] and it was still the legislature who provided funds for military purposes.

As in any military institution the Massachusetts militia faced the problem of procuring men and supplies, and paying for them. The volunteer method, at one time or another, was tried in Massachusetts, but was a failure financially, and from a disciplinary point of view.[157] The General Court then turned to the draft as a means of obtaining militia personnel.

Draftees generally included the men on the company lists.[158] But even more eligible were unemployed single males,[159] transients,[160] and smiths.[161] In times of trouble all persons were likely candidates for duty in work gangs repairing forts.[162] However, except in emergencies, the draft was a local affair, and men could not be ordered beyond the borders of the colony.[163]

Nor was the art of draft dodging entirely unknown to the Massachusetts colonial. During King Philips war £ 4 and £ 6 fines were set for the evasive,[164] and to the town constables fell the delicate task of collecting the fines.[165] Yet it was not entirely impossible to defy the draft. In 1687 the men questioned the pay and the legality of the empressment with the result that few appeared for active duty.[166] But direct opposition was not the only means available to avoid the inconveniences of military duty. Draftees could hire substitutes,[167] and company drill could be avoided if a magistrate would accept 4 to 6d in lieu of marching time.[168] Special contributions such as firearms also tended to reduce a man's liability for service.[169]

Edward Johnson was most optimistic in his estimate of the draft's all inclusive extent. Said he, "there are none exempt, unless it be a few timerous persons that are apt to plead infirmity, if the Church chuse them

---

[151]*Cal. State Papers,* 1677-1680, 332.
[152]*Ibid.,* 1681-1685, 31-32.
[153]*Publications of the Colonial Society of Massachusetts,* II, 41-42. Hereafter cited as *Pub. CSM.*
[154]*Pub. CSM,* II, 50.
[155]*Ibid.,* II, 71-75.
[156]*Ibid.,* II, 26-27; *Colony Records of Mass.,* p. 157.
[157]*Cal. State Papers,* 1675-1676, 252; *Mass. Colony Records,* V, 71, 76; *Ply. Colony Records,* X, 360; E. W. Peirce, *Indian History,* p. 81.

[158]*Mass. Colony Records,* IV, Pt. II, 575.
[159]*Ibid.,* V, 144-145.
[160]*Ibid.,* V, 123.
[161]*Ibid.,* II, 222.
[162]*Ibid.,* V, 48.
[163]W. H. Whitmore (ed.), *The Colonial Laws of Masachusetts Reprinted from the Edition of 1660, with the Supplements to 1672. Containing also, the Body of Liberties of 1641,* p. 35. Hereafter cited as *Colonial Laws;* A. B. Hart, *Commonwealth History,* I, 201.
[164]*Mass. Colony Records,* V, 78-79.
[165]*Ibid.,* V, 79.
[166]*Cal. State Papers,* 1689-1692, 111, 120.
[167]*Pub. CSM,* XXX, 683.
[168]*Mass. Colony Records,* I, 212; III, 368.
[169]*Ibid.,* V, 48.

not for the Deacons, or they cannot get to serve some Magistrate or Minister."[170] But this view seems slightly exaggerated when one examines the exemption laws.

Generally speaking, one who suffered a "natural or personal impediment" such as "want of yeares, greatness of age, defect of minde, fayling of sences, or impotence of Lymbes"[171] was exempt from military duty. Of these plying the profession of politician the following were exempt: magistrates, deputies, officers of the General Court, treasurers, the public notary, one servant for each magistrate and elder, the Surveyor-general, and the sons and servants of the Major-general. Among the religious, the elders and deacons stood exempt. Educators free of obligation included the president, fellows, students and officers of Harvard College, ten servants for Harvard,[172] and professed school teachers. Among professional people physicians and surgeons were exempt, and among the tradesmen the following were not obligated by militia laws: masters of ships over twenty tons, fishermen employed all year, constant herdsmen, ship carpenters, millers,[173] and ferry men.[174] Property owners of twenty acres and twenty cattle could get one man exempted. Also free from call were dwellers on remote farms, those having a ferry to cross, and those living more than four miles from town.[175]

The military status of certain of the trades varied over the years. For example, there was an increasing tendency to make fishermen liable for service,[176] especially in view of the seasonal nature of their trade.[177]

When specific exemptions were made they most often came from the County Court. Old age was frequently cited as the reason for exemption of the individual, but family sickness and certification from a captain were acceptable reasons as well.[178]

Next in importance to the problem of obtaining the men was the problem of securing supplies. The commissary officer was usually in charge of procurement.[179] Items always in demand included bread, beef, fish, pork, corn, strong water, rum, wine, nad beer. Non-edibles included shoes, shirts, canvas, and hardware.[180] Contracts for arms usually went to private individuals. At first, body armor of various sorts was in great demand, but in time the requirements of war shifted the emphasis to firearms and building supplies.[181] After the colony had accumulated some degree of capital wealth the procurement problem was eased somewhat by the expedient of impressment of goods.[182] Usually an effort was made to obtain goods on six month terms, but when this failed the materials were seized.[183]

Not quite as arbitrary, and under more direct regulation from England was the procurement of gun powder. The home government would issue licenses of warrants to private traders through the Council of State whose enforcement agency was the Committee of Admiralty.[184] From the demands for security[185] required by England it could be assumed that the home government felt suspicious that the powder might not reach its destination, or even in doing so it might be misused.[186]

[170]Coll. MHS, 2nd Ser., VII, 53.
[171]Colonial Laws, p. 135.
[172]Mass. Colony Records, IV, Pt. I, 14; Pub. CSM, XV, 26, 27, 42, 43, 183, 184, 338; XXXI, 5.
[173]Mass. Colony Records, I, 258.
[174]Ibid., V, 51.
[175]Ibid., I,210; II, 221-222;Mass. Colony Records, 160.
[176]Mass. Colony Records, I, 258; 119; III, 320.
[177]Ibid., IV, Pt. II, 552.

[178]Pub. CSM, XXIX, 111, 145, 147, 188. 409; XXX, 579, 676.
[179]Mass. Colony Records, V, 74, 85.
[180]Ibid., II, 124; V, 74; Cal. State Papers, 1661-1668, 435.
[181]Mass. Colony Records, I, 31, 36; Cal. State Papers, 1661-1668, 189.
[182]Mass. Colony Records, II, 124.
[183]Ibid., V, 123.
[184]Cal. State Papers, 1574-1660, 335, 336, 341, 344, 348, 349, 377 400; 1689-1692, 273, 549.
[185]Ibid., 1574-1660, 336, 344, 348, 349.
[186]Ibid., 1574-1660, 335, 337.

The establishment of powder mills at Neposet,[187] Dorchester, Milton,[188] and Rehoboth[189] reflected colonial efforts to ease the need for powder. Fines were one source of income for local powder purchases,[190] but a more dependable source of revenue was the powder tax levied against all foreign ships entering Boston harbor.[191] This was most fitting for one of the principal strains on the powder supply was the common salute given to ships entering the harbors of Massachusetts.[192]

Though fines bore a share of the financial burden,[193] it was necessary to find other means to pay for war activities. One obvious means was the establishment of rates[194] by the county governments.[195] This was usually done when the General Court needed money for specific campaigns.[196] It was possible to borrow money from merchants when land was offered as security.[197] Tariffs on rum, cider, and beer helped to fill a treasury depleted by wars,[198] and boycotts were used to conserve goods.[199] However, on the more cheerful side of the ledger in one instance a private contribution amounted to £ 1,000 for the purchase of artillery.[200]

To save money in time of war the economy-minded Court would indulge in price fixing to stabilize the charge for horses, billeting, and provisions.[201] Script was used to pay wages.[202] Massachusetts obtained money from the New England Confederation,[203] and there was a certain economy in requiring soldiers to provide their own arms.[204]

Even though the purchase of ammunitions, powder, guns, supplies, cannon, and food-stuffs all swelled the expense list, no item was so persistent in its demand for payment as the soldier for his wages. And from the very beginning the trend in wages was upward. The wage of the foot-soldier rose from a pound per month in 1637 to a pound and ten shillings in 1676. Sergeant's wages appreciated fourfold in value in sixteen years, while the pay of captains, curiously enough, dropped off by one-third. Perhaps this is explained by the fact that captains sometimes were paid by the campaign. The salary of a captain in a campaign could run anywhere from £ 5 to £ 170.[205] But in spite of all the barrel scraping by the General Court an annual military budget for a peace-time year like 1665 amounted to £ 1,200.[206]

The arms of the militia, like so many aspects of colonial life, reflected the influence of European traditions. This was also true of the "fort psychology" cultivated by colonial military thinking. However, in either case both aspects of militia life were modified somewhat by American conditions which differed from the European scene.

In 1628 arms for one-hundred men included drums, ensigns, partizans for officers, halberds for sergeants, muskets, fowling pieces, rests, bandoleers, horn flasks, swords, belts, corselets, pikes, half-pikes, culverins, demi-culverins, and sakers.[207] The muskets were

[187]*Mass. Colony Records*, V, 73.
[188]*Ibid.*, V, 51.
[189]*Cal. State Papers*, 1675-1676, 443.
[190]*Colony Records of Mass.*, p. 167.
[191]*Mass. Colony Records*, IV, Pt. II, 331.
[192]*Ibid.*, II, 150; III, 286.
[193]*Ibid.*, I, 212.
[194]*Randolph Correspondence*, IV, 297.
[195]*Mass. Colony Records*, V, 76; *Pub. CSM*, XXIX, 560.
[196]*Mass. Colony Records*, II, 124.
[197]*Ibid.*, V, 71.
[198]*Coll. MHS*, 3rd Ser., VIII, 338-339.
[199]*Mass. Colony Records*, V, 52.
[200]*Coll. MHS*, 2nd Ser., xxix.
[201]*Mass. Colony Records*, V, 79, 137.
[202]*Ibid.*, II, 124.

[203]*Ply. Colony Records*, X, 367.
[204]*Cal. State Papers*, 1675-1676, 221.
[205]*Mass. Colony Records*, I, 192-193; II, 137; III, 321; IV, Pt. I, 217; V, 147; *Cal. State Papers*, 1576-1660, 424; 1661-1668, 196; 1675-1676, 465.
[206]*Coll. MHS*, 2nd Ser., VIII, 71-72.
[207]*Mass. Colony Records*, 1, 26. Ensigns—flags; Partizansa kind of pike; Halberd—an axe; Fowling pieces—shotguns; Rests—forked sticks to support guns; Bandoleers—ammunition belts; Culverins—sixteenth century cannon; Demiiculverins—heavy cannon; Sakers—small cannon.

of two types, bastard muskets and full muskets. The former had a spring lock and the latter a flint lock. The law required that the individual militiaman who had a musket must also provide himself with a pound of powder, twenty bullets, and two fathoms of match.[208] Later, swords, bandoleers, and rests were added to this list.[209] The pikemen were required to have a good pike well headed, a corselet, headpiece, sword, and knapsack.[210] In practice, the men actually were able to obtain only muskets, rests, swords, corselets, and bandoleers.[211] Providing the poor with this elaborate equipment posed a problem, so a law was framed to permit the poor to present corn instead of arms at the inspections. The corn was then sold to provide money to arm the unfortunate, but failing in this the poor people were put to work by the constable till they earned the value of the arms.[212]

The effectiveness of this heavy European equipment was questionable, and the passage of time marked the evolution of certain new types of arms. The early Massachusetts soldier was practically a walking fortress and had little to fear from the primitive weapons of the Indians if he had the strength to wear all his armor.[213] The Indians had difficulty in figuring where to strike the heavily armored soldier, but the soldier was no match for the Indians when it came to pursuit.[214] Gradually the use of armor was discontinued and the musket, bandoleer, powder, and shot became the popular weapons of colonial warfare.[215] But Captain John Mason could still see some value in body armor when he observed that one of his officers was

saved great bodily pain from an Indian arrow simply because he carried lumps of cheese in his rear pockets.[216]

A good deal of militia fighting was done from fortified positions, and the colonials seemed to have a profound respect for forts. The settlers felt, for example, that two-hundred men could hold ten thousand at bay in a position such as Quebec.[217] Usually the committees of militia were in charge of fort building, and for this work they could use soldiers on training days.[218] And at times it was recommended that all country rates for a year be devoted to fortification of such strategic positions as Boston, Charlestown, and Salem.[219]

Between Indian wars the operation of the militia in Massachusetts consisted mainly in drilling for the next conflict when it was possible to take time from business or husbandry.[220] In 1631 enthusiasm for drill was sufficient for the law to require meetings once a week,[221] but before the year was out ardor had cooled to the point where the drill sessions had been reduced to once a month.[222] By 1637 drill was required eight days a year.[223] In 1660 the period was cut to six days,[224] and then ultimately to four days.[225] Regimental drill was required once a year,[226] but the time was deductible from the year's total requirement for practice. On occasion, however, there would be a sudden spurt of interest in drill. During King Philips War drill sessions were held twice a week.[227]

[216]Coll. MHS, 2nd Ser., VIII, 152.
[217]Cal. State Papers, 1564-1660, 139.
[218]Mass. Colony Records, IV, Pt. II, 332; V. 73.
[219]Mass. Colony Records, IV, Pt. II, 510-511.
[220]Ibid., I, 327.
[221]Ibid., I, 85; A. B. Hart, Commonwealth History, V, 570.
[222]Mass. Colony Records, I, 90, 102, 124.
[223]Ibid., I, 210.
[224]Ibid., IV, Pt. I, 420; Colony Records of Mass., p. 159.
[225]Mass. Colony Records, V, 211-212; A. B. Hart, Commonwealth History, V, 570.
[226]Mass. Colony Records, II, 43, 118, 216.
[227]Cal. State Papers, 1675-1676, 221.

[208]Ibid., I, 85.
[209]Colony Records of Mass., p. 159.
[210]Ibid.
[211]Coll. MHS, 3rd Ser., VI, 12.
[212]Mass. Colony Records, II, 222; Colony Records of Mass., pp. 159-160.
[213]Pub. CSM, XII, 38.
[214]Coll. MHS, 2nd Ser., IV, 44; Pub. CSM, XII, 38.
[215]Ibid., XII, 39.

The scene of practice was usually at a place in or near the town. Sometimes the drills were held near the Indian wigwams.[228] Regimental drills at Boston took place at Fox Hill[229] or on the Common.[230] The soldiers were called into close order and a prayer was recited.[231] Then the men might commence their practicing at marching, skirmishing, retiring, ambuskado, and forming in battalia,[232] under the direction of captains who "shewed themselves very skillful in divers sorts of skirmishes, and other military actions."[233] Ordinarily this display of military pageantry was performed to the accompaniment of a drum.[234]

One of the most remarkable aspects about the militia drill was the fifty-six count manual of arms required by a book called Elton's Tactics or "The Compleat Body of Art Military."[235] Crucial item number forty-three read "Give fire breast high." Though the magnificent variety of motions found in this manual may have served as an exhaustive means of discipline for soldiers at drill, it is difficult to understand how the militiaman managed to avoid the scalping knife of some reasonably competent Indian while he struggled to reach number forty-three.

Usually the drill was concluded about three o'clock with another prayer. After the prayer a meal was sometimes served for the soldiers, and to this dinner the clergy was invited.[236] At other times, to the disgust of the clergymen, the soldiers would retire for a mug of rum. Nor was the holiday spirit lacking among the non-combatants on train-ing day. By 1679 the celebrating was getting out of hand so the General Court required licenses of those selling liquor at the drill field. To enforce this law the constable needed his own force of men.[237]

Another curious social aspect about militia life was legal provision for training of children, Negroes, Scotsmen, and Indians.[238] However, this law was reversed and Indians and Negroes were forbidden to train or be armed.[239]

In combat the tactics employed by the militiamen generally failed to follow any particular pattern. When under attack the men formed a single file and the musketeers fired on the enemy while the pikemen stood ready to prevent the enemy from breaking into the file. Those without a gun also kept busy gathering up the arrows shot by the Indians.[240] In surprise attacks on Indian camps the soldiers would surround the wigwams and fire their first shot toward the floor of the shelter because they knew the Indians slept on the ground.[241] Though great guns and dogs were a terror to the Indians,[242] the colonials were not without their own fears as they sniped at brush full of imaginary Indians, thus wasting ammunition and giving away their own position.[243] But the militia knew the art of ambush as well as the Indians,[244] and the location of Indian positions was obtained through the use of Indian spies.[245] Intelligence on enemy whereabouts was also sent to what was called a "flying army" but actually consisted of fast moving cavalry units.[246]

The most extensive intelligence system developed by the colony was the watch. In

[228]Mass. Colony Records, I, 90.
[229]Coll. MHS, 3rd Ser., I, xxiv.
[230]Ibid., 1st Ser., III, 243.
[231]Dunton Correspondence, p. 141.
[232]Coll. MHS, 3rd Ser., III. 50. Battalia—Order of battle; troops arranged in their proper brigades, regimants, and battalions.
[233]Ibid., 2nd Ser., I, xxiv.
[234]Pub. CSM, XII, 39.
[235]E. W. Peirce, Indian History, p. 79.
[236]Dunton Correspondence, p. 141.
[237]Mass. Colony Records, V, 211.

[238]Ibid., II, 99; III, 268.
[239]Ibid., III, 397.
[240]Coll. MHS, 2nd Ser., V, 252.
[241]Ibid., IV, 48.
[242]Cal. State Papers, 1675-1676, 253.
[243]Cal. State Papers, 1675-1676, 442.
[244]Ibid.
[245]Ibid., 1675-1676, 351.
[246]Ibid., 1689-1692, 263.

peace time the watch was a civil matter,[247] but in time of emergency it became a military activity.[248] Usually two men stood watch,[249] a pikeman and a musketeer.[250] The sentinels examined all persons who came within their watch or rounds, and had orders to fire on those who resisted investigation; but they were warned not to kill unnecessarily. If there was real danger they were to retire and give the alarm.[251]

The system of alarms centered about a beacon at Boston which would signify a general alert.[252] Other methods of spreading a general alert were the discharge of guns or ordnance, the beating of drums,[253] or the shout of a messenger "arm, arm."[254] The messenger's shout or the shot of a musket was thought sufficient for local warnings.[255] During those periods when military watches were maintained throughout the colony special groups of thirty men were held in readiness to go into action on a half-hour's notice.[256]

No particular system of medical treatment was maintained by the Massachusetts militia though physicians and surgeons accompanied regiments. Shelters were built for the wounded,[257] and in the medicinal line suger was recommended for the sick.[258] However, the smell of an empty rum flask was recommended as a comfort for those who fainted along the way.[259] Those who became seriously ill were sent home.[260]

Maintenance of discipline was based upon the punishment customary to the period.

The most likely place to incur a penalty was at drill or watch. Common offenses included disobedience, disorder, and contempt.[261] Other common offenses included delinquency in arms,[262] and firing guns after the watch was set, at drill without command, or without bullets.[263] Most of these offenses were punished by fines of a few shillings,[264] but during King Philips War many offenses were punished with great severity. For example, to resist, lift arms against, or strike an officer, to desert, engage in sedition or mutiny, or to indulge in rape, unnatural abuses, adultery, or murder meant death. Blasphemy was punished by boring the tongue with a red hot iron, but the punishment for fornication was left to the discretion of the officers.[265] Other brutal punishments included whippings, running the gauntlet, the stocks, brandings, and wearing shackles.[266] Of lesser severity were admonition before the company, discharge from the commissioned ranks, and jail.[267] However, the soldier could take an officer to court if he thought he had a case.[268]

One aspect of the operating militia which cannot be overlooked is its phenomenal inefficiency. In the United Colonies troops were supposed to be under the command of officers of the colony within whose borders they were serving.[269] Also, troops from member colonies could not be called until all aspects of the war were considered by the commissioners of the New England Confederation.[270]

[247]Mass. Colony Records, II, 151, 224.
[248]Ibid., II, 121-123.
[249]Ibid., I, 120.
[250]Ibild., II, 120.
[251]Colony Records of Mass., p. 163.
[252]Mass. Colony Records, I, 137.
[253]Colony Records of Mass., p. 163.
[254]Mass. Colony Records, V, 242.
[255]Mass. Colony Records, II, 29, 223.
[256]Ibid. II, 121-123.
[257]Ibid., V, 75.
[258]Ibid., II. 124.
[259]Coll. MHS, 2nd Ser., VIII, 151-152.
[260]Mass. Colony Records, V, 93.

[261]Ibid., II, 223; Colony Records of Mass., p. 159, 166.
[262]Ibid., pp. 169-170.
[263]Mass. Colony Records, I, 85, 98, 125.
[264]Ibid., V, 212, 243.
[265]Mass. Colony Records, V, 49-50; Cal. State Papers, 1675-1676, 299-300.
[266]Mass. Colony Records, I, 85, 270; IV, Pt. II, 511; Pub. CSM, III, 56, 63.
[267]Mass. Colony Records, I, 165; II, 23; IV, Pt. II, 97.
[268]Pub. CSM, XXX, 1108-1109.
[269]Ply. Colony Records, I, 360; A. B. Hart, Commonwealth History, II, 74-75.
[270]Ply. Colony Records, IX, 27.

On the question of supply John Endicott spoke of the unfurnished state of the country,[271] and Edward Randolph used the same gloomy tone when he wrote of a possible French attack.[272] And on one occasion the second expedition against the Narragansetts in 1676 bogged down completely when Boston refused to send out supplies.[273]

On the frontier it was difficult to obtain officers,[274] and even when present the officers had to do what they could by "persuasion and advice" because they had no authority.[275] Also, the towns on the frontier were reluctant to help one another in times of distress.[276]

The officers were not always complimentary as regards the military talent of their charges. Lion Gardiner spoke of "twenty insufficient men,"[277] and John Underhill mentioned "soldiers not accustomed to war," and "unexpert in the use of their arms."[278] Men would go hunting while they were on duty,[279] and casting away arms while in flight appeared common.[280] And the insufficiency of training was never so evident as at the Black Point massacre where inexperienced troops attempted individual escapes when ambushed by Indians.[281] Nor was the blame all with the common soldier. William Phips, with profound hindsight, estimated that he would need one-thousand barrels of powder to carry a second assault against Quebec, after the French had repulsed his first seventy-barrel attack.[282]

The General Court was conscious of this inefficiency and repeatedly sent orders to the sergeant-majors to tighten up the training.[283] However, this protest by a legal body did little to influence the militiamen to change their ways. Still, in spite of its bungling and occasional heavy losses, the Machasetts militia won all the important wars undertaken during the colonial period.

The military mentality of the Massachusetts colonial can in great part be accounted for by his desire to survive the attacks of his enemies. And this aggressiveness was tempered by the annoyance engendered by the local war games. The delay and procrastination in falling out for drill lends constant testimony to this fact. But it was more than the crude requirements of physical and economic survival which shaped the colonial soldier into a passable fighting man. Part of the answer is to be found in the churches which served as a spiritual center for the growing villages.

At the time of the Puritan migration war was taken for granted like private property and the family.[284] In fact, to deny war's legitimacy was heresy.[285] According to Nathaniel Appleton there was no moral basis for a man contending that he was a conscientious objector, for war "is an Affair with the Prince and Councils of a Nation; and the Soldier is to presume that the Government have good Reasons to justify their proclaiming and engaging in a war."[286] Only Cotton Mather sounded a sour note in holding that a man should bear suffering rather than serve in a conflict he knows to be unjust.

The General Court would justify fort repairs by holding that the strongholds should be ready for service "if God should

[271]Coll. MHS, 4th Ser., VI, 150.
[272]Randolph Correspondence, VI, 300.
[273]Pub. CSM, XXVI, 257.
[274]Randolph Correspondence, VI, 281.
[275]Cal. State Papers, 1685-1688, 592.
[276]Ibid., 1685-1688, 591-592.
[277]Coll. MHS, 3rd Ser., III, 149.
[278]Ibid., 3rd Ser., VI, 3, 23.
[279]Ibid., 2nd Ser., V, 253.
[280]Ibid., 3rd Ser., III, 143-144; Randolph Correspondence, VI, 294.
[281]Coll. MHS, 2nd Ser., VI, 634-635.
[282]Cal. State Papers, 1689-1692, 478.

[283]Colony Records of Mass., pp. 166-167.
[284]Pub. CSM, XXVIII, 68. These citations concerning religion from the Publications of the Colonial Society of Massachusetts are taken from a very excellent article by Arthur H. Buffinton.
[285]Ibid., XXVIII, 71; Cal. State Papers, 1675-1676, 221.
[286]Pub. CSM, XXVIII, 79.

Call thereunto."[287] And the New England Confederation, irked by lack of Massachusetts zeal for its expeditions, could piously barb its reluctant member with "We may comfortably Comit ourselves unto the Lord waighting upon Him in a posture of Defense and Reddiness for action as need shall Require hoping that the Lord will not suffer His people to loose by their tenderness of conscience in being slow to sheed blood."[288] The sermons to the Ancient and Honorable Artillery Company on "Anniversary Day" reflected the Puritan attitude on justification for war,[289] and it was the first minister of Boston who donated a substantial sum of money to the colony for purchase of artillery.[290]

The principle in theology which gave the Puritan the basis for his thinking was the fact that whatever is, is so by the permission or the ordinance of God. The disorder of war was thought to be a natural consequence of sin, and like all other human ills, was the result of the fall of man.[291]

One curious and egotistic twist in the Puritan interpretation of original sin was the assumption that they were another chosen people transplanted to a new land miraculously preserved and cleared of its inhabitants.[292] Edward Johnson stated the position with precise if wordy clarity when he said:

These souldiers of Christ Jesus, having made a fair retreat from their Native Country hither, and now being come to a convenient station, resolved to stand it out (the Lord Assisting) against all such as should come to rob them of their privileges, which the Lord Christ had purchased for them at a very high rate, and now out of the riches of his grace was minded to give them, yet woud he have them follow him into this Wilderness for it. Although the chiefest work of these select bands of Christ, was to mind their spiritual warfare, yet they knew right well the temple was surrounded with walls and bulworks, and the people of God in re-edifying the same, did prepare to resist their enemies with weapons of war, even while they continued building.[293]

While the chosen people prepared themselves to be "expert and fitt for such services as by the providence of God they shall be called unto,[294] they had the feeling that divine providence was on their side. When supplies failed to arrive in support of infantry during the Phips assault on Quebec the explanation was that God prevented the troops from advancing against hopeless odds by withholding the needed items.[295] On the other hand, Samuel Myles called the Quebec disaster a punishment sent by the Almighty.[296]

From a purely natural point of view Cotton Mather could argue that "Men have their Lives, Liberties, Properties, which the very light of nature teaches them to maintain by stronger arms against all Forreign Injuries. Christianity never instructed men to lay down that Natural Principle of Self-Preservation."[297] Samuel Nowell listed self-defense, recovery of property, punishment for injuries, and helping allies as causes for war.[298] This type of thinking was particularly common to Catholic kings, and especially the King of France.[299] Perhaps Edward Johnson was giving expression to this sentiment when he said:

Thus are these people with great diligence provided for these daies of war, hoping the day is at hand wherein the Lord will give Antichrist the double of all her doings . . . and now woe be to you, when the same God that directed the stone to the forehead of the Philistine, guides every bullet that is shot at you, it matters not for the whole rabble of Antichrist on your side, the God of Armies is for us a refuge high. Chela.[300]

---

[287]*Colony Records of Mass.*, p. 169.
[288]*Ply. Colony Records*, X, 57.
[289]*Pub. CSM*, XXVIII, 72.
[290]*Coll. MHS*, 2nd Ser., I, xxix.
[291]*Pub. CSM*, XXVIII, 73.
[292]*Pub. CSM*, XXVIII, 69-70.
[293]*Coll. MHS*, 2nd Ser., VII, 52-53.
[294]*Mass. Colony Records*, IV, Pt. II, 27-28.
[295]*Cal. State Papers*, 1689-1692, 386.
[296]*Ibid.*, 1689-1692, 368.
[297]*Pub. CSM*, XXVIII, 75.
[298]*Ibid.*, XXVIII, 76.
[299]*Ibid.*, XXVIII, 74-75.
[300]*Coll. MHS*, 2nd Ser., VIII, 57-58.

Nor were moral considerations on the basis of natural law and scriptural theology the ultimate in the Puritan analysis of war. In weighing the factors of good and evil as regards war John Richardson write "War is an Ordinance appoynted by God for subduing and destroying the Churches Enemies upon Earth."[301] Cotton Mather also argued that God permits war to refine and purify His church,[302] and stated further that "there is no war for the most part, which has not some injustice on one side giving Rise unto it."[303]

Perhaps the ultimate in this self-confident religious attitude on war is an example of sermons which Edward Johnson claims were presented to militia troops. The "reverend Ministers" might speak as follows:

Fellow-Souldiers, Country-men, and Companions in this wilderness-worke, who are gathered together this day by the inevitable province of the Great Jehovah, not in a tumultuous manner hurried on by the floating fancy of every high hot headed braine, whose actions prove abortive, or if any fruit brought forth; it hath been rape, theft, murther, things inconsisting with natures light then much less with a Souldiers Valour; but you my deare hearts, purposely pickt out by the godly grave Fathers of this government that your prowesse may carry on the work, where there Justice in her righteous cause is obstructed, you need not question your authority to execute those whom God, the righteous judge of all the world, hath condemned for blaspheming his sacred Majesty, and murthering his servants: every common Souldier among you is now installed a Magistrate.[304]

But the Puritan could bow his head as well as thunder his self-righteousness. On days of humiliation declared by the General Court the people would pray to God for a blessing on their military efforts. At such times men were "to humble or soules before God" in order to gain "a reconciliation with him, & his blessing on our forces."[305] And the commissioners of the New England Confederation would ask for prayers for "successe in our Indeavors for Repelling the Rage of the enemy."[306] Apparently the prayers of the militia were answered. For although their dead were strewn along the New England trails the colonial Massachusetts militia on no occasion failed to achieve its ultimate objective.

Though it would not be correct to say that the militia was the most important single institution in the life of the early Massachusetts citizen, or that it was even as important as the Congregational Church, in view of available evidence it becomes quite apparent that the militia was a very deep rooted and organic part of colonial life in the Bay Colony. Since the need for organized military protection was genuine and immediate, the only remaining problem was to adopt the most convenient means. This was the militia system as the settlers had known it in England. Once established, the militia became important as an avenue to political and military prominence for the soldier-politician. Economically and financially the militia was annoying to most citizens who were burdened with the expense of providing themselves with arms. Socially, the militia provided a break in the otherwise grueling process of earning a living; and sometimes this break was gay and colorful. After drill a man could enjoy some rum with his fellow soldiers even though most of the ministers disapproved. But in the serious business of war the ministers could only nod their approval, for in Massachusetts the licitness of waging war was guaranteed by God as well as man. Delicately interwoven with other aspects of colonial life, the militia, as an institution, was extremely important in shaping the men who were to father the founders of a new nation.

301 *Pub. CSM*, XXVIII, 74.
302 *Ibid.*
303 *Ibid.*
304 *Coll. MHS*, 2nd Ser., IV, 45-46.
305 *Mass. Colony Records*, V, 69.

306 *Ply. Colony Records*, X, 358.

# THE COLONIAL MILITIA
## AS A SOCIAL INSTITUTION:
## SALEM, MASSACHUSETTS 1764-1775

By Ronald L. Boucher*

THE Militia system established by English settlers in America became in time one of the most important institutions in colonial life. By the eighteenth century a pattern of development by the militia was clearly evident. In the beginning the militia was a necessity in safeguarding small and isolated communities against a hostile and threatening environment. By the end of the Great War for Empire, its military vigor and effectiveness had seriously declined, only to be revived again during the Revolutionary crisis. These changes reflect the growth and maturity of the American colonies.

When the colonies became more secure and permanent, and the militia's defense activities decreased, its importance within colonial communities became increasingly social. John Adams, for instance, noted in 1782 that four institutions—the towns, congregations, schools and militia—provided the key to understanding American history. To Adams, these institutions "produced the American Revolution," and were the foundations of the liberty, happiness and prosperity of the American people.[1] The militia was one of the most enduring colonial institutions, theoretically including almost all white males, and was active or present in nearly every community. Since it was so thoroughly integrated into the complex pattern of colonial society, an investigation into the militia's social aspects offers new insights into colonial history, particularly the changes and conflicts as the Revolution approached. The legal structure and regulations of the militia have been thoroughly studied, but its importance as a social institution often has been neglected.[2]

Such an inquiry demands that the militia be studied in specific geographic settings because it was basically a local institution. Community attitudes and conflicts regarding the militia and its relationship to other social organizations and processes undoubtedly more important than its legal framework in revealing the social significance of the militia. The community of Salem, Massachusetts provides a unique opportunity to examine the colonial militia as a social institution. As a result of Salem's location on the seacoast, the military functions of its militia were very limited by the eighteenth century, but its social importance was increased. The Salem militia was also a focus of conflict and dramatic change in the Revolutionary period, and this attempt to revive the militia as an effective military force, only partly successful in Salem, illustrates the difficulties of the Revolutionary movement.

The militia was first organized in Salem in 1630, and by the mid-eighteenth century it had gradually expanded to include four companies in the First Essex Regiment. Both active and inactive militia titles were commonplace in Salem. Yet, there were so many exemptions from militia service in this seacoast town, such as fishermen and seamen, that its militia was smaller than that in many other communities. Due to Salem's impor-

---

*Dr. Ronald Boucher is Professor of History, Clark University.

[1]Charles F. Adams, ed., *The Works of John Adams* (Boston, 1851), V, 494-5.

[2]John Shy, "A New Look at Colonial Militia," *William and Mary Quarterly,* 3rd Series, XX (1963), 185; see also Ellery B. Crane, "The Early Militia System of Massachusetts," *Proceedings of the Worcester Society of Antiquity,* IX (1888), 105-127, Jack S. Radabaugh, "The Military System of Colonial Massachusetts," (unpublished Ph.D. dissertation, University of Southern California, 1965), and Richard H. Marcus, "The Militia of Colonial Connecticut, 1639-1775," (unpublished Ph.D. dissertation, University of Colorado, 1965).

tance in Essex County, however, it was able to dominate important officer positions of leadership in its militia regiment.

Many community attitudes in Salem were related to its militia. The colonists, in general, viewed a standing army as a threat to their liberties and rights. And in Salem, the most vociferous militia analyst, Timothy Pickering, contended in his first letter written as "A Military Citizen," and published in the *Essex Gazette*, that a well-organized militia rendered permanent professional armies unnecessary on American soil.[3] When British regulars were stationed in Boston in 1768, the *Essex Gazette* stated: "The thoughts of a Standing Army are more and more alarming to this People, who hitherto supported the due Execution of constitutional Law without the Necessity of such Aid." As the Revolution approached these beliefs had important implications for the colonial militia because, as will be shown, the initial defense efforts of the colonists reemphasized the militia system of earlier days.

The public often took an active interest in Salem's militia, at times responding with pride and enthusiasm on muster days. In fact, public approval appears to have been one of the main concerns of these events held four times each year. In 1770, in the *Essex Gazette*, it was reported that "The good Order and Regularity with which they performed all parts of their Duty, very sensibly pleased a numerous crowd of Respectable Spectators, and reflected great Honor on the Assiduity and military Skills of their Officers." Training days were secular holidays when the militia "performed their Exercises to such general Acceptance as would do Honor to any Militia."

To Salem's militia leadership such occa-

sions were also socially important. Muster days were opportunities to gather together as a group and reinforce their distinctive importance as militia leaders. After one day of training, for instance, it was reported, "the officers prepared an elegant dinner at Mr. Goodhue's Tavern . . . (and) they spent the Evening together at the same House, when they made a Collection and released a Debtor from Prison." On special occasions in Salem, such as a visit by the governor in 1774, the mustering and review of the militia was usually an integral part of civil celebrations. In the decade prior to the Revolution, social interest in militia activities often outweighed military purposes.

An anonymous letter to the *Essex Gazette*, however, indicates that not everyone in Salem was so interested in the militia. "F," a correspondent in the *Essex Gazette*, took ". . . the Freedom to mention the Fault that some of my Neighbors find with it." He thought that the militia held only slight interest for the average person (those who "have time only in the Evening to read News."). It was a vital concern only to men "impatient to be promoted." "F" implied that persons active in militia affairs were seeking their own social or individual aims, and asked the printer, referring to Pickering's letters, "If the Old Gentleman should come again (as I fear he will after the next Training) pray desire him to have Pity on your Readers, and not be so lengthy."

The militia in Salem also came in for some criticism. Timothy Pickering's interest was highly critical, and even before the prospect of armed conflict with England became likely, he agitated for militia reforms. According to Pickering, one of the main reasons why the militia was so "truly contemptible" in 1770 was because it was now mainly composed of "Children, Apprentices and Men of Low Rank." The lower classes had come to dominate the militia because "everyone who could pay a small Fine, thought it beneath them to appear on a Muster."

The militia's leadership also drew criticism. One attitude reported in the *Essex Gazette* was voiced by "A Common Soldier," who thought

---

[3]This and other quotes from Pickering's comments on the militia, along with other quoted and paraphrased comments and descriptions of the militia by its contemporaries are largely from the *Essex Gazette* and the *Salem Gazette*. In most instances, to conserve space, the issue will not be cited, but this information, along with more extensive footnotes, is available from the author. The identification of Timothy Pickering as "A Military Citizen" is provided by Octavius Pickering, *The Life of Timothy Pickering* (Boston, 1867), I, 16.

"the conduct of the officers of that company to which I have the misfortune to belong," was so neglectful of militia affairs that it actually discouraged many young men from taking interest or pride in their own defense. With disgust he declared that the present officers were "so lazy and imcompetent" that they actually ridiculed those sincere militiamen who tried to improve themselves. This critic attributed the problem to "an amazing infatuation of many militia officers . . . that the only end of giving them commissions was that they might be addressed by the title of captain, lieutenant or ensign." The importance of titles was emphasized in town meetings, he cynically noted, where moderators were extremely careful "lest they should offend their honors by omitting these notable marks of distinction." To "A Common Soldier," the militia was being misused by those who saw it as a means of securing or maintaining social recognition.

Timothy Pickering declared that the main problem was that "Officers in the Militia have sometimes descended from Persons of Interest, Influence and Abilities, to others Inferior in all those Respects, and these last to a Class still lower, and so on till at length, in the Course of a few Years, the Officers have gotten into the lowest Hands." The best gentlemen have mistakenly paid "little attention to military exercises, though it behooves *them* more than any others." The better classes should be involved in the militia greater in Proportion to the greater Interests they have to be defended and guarded." The solution according to Pickering was to attract more men of "Fortune, Weight and Figure." The social structure of the militia should conform more closely to the hierarchical

| TABLE 1 TAXES FOR 1764, 1765 AND 1773 | | | |
|---|---|---|---|
| Militia Officers | | Town Officers | Town Mean |
| **1764:** | | | |
| Range (R. Foster) | £ 0.12/6½ | £ 1.18/10 (Jon Gardner) | |
| (B. Pickman) | 45. 4/11 | 37.13/4 (R. Derby, Jr.) | |
| Average | 8. 8/10 | 9. 3/2 | £2. 8/2 |
| **1765:** | | | |
| Range (E. Procter) | 0.17/10 | 0.17/3 (S. Higginson) | |
| (B. Pickman) | 42.10/½ | 42.10/½ (B. Pickman) | |
| Average | 7. 5/1½ | 7. 3/2 | 0.19/10 |
| **1773:** | | | |
| Range (B. Ward) | 0.13/2 | 0.14/1 (E. Beckford) | |
| (R. Derby, Jr.) | 33. 1/6 | 33. 1/6 (R. Derby, Jr.) | |
| Average | 6.18/7 | 0.17/3 (S. Higginson) | 1. 5/5 |

(This table is based upon an analysis of the Salem tax records preserved in the Salem City Hall. These tax lists include 1008-1100 individuals each year, usually the heads of households. Only four militia officers and one town leader could not be identified with certainty. The figures in this table are a summary of three different tax authorities, the province, county and town. And three separate tax bases were used at that time to compute each individual's burden, "For Polls," "For House and Lands," and "For Personal Estate and Income by Trade and Faculty.")

social order prevailing in colonial society.

The efforts to rejuvenate Salem's militia provide insight into the colonial attitudes towards warfare. Many problems such as tardiness, absenteeism and drunkenness were identified, but the basic failing appeared to be a lack of "military discipline," i.e. the ability to perform many complicated exercises and maneuvers in large formations. In one respect, therefore, the militia leaders of Salem reflected the rigid, mechanistic views of the British. On the other hand, the military manual most strongly recommended was the "Norfolk Manual" which presented military discipline in a simplified manner, compared to other eighteenth century manuals. The difficulties of teaching military discipline under colonial conditions was often recognized, and therefore the colonials sought the most practical guidelines. At least one Salem officer, Captain Samuel Barton, Jr., made a brief attempt at improving and standardizing militia drills at the "Exercises of the 2nd Day."[4] But the most important effort was made by Timothy Pickering who in 1775 published *An Easy Plan of Discipline for a Militia*. Pickering's approach was clearly pragmatic. Because of the limited time available for training, he sought to simplify earlier manuals even more by eliminating "the custom and prejudice (that) are the foundations of many practices among the military, and maxims . . . blindly adopted without any examination of the principles upon which they are founded."[5] The ordinary militiaman must understand the exercises performed, and if the motions are taught because they are "convenient, useful and necessary," they will be accepted and learned more easily.

The social importance of the militia also may be investigated by examining the relationship of its leaders to other aspects of Salem society. For example, a variety of typical occupations were represented by the militia leaders. Although "merchant" was the most commonly identified occupation, the list also includes several "gentlemen," a draper, blacksmith, anchorsmith, gristmill operator, farmer and chairmaker. It must be remembered that the colonials frequently did not specialize and many of these individuals may have been engaged in several activities. Yet, it is evident that this group included a broad spectrum of Salem's economy in the 1760s and 1770s.

The wealth of the militia officers also indicates their relative position in Salem. A reasonably accurate measurement of this wealth may be found in the Salem tax records. Table 1, summarizing the data for selected years, reveals the following patterns. The average total tax paid by militia officers was £7.10/11, and by town officers £7.16/10. For the same years a random 7-8 percent sampling of the town's population shows the average tax paid by Salem's residents was £1.11/02. The range of taxes levied, moreover, was similarly distributed. In the average year only three of eighteen militia officers and two of thirty town officers paid less than the town mean. In general, militia and town positions of authority were filled by men of approximately equal economic means and, despite a few obvious exceptions, the wealth of both groups was far above that of the average citizen.

The rate of turnover among Salem's militia officers is another factor in analyzing its leadership. Major appointments were made in 1765-1767, and again in 1771 (commissions were given irregularly and were held for an indefinite term). Fifteen men were commissioned at the earlier dates, but only four were reappointed in 1771. The last group of militia commissions prior to the Revolution therefore included fourteen out of eighteen individuals who had not previously held military office.[6] In 1771 there was only one town officer who had belonged to the same group during the years 1765-1767. There was a basically similar pattern of leader turnover in the militia and town even though the method of selection to each group was fundamentally different. These facts reflect, in part, the

---

[4]Samuel and John Barton, "Letters, 1758-1798," (manuscript, The Essex Institute).

[5]Timothy Pickering, Jr., *An Easy Plan of Discipline of a Militia* (Salem, 1775), 3-4, and 11-12.

[6]*Massachusetts Archives—Muster Rolls, 1761-1774*, IC, 84-5, and 424-5. Six names were illegible in these official records and could not be located in other sources.

colonial attitude that obligated a man to serve his community. This idea of duty demanded that an individual serve in public office when requested or expected to do so. But many also sought to restrict such duty to as short a time as possible. This rapid rate of turnover implies that militia commissions probably were often based upon non-military considerations determined at the provincial level of government rather than by local military concerns for the effectiveness of the militia.

A further indication of the social recognition given to militia officers is the frequency of plural office-holding by these men. Of the twenty-nine active militia officers between 1765 and 1774, twelve also held positions of civil importance in Salem. Conversely, 39 per cent of the town leaders held militia commissions during the same period. This integration of leadership again indicates that non-military considerations were an important factor in the selection of militia officers. Contrary to the assertions of Timothy Pickering, whose opinions were influenced mainly by the problems of military effectiveness, the militia leadership obviously included the wealthier men of Salem, and while this was a rapidly changing rather than static group, these were also men who generally enjoyed more than the usual social recognition.

During the decade after 1764 political interests and factions appear to have exercised a decisive influence upon the Salem militia. Since appointments were the responsibility of the provincial government, there was frequently a conflict between it and town authorities. Two incidents involving William Browne illustrate the importance of provincial control over militia commissions. In 1768 Salem had instructed its representatives to the General Assembly, Browne and Peter Frye, to support the "rescinding petition" from Massachusetts against English duties. When Browne and Frye disobeyed these orders they were quickly removed from their posts by the town.[7] Salem's sentiments were

indicated by their replacements, Richard Derby, Jr. and John Pickering, both ardent patriots during the 1770s and annually returned to office for the next six years. However, both Browne and Frye retained their militia posts, and in 1771 were promoted to colonel and major respectively in the First Essex Regiment.

In a second episode, William Browne was arrested in 1769 in connection with the beating of James Otis by John Robinson in a Boston tavern. When Otis was strongly supported by the *Essex Gazette*, which also printed Robinson's apology for his actions, Browne discontinued his subscription to Salem's local newspaper on the grounds that it had become too radical. He was publicly criticized for this behavior. It is clear that Browne, Frye and others leaning towards Toryism were becoming politically unacceptable in Salem. However, because militia appointments were controlled by provincial authorities, this group of future Loyalists remained in their militia posts for several more years. Provincial officals indicated their attitude in 1771 when three of the only four re-appointments to the Salem militia were men who would soon decide on loyalty to England.

The label of Tory was a serious charge in Salem even several years before the Revolution. As early as 1770 Timothy Pickering became embroiled in a newspaper controversy when "Y" accused him of leading a pro-British party that sought its own self-interest rather than the public good. In three vigorous replies Pickering denied these charges, asserting that he had long since disassociated himself from his earlier Tory friends, supported colonial resistance to British infringements of American rights, and had never embraced Tory principles. He offered his constant endeavors to improve the militia as proof of his patriotism.[8]

[7]"Essex County Loyalists," *Essex Institute Historical Collections*, XLIII (1907), 290; Clifford K. Shipton, *Sibley's Harvard Graduates* (Boston, 1965), XIII, 552; and E.

Alfred Jones, *The Loyalists of Massachusetts, Their Memorials, Petitions and Claims* (London, 1930), 58-9.

[8]*Essex Gazette*, 9-16 Oct. 1770, and 23-30 Oct. 1770. Apparently only "R" still doubted Pickering, for he went on to become one of the most important revolutionary leaders in Salem, see *ibid.* 23-40 Oct. 1770.

In most respects, the militia resembled Salem society in the eighteenth century, with one important difference—local communities had only limited control over militia commissions. In times of crisis, conflict over the militia between the colonists and the British was almost certain. The resolution of this conflict and the hurried attempts to prepare the militia for an active military role must be analyzed to understand the intial impact of the Revolution upon the militia in Salem.

One important aspect of the militia as a social institution has remained obscure. Little is known of the "common man" in the militia. As recent efforts to study the common man in American history have indicated, this is usually a difficult task.[9] The brief glimpses offered by contemporary observers, such as Timothy Pickering, are undoubtedly biased. During peaceful years inadequate militia records were kept or preserved to investigate the socio-economic status of the average militia member, and their attitudes towards the militia have also remained largely unknown.

As the American Revolution approached, the militia became increasingly important to the colonists. An investigation of its role in this crisis is a revealing study of institutional change. The dramatic changes in the militia after 1774 stemmed partly from the sudden demand that it become militarily more effective, but the colonists also sought to make the militia conform with patriotic attitudes. This second motive for change was especially important in Salem where partisan politics influenced almost every aspect of life.

In the years prior to the Revolution Salem's attitudes towards the British changed significantly. While joining the protests over the Stamp Act in 1765, for instance, Salem maintained its loyalty to England. Ten years later the transformation had been so complete that it was declared: "The Colonies are convinced that their Liberties depend upon their Power, and are generally attentive to military Discipline."[10]

Many members of the militia in Salem reflected this shift in attitudes by their involvement in organized protest. Forty percent of the committee elected to draft Salem's protest concerning the Stamp Act held military titles. Militia leaders also comprised 66 per cent of the Boycott Committee in 1770 and 55 per cent of the Committee of Correspondence. In 1774 militia officers made up 63 per cent of the delegates to the Essex County Convention and provided both of Salem's representatives to the Provincial Congress in the same year. These facts become more meaningful when compared to the letter welcoming Governor Gage to Salem in 1774; only eight of forty-eight signatures belonged to militia officers, three of whom soon after apologized for this mistake. There was a significant group of at least twelve militia officers, however, who did not participate in any rebellious activities. A sharp division had therefore developed within the militia's leadership. Despite the fact that its leaders comprised a high percentage of those involved in organized patriotic activities, they still constituted slightly less than half of the militia officers in Salem. Most of these pro-patriot leaders had emerged in the years after 1765 and were part of a three-way split within the militia—patriots, Tories and undecided. Therefore, prior to its reorganization in 1774 it is doubtful that the militia could have acted as a unified body because of these political divisions.

Salem became inescapably involved in the forces leading to the decisive break with

[9]A brief discussion of these difficulties may be found in Tamara K. Hareven, ed., *Anonymous Americans: Explorations in Nineteenth Century Social History* (Englewood Cliffs, New Jersey, 1971), ix. Jesse Lemisch has criticized American historians and the American Historical Association (through the National Historical Publications commission) in "The Papers of Great White Men," *AHA Newsletter* (November 1971), pp. 7-21, and received a reply from Boyd C. Shafer, *ibid.*, (May 1972), p. 25. Lemisch's efforts to redress this imbalance may be found in "The American Revolution Seen from the Bottom Up," in Barton J. Bernstein, ed., *Towards a New Past: Dissenting Essays in American History* (New York, 1968), pp. 3-45, and "Jack Tar in the Streets: Merchant Seamen in the Politics of the American Revolution," *William and Mary Quarterly*, 3rd Series, XXV (1968), 371-407.

[10]*Salem Town Records, 1765*, pp. 542-43, and *Essex Gazette*, 17-24 Jan. 1775.

England when Governor Thomas Gage attempted to escape the unsettled, radical atmosphere of Boston by moving the General Court to Salem in 1774. Conflict within Salem was quickly apparent. After being welcomed at a ball hosted by Colonel William Browne, Gage received two contradictory letters, the *Salem Gazette* reported. One expressed the support of many citizens for Gage's recent actions, and the other criticized British policies with uncompromising harshness. Tensions were further heightened when the justices of the Essex County court assured Gage that they would preserve "law and order" in Salem, and also upon the removal of British troops from Boston to Salem.

The General Court that convened in Salem confronted Gage with a legislature as stubbornly resistant to his wishes as any he had faced in Boston. Realizing that he could not control this legislature, and fearful that they might decide to defy British authority, he issued a message of dismissal to the lower house. But it refused to bow to his orders, and proceeded to endorse the motion for a provincial congress to meet that Fall.[11]

Gage then turned his frustrated anger upon Salem. In August 1774, the Committee of Correspondence had announced a special town meeting to select delegates to the Essex County Convention that was to be held soon. As the meeting was assembling, Gage informed the Committee that it was illegal and should be immediately dispersed. When the Committee refused to cooperate and Salem proceeded to elect its representatives, Gage issued a warrant for the Committee's arrest, delivered by Peter Frye. Two Committee members were arrested as a result, but realizing the futility of his position Gage soon dropped the charges against them. For the future of the militia, however, these events were decisive.

The Essex County Convention met at Ipswich on 6 and 7 September 1774. Its decisions concerning the militia clearly were influenced by recent events in Salem which required "immediate opposition." The Con-

vention resolved that any officers or magistrates who cooperated with England to restrict American liberties "are and will be considered its unnatural and malignant enemies." William Browne and Peter Frye, both regimental militia officers in Salem, were singled out for special criticism. Condemnation of Frye for his part in the arrest of two members of the Committee of Correspondence was suspended awaiting his apology and pledge to reform. Browne was censured more severely for his acceptance of a position as Mandamus Councilor, and the Convention demanded that he resign his current offices and refuse other appointments.

Frye quickly deferred to the Convention and assured Salem that, "I will not accept any Commission under said Act of Parliament. . . and therefore hope to be restored to that Friendship and Regard with my Fellow-Citizens and Countrymen which I heretofore enjoyed."[12] Despite these efforts, Frye's patriotism remained doubtful in Salem, and soon after his house and store were set afire and totally destroyed. Frye was left with little choice but to join the Loyalists and flee Massachusetts when the Revolution began.

Browne, however, steadfastly refused to alter his stance. Even after conferring with a special committee and receiving public encouragement to associate himself with the patriots, he stated, "I cannot consent to defeat His Majesty's Intentions and disappoint His Expectations by abandoning a Post to which He has Graciously pleased to appoint me . . . I will therefore give Him no Cause to suspect my Fidelity."[13] Browne's property was also damaged by zealous patriots and he was forced to leave Salem for the safety of Boston.[14]

---

[11]Gilbert L. Streeter, "Salem Before the Revolution," *Essex Institute Historical Collections*, XXXII (1896), 80.

[12]*Ibid.*

[13]*Essex Gazette,* 13-20 Sept. 1774; see also the replies of "Johannes in Eremo," and "An American," in *ibid.,* 20-27 Sept. 1774.

[14]The third important militia officer to become a Loyalist, Benjamin Pickman, expressed the conflict of many Tories when he wrote to his wife from exile, . . . " 'twas death to leave you, 'twas worse to stay and enter into measures which my conscience totally disapproved of." George Francis Dow, ed., *The Diary and Letters of*

The Provincial Congress which met in Concord stressed the need for increased defense preparations and ordered county and town militia units to be reorganized. An important feature of their recommendations revived the practice of local election of officers. On 26 October, 1774, it suggested that those companies which "have not already chosen and appointed officers, that they meet forthwith and elect officers to command their respective companies."[15]

Colonel Browne's refusal to resign his various offices had given Essex County the opportunity to take militia affairs into their own hands even before this decision by the Provincial Congress. On 4 October 1774, many of the militia officers resigned their commissions because of Browne's "exertions for carrying into execution acts of Parliament calculated to enslave and ruin his native land."[16] The militia in effect was dissolved and could now be reorganized free of British influence. Only through such direct and radical action were the Essex County towns able to exert sufficient power to determine the political persuasion of its militia officers. A minority of the county's militia leaders were responsible for the action. Less than half of the officers resigned (twenty-three in all, nine from Salem). There is nothing to suggest that either Tories or even those who were at the time moderates or undecided participated in this decision. The reorganized militia, as might be expected, consisted mainly of the most enthusiastic supporters of independence from England.

While many Essex County towns quickly elected new officers and intensified militia training, little of this activity was evident in Salem for many months. An attempt to select officers in December 1774, was apparently unsuccessful because when Timothy Picker-

ing was appointed Colonel of the First Essex Regiment two months later, he was compelled to instruct the militia companies of Salem "to hold themselves in readiness to march at the shortest notice under the command of such officers as they shall choose."[17] Unlike other towns, it took a minor crisis to prod Salem into serious military preparations.

In February 1775, the British received rumors of cannon placements in the Salem area, and dispatched a small unit from Boston to investigate. The British troops confronted a hastily assembled group of militiamen at the North Bridge entrance to Salem. With little hope of accomplishing their purpose, the British avoided armed conflict. The disorganized response of the Salem militia, particularly its leadership, demonstrated its inadequate preparation. Soon afterwards the first general training session was held at which "Every person liable by law to train, and to muster upon an Alarm, belonging to the Militia of this Town, have been warned to appear in School Street . . . with Arms Ammunitions and Accoutrements." Two minutemen companies were formed, additional money was appropriated for defense and Salem "Voted that there be a constable's watch kept in the town consisting of ten persons nightly."[18]

But events moved swiftly, and when the "British commenced hostilities upon the People of this Province," the Salem militia was still not completely prepared. On 19 April 1775, several hundred militiamen under the command of Timothy Pickering rather than their elected captains failed to intercept the British retreat from Lexington and Concord.[19] The transformation of Salem's

---

*Benjamin Pickman (1740-1819) of Salem, Massachusetts* (Newport, Rhode Island, 1928), p. 97.

[15]For a detailed discussion of militia reorganization at this time, see David R. Millar, "The Militia, The Army and Independence in Colonial Massachusetts," (unpublished Ph.D. dissertation, Cornell University, 1967), p. 284 *passim.*

[16]*Essex Gazette,* 18-25 Oct. 1774.

[17]*Ibid.,* 13-20 Dec. 1774; and Timothy Pickering, Jr., "Letter to the Captains and Subalterns of the First Company of Militia in Salem," *Essex Institute Historical Collections,* II (1860), 155.

[18]*Ibid.,* 29 Feb-6 March 1775; and *Salem Town Records,* 1775, p. 29.

[19]A great deal of controversy resulted from the failure of the Salem militia to engage the British in their retreat. For a discussion of this issue in which Salem sought to ". . . take effectual steps to vindicate its innocence, and

militia into an effective military force was not a task that was easily or quickly accomplished, but there could be no doubt regarding its attitude towards Independence.

By April 1775, the Salem militia had been significantly changed by the events of the previous decade. During most of that time the militia had lapsed as a military organization, and much of the interest in it was non-military. Beginning in mid-1774, however, renewed emphasis was placed upon the militia's original purpose—the defense of Salem. This caused the militia to assume new importance, and indicates why Adams thought it continued to be one of the most fundamental colonial institutions. The alternative to a militia defense system, a professional standing army, again was proven unnecessary, for the time being at least.

The importance of the militia, however, cannot be assessed solely in military terms. The militia reflected many of the issues and conflicts that were crucial in pre-Revolutionary colonial society. Through both its leadership and the increased importance placed upon its role in the colony, the militia was directly involved in the crises in Salem and Essex County as the Revolution approached. It was a focus of conflict that witnessed a growing polarization and struggle for control, and by 1774 had reached a point in which the opposing factions were virtually irreconcilable. These divisions, scarcely evident in the early 1760s, increased and be-

came determining forces as the complex interplay of revolutionary events and issues quickened.

While the militia was being transformed into a more effective military organization, it remained an important social institution. In fact, social and political concerns had become more decisive, as was the case in many other aspects of colonial life in the 1770s. The developments and changes in the militia, and the conflicts in which it was involved, are an interesting study of institutional transformation in revolutionary America. But while this study suggests several important aspects of the militia as a social institution, it also serves to raise further questions. Important insights, for example, might arise from a more extensive comparison of the new militia officers after 1774 with the earlier leadership. Greater understanding of the social impact of the American Revolution upon the colonies might be gained by examining the continuing transformations of the militia during the Revolution.

The conclusion reached in 1775, when it was generally agreed to revive the earlier and basically seventeenth century militia structure is particularly important. Greater universality of service was required, the urgency of day-to-day preparedness was emphasized, and most importantly, the direct control of each community over its militia was reasserted. This reorganization of the militia demonstrates a distinctive thrust of the American Revolution that sought to return to simpler, more direct institutions—the militia included—that many Americans felt had always been successful in preserving their rights and liberties.

procure a redress of these grievances which are too many and too heavy any longer silently to be endured," see *Salem Town Records*, 1775, pp. 54-63.

# COLONIAL OPPOSITION TO THE QUARTERING OF TROOPS DURING THE FRENCH AND INDIAN WAR

By J. Alan Rogers*

NEARLY a century and a half of resistance to arbitrary military power was ignored when the Crown left the quartering of troops in America to the British army during the French and Indian War. Americans vigorously opposed the forced quartering of troops as a violation of the constitutional guarantee that the army should be subordinate to civil authority. Moreover, the colonists went beyond legalistic objections to the actions of the British army to a defense of the underlying principle articulated by that provision of the constitution. Specifically, they feared that if British military power were allowed to reign unchecked in America—as the Crown's new policy seemed to threaten—liberty itself would be destroyed.

Students of colonial history have not defined the issue as clearly as the colonists did. Historians of the French and Indian War who are interested in the problems faced by British leaders in its prosecution usually picture the colonists who spoke out against forced quartering as shortsighted obstructionists whose petty arguments undermined the war for empire. Those historians intent on tracing the development of political ideology have described the controversy over quartering simply as one more milestone on the colonists' march to democracy. Other historians have viewed the whole business as a power struggle masquerading as a constitutional debate. For instance, it is maintained that the Pennsylvania Assembly used the quartering issue to make gains in its contest for political supremacy with the governor. Another view is that the bitterness stirred up in the early years of the war was forgotten when General Jeffery Amherst assumed command in America. And finally, one student finds that the "'ideological' differences were over-shadowed by the sure consequences of appearing laggard in the King's service." While this interpretation explains generally why the struggle over quartering was not more divisive than it was, it does not account for the widely held view that the British army's actions presented a real danger to American liberty.[1]

Since the revolutionary settlement of 1689, Parliament had enacted an annual Mutiny Act which among other things expressly prohibited quartering on private citizens against their will. In 1723, 1754, and 1756 certain provisions of the Mutiny Act were specifically stated by Parliament to be applicable in the colonies, but the sections on quartering were not extended to America until the war there had ended. During the war Americans were told only that they must

*Dr. J. Alan Rogers is Assistant Professor of History, University of California, Irvine.

[1]See, for example, Lawrence Henry Gipson, *The Coming of the Revolution* (New York, 1959), p. 128, and the more sympathetic but similar treatment of the colonists' arguments in Stanley M. Pargellis, *Lord Loudoun in North America* (New Haven, 1933), p. 210- Theodore Thayer, *Pennsylvania Politics and the Growth of Democracy, 1740-1776* (Philadelphia, 1948), p. 60; John Zimmerman, "Governor Denny and the Quartering Act of 1756," *Pennsylvania Magazine of History and Biography*, XCI (1967), 280-381; Nicholas B. Wainwright, "Governor William Denny in Pennsylvania," *ibid.*, LXXXI (1957), 178-79; John Shy, *Toward Lexington: The Role of the British Army in the Coming of the American Revolution* (Princeton, 1965), p. 143; John Schutz, *Thomas Pownall, British Defender of American Liberty* (Glendale, Calif., 1951), pp. 109, 115; Ralph L. Ketcham, "Conscience, War and Politics in Pennsylvania, 1755-1757," *William and Mary Quarterly*, 3rd ser., XX (1963), 419; Bernard Bailyn, *Ideological Origins of the American Revolution* (Cambridge, Mass., 1967), pp. 61-64, brilliantly demonstrates how much the political culture of America was shaped by the ideas and fears of England's radical Whigs. In particular, they pointed out the dangers of arbitrary military power.

follow the orders issued by the commanders-in-chief for quartering soldiers.

Early in 1755 General Edward Braddock acridly told the Pennsylvania Assembly that, as the assigning of quarters for the army was his province, he would "take due care to burthen those colonies the most, that show the least loyalty to his Majesty." Edward Shippen, a wealthy Pennsylvania merchant, wrote his son:

The Assembly know not how to stomach this military address, but tis thought it will frighten them into some reasonable measures as it must be a vain thing to contend with a General at the head of an army, though he should act an artibtrary part; especially in all probability he will be supported in everything at home.[2]

The general did not live to carry out his threat. He and nearly half his men were killed in an ambush near the banks of the Monongahela River in July 1755.

Lord Loudoun, who arrived a year later to resume the military campaign in America, was well aware that the legal basis of his demands for quarters was ill-defined; but he was determined to get what he needed, by force if necessary. "As to quarters at Philadelphia and every other place," he instructed one of his senior officers in September 1756, "where I find it Necessary to have Troops, I have a Right to them, and must have them; I would have you go gently with the People at First, but [you] must not give up. . . . "[3]

In October Loudoun wrote Governor William Denny of Pennsylvania informing him that one battalion of royal troops was to be quartered in Philadelphia. Loudoun disingenuously added that he thought it unnecessary to spell out the army's needs because, as an ex-army officer, Denny was "so thoroughly

acquainted with the Quartering in England in Time of Peace, and what Things are furnished in Quarters, for the Officers and Soldiers, and how much further Quartering extends in Time of War, and even must do so from the Nature of Things." In fact, neither Denny nor anyone else, including Loudoun, knew what effect war had on the provision of the Mutiny Act, because there had been no clear precedents for quartering in Great Britain in wartime since 1689.

Even the Privy Council's veto of a quartering act passed by the Pennsylvania Assembly in 1755 provided little positive help. The Council's negative opinion seemed to be provoked as much by its hostility to Pennsylvania pacifist tendencies as by the idea that the rights of Englishmen in regard to quartering were not applicable in America. Thus, when the Assembly's new bill was sent to Governor Denny in December 1756 it contained the customary guarantee that citizens would not be forced to take soldiers into their homes. Denny refused to sign the bill, insisting that the Privy Council had rejected the first quartering act simply because it had included such a provision. When the bill was reconsidered by the Assembly on 8 December the objectionable passage was omitted, but so too was any reference to quartering in private homes. The new act outlined a procedure for lodging soldiers only in public houses.[4]

It was soon apparent, however, that there was a serious shortage of quarters. On 15 December Denny reported to the Council that despite his orders to city officials and the Assembly, "the King's Forces still remained

---

[2]Edward Shippen to Joseph Shippen, 19 Mar. 1755, "Military Letters of Captain Joseph Shippen of the Provincial Service, 1756-1758," *Pennsylvania Magazine of History and Biography*, XXXVI (1912), 35.

[3]Loudoun to Col. John Stanwix, 23 Sept. 1756, Loudoun Papers (Henry E. Huntington Library, LO 1885 [hereafter cited as LO]). Loudoun had already received reports from John Rutherford that made it clear there was going to be trouble between the army and the Pennsylvania government; see Rutherford to Loudoun, 12, 14, 16 Aug. 1756, Lo 1473, 1485, 1499.

[4]Attorney General William Murray told the Privy Council that Pennsylvania's 1755 quartering law should be disallowed because "the application of such propositions to a Colony in time of War, in the case of Troops raised for their Protection by Authority of the Parliament of Great Britain made the first time by an Assembly, many of whom plead what they call Conscience, for not making or assisting Military operations to resist the Enemy; should not be allowed to stand as Law." *Acts of the Privy Council*, IV, 337-39. Samuel Hazard, *et al., eds., Pennsylvania Archives*, 9 ser., 138 vols. (Philadelphia and Harrisburg, 1852-1949), 8th ser., VI, 4440, 4442, 4447, 4450.

in a most miserable Condition, neither the Assembly, Commissioners, nor Magistrates, having done anything to relieve them, tho' the Weather grew more pinching, and the small Pox was encreasing [sic] among the Soldiers to such a Degree that the whole Town would soon become a Hospital. . . ."[5]

Col. Henry Bouquet, the officer in command of British troops in Pennsylvania, had orders from Loudoun to take whatever quarters he needed by force and to march in as many more troops as necessary to carry out the orders. Bouquet was loath to use force, however. Instead, he asked Denny to issue a warrant to the sheriff authorizing him to quarter soldiers in private homes. The governor deliberately left the warrant blank, so that Bouquet could have a free hand.[6]

The Pennsylvania Assembly was outraged; the legislators "did not think it possible your Honour could be prevailed with to issue Orders so diametrically opposite to an express Law passed by yourself but a few Days before. . . . " They insisted that Denny compel the city officials to reconsider their earlier estimate of the number of troops that could be quartered in public houses, but Denny's terse reply, delivered to the Assembly on 18 December, was "The King's Troops must be quartered."

For the first time in the colony's history, the Assembly met on a Sunday. A reply was drafted to the governor's demands, and carried to him "when the Streets were full of People going to their respective Places of Worship." The Assembly's reply reviewed the whole dispute and concluded by placing the blame for the present difficulties squarely on Denny and Loudoun. Neither had given the House specific information about exactly what should be provided, nor had they indicated how many troops were to be quartered. The Assembly's confusion was evident: "We

thought we had by the late Law provided well for their Quartering in this Province; especially as we had exactly followed the Act of Parliament made for the samé Purpose."[7] Although Denny found the message "a long Narrative filled with Abuses," he agreed to meet with a committee from the Assembly the following day in order that the dispute between them might be resolved.

Benjamin Franklin opened the conference by suggesting that soldiers might be quartered in public houses in the suburbs, or in the neighboring towns, but Denny answered bluntly that the commander in chief had demanded quarters in Philadelphia. If the people were unhappy about this arrangement, they should complain to Lord Loudoun. At this, the committee retorted that they "wished the Governor would consider himself somewhat more in his civil Capacity as Governor of the Province." He should protect the people, and, if a matter needed to be brought before Loudoun, the governor should present it. In other words, the committeemen wanted Denny to help them protect the constitutional rights of the people.

The committee then posed a question which came to the heart of the controversy. "What was to be understood," the legislators asked, "by Quartering being extended farther in Time of War, than in Time of Peace?" Denny said he did not know, "unless it was Quartering on private Houses." That would be permissible, the committee said, if the people voluntarily offered quarters, but certainly no one should be forced to provide for soldiers. The governor replied that the general would decide if troops were to be forcibly quartered. One committeeman angrily reminded Denny what might happen if generals were allowed such power. A military officer "might say it was necessary to quarter the whole Army, not only in one City, but in one Square or one Street; and thereby harrass the Inhabitants excessively." At this point the governor broke in and declared he was interested only in facts.

---

[5] 15 Dec. 1756, *Minutes of the Provincial Council of Pennsylvania*, 10 vols. (Philadelphia, 1851-1853), VII, 358-59 [hereafter cited as *Pennsylvania Colonial Records*]. Doctor James Stevenson had asked Col. Bouquet to see to it that a hospital was provided for those soldiers suffering from small pox.

[6] *Ibid.*, 18 Dec. 1756, VII, 361-62.

[7] Assembly to Denny, 20 Dec. 1756, *ibid.*, VII, 364-69.

This uproarious conference did much more than raise tempers. It served as concrete evidence to Pennsylvania's political leaders that Loudoun's demands for quarters were a clear threat to American liberty. Indeed, Franklin summed up this fear when he called Denny—who was nothing more than the general's go-between—"a meer Bashaw or worse." To Americans like Franklin, who were familiar with the writings of radical Whigs, there was no worse example of despotism than those Turkish bashaws whose armies allowed them to rule without the consent of the people.[8]

The following day the Assembly invoked the spirit, if not the rhetoric, of Franklin's charge. When Denny told the legislators that the mayor of Philadelphia was certain there was not enough public housing to quarter Loudoun's soldiers, the Assembly insisted that the governor could do no more than enforce existing law. That was all any Englishman concerned with the preservation of liberty could do. Of this the House was confident. "We are contented," the Assemblymen declared, "that the King's Ministers should judge of these Proceedings and that the World should judge of the Decency of our last Message."

When Loudoun heard that his troops still had not been adequately housed in Philadelphia, he sent Denny a message on 22 December reiterating his demand that his soldiers be quartered. If Pennsylvania did not comply immediately, he intended to seize quarters; to "instantly march a Number sufficient for that purpose and find Quarters for the whole." With that sword dangling over their heads, Franklin and other provincial commissioners quickly agreed to rent additional housing and to make hospital space available for soldiers suffering from smallpox.[9]

The bitter, raucous quarrel between the Assembly and the governor and Lord Lou-

doun was more than just another dispute between the legislature and the executive, or the Crown. It was more than a simple struggle for political power. It was a contest for political liberty which in this case had been clearly defined in England by Parliamentary statute and the charters of rights issued in 1628 and 1689. But during the winter of 1756 Pennsylvania's leaders learned that they did not have the same rights as other Englishmen. They saw that British bayonets, or the threat of them, would be used to dictate solutions and enforce measures which were resisted by local governments.[10]

Wherever the British army violated what the colonists believed to be the rights of Englishmen as to quartering, local political agencies reacted with hostility. The city officials of Albany also clashed sharply with the army during the latter half of 1756, for, although the New York Assembly had appropriated £1,000 to build barracks in Albany, nothing actually had been accomplished when the troops arrived. Without the barracks, troops would have to be quartered in private houses, for there were not nearly enough public houses in Albany to house two regiments. But the Assembly had not enacted legislation to cover this situation, and the mayor of Albany therefore refused to quarter Loudoun's troops. He told the general that he "understood the Law; that [Loudoun] had no right to Quarters or Storehouses, or anything else from them; and that [Albany] would give none." Loudoun promptly labeled the mayor "a fool" and thereafter communicated only with one of the mayor's staff, tersely informing him that as a military officer he "must Follow the Custom of Armies and help myself [to quarters]." When the mayor and his

[10]Not all of Pennsylvania's political leaders were willing to press their claim to the rights of Englishmen, if it meant damaging the war effort. Joseph Shippen, for example, seemed to support the Assembly's position on quartering, but he was anxious that the quarrel should not persist. It was this concern for the well-being of the Empire, rather than any basic disagreement over the quartering issue that was one of the key factors separating Pennsylvania's politicians. Joseph Shippen to Edward Shippen, 19 Jan. 1757, Shippen Family Papers (Historical Society of Pennsylvania), II, 99.

[8]*Ibid.*, pp. 371, 373-74; Richard Peters to Thomas and Richard Penn, 26 Dec. 1756, Penn Papers (Historical Society of Pennsylvania); Bailyn, *Ideological Origins,* pp. 63-64n.

[9]Richard Peters to Provincial Commissioners, 26 Dec. 1756, *ibid.,* VII, 380.

council remained adamant, Loudoun ordered his quartermasters to forcibly place soldiers into homes.[11]

Loudoun forced the residents of Albany to meet his demands, but he could not make them accept the arguments he used to justify his high-handed actions. In September 1756 the New York Assembly framed a bill which it hoped would protect homeowners from further forcible quartering. At first, Governor Charles Hardy demanded that the bill be amended to allow the military authorities more lattitude, but after a month of debate Hardy swung over to the Assemblymen's position. He had become convinced, he told Loudoun in November, that it would be a great hardship for many families to have soldiers thrust into their homes. Loudoun was not sympathetic. He simply repeated his dogmatic contention that in wartime "no house has been exempt from Quartering the Troops the General thought Proper to have in any Place for carrying on the Service. . . ."[12]

Once again, therefore, in the winter of 1756, Loudoun threatened to send additional soldiers to Albany in order to compel the people there to house his troops. The mayor of that city told Loudoun that the people were opposed to such an illegal act; but, faced with British bayonets and political pressure from Lieutenant-Governor James de Lancey, the mayor's resistance collapsed. By the end of the day British solders were quartered in every house in Albany.[13]

Just as in Philadelphia, those who resisted forced quartering in Albany argued that a fundamental principle was at stake. Loudoun privately acknowledged the long-range implications of the conflict. Opposition to the army's tactics, he observed in a letter to the Duke of Cumberland, "seem not to come from the lower People, but from the leading People, who raise the dispute in order to have merit with the others, by defending their liberties, as they call them." In short, the clash between the British army and the people of Albany was not merely a petty local dispute but the thin edge of the wedge that was being driven between the colonies and the home country.

Governor Thomas Pownall of Massachusetts was one of the first English officials to grasp this fact. By the end of 1758 he had concluded that Loudoun's behavior was alienating the American people from the British Empire. He condemned Loudoun's aggressive methods as repulsive and unconstitutional; no military man had a right to interfere in civilian affairs, according to Pownall. A number of Massachusetts politicians, including Thomas Hutchinson and a substantial part of the lower house, were also disturbed by Loudoun's methods. A crisis did not arise until 1757, however, because Pownall's predecessor, Governor William Shirley, had convinced the Massachusetts legislature that in order to avoid trouble it should build barracks for British troops. Thus, by mid-1755 soldiers were safely quartered on an island in Boston harbor.

This amicable arrangement was upset in January 1757 when Loudoun told a legislative committee that during a war soldiers might very well be quartered in private homes as well as in barracks.[14] In speeches to the House, several committee members demanded an investigation into the army's right to seize quarters. Only a clever move by Jere-

[11]Governor Hardy to Assembly, 6 July 1756; Assembly to Hardy, 8 July *Votes and Proceedings of the General Assembly of the Colony of New York,* Public Record Office/ Colonial Office, 5/1216; Loudoun to the Duke of Cumberland, 29 Aug. 1756, LO 1626.

[12]The Assembly's bill may be found in *Votes and Proceedings of the General Assembly of the Colony of New York,* Public Record Office/ Colonial Office, 5/1216, 9 Oct. 1756; Hardy's initial reaction to the bill is contained in his letter to the Lords of Trade, 13 Oct. 1756, in E. B. O'Callaghan, ed., *Documents Relative to the Colonial History of the State of New York,* 15 vols. (Albany, 1856), VII, 163; Hardy's letter to Loudoun on 11 Nov. 1756 reveals his change, LO2199; Loudoun to Hardy, 21 Nov. 1756, LO2250.

[13]Loudoun to the Duke of Cumberland, 22 Nov. 1756, LO2262; according to a survey Loudoun ordered

made, there were 329 households in Albany. He calculated that it would be possible in a pinch to quarter 190 officers and 2,082 soldiers in Albany's 329 homes. This meant there would be approximately five soldiers to each home, LO3515.

[14]Loudoun, Diary, II (26 Jan. 1757).

miah Gridley, who belonged to the prerogative faction in the House, prevented a full debate on the matter. Gridley asked that a joint committee be formed to consider the problem, hoping that such a move would not only win time for those who supported the army but would also put the question in safer, more conservative hands.

For a while at least Gridley's maneuver seemed likely to be upset by Thomas Hutchinson. When the joint committee to discuss quartering met, Hutchinson read a prepared statement which asserted that only civil authorities had the right to determine what should be done to meet the army's needs. "With great warmth and Sputter," Hutchinson, according to Gridley's biased account, "began to catechise . . . about English rights." Gridley countered by pointing out that Loudoun had not demanded, but had asked the Massachusetts legislature to make quarters available. In this particular instance Gridley was correct, but Hutchinson must have known that Loudoun had threatened to seize quarters in Philadelphia and Albany when those governments refused to comply with his specific demands. Still, this was Massachusetts and so far Loudoun had abided by local law. Therefore, first Hutchinson and then the other members of the committee backed off from their hostile position and recommended that the House implement Loudoun's requests.

It soon became apparent how unimportant words were, for whether he "demanded" or "requested" the fact was that Loudoun held a powerful hand. Early in August he asked Pownall to quarter a regiment of soldiers. Realizing the significance of the situation, Pownall urged the House to pass a bill empowering Boston officials to assign quarters, thus maintaining local governmental control over the army. The governor warned the legislators that if this were not done the army would "plead necessity and provide for themselves." The threat worked; on 27 August the House appropriated money to build additional barracks for 1,000 men on Castle William. Although this was an expensive solution, it allowed the legislators to prohibit any

quartering in Massachusetts' towns. Now, Pownall tried to convince Loudoun to play along. He pleaded with the general to work through local officials as the law stipulated, reminding him that this was constitutional procedure.

Everything went smoothly until two recruiting officers came to Pownall complaining that local officials had refused them quarters in Boston. The governor promptly communicated with the city's selectmen. They were sympathetic, but they reminded the governor that Massachusetts law prohibited any quartering in public or private houses. As an immediate and temporary solution to the problem, Pownall suggested that the recruiters use the barracks on Castle William. At the same time, he sent Loudoun a detailed report outlining the steps he had taken and explaining Massachusetts' quartering law. The law was designed to safeguard "an Essential right of the Subject that no one could be quartered upon, unless by Law and there was no Law. . . . "[15]

Under almost any circumstances Loudoun would have been angered at this situation, and Pownall's letter reached the general at an especially bad time. He faced a frontier crisis in northern New York: French and Indians had overrun the colony's defense perimeter. According to Loudoun's view, therefore, the military situation was too serious to allow civilian authorities to obstruct military activities. There was no excuse for Massachusetts' disobedience, he stated in his letter to Pownall. He insisted that he had a right to quarters which superseded any provincial law, and he threatened to march three regiments into the city unless the recruiters were housed in Boston within 48 hours.

Loudoun's ultimatum arrived in Boston on the evening of 25 November. Early the next day, Pownall sent a brief message to the General Court, telling the legislators that the defense of the colonies depended upon compliance with his demand. The House remained in session well into the night and reconvened on Sunday in order to hammer out a

[15]Pownall to Loudoun, 4 Nov. 1757, LO4757.

bill which would, at once, satisfy their principles, their constituents, and Loudoun. On Monday afternoon the bill was presented to the governor for his signature. The act made it clear that the legislators believed a colonial law was the prerequisite to any quartering. Moreover, although it provided for quartering in public houses, the law allowed innkeepers to complain to a justice of the peace if they thought too many soldiers had been quartered upon them. In this way, the legislators preserved at least a modicum of the essential right of Englishmen to refuse to billet soldiers.

Neither the new law nor Pownall's explanation of his reasons for signing it pleased Loudoun. He renewed his threat to march troops into Boston and force the people to acknowledge his right to quarters wherever he chose them. Indeed, as he wrote Pownall on 6 December, the Massachusetts legislature had no business even debating the matter; the army's absolute right to quarters was "settled and regulated by an Act of the British Parliament, which no Act of theirs can infringe or diminish."

When Loudoun's latest condemnation of civil government became known, there was an outburst of public indignation. Pownall was accused of leading a military faction bent on subverting the Massachusetts constitution. "Were this Government [by] Elections as Rhode Island is," Pownall wrote to Loudoun, "I should next year be turn'd out. . . ." Similarly, an Assembly committee reminded the general on 16 December that the "inhabitants of this Province are intitled [sic] to the Natural Rights of English born Subjects. . . . " The rest of the committee's report was more conciliatory, though it recommended that Massachusetts' law remain unchanged.

By the end of December Loudoun's temper had cooled and he accepted the Assembly's report as sufficient evidence of its acquiescence to his demands. In a letter to William Pitt on 4 February he boasted that, while the other colonies watched, he had settled the Massachusetts controversy in the army's favor. In fact, Massachusetts was the

clear winner. Despite Loudoun's bluster, the quartering of troops was still dependent upon an act of the Massachusetts legislature, without which it was legally impossible to quarter troops anywhere other than in the barracks on Castle William. Thus, Massachusetts had effectually upheld the procedural political forms which allowed the colonists to continue to lay claim to the rights of Englishmen in regard to quartering.[16]

A quartering act for America was finally passed by Parliament on 3 May 1765. The act stipulated that soldiers were to be quartered in barracks; if there were not enough barrack space, they were to be billeted in public houses and inns. If these accommodations were insufficient, the governor and council were to hire vacant buildings. Quartering in private homes was scrupulously avoided. In this way, the Grenville ministry thought to quiet American complaints. But the law missed the most important point; namely, that Americans had insisted that only their own legislatures could enact such laws. This was the assumption underlying the opposition to the Quartering Act that developed in Massachusetts, New York, New Jersey, South Carolina, and Georgia. About a decade later the First Continental Congress reiterated this same position when it listed the Quartering Act as one of those arbitrary laws "which demonstrate a system formed, to enslave America." In short, as a direct result of one part of their experience during the French

[16]Pownall was in complete agreement with the Assembly's position. See, for example, Pownall to the General Court, March 1758, LO5941; Abercromby to Amherst, 19 Oct. 1758, Abercromby Papers (Henry E. Huntington Library), AB 778. General Jeffery Amherst expressed his views on quartering in a letter to Governor Denny, 7 Mar. 1759, *Minutes of the Provincial Council of Pennsylvania from the Organization to the Termination of the Proprietary Government*, 10 vols. (Philadelphia, 1851-1853), VIII, 285; for the Pennsylvania Assembly's reply, *ibid.*, 330-31. Other lower houses opposed forced quartering in the late 1750's; Captain Anthony Wheelock to Abercromby, 2 May 1758, Abercromby Papers, Ab 227, for New Jersey's quartering law; Ensign Richard Nickleson to Col. John Forbes, 9 Dec. 1757, LO 4976, for New Hampshire's law; and the South Carolina Assembly to Governor Lyttleton, 18 Mar. 1758, LO 5763.

and Indian War, Americans had come to believe that an assertive English imperialism presented a real danger to American liberty.[17]

[17]New York's flat refusal to make any military appropriation is well known (O'Callaghan, *Doucments Relative to the State of New York,* VII, 845-46, 867-68); New York merchant John Watts insisted that the question was not whether the Quartering Act was constitutional, but whether "People . . . had rather part with their Money, tho' rather unconstitutionally, than to have a parcel of Military Masters put by Act of Parliament a bed to their Wives and Daughters" (Watts to James Napier, 1 June 1765, New York Historical Society, Collections [1928], p. 355); the New Jersey legislature contended that the act was "as much an act for laying Taxes on the Inhabitants as the Stamp Act," (William A. Whitehead, ed., *Archives of the State of New Jersey,* 33 vols. [Newark, 1880-1928], IX, 577); William W. Abbot, *The Royal Governors of Georgia, 1754-1775* (Chapel Hill, N.C., 1959), pp. 126-44; Merrill Jensen, ed., *English Historical Documents* (London and New York, 1955), IX, 805-808.

The controversey between the British army and colonial governments over quartering helped to create a lasting resentment and a hardening of political attitudes which contributed to the alienation of the colonies from Great Britain. Colonial political leaders would not quickly forget that military power had been used to force them to comply with what they considered an unconstitutional procedure, a practice which posed a grave danger to political liberty in America. Indeed, those who observed how British generals settled the quartering problem by threatening to use the King's soldiers against recalcitrant colonials could scarcely avoid the conclusion that in the event of future serious differences with the Crown the colonies would either have to submit to royal force or devise a resistance in kind.

# "FOR MILITARY MERIT"

## By Allen Pennell Wescott

IN an Exeter, New Hampshire, museum hangs a worn and faded uniform of dark blue homespun, the property of the Society of the Cincinnati. Who the soldier was who wore this uniform during the Revolution is unknown, but we know that he possessed such virtues as valor, fidelity, and fortitude because on the left breast, over the heart, is a badge of purple sprigged silk, faded to steel gray, edged in tarnished silver. It is the only known specimen of a decoration designed by George Washington and designated by him as the Badge of Military Merit—America's first military decoration, the second oldest in the world (the Cross of St. George of Russia was established in 1769) and unique in that it was obtainable only by non-commissioned officers and privates.

On August 7, 1782, at Newburgh, General Washington caused the following general order to be issued:

The General ever desirous to cherish virtuous ambition in his soldiers, as well as to foster and encourage every species of Military merit, directs that whenever any singularly meritorious action is performed, the author of it shall be permitted to wear on his facings over the left breast, the figure of a heart in purple cloth, or silk, edged with narrow lace or binding. Not only instances of unusual gallantry, but also of extraordinary fidelity and essential service in any way shall meet with a due reward. Before this favour can be conferred on any man, the particular fact, or facts, upon which it is to be grounded must be set forth to the Commander in chief accompanied with certificates from the Commanding officers of the regiment and brigade to which the Candadate for reward belonged, or other incontestable proofs, that upon granting it, the name and regiment of the person with the action so certified are to be enrolled in the book of merit which will be kept at the orderly office. Men who have merited this last distinction to be suffered to pass all guards and sentinals which officers are permitted to do.

The road to glory in a patriot army and a free country is thus open to all. This order is also to have retrospect to the earliest stages of the war, and to be considered as a permanent one.[1]

[1]John C. Fitzpatrick, ed., *The Writings of George Washington from the Original Manuscript Sources, 1745-1799* (Washington, 1931-38), XXIV, 488.

Evidence that the Badge of Military Merit carried with it certain privileges is signified by an order issued at Verplanks Point, August 31, 1782, to the effect that "No Noncommissioned Officer or soldier except those having the badge of Military merit is to go off the Island or peninsula on which we now are encamped without a pass in writing from the Commanding officer of the regiment to which he belongs. If any should be found off it contrary to this order they are to be deemed Deserters and tried accordingly . . . ."[2]

The book of merit unfortunately having been lost, few records of Revolutionary soldiers so decorated survive, but in a general order dated April 27, 1783, we find this entry:

The Board appointed to take into consideration the claims of the Candidates for the Badge of merit. Report. That Serjeant Churchill of the 2d regt. of Light Dragoons and Sergeant Brown of the late 5th Connecticut regt. are in their opinion severally entitled to the badge of Military merit and do therefore recommend them to His Excellency the Commander in chief as suitable characters for that honorary distinction.

The Commander in chief is pleased to order the before named Serjt. Elijah Churchill of the 2d. regt. of Light Dragoons and Serjt. Brown of the late 5th Connecticut regiment to be each of them invested with the badge of merit. They will call at Head Quarters on the third of May, when the necessary Certificates and Badges will be ready for them.[3]

Sergeant William Brown[4] was awarded the Badge of Military Merit because "in the assault of the enemy's left redoubt at Yorktown, in Virginia, on the evening of October 14, 1781 [he] conducted a forlorn hope with great bravery, propriety and deliberate firmness and that his general character appears unexceptionable."[5]

[2]*Ibid.,* XXV, 97.
[3]*Ibid.,* XXVI. 363-64.
[4]This may have been Daniel Brown.
[5]John C. Fitzpatrick, *The Spirit of the Revolution: New Light from SoSme of the Original Sources of American History* (Boston, 1924), p. 202. This volume, pp. 190-204, also describes the exploits which won the order for Churchill and Bissel.

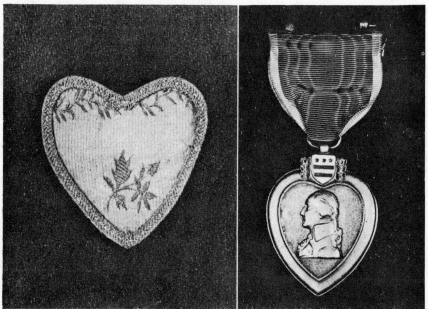

*THE PURPLE HEART*
*Left, the original Badge of Military Merit, courtesy of the Fort Ticonderoga Museum.*
*Right, the present Purple Heart.*

The citation of Sergeant Churchill of the 2d Continental Dragoons, also a Connecticut regiment, describes his service as follows:

That Serjeant Elijah Churchill of the 2d Regiment of Light Dragoons, in the several Enterprizes against Fort St. George and Fort Slongo on Long Island, in their opinion acted a very conspicuous and singularly meritorious part; that at the Head of each Body of Attack, he not only acquitted himself with great gallantry, firmness and address; but that the Surprize in one instance, and the success of the attack in the other, proceeded in a considerable degree from his Conduct and management. . . .[6]

Sergeant Daniel Bissel of the 2d Connecticut Regiment of the Continental Line also received this honor badge. He enlisted from Windsor, Connecticut, but "deserted" in August 1781. Nearly two years later the Badge of Military Merit was conferred upon this "deserter" who, it seems, had been entrusted by Washington to spy upon the enemy within their own lines. Bissel had proceeded to New York and enlisted in a British regiment. More successful than Captain Hale, Bissel escaped from the British and

[6]*Writing of George Washington*, XXVI, 373.

returned to Washington's army after an absence of thirteen months with a wealth of valuable information gathered while on his hazardous mission. He was cited in general orders of June 8, 1783:

Serjeant Bissel of the 2d Connecticut regt. having performed some important services, within the immediate knowledge of the Commander in chief, in which the fidelity, perseverence, and good sense of the said serjeant Bissel were conspicuously manifested; it is therefore ordered that he be honored with the badge of merit; he will call at Head Quarters on Tuesday next for the insignia and certificate to which he is hereby entitled.[7]

After the Revolution the Order of Military Merit, or of the Purple Heart as it came to be called, fell into disuse and eventually vanished from public sight. For years it had been practically unknown except to a few historians until in recent years interest in the decoration was aroused by the publication of articles calling attention to its existence.[8] For some time a number of individuals sought to

[7]*Ibid.*, XXVI. 481.
[8]For instance, *The Badge of Military Merit of the Continental Army*, published by the Society of the Cincinnati of the State of New Hampshire in 1925.

have the order revived and perpetuated. among these being Carleton S. Gifford of Boston, Stephen H. P. Pell of New York, and Lynde Sullivan of the Society of the Cincinnati. The bicentennial anniversary of the birth of George Washington was selected as the most appropriate time for the reinstitution of the order, and on February 22, 1932, the Purple Heart was officially revived out of respect to his memory and military achievements.[9]

The Purple Heart is awarded for acts or

[9]General Orders No. 3, War Department, February 22, 1932.

services performed prior to February 22, 1932, by persons who, as members of the Army, had received a Meritorious Service Citation Certificate from General Pershing or who were wounded in an action against an armed enemy of the United States. The present decoration is a heart-shaped medal of bronze, with a center of purple upon which is superimposed a bust of Washington and above which appears the Washington family coat-of-arms. Upon the reverse appear the words "For Military Merit." The medal is suspended from a purple ribbon edged in white.

# THOMAS JEFFERSON ON UNIVERSAL MILITARY TRAINING

By Sidney Forman*

Polemicists on both sides of the issues of universal military training have naturally appealed to American history and tradition as a basic support of their respective positions. In reviewing the historical arguments it seems that there is general acceptance of the fact that such founding fathers as Washington, Hamilton and Knox would approve of universal military training. But by inference and suggestion the Jeffersonian tradition is brought forward in opposition to any such proposal. In the light of the fact that several of the more recent students of Jefferson have neglected his policy on military training — a policy which was an integral part of the achievement of his Presidential administration and which may serve to guide us today — a statement of Jefferson's thinking is enlightening.

When Jefferson took office in 1801 he was faced with certain practical political problems in which America's very honor was at stake. Faced with the pirates of Morocco, Algiers, Tunis and Tripoli, with French machinations on our southern borders, in Louisiana and the Floridas, and English threats to the north via Canada, Jefferson took practical measures for defense as quickly as possible. Jefferson, a man whose philosophical background and Revolutionary experience had made him a forthright foe of

European militarism, saw no contradiction to his views in encouraging the construction of a system of coastal fortifications and in approving the organic act, on March 16, 1802, establishing the Corps of Engineers and the United States Military Academy. He felt that only in this way could he strengthen and support America's new-born liberty and independence and logically fulfill his earlier career as Revolutionary Governor of Virginia. In terms of lasting influence these acts certainly rank among Jefferson's most important achievements.

In 1802 Jefferson wrote to Jonathan Williams, Chief of the Corps of Engineers and Superintendent of the Military Academy at West Point, an appreciation of Williams' energetic promotion of the study of military art. Jefferson expressed the opinion that such study was very important considering the inadequately small size of the Regular Army. He continued his encouragement throughout his administration.[1]

*Sidney Forman is Archivist, U.S. Military Academy.

[1]"MS Minutes and Records of the United States Military Philosophical Society, 1802-1813," New York Historical Society, include two hitherto unpublished letters of Jefferson, dated 1802 and 1805, showing his support of the objective of the Society which was "... promoting Military Science." See also Sidney Forman, "The United States Military Philosophical Society, 1802-1813," *The William and Mary Quarterly* (July, 1945).

55

Jefferson, in 1810, wrote from Monticello to General Thaddeus Koskiusko, giving an account of his stewardship in building up a system of defense. He tells of having repeatedly recommended to Congress to have "... the whole territory of the United States organized by such a classification of its male force, as would give to the benefit of all its young population for active service, and that of a middle and advanced age for stationary defence."[2]

Jefferson's views were elaborated in a letter to his friend James Monroe on June 18, 1813. He wrote then: "It is more a subject of joy that we have so few of the desperate characters which compose modern regular armies. But it proves more forcibly the necessity of obliging every citizen to be a soldier; this was the case with the Greeks and the Romans, and must be that of every free State. Where there is no oppression there will be no pauper hirelings. We must train and classify the whole of our male citizens, and make military instruction a regular part of collegiate education. We can never be safe till this is done."[3]

Jefferson's testimony manifested in his writings piles up to leave no room for uncertainty or equivocation. It was Jefferson who wrote the Rockfish Gap Report of the Commissioners for the University of Virginia which recommended "... and the manual exercise, military manoeuvres, and tactics generally, should be the frequent exercises of the students in their hours of recreation. It is at that age of aptness, docility, and emulation of the practices of manhood, that such things are soonest learned and longest remembered."[4] His views were written into the regulations of the University of Virginia and before his death military training was regularly given at the University.

At least on this issue American tradition reveals Washington, Hamilton, Knox and Jefferson standing united.

SIDNEY FORMAN,
*Archivist, U. S. Military Academy*

# MILITARY JUSTICE
# UNDER GENERAL WASHINGTON

By Maurer Maurer*

T HE army was in a sad state when
George Washington assumed command
on July 3, 1775. In the camp there were
many brave and ardent patriots, good men
who would make good soldiers. But they
lacked uniforms and equipment. They needed training. They had to be brought under
control.

Soldiers wandered about, shooting their
guns into the air, wasting precious ammunition and raising false alarms. Many neglected
their duties and refused to obey orders. They
got drunk, fought, rioted, mutinied, and deserted. Some of the officers were no better.
In short, the General found himself in command of a disorganized and undisciplined
mob that scarcely deserved to be called an
army.[1]

Although conditions began to improve
within a short time, Washington was to learn
that a disciplined fighting force could not be
developed in "a day, a month or even a
year." These Americans were "accustomed
to unbounded freedom." They could not
"brook the Restraint which is indispensably

necessary to the good order and Government
of an Army." Yet, somehow or other, "Subordination and Discipline," which Washington regarded as "the Life and Soul of an
Army," had to be established and maintained, for these were qualities which would
"make us formidable to our enemies, honorable to ourselves, and respected in the world."
Without "Order, Regularity and Discipline,"
he said, an army "is no better than a Commissioned Mob."[2]

The Commander-in-Chief told his troops
that he required "exact disciplines." He
pleaded "the importance of the cause . . .
and the necessity there is of their behaving
like men, who are contending for everything
that freemen should value." He held up
recognition and honor as rewards for the
good and the brave. He threatened, and
promised, to "punish every kind of neglect,
or misbehaviour." And he warned that "no
Connections, Interests or Intercessions . . .
will avail to prevent strict execution of justice."[3]

Justice, which often was found in the "Cat
o'Nine Tails" or the hangman's noose, was
administered in accordance with a code derived from British law and custom. It was
natural that the Revolutionists should turn
to Britain for laws to govern their army.
Washington and many others who had served
during the colonial wars were familiar with
the British military code. Some, like Daniel
Morgan, whose back carried the scars of 499

*Dr. Maurer Maurer is Professor of Military History
at the Air University and Chief of the Historical Studies
Branch of the USAF Historical Division. Personal
views expressed or implied in this article are not to be
construed as carrying official sanction of the Air University, the Department of the Air Force, or the Department of Defense.

[1]Nearly everyone who has written about the army of
1775 has commented on the lack of discipline. See, for
example, Douglas Southall Freeman, *George Washington: A Biography* (New York, 1948-1954), III, 489,
*et seq.* Washington's views are found in his correspondence and military papers, which constitute the primary
sources for this article. In the notes which follow,
the author has cited the primary documents, all of
which, unless indicated otherwise, may be found in
chronological order in John C. Fitzpatrick (ed.), *The
Writings of George Washington* (Washington, 1931-
1944).

[2]Washington to President of Congress, Sept. 24,
1776; General Orders (hereafter cited as GO), Jan.
1, 1776. For improvement in discipline, see Freeman,
*Washington*, III, 544.

[3]GO, July 4, 1775, Oct. 1, 1776, July 7, 1775, Jan.
1, 1776, July 7, 1775.

stripes laid on for striking an officer, had first-hand experience with British justice.[4]

The articles of war in effect at Cambridge when Washington took command had been enacted by the Provincial Congress of Massachusetts two weeks before Minutemen and Redcoats had met at Lexington. Most of these articles had been copied from British law, but in many instances they had been modified to make the punishment less severe. The military code adopted by the Continental Congress on June 30, 1775, and placed in effect on August 10, 1775, was derived more from the Massachusetts articles than from the British. Congress amended this code on November 7, 1775, and revised it completely on September 20, 1776, bringing it more in line with British law.[5]

Military law, one of the most powerful instruments available to Washington for establishing and maintaining discipline, extended over both enlisted men and officers, as well as over civilians who served with or accompanied the army in the field. Americans, however, cherished the privileges of the common law and objected to a legal system in which indictment by grand jury and other fundamental rights were unknown. They were familiar with the long struggle of the English people against military law, and the war they were fighting was itself a protest against arbitrary government. Thomas Jefferson and other Americans had read Sim Matthew Hale's *History of the Common Law of England,* in which the Lord Chief Justice had asserted that military law was "something indulged, rather than allowed as law." Hale explained, "The necessity of Government, Order and Discipline in an Army, is that only which can give those laws a Countenance."[6] Military necessity, then, was jutification for military law. As Washington's judge advocate said, "when a man assumes the soldier he lays aside the citizen, and must be content to a temporary relinquishment of some of his civil rights."[7]

An enlisted man accused of an offense against military law was taken into custody by the provost and held under guard for trial by court-martial. An officer was arrested and restricted to his tent, or to some particular area of camp, until his case had been decided. Courts of inquiry were convened on occasion to investigate complaints against officers. If the inquiry produced evidence of a violation of military law, the officer was brought to trial by court-martial; if not, the charges were dropped and the officer was "honorably acquitted."

Under the law, an officer or soldier who had been arrested or confined had to be brought to trial within eight days, or as soon thereafter as a court could be conveniently assembled. Movements of the army and enemy actions made it impossible at times to obtain prompt hearings, but Washington insisted that every effort by made to bring the accused to trial without undue delay. As the need arose, officers were designated to sit as a court to try a specific case or to hear such cases as might be brought before them.

A person charged with a minor offense was

---

[4] Washington to Dinwiddie, April 29, 1757; North Callahan, *Daniel Morgan: Ranger of the Revolution* (New York, 1961), 24-25. Referring to the British articles of war, John Adams said, "It would be in vain for us to seek in our own invention, or the records of warlike nations, for a more complete system of military discipline." *Journals of the Continental Congress* (Library of Congress edition, 1904-1937), V, 670, n. 2, quoting Adams, Autobiography, in *Works,* III, 68-83.

[5] The British articles of 1765, the Massachusetts articles of April 5, 1775, and the American articles of June 30, 1775, Nov. 7, 1775, and Sept. 20, 1776, are printed in William Winthrop, *Military Law and Precedents* (Washington, 1920), 931-971. The American articles are found in *Journals of the Continental Congress,* II, 111-123, III, 331-334, V, 788-807, VII, 265-266.

[6] Hale, *History of the Common Law* (1713), as quoted by Justice Hugo Black in *Reid v. Covert,* 1 L ed 2d, 1169, n. 48.

[7] Memorial of Judge Advocate [William Tudor, Oct., 1775], in Peter Force (ed.), *American Archives* (Washington, 1837-1853), 4th ser., III, 1164.

tried by a regimental or garrison court, consisting normally of five officers appointed by the commander of the regiment or garrison. One accused of a more serious offense was tried by a general court-martial, which normally was made up of thirteen officers. Although the articles of war did not give Washington power to convene general courts, he did so, presumably under the authority of his commission, which made him responsible for order and discipline in the army. General courts also were convened by brigade and division commanders, by generals commanding in the various departments and states, and, on occasion, by Congress or the Board of War. If the accused believed that a member of the court was prejudiced against him, he was permitted a challenge, in which event the convening officer designated another member to take the place of the one rejected.

When a general court had been convened and the members sworn, the judge advocate, who served as prosecutor, called his witnesses and presented his evidence. These witnesses testified under oath and could be cross-examined by the accused, who also could call other witnesses to testify in his behalf. The defendant was permitted to bring a lawyer or some other person into court to give him advice either in writing or in a quiet voice, but the counselor was not permitted to address the court. Responsibility for making the defense rested with the accused. Sometimes his inept pleading had disastrous results.[8]

When the evidence was in and the vote had been taken, the court announced its verdict. The officer who had neglected his duties, disobeyed orders, behaved in a man-

ner unbecoming a gentleman, or committed some other offense against military law, might escape with no more than a reprimand which might be given in private, delivered in public, or published in a general order. For example, a captain guilty of speaking disrespectfully to a major was reprimanded before the officers of his regiment and required to ask the major's pardon.[9]

Sometimes the offender was fined, as in the case of an ensign who was mulcted one month's pay (the maximum permitted by the Continental articles) for being absent without leave. An enlisted man who was found guilty of stealing and of using abusive language to the quartermaster was assessed twenty shillings. A deserter was given fifteen lashes and fined one month's pay "to defray the expense of apprehending and bringing the Prisoner to Camp."[10]

Confinement on bread and water was a common sentence for enlisted men. One man received six days for raising a disturbance in the streets. Another received eight for threatening the life of a lieutenant. Another, a deserter, was put on bread and water for a month.[11]

Noncommissioned officers frequently were "reduced to ranks" for their crimes. A deserter was demoted from corporal and fined one month's pay. A sergeant who deserted was whipped and broken to private, as was

the court convened to try him, Washington found that the articles were silent on the subject. Washington therefore appointed a council of general officers to recommend principles to govern challenges in "the present and all future cases." (Washington to Council of General Officers, June 1, 1779.) The paragraphs above which summarize court-martial procedures are based upon the articles of war, court-martial reports, general orders, and the enlightening notes scattered through Winthrop, *Military Law*. For information concerning counsel for the defense, the writer is indebted to the Office of the Judge Advocate General of the Army for a copy of a memorandum which that office prepared for Douglas Southall Freeman in 1950.

[9]GO, Sept. 2, 1775.

[10]GO, Oct. 3, 1775, Nov. 29, 1775, Feb. 24, 1776.

[11]GO, May 10, 1776, May 14, 1776, Jan. 3, 1780.

[8]The courts were authorized by the articles of war, but neither the articles nor other enactments of Congress detailed the procedures to be followed. The procedures employed were derived from British practice and custom, as well as from the experience of French and other foreign officers who served with the Continental Army. Questions of procedure arose frequently. For example, when Arnold challenged some members of

another who was convicted of abusing and striking a captain. For mutiny a sergeant was reduced to private and fined forty-eight shillings, while a corporal involved in the same affair was whipped and demoted.[12]

Tried for misbehavior at the Battle of Bunker Hill, one colonel was cashiered, two colonels were acquitted, a lieutenant was dismissed and prohibited from further service in the Continental Army, and a major was cashiered but was not rendered incapable of holding a commission if the general officers recommended him to the Commander-in-Chief. Officers were dismissed for such offenses as leaving their posts, disobeying orders, and, among other things, defrauding their men. The sentence of a captain dismissed for cowardice stated that his name, place of residence, and punishment were to be published in the newspapers of his state, "After which, it shall be deemed scandalous for any officer to associate with him." In a few cases, officers were suspended, three months being the period specified for a captain convicted of conduct unbecoming an officer and a gentleman.[13]

A lieutenant was sentenced "to have his sword broke over his head on the grand parade at guard mounting" before he was dismissed from the service. One who was to be dismissed "with Infamy" was to be "drummed out of Camp tomorrow morning by all drummers and Fifers in the Army and never to return." A man convicted of theft was to be "mounted on a horse back-foremost, without a Saddle, his Coat turn'd wrong side out, his hands tied behind him, and drummed out of the Army (never more to return) by all of the drums of the division to which he belongs and that the above sentence be published in the News-Papers." A sergeant was drummed out "with a Label on his back, with the word *Mutiny* on it." Another was "to be deprived of his Arms and Accoutrements, put on a Horse Cart, with a Rope round his neck, and drum'd out of the Army."[14]

Early in the war, men sometimes were sentenced to "ride the wooden horse,"[15] but this cruel punishment was not authorized by the Continental articles. Flogging, on the other hand, was common all during the war. British courts-martial could, and did, impose sentences of five hundred, one thousand, or even two thousand lashes,[16] but both the Massachusetts code and the Continental articles of June 30, 1775, limited the number of stripes to thirty-nine. Disobedience, neglect of duty, drunkenness, theft, sleeping on guard, and desertion were some of the offenses that could lead to an enlisted man's being whipped before his regiment. Sometimes the flogging was administered in increments, as it was in the case of a corporal who, for "speaking disrespectfully and villifying the Commander in Chief," was given thirteen lashes on three successive days.[17]

The threat of thirty-nine lashes was insufficient, however, to preserve order. In October, 1775, Judge Advocate William Tudor suggested that the limit be raised to one hundred. He said that "Nine-tenths of the officers . . . think this addition absolutely necessary."[18] When Congress complained about the lack of discipline, Washington replied that the articles of war were "Relaxed, and unfit, . . . for the Government of an Army," For one thing, the limit on the number of lashes made "this punishment inadequate to

---

[12]GO, May 12, 1776, Feb. 21, 1777, Sept. 11, 1776, Nov. 15, 1776.
[13]GO, Sept. 15, 1775, July 18, 1775, Sept. 11, 1775, Oct. 13, 1775, Sept. 24, 1775, Aug. 2, 1775, June 16, 1776, Oct. 8, 1776, Oct. 19, 1777, Jan. 19, 1783.

[14]GO, Feb. 8, 1778, March 14, 1778, Jan. 5, 1778, May 11, 1783, Sept. 16, 1775.
[15]GO, July 10, 1775.
[16]Winthrop, *Military Law*, 439.
[17]GO, Sept. 8, 1776.
[18]Memorial of Judge Advocate, *loc. cit.*

many Crimes it is assigned to." Some of the men who had been whipped were so tough that "for a bottle of Rum they would undergo a Second operation."[19]

In revising the articles of war on September 20, 1776, Congress increased the number of stripes to one hundred. This maximum often was imposed, sometimes in increments. A soldier found guilty of deserting and reenlisting was sentenced to "one hundred lashes on his naked back, to be inflicted at four different times." Another sentence called for fifty stripes to be administered on each of two successive days, with the culprit's "Back to be well washed with Salt and water after he has received the last fifty."[20]

Courts sometimes tried to get around the limitation on the number of lashes by awarding a hundred for each of two or more charges against a man. For example, a soldier found guilty of deserting and of attempting to escape to the enemy was sentenced to receive two hundred. Washington regarded such sentences as illegal and would not approve more than one hundred lashes, the number he authorized for a man who had been sentenced to receive three hundred.[21]

There were times when one hundred lashes apparently were not enough, but there was no penalty between that and death. To fill this gap, Washington suggested in 1781 that the limitation on whipping be removed or that the maximum number of stripes be raised to five hundred, but Congress rejected the idea.[22]

Whipping often was accompanied by some other penalty, such as fine or imprisonment. A man convicted of desertion was given a hundred lashes and sent to the navy, where opportunities to desert were fewer. Another,

found guilty of being drunk and asleep while he was supposed to be guarding prisoners, was sentenced to receive one hundred lashes and "to have the hair from the front part of his head shaved off without soap, and tar and feathers substituted in the room of the hair." A matross also had his head tarred and feathered, after which he was forced to "run the Gauntlope in the company to which he belongs." A man who deserted after having been decorated for faithful service was sentenced "to have his honorary Badge taken off by the Drum Major at the head of the regiment and receive fifty lashes on his naked back."[23]

Under the British articles of war, the death penalty could be invoked for many crimes, including mutiny, striking a superior, disobeying an order, deserting, sleeping on guard, raising a false alarm, corresponding with the enemy, plundering, misbehaving in battle, revealing the watchword, and forcing a commander to abandon his post to the enemy. Only the last three of these were capital offenses under the Massachusetts code and the Continental articles of June 30, 1775.

When a charge of corresponding with the enemy was brought against Dr. Benjamin Church, Director General of Hospitals, in the autumn of 1775, Washington found that the punishment available for the crime was inadequate. He laid the case before Congress with the suggestion that some alteration of the law was needed. Judge Advocate William Tudor believed that the offense called for capital punishment. He also wanted the death penalty for mutiny and desertion, of which there had been many cases. On November 7, 1775, Congress amended the articles of war to provide sentences of death for the crimes mentioned by Tudor. The following year, after Washington and others

[19]Washington to President of Congress, Sept. 22, and Sept. 24, 1776.

[20]GO, Jan. 3, 1780, March 25, 1778.

[21]GO, May 29, 1778; Washington to Col. Thomas Bartley, May 29, 1778, GO, June 11, 1778.

[22]Washington to President of Congress, Feb. 3, 1781.

[23]GO, Sept. 2, 1777, Sept. 3, 1777, March 15, 1783.

had complained about the ineffectiveness of the military code, Congress revised and re-enacted the articles of war, extending the death penalty to all those offenses for which the British military law provided capital punishment.[24]

The first instance in which Washington approved a sentence of death came nearly a year after he assumed command. The culprit was Thomas Hickey, a member of the General's guard, who was involved in a plot to enlist soldiers of the Continental Army into British service, and to start an uprising when the British army arrived at New York. There were rumors that the plot had also included the assassination of Washington. At any rate, when a court-martial sentenced Hickey to death, Washington submitted the matter to a council of generals, who unanimously advised the Commander-in-Chief to approve the sentence. Accordingly, Washington ordered Hickey hanged the following day, June 28, 1776, at eleven o'clock in the morning.[25]

During the war, military courts sentenced many persons to death by hanging or shooting. Many of the sentences were carried out, but Washington frequently granted stays and often pardoned the offenders.

The sentence of a court-martial actually was no more than an opinion, for the proceedings and sentence was subject to review and approval by the officer who had ordered the trial. If Washington found irregularity in the constitution of the court or in the proceedings, he ordered a new trial. In most cases he approved the sentence, but he often exercised his power to pardon offenders or mitigate punishment.

When an artillery officer was sentenced to be reprimanded for cowardice at Brandywine, Washington could not find sufficient evidence to support the verdict; he ordered the captain "discharged from arrest without Censure." Discovering that a man who was under sentence for sleeping on his post was a "good orderly, well-behaved soldier, and was probably unwell when on sentry," the Commander-in-Chief remitted the sentence of twenty-five lashes. In awarding two men fifteen lashes each for quitting their posts, the court recommended mercy because the prisoners were young and did not understand their duties; Washington pardoned the men but warned that "such a crime will not meet with Mercy in the future."[26]

Cases involving capital punishment received a special attention. On October 26, 1777, Washington ordered the execution of a man sentenced to death for desertion. Later the same day he granted a postponement for three days. On the 30th he granted another stay. On November 1 he pardoned the man, saying that he expected him to "show himself worthy of this act of clemency." In pardoning a number of men who were under sentences for various offenses Washington said that he hoped that "Gratitude to his Clemency will induce them in the future to behave like good soldiers." In 1779, on the "Anniversary of our glorious Independence," the Commander-in-Chief pardoned all prisoners then under sentence of death.[27]

While Washington could pardon an offender or reduce the sentence of a court-martial, he did not have the authority to increase the punishment set by a court. He was free, however, to express his displeasure

[24]Washington to President of Congress, Oct. 5, 1775; Memorial of Judge Advocate, *loc. cit;* Washington to President of Congress, Sept. 22, and Sept. 24, 1776; Col. Joseph Reed to President of Congress, July 25, 1776, in Force, *American Archives,* 5th ser., I, 576; Maj. Gen. Horatio Gates to President of Congress, in Force, *American Archives,* 5th ser., I, 795; Articles of War, Sept. 20, 1776, in Winthrop, *Military Law,* 961-971.

[25]GO, June 27, 1776; Washington to President of Congress, June 28, 1776.

[26]GO, Jan. 3, 1778, July 13, 1777, Nov. 21, 1775.
[27]GO, Oct. 26, Oct. 30, and Nov. 1, 1777, May 6,

if he believed a sentence was inadequate for a crime. When a court sentenced a captain to be reprimanded privately for refusing to comply with an order, Washington said, "The mutinous and dangerous spirit which actuated Captn. Norwood merited in his opinion the most exemplary Punishment. He is to be released from Arrest." In another instance, a colonel charged with failure to obey an order was acquitted because the order had not been issued properly; although Washington regarded the order as valid, there was nothing he could do but release the colonel from arrest.[28]

In rare instances the Commander-in-Chief sent a case back to a court for reconsideration. An example concerns an ensign who, with a group of men, robbed a house, carry-off "four large Pier looking Glasses, Women's Cloaths, and other articles which one would think could be of no Earthly use to him." When a brigade major ordered the goods returned, the ensign "swore he would defend them at the hazard of his Life." Washington had the ensign arrested and tried. The court found him not guilty of plundering but guilty of insubordination and disrespect to his superiors. His sentence was to apologize and be reprimanded before the regiment, a sentence that "appeared so exceedingly extraordinary" that Washington "ordered a Reconsideration of the matter." With some new evidence, the court "made Shift to Cashier him." Washington ordered the ensign turned out of the army immediately. Congress directed the Commander-in-Chief to obtain the names of the men who had voted for acquittal, but the court, asserting its independence, refused to supply the information. Washington suggested to Congress that the matter be permitted to "rest where it is." Some months later, when

Washington found himself "under the disagreeable necessity of directing a reconsideration" of another case, the court held to its verdict.[29]

Appeal from a regimental to a general court was permitted but seldom taken. When two men, convicted of theft, appealed in September, 1775, one was acquitted and the other sentence to receive thirty-nine lashes. An officer tried by a brigade court sometimes appealed to a general court-martial of the line. A lieutenant under sentence to be dismissed from the service was acquitted on appeal, but in another case the appellate court affirmed the trial court's finding that a captain was guilty of acting in a cowardly manner.[30]

A lieutenant colonel who was cashiered in August, 1779, carried his case to Congress. In December, 1780, Congress referred it to Washington. The following April the Commander-in-Chief informed the ex-officer that a new trial could not be granted. The proceedings of the court had been fair and regular, and the judgment was well supported by the evidence. If a new trial were granted in this case, similar relief could not be denied others. Washington pointed out that "no determination can ever be final, if, months after the sentence is passed and approved, a cashiered officer, under the plea of fresh evidence . . ., can by demanding a new trial, take the chance of a second decision by a court composed of officers different from the first." A cashiered officer had nothing to lose but everything to gain from a new trial. The government, however, would be subjected to "great, unnecessary, and probably frequent expenses," and officers would be involved in the "unnecessary and irksome duty" of rehearing such cases.[31]

1778, July 4, 1779.
[28]GO, June 11, 1778, April 2, 1778.

[29]GO, Sept. 22, 1776; Washington to President of Congress, Sept. 24, and Oct. 5, 1776; GO, Oct. 5, 1776; Washington to President of Congress, Oct. 8, 1776; GO, June 16, 1777.
[30]GO, Sept. 28, 1775; Jan. 15, 1776, Jan. 25, 1778.
[31]Washington to Jotham Loring, April 6, 1781.

All through the war the courts were busy. It is no wonder that the judge advocate complained that his duties were "arduous and difficult." Officers sometimes found, however, that discipline could not be "maintained by a regular course of proceedings." Consequently, they were "tempted to use their own discretion," which, Washington said, "sometimes occasions excesses." The Commander-in-Chief intervened when a brigadier was about to dismiss a major "without his having had a fair trial, and the charges against him being properly proved." When two captains were tried for beating a sentry and the corporal of the guard, the court-martial saw justification and delivered an acquittal. Washington disagreed. The sentry and corporal "were insolent and merited punishment,," but their punishment "ought not to have been of an arbitrary kind." Holding that the two men should have been "confined and punished in a regular way," Washington said, "The Idea of inflicting personal punishment for personal insult was, in this instance, carried too far, and if the principle was established it would be subversive of all military discipline." At another time, a court-martial sentenced a captain to be reprimanded for "immoderately beating" a soldier "without sufficient cause to Justify such correction." Washington expressed "dissatisfaction at any instance of conduct where violence is made use of without sufficient cause," but he went on to say that "the laudable motive of preserving public property from abuse" had been responsible for the captain's action and was "a palleation for the Deed."[32]

Washington found that "Prompt, and therefore arbitrary punishments are not to be avoided in an army." On several occasions he deemed it necessary to dispense with legal proceedings and resort to summary action. At Valley Forge he ordered: "Any soldier who shall be found discharging his musket without leave, and in an irregular manner, is to receive 20 lashes immediately on the spot." Straggling, a "Practice subversive of all discipline and pernicious in every point of view," also called for strong measures. Officers were authorized to order as many as fifty lashes on the spot. To suppress marauding, Washington directed that each "delinquent [be] punished immediately on the spot with any number of lashes not exceeding one hundred." While attempting to hold his position on Harlem Heights in September, 1776, Washington took the view that a coward was not entitled to his day in court: "Any Officer, or Soldier . . ., who (upon the Approach, or Attack of the Enemy's Forces, by land or water) presumes to turn his back and flee, shall be instantly Shot down, and all good officers are hereby authorized and required to see this done, that the brave and gallant part of the Army shall not fall a sacrifice to the base and cowardly part, or share their disgrace ina cowardly and unmanly Retreat." Ten days later he ordered his brigadiers to select some good officers and place them at the rear of the battalions with orders "to shoot any Officer, or Soldier, who shall presume to quit his Ranks, or retreat, unless the Retreat is ordered by proper Authority." When Major General Anthony Wayne had some of the mutineers of the Pennsylvania line shot in May, 1781, Washington agreed that "Sudden and exemplary Punishments were certainly necessary."[33]

Washington had to act carefully in attempting to establish and maintain discipline, for drastic measures might discourage re-

---

[32]Tudor to Washington, Aug. 23, 1775, in Force, *American Archives*, 4th ser., III, 245-246; Washington to President of Congress, Feb. 3, 1781; Washington to Brig. Gen. Preudhome de Borre, Aug. 3, 1777; GO, May 8, 1779, June 5, 1782.

[33]Washington to President of Congress, Feb. 3, 1781; GO, Dec. 22, 1777, June 11, 1780, Nov. 19, 1782, Sept. 20, 1776, Oct. 1, 1776; Washington to Wayne, June 9, 1781.

enlistments or provoke disorders greater than those he was trying to correct. He had to use great care, for example, in dealing with the insolent and arrogant riflemen from Pennsylvania. When thirty-three were tried for mutiny, each was fined twenty shillings, with the ringleader being sentenced also to six days in prison. If the penalty had been fitted to the crime and the men had been whipped, Washington might have been faced with mutiny on a much larger scale.[34]

The General distinguished "between enormous and premeditated crimes and slight offenses . . . committed through Levity and inconsideration." The latter required special treatment in order to "reclaim those who are not lost to all sense of virtue and military pride." The Commander-in-Chief was "more desirous to reclaim than punish Offenders."[35]

Although Washington sometimes regarded punishment as retribution for a crime committed, or as an instrument for reforming an offender, he more often regarded it as a deterrent against crime. In fact, he stated that he did not "wish to inflict punishment, especially capital, but for the sake of example." On June 28, 1776, he told his men he hoped that the "unhappy Fate of Thomas Hickey, executed this day for Mutiny, Sedition and Treachery . . . will be a warning to every Soldier, in the Army." The spectacle of the guardsman swinging from the gallows would, he believed, "produce many salutary consequences and deter others from entering into like practices." When three men were sentenced to death for desertion, he said, "Examples must be made, to put a stop to that prevailing Crime; or we may as well disband the Army at once." Shocked by the number of men who engaged in plundering, he was "determined to make Examples which will deter the boldest and most harden'd offenders."[36]

Washington was aware, however, that restraint was necessary "lest the frequency of punishment should take off the good effects intended by it." He warned one brigadier "not [to] introduce Capital executions too frequently," and he told another that if executions were too common they would "lose their intended force and rather bear the Appearance of cruelty than Justice."[37]

Washington, who took no pleasure in punitive measures, begged his men to "save him the anguish of giving Guilt the chastisement it demands." He could not understand why some men misbehaved as they did. "Why," he asked, "will Soldiers force down punishment upon their own heads? Why will they not be satisfied to do their duty, and reap the benefits of it? . . . Why will they abandon, or betray so great a trust? Why will they madly turn their backs upon glory, freedom and happiness?"[38]

He expected too much, however, for no commander, in any age, has attained the goal that Washington set for himself, that of having "the business of the Army conducted without punishment." It was with "inexpressible regret" that he invoked military law to do those "severe, but necessary acts of Justice" which he believed were required if he were to discharge his responsibilities as Commander-in-Chief of the Revolutionary Army, an army which, he said, was "engaged in the greatest cause men can defend."[39]

[34]GO, Sept. 13, 1775; Freeman, *Washington*, III, 525-526.
[35]GO, Nov. 12, 1782, May 6, 1778.

[36]Washington to Col. Christopher Greene, Oct. 21, 1780; GO, June 28, 1776; Washington to President of Congress, June 28, 1776; Washington to Maj. Gen. Joseph Spencer, April 3, 1777; GO, Oct. 23, 1778.
[37]Washington to Col. Goose Van Schaick, Oct. 27, 1778; Washington to Brig. Gen. Samuel Holden Parsons, April 25, 1777; Washington to Brig. Gen. George Clinton, May 5, 1777.
[38]GO, June 10, 1777.
[39]GO, Jan. 1, 1776, June 10, 1777.

# THE OPENING PHASES

# THE PAPERS OF THE
# BRITISH COMMANDERS IN CHIEF
# IN NORTH AMERICA, 1754-1783*

By Henry P. Beers

## The Office of Commander in Chief

In the British colonies in America prior to the French and Indian War, the colonial governors and assemblies had the responsibility in time of peace in Europe for the defense of their frontiers.[1] During the inter-colonial wars that had been fought previously, British troops had been provided and withdrawn upon the conclusion of hostilities. The inability of the British Government, however, to induce the colonies to cooperate for their defense had forced it to keep small garrisons of regular troops in New York and South Carolina during the eighteenth century.

The defense of the colonies became a problem for the British Government in 1754 following the defeat of the Virginia forces under George Washington by the French at Fort Necessity. Governor Robert Dinwiddie of Virginia had taken the lead in opposing the French intrusion on the Ohio. He communicated with the governors of neighboring colonies in an effort to obtain succor, and appealed to London for military aid. The decision was reached in July 1754 by the British ministry to replace Dinwiddie by Governor Horatio Sharpe of Maryland as temporary commander in chief and to appropriate funds for an expedition to the Ohio.[2] Sharpe's appointment was dated July 5, and he received it on October 7, 1754, but he was not destined to hold the command long.

Even before Sharpe had received his commission, a British officer had been selected to fill on a permanent basis the position of Commander in Chief of His Majesty's Forces in North America. The officer designated was Major General Edward Braddock, a professional soldier and a favorite of the Duke of Cumberland, the captain general of the British land forces. At the time of his appointment on September 24, 1754, General Braddock was aboard ship en route from Gibraltar to Marseilles, and he did not reach America at Hampton Roads, Virginia until February 1755. He was instructed to assume command not only of all the forts and military forces but also to take control of Indian relations and to secure the cooperation of the colonial governments in raising men, obtaining supplies and arms, and furnishing transportation.[3] Braddock's headquarters during the few months that he held command were with his army in the campaign against Fort Duquesne.

[1] George L. Beer, British Colonial Policy, 1754-1765 (New York, 1907), 10; Lawrence H. Gipson, Zones of International Friction North America, South of the Great Lakes Region, 1748-1754 (New York, 1939), 290.
[2] Beer, op. cit., 27; Lawrence H. Gipson, The Great War for the Empire, the Years of Defeat, 1754-1757 (New York, 1946), 50-55; Ella Lonn, "Horatio Sharpe," in Dictionary of American Biography, ed. by Allen Johnson, Dumas Malone and Harris E. Starr (New York, 1928-1944, 22 vols.), XVII, 25-26; Herbert L. Osgood, The American Colonies in the Eighteenth Century (New York, 1924-1925, 4 vols.), IV, 339.
[3] Osgood, op. cit., IV, 342-343; Clarence E. Carter, "The Office of Commander in Chief: a Phase of Imperial Unity on the Eve of the Revolution," in The Era of the Revolution; Studies Inscribed to Evarts Boutell Greene, ed. by Richard B. Morris (New York, 1939), 175.

*This article is part of a longer study entitled: A History of the Colonial Records of American Territories, for work on which a grant in aid has been received from the Social Science Research Council.

After General Braddock's death in July 1755, following his defeat in the battle with the French on the Monongahela River, the post of commander in chief devolved temporarily upon William Shirley, who was Braddock's choice for the succession.[4] Governor of Massachusetts since 1741, Shirley had become the most prominent military figure in the colonies, having led a successful attack upon Louisbourg in 1744-1745. At the time of his appointment as commander in chief, he was leading the British forces against Fort Niagara. Because of circumstances beyond his control, he was unsuccessful in this campaign and in the operations of 1756. He was replaced largely as a result of the representations of his enemies to the British Government.[5]

A general in the British army, John Campbell, Fourth Earl of Loudoun, was picked to succeed Shirley. James Abercromby, a close friend of Loudoun, was designated as second in command and Colonel Daniel Webb as the next in line. Since Loudoun could not proceed immediately to America, a temporary commission as commander in chief was issued to Colonel Webb.[6] On reaching New York early in June 1756, however, he waited there for the arrival of General Abercromby. They proceeded together to Albany where Abercromby relieved Shirley on June 25, 1756. His command was of short duration, for near the end of the next month he was followed by Lord Loudoun, who had received a permanent commission as commander in chief in March 1756.[7] Loudoun made considerable progress in organizing the army but suffered defeat in battle; a letter of recall was addressed to him on December 30, 1757.[8] General Abercromby, who had remained as second in command, was sent an appointment as his successor on the same date. Abercromby took over command in New York in March 1758.[9] His was actually only a partial command, for the successful expeditions against Louisbourg under Amherst and against Fort Duquesne under Forbes were planned by William Pitt. The disastrous defeat of Abercromby at Ticonderoga in July 1758 led to his recall to England.

Major General Jeffery Amherst, the next commander in chief, proved to be an outstanding military leader. He had already gained fame as the captor of Louisbourg when chosen by William Pitt for the top military command in America. After receiving his appointment at Halifax in November 1758, Amherst went to New York where he thenceforth maintained his headquarters when not commanding operations in the field.[10] The campaigns of 1759 and 1760 resulted in the conquest of Canada. The office of commander in chief was continued thereafter in order to protect British interests in North America. The new acquisitions of territory, including the eastern half of the Mississippi Valley and the Floridas as well as New France, had to be occupied, garrisoned,

[4]Osgood, op. cit., IV, 361; Gipson, Great War for the Empire, 180-181; Charles H. Lincoln, ed., Correspondence of William Shirley (New York, 1912, 2 vols.), II, 215, 241.

[5]Gipson, Great War for the Empire, 180-188; Osgood, op. cit., IV, 381; Lincoln, op. cit., I, xxvii, II, 425; John R. Alden, General Gage in America, being Principally a History of His Role in the American Revolution (Baton Rouge, 1948), 32-36; James T. Adams, "William Shirley," Dict. Amer. Biog., XVII, 122; Gertrude S. Kimball, ed., Correspondence of William Pitt when Secretary of State, with Colonial Governors and Military and Naval Commissioners in America (New York, 1906, 2 vols.), I, xxvii.

[6]Stanley M. Pargellis, Lord Loudoun in North America (New Haven, 1933), 74; Lincoln, op. cit., II, 425.

[7]Pargellis, op. cit., 42 ff.; Gipson, Great War for the Empire, 188, 193; Lincoln, op. cit., II, 483 nl.

[8]Osgood, op. cit., IV, 410; Kimball, op. cit., I, 134; Pargellis, op. cit., 336-351.

[9]Stanley M. Pargellis, "James Abercromby," Dict. Amer. Biog., I, 29.

[10]John C. Long, Lord Jeffery Amherst, a Soldier of the King (New York, 1933), 79-80, 119-122, 139, 153; Kimball, op. cit., I, 354, 430.

and governed. These activities were directed by the commander in chief from New York. Upon General Amherst's return to England in November 1763, he was succeeded by Major General Thomas Gage, who had seen service throughout the war in the colonies.[11]

General Gage served on an acting basis until September 1764 when he was given a regular commission after Amherst decided not to return to America. For almost ten years General Gage devoted himself to the duties of the position of commander in chief before he took leave of absence to visit England. His place in New York was filled by Major General Frederick Haldimand from June 1773 to May 1774.[12] Upon his return to America in May 1774, General Gage landed at Boston, having been appointed vice admiral, captain and governor in chief of Massachusetts. He journeyed to New York in the summer of 1774, but during the rest of his command in America he was stationed at Boston overseeing the rebellious colony of Massachusetts. Further consideration of the situation in the colonies led the British cabinet to decide upon the dispatch of additional generals. General Gage was continued in command, but three younger major generals, William Howe, Henry Clinton, and John Burgoyne, were chosen to assist him.[13] These officers and a fleet of troop transports reached Boston in May 1775.

Not long after the outbreak of hostilities in Massachusetts and the receipt of the news of Bunker Hill in England, the recall of Gage was decided upon. His departure in

October 1775 made way for Sir William Howe, who was placed in command of the British forces south of Canada. Sir Guy Carleton was given charge of operations on the St. Lawrence. Howe commanded the British forces opposing General Washington until May 25, 1778. Henry Clinton, who had been with Howe since 1775, then filled the chief command. Not more successful than his predecessor, General Clinton resigned in May 1782 and returned to England. By this time Cornwallis had been defeated at Yorktown, and there was little for the next commander in chief, Guy Carleton, to do but to await at New York the conclusion of peace negotiations. On November 23, 1783, over two months after the signing of the treaty of Paris, General Carleton evacuated New York.

For military affairs in British North America the most important manuscripts are the papers of the commanders in chief. These are more significant than the documents in the British Public Record Office, for they contain not only communications to and from the British Government but also communications with correspondents in North America as well as other types of records. It was the custom for the generals to retain their papers upon the termination of their service in America and to carry them off to their own estates in England. Most of these collections have survived the passage of time and are among the most important documentary sources for the history of colonial America. Though they remained in private hands, these papers are more official than personal in character.

### List of Commanders in Chief

The commanders in chief are listed below in chronological order. Tenures are reckoned from assumption of command to assumption of succeeding command, ignoring dates of

[11]Carter, loc. cit., 177; Clarence E. Carter, ed., The Correspondence of General Thomas Gage with the Secretaries of State and with the War Office and the Treasury, 1763-1775 (New Haven, 1931, 1933, 2 vols.), II, 9 n48, 259; Alden, op. cit., 61.

[12]Carter, Correspondence of General Thomas Gage, I, 353, 355, II, 158 n45, 159, 640; Alden, op. cit., 192.

[13]Alden, op. cit., 236; Troyer S. Anderson, The Command of the Howe Brothers during the American Revolution (New York, 1936), 43.

appointment. Military rank is given as of date of assumption of command. Amherst and Howe became lieutenant generals while in office. Governor Dinwiddie is omitted from this list because of insufficient information.

---

| | | |
|---|---|---|
| Governor Horatio Sharpe of Maryland . . . . (Temporary) | | Oct. 1754 - Feb. 1755 |
| Maj. Gen. Edward Braddock . . . . . . . . . . . . | | Feb. 1755 - July 1755 |
| Governor William Shirley of Massachusetts . . (Temporary) | | July 1755 - June 1756 |
| Maj. Gen. James Abercromby . . . . . . (Temporary) | | June 1756 - July 1756 |
| Maj. Gen. Lord Loudoun . . . . . . . . . . . | | July 1756 - Mar. 1758 |
| Maj. Gen. James Abercromby . . . . . . . . . | | Mar. 1758 - Nov. 1758 |
| Maj. Gen. Jeffrey Amherst . . . . . . . . . . | | Nov. 1758 - Nov. 1763 |
| Maj. Gen. Thomas Gage . . . . . . . . . . . | | Nov. 1763 - June 1773 |
| Maj. Gen. Frederick Haldimand . . . . . . (Temporary) | | June 1773 - May 1774 |
| Maj. Gen. Thomas Gage . . . . . . . . . . . | | May 1774 - Oct. 1775 |
| Maj. Gen. Sir William Howe . (For area *excluding* Canada) | | Oct. 1775 - May 1778 |
| Lt. Gen. Henry Clinton . . . (For area *excluding* Canada) | | May 1778 - May 1782 |
| Lt. Gen. Sir Guy Carleton . . . . . . . . . . . | | May 1782 - Nov. 1783* |

*After Gen. Carleton evacuated New York on 23 November 1783, the title of Commander in Chief in North America pertained to Canada only.

---

## The Papers of Governor Dinwiddie

The early military efforts of the British in the Ohio country are documented in the papers of Robert Dinwiddie. As Governor of Virginia from 1751, he energetically pushed the British claim to that region and urged action on the part of the British Government. Ill health forced his return to England in 1758. His papers were in London in 1829 in the possession of a J. Hamilton.[14] They passed into the hands of an American dealer in London, Henry Stevens, who in 1881 sold them to William W. Corcoran of Washington, D. C. By the latter they were presented to the Virginia Historical Society in Richmond, and that institution soon published them.[15] This collection comprises letters, addresses, reports, commissions, and in-

[14] Justin Winsor, ed., *Narrative and Critical History of America* (Boston, 1884-1889, 8 vols.), V, 572.

[15] R. A. Brock, ed., *The Official Records of Robert Dinwiddie ... 1751-1758* (Richmond, 1883-1884, 2 vols.).

structions. Many of the letters addressed to William Trent, George Washington, the governors of other colonies, British ministers, the Board of Trade, and to General Braddock related to Virginia activities connected with the upper Ohio. Though one of the principal sources on this subject, these papers must be supplemented by other official documents.

## Governor Horatio Sharpe

Further record of the early years of the French and Indian War is to be found in the papers of Governor Horatio Sharpe of Maryland. With a temporary appointment as British commander in chief, Governor Sharpe continued Dinwiddie's activities during the second half of 1754 and later cooperated with General Braddock. Upon his retirement from the governorship in 1769 he established a home near Annapolis, but in 1773 he was recalled to England on family affairs and never returned to Maryland. His

Maryland home was thereafter occupied by John Ridout, who had come to America with the governor as his secretary, and when Sharpe died in 1790 the place was bequeathed to Ridout.[16] Governor Sharpe's papers were eventually given by one of Ridout's sons to Robert Gilmor of Baltimore, by whom they were presented to the Maryland Historical Society.[17] The Gilmor collection of Sharpe papers relates to the whole of the governor's administration and includes letters from a number of military officers and correspondence with the governors of the neighboring colonies. The Maryland Historical Society also became the depository by a resolution of the state legislature of 1846-1847 of two letter books of Governor Sharpe for 1754-1756 and 1767-1771.[18] Both collections of Sharpe papers in the society, the Calvert papers, and other state records were drawn upon for the Sharpe correspondence which was published in the *Archives of Maryland*.[19] Other letters of Governor Sharpe can be found in the published papers of Robert Dinwiddie and in the colonial records of Pennsylvania.

## General Edward Braddock

For documents pertaining to General Braddock's ill-fated command resort must be had to various archival and manuscript collections, for no group of his own papers exists. Papers of Braddock captured by the French at the time of his defeat revealed the plans of the British.[20] In an effort to show that the British were the aggressors in the war, the French published in 1756 a collection of French and British documents which included Braddock's captured papers.[21] There were two sets of instructions, both dated November 25, 1754, one secret[22] and the other general.[23] The French also captured letters and a plan of Fort Duquesne sent to Braddock by Major Robert Stobo, a Virginia officer held by the French as a hostage following Washington's defeat at Fort Necessity.[24] Communications from Braddock and subordinate officers to Robert Napier, Adjutant General to the Duke of Cumberland, are in the Cumberland papers.

16Matilda Edgar, *A Colonial Governor in Maryland, Horatio Sharpe and His Times, 1753-1773* (London, New York, 1912), 250, 268, 278-280.

17Maryland Historical Society, *Catalogue of the Manuscripts . . .* (Baltimore, 1854), 10.

18*Ibid.*, 5-7.

19William H. Browne, ed., *Correspondence of Governor Horatio Sharpe, 1753-1771* (*Archives of Maryland*, vols. VI, IX, XIV, XXXI) (Baltimore, 1888, 1895, 1911).

20New York (Colony), *Documents Relative to the Colonial History of the State of New York; procured in Holland, England and France, by John Romeyn Brodhead, Esq., Agent, . . .* ed. by Edmund B. O'Cal-

laghan and Berthold Fernow (Albany, 1856-1887, 15 vols.). (Hereafter cited as *N. Y. Col. Doc.*). X, 311-312.

21Jacob N. Moreau, *A Memorial Containing a Summary View of Facts, with Their Authorities, in Answer to Observations sent by the English Ministry to the Courts of Europe* (Philadelphia, 1757). Several editions of this publication appeared in French and English in Paris, London, and New York. Braddock documents published therein include his general instructions of November 25, 1754, a letter of the same date written by Robert Napier, and a number of letters to the British ministers taken from a copybook.

22*N. Y. Col. Doc.*, VI, 920-922; Stanley M. Pargellis, ed., *Military Affairs in North America, 1748-1765; Selected Documents from the Cumberland Papers in Windsor Castle* (New York, London, 1936), 53-54.

23Pennsylvania (Colony), *Pennsylvania Archives*, ed. by Samuel Hazard and others (Philadelphia and Harrisburg, 1852-1907, 6 series in 91 vols.), 1st ser., II, 203-207; Winthrop Sargent, ed., *The History of an Expedition against Fort DuQuesne, in 1755, under Major-General Edward Braddock* (Philadelphia, 1855), 393-397; Quebec (Province) Archives, *Rapport de l'Archiviste de la Province de Quebec, 1932-1933* (Quebec, 1933), 310-314; Israel D. Rupp, *Early History of Western Pennsylvania, and of the West, and of Western Expeditions and Campaigns . . .* (Pittsburgh, 1846), 53-57.

24The letters were written to Colonel Innes, of the Virginia forces, and were sent by two Indians to Aughwick, Pa., where George Croghan opened them and made copies which he forwarded to Governor Hamilton of Pennsylvania. The letters were published in the *Minutes of the Provincial Council of Pennsylvania* in 1851 (vol. VI, 141-143) and the map in *Pennsylvania Archives* in 1852 (vol. II, 146), and in Sargent, *op. cit.*, 182. Both appeared in Neville Craig, *Memoirs of Major Robert Stobo, of the Virginia Regiment* (Pittsburgh, 1854). Cf. G. M. Kahrl, "Robert

These are preserved in Windsor Castle, the principal royal residence near London. The American documents in the Cumberland papers have been published.[25] The Loudoun papers also contain material relating to the Fort Duquesne expedition, including a number of pieces by Braddock himself. Additional letters of the general are in the Nead collection in the Historical Society of Pennsylvania. For the purpose of publication a collection of the papers of General Braddock has been initiated by Professor Alfred P. James of the University of Pittsburgh.

Orderly books covering Braddock's march kept under the direction of George Washington found their way into the hands of Peter Force. After their acquisition by the Library of Congress upon the purchase of the Force collection, the orderly books were printed.[26]

The sources pertaining to Braddock's defeat are extensive and have been subjected to different interpretations.[27] The official story was presented in a series of letters written by Captain Robert Orme, Braddock's aide de camp, following the general's death. Telling the same story, these were addressed to the officials in England, to Commodore Augustus Keppel, and to the governors of Virginia, Maryland, and Pennsylvania.[28] A journal which Captain Orme kept for the whole expedition was sent with a set of maps

to the Duke of Cumberland. These became part of the King's MSS. in the British Museum,[29] and they were obtained and published by the Historical Society of Pennsylvania upon the hundredth anniversary of the battle on the Monongahela.[30] Young George Washington wrote an account which was not of a professional character; he had joined to gain experience with professionals. In the British Museum are two copies of the same letter written by Adam Stephen, a Virginian with the rear guard, to different persons.[31] The officer in charge of the vanguard, Thomas Gage, communicated his explanation of the rout to Admiral Keppel, who commanded the British fleet off the Virginia coast.[32] In the Cumberland papers are other descriptions, including that sent by Sir John St. Clair, who commanded the working party which followed the vanguard, to Robert Napier; a letter by Harry Gordon, an engineer, to his brother; and by an anonymous officer who served as an amanuensis to St. Clair.[33] Parts of a letter by Horatio Gates, who captanied a New York independent company under Gage, to Robert Monckton were copied in a letter of Major Hale, which is in the Loudoun papers. In the fall of 1755 after

Stobo," in *Dict. Amer. Biog.*, XVIII, 35-36. The copies that fell into French hands apparently found their way into the French archives — cf. Nancy M. Surrey, comp., *Calendar of Manuscripts in Paris Archives and Libraries Relating to the History of the Mississippi Valley to 1803* (Washington, 1926, 1928, 2 vols.), II, 1249.

25Pargellis, *Military Affairs in North America.*

26"Major General Edward Braddock's orderly books, from February 26 to June 17, 1755," in William H. Lowdermilk, *History of Cumberland, (Maryland) from the Time of the Indian Town, Caiuctucuc, in 1728, up to the Present Day* (Washington, D. C., 1878).

27Stanley M. Pargellis, "Braddock's Defeat," *Amer. Hist. Rev.*, XLI (Jan. 1936), 253-269. This article presents a critical evaluation of the sources.

28Orme's letters to Robert Napier and Henry Fox, the Secretary at War, are published in Pargellis, *Military Affairs*, 98-101. For references to the places of publication of his other letters, see *ibid.* 101 n1 and the same author's "Braddock's Defeat," 254, n3.

29Sargent, *op. cit.*, 281; Charles M. Andrews and Frances G. Davenport, *Guide to the Manuscript Materials for the History of the United States to 1783, in the British Museum, and in Minor London Archives, and in the Libraries of Oxford and Cambridge* (Washington, 1908), 28.

30"Captain Orme's Journal," in Sargent, *op cit.*, 281-358.

31Pargellis, "Braddock's Defeat," *Amer. Hist. Rev.* XLI, 255-256.

32This is printed in Thomas Keppel, *The Life of Augustus Viscount Keppel* (London, 1842, 2 vols.), I, 213 ff. Commodore Keppel upon the arrival of Admiral Boscawen carried the news of Braddock's defeat to England.

33Pargellis, "Braddock's Defeat," 256. These are published in Pargellis, *Military Affairs.*

the remnant of the army reached Albany, the officers held a court of inquiry on the battle.[34] At the command of General Shirley maps were prepared by Patrick Mackellar, an engineer with the expedition, showing the formation of the troops on the march and their disposition during the battle.[35] Several accounts by contemporaries who were not eye-witnesses have been published in various places.[36] Among these was the "Journal of the Proceedings of the Seamen (a Detachment) Ordered by Commodore Keppel to Assist on the Late Expedition to the Ohio."[37]

### Governor Shirley

Less than a year of William Shirley's long career in America was spent as commander in chief of the British army. No collection of Shirley's letters has survived. Some original letters written by him to Colonel John Stoddard are in the Massachusetts Historical Society which also has copies in the Parkman transcripts. William Alexander, known during the Revolutionary War as Lord Stirling, served during the early years of the French and Indian War as commissary, aide, and secretary to General Shirley. His correspondence for this period is preserved in the New York Historical Society and includes letters of Shirley and others which are valuable for Shirley's command.

When the publication of Shirley's correspondence was undertaken by Charles H. Lincoln for the Colonial Dames of America in 1910, he was obliged, for lack of a collection of Shirley papers, to draw upon other archival and manuscript collections.[38] He found, however, an abundance of material in the British Public Record Office, the British Museum, the Massachusetts Archives, the Library of Congress, the historical societies of Massachusetts, Connecticut, Pennsylvania, and Maryland, the William Johnson papers, and other places. The publication that resulted is comprised chiefly of selected letters and other documents sent out by Shirley hitherto unpublished and a smaller number of incoming letters. The portion of the second volume covering the period when Shirley was commander in chief (July 1755 to June 1756) contains letters to and from the governors of colonies, officials of the British Government, military officers, and William Johnson.[39] His earlier correspondence is also important for military affairs, for he had been commander of the New England forces engaged in fighting the French.

---

[34]Printed in Lincoln, *Correspondence of William Shirley*, II, 311-213.

[35]These maps are printed in Pargellis, "Braddock's Defeat," 258-259 and in his *Military Affairs*, 114. They had previously been published by Francis Parkman in his *Montcalm and Wolfe*. The original maps are in the Cumberland papers, and other sets are in the Public Record Office and the Public Archives of Canada.

[36]The writers were James Burd, John Rutherford, William Johnston, Matthew Leslie, and Dr. Walker. Cf. Pargellis, "Braddock's Defeat," 254. Governor Dinwiddie of Virginia wrote the Earl of Halifax an account on October 1, 1755, based on information obtained from officers he had seen. This is published in his *Official Records*, II, 220-226.

[37]This journal was given by Captain Hewitt, R.N. to Captain Henry G. Morris, R.N., and a copy of it was obtained from the latter's son, the Rev. Francis-Orpen Morris of Yorkshire, by Joseph R. Ingersoll, who presented it together with maps and plans of the route of Braddock's army to the Historical Society of Pennsylvania. This journal was published by Sargent, *op. cit.*, 359-389. Subsequently Archer B. Hulbert published extracts from another version obtained from the Royal Artillery Library at Woolwich, to which it had been presented by a Colonel Macbean. (A. B. Hulbert, *Braddock's Road* (Cleveland, 1903), 83-107). Hulbert believed the Morris journal to be the work of Harry Gordon, an engineer on the expedition, impersonating a sailor. He did not ascertain the authorship of the other journal. Pargellis, however, considered that the author of the Morris journal was the midshipman who had been left behind in the hospital at Will's Creek, but that Gordon may have contributed to it.

[38]Carnegie Institution of Washington, Department of Historical Research, Correspondence Files, Correspondence between Lincoln and J. F. Jameson, 1910-1912.

[39]Lincoln, *op. cit.*, II, 215-468.

## Lord Loudoun

The papers of Lord Loudoun remained in the possession of the family until their sale in 1923 to Mr. Henry E. Huntington. A nephew of Collis P. Huntington of Southern Pacific Railroad fame and his successor as the president of that line, Henry E. Huntington became in the first quarter of the present century one of the foremost American private collectors. Specializing in English literature and Americana in both printed and manuscript form, he purchased whole libraries gathered by others in both the United States and England, and in 1920 opened his treasures to the public in the Henry E. Huntington Library and Art Gallery in San Marino, California.[40]

The bulk of the 10,000 pieces in the Loudoun collection relate to the general's service in America during the French and Indian War.[41] Among these papers are 1500 dealing with the period from 1740 to 1756, and, with the exception of a group in the 1740's relating to French and Indian affairs, are largely copies of papers of Braddock and Shirley which were handed over to Loudoun. Besides over 1200 letters written by Loudoun, there are many letters and reports from governors, military officers, Indian superintendents, and naval officers. Records of various types pertaining to the British Army include returns, lists, accounts, orders, and warrants. Over a hundred communications from Loudoun to the Duke of Cumberland have been printed.[42]

The Huntington Library also possesses the papers of James Abercromby for the period of his service during 1758 as British commander in chief in North America. These were purchased from Lathrop C. Harper, a New York dealer, in 1923.[43] Numbering approximately 1,000 documents, these are similar in variety and subject matter to the Loudoun papers. Communications sent by Abercromby and retained for his files in copies made by his secretaries number 446. Other Abercromby letters are to be found in the Loudoun papers.

## General Amherst

Upon General Amherst's departure for England, his brother, William, who had served with him in America, attended to the packing of the general's records and their shipment to England. These voluminous papers remained undisturbed in the cellar of the country home of the family, Montreal House, in Sevenoaks, Kent, until brought to light by the approaching sale of the house in 1925.[44] Lord Amherst's long service of over five years in America is well recorded in his papers comprising over 85,000 items. More than 80,000 of these in 250 packages are concerned with public affairs. This portion of the collection has been loaned to the British Public Record Office where it is classified as *War Office 34*. Of the private letters which remained in the possession of the family, the Public Archives of Canada has prepared an index. The manuscripts include the journals of both the general and his brother.[45]

Reproductions of many of the Amherst

[40]Carl L. Cannon, *American Book Collectors and Collecting* (New York, 1941), 302-317.

[41]Henry E. Huntington Library and Art Gallery, *American Manuscript Collections in the Huntington Library for the History of the Seventeenth and Eighteenth Centuries,* comp. by Norma B. Cuthbert (San Marino, 1941), 37.

[42]Pargellis, *Military Affairs in North America,* xiii, passim.

[43]Huntington Library, *op. cit.,* 3.

[44]John C. Long, *Lord Jeffery Amherst, a Soldier of the King* (New York, 1933), vii-ix, 327.

[45]The journal of General Amherst has been published: J. C. Webster, ed., *The Journal of Jeffery Amherst, Recording the Military Career of General Amherst in America from 1758 to 1763* (Toronto, 1931).

papers have been obtained by institutions in the United States and Canada. The Library of Congress has photostats of the most important correspondence volumes.[46] Amherst College, which derived its name from the British general, has photostatic copies of the bulk of the Amherst papers. Extensive copying from this collection has also been executed by the Public Archives of Canada. The University of Michigan Library has a microfilm copy of the Amherst correspondence. A calendar of the papers prepared by John C. Long in five volumes is in the William L. Clements Library. Copies of an index to the papers prepared by the same biographer are in Amherst College Library, the British Public Records Office, the Library of Congress, the New York Public Library, and the Public Archives of Canada.

Certain correspondence and other papers relating to unfinished business were turned over to Gage when he succeeded General Amherst in 1763. Though purchased by the William L. Clements Library with the Gage papers, these are bound and classified separately in two portfolios and seven volumes.[47] The collection includes letters and petitions addressed to Amherst, letters from Amherst to Gage, letters to Amherst received after his departure, and letters between Amherst and various correspondents. The last named series is composed particularly of correspondence with subordinate officers and contains letters from Major Henry Gladwin of Detroit and other post commanders relating to

Pontiac's War. The inclusive dates for the group are 1758 to 1764.

Letters of General Amherst exist in other places.[48] In various collections in the Division of Manuscripts of the Library of Congress are some 500 letters. A folio in the "additional manuscripts" of the British Museum contains others. The original letters from Amherst to Haldimand, Bouquet, Monckton, and William Johnson exist in the collections of the papers of those men. Numerous letters from Amherst to William Pitt have been published.[49]

## General Gage

General Gage took home to England with him in 1775 the papers accumulated during his long service as British commander in chief in North America. They were deposited and remained for 150 years in the country seat of the Viscounts Gage, Firle Place, in Lewes, Sussex.

The discovery of the Gage papers resulted from combined English and American interest. Dr. Clarence E. Carter of Miami University, historian of the British period in Illinois, had been collecting copies of Gage's correspondence for publication for some years when he learned in 1926 through correspondence with Dr. J. F. Jameson of the Carnegie Institution of Washington that the papers of General Gage had been deposited in the British Public Record Office by the Viscount Gage, in order that a report could be prepared upon them by the British Historical Manuscripts Commission.[50] Dr. Carter finally

[46]Grace G. Griffin, *A Guide to Manuscripts Relating to American History in British Depositories Reproduced for the Division of Manuscripts of the Library of Congress* (Washington, 1946), 82-83. The Force transcripts in this library also contain Amherst correspondence for 1759 to 1764.

[47]Howard H. Peckham, *Guide to the Manuscript Collections in the William L. Clements Library* (Ann Arbor, 1942), 12; S. Morley Scott, "Material Relating to Quebec in the Gage and Amherst Papers," *Canadian Hist. Rev.*, XIX (Dec. 1938), 385.

[48]A volume of correspondence between Amherst and Colonel John Bradstreet presented to the New York State Library by the Rev. William B. Sprague in 1851 was lost in the Capitol fire of 1911. Winsor, *op. cit.*, V, 233; Letter from Edna L. Jacobsen, Manuscripts and History Section, New York State Library, September 21, 1948.

[49]Kimball, *op. cit.*

[50]Carnegie Inst. Wash., Correspondence between Carter and Jameson, 1915-1928; A. E. Stamp, Secretary of

got to London in the summer of 1928 and spent several months examining the Gage papers. Upon his return to the United States he informed Mr. William L. Clements of the great value of the papers. Negotiations were opened for Mr. Clements by Randolph G. Adams and in 1930 the papers were purchased from the Sixth Viscount Gage, brought back across the Atlantic, and deposited in Mr. Clement's home at Bay City, Michigan.[51]

A graduate of the University of Michigan, William L. Clements had begun early in his life the collection of Americana. A successful business career as a manufacturer and a banker brought him wealth and enabled him to build up an extensive library of Americana for the years before 1800. He presented the collection in 1922-1923 to the University of Michigan together with a building to house it. The acquisition of the papers of Lord Shelburne[53] in 1922 turned his attention to the manuscripts relating to the British side of the War of Independence. Continuing his quest of manuscripts, particularly after his retirement in 1924, Mr. Clements acquired in subsequent years the papers of a number of British statesmen and generals of that period. These collections were purchased from the estate of Mr. Clements by the University of Michigan in 1937 for $300,000 and moved from Bay City to the William L. Clements Library at Ann Arbor.[54]

The Gage papers constitute the most important collection for the general's career in America and for the operations of the British Army during the period when he was commander in chief.[55] The 21,000 pieces have been bound into 175 three-quarters red morocco bindings. Thousands of documents not available elsewhere are to be found in the collection. The major part of the correspondence relates to the years 1763-1775 when Gage was commander in chief.

The correspondence, reports, and financial papers in the Gage papers document not only the administration of military affairs, the operations of the British Army, and Indian affairs, but also political events in the colonies. A voluminous correspondence was carried on by the general with British ministers, colonial governors, Indian superintendents and agents, and army officers attached to military districts and posts throughout the British domain. By means of these letters and of the returns, lists, vouchers, warrants, and other documents can be derived a knowledge of occurrences at the posts in the West and in the Floridas. Communications from officers commanding at Fort Pitt, Detroit, and Fort Chartres disclose much detailed information. The occupation of St. Augustine and Pensacola, and other points, military administration, and the disputes with civil officials are some of the subjects treated in the voluminous correspondence with the military commanders in the Floridas.[56] Since the

the Hist. MSS. Com., to Jameson, Nov. 20, 1924, apprising him of the fact that the Viscount Gage had consented to the deposit; Jameson to Stamp, April 6, 1926, informing him of Carter's interest.

[51]Randolph G. Adams, "A New Library of American Revolutionary Records," *Current History*, XXXIII (Nov. 1930), 238; Peckham, *op. cit.*, 85. Adams became custodian of the Clements Library in 1923.

[52]Randolph G. Adams, "William L. Clements," *Dict. Amer. Biog.*, XXI, 180.

[53]William Petty Fitzmaurice, Earl of Shelburne and First Marquis of Lansdowne, served as Secretary of State for the Southern Department, 1766-1768.

[54]The acquisitions by Mr. Clements included papers of the following men: Henry Clinton, Thomas Gage,

George Germain, William Howe, William Knox, Lord Shelburne, John G. Simcoe, and John Vaughan. Mr. Clements had intended to present the remaining collections to the William L. Clements Library, but financial reverses suffered after 1929 rendered this difficult and the University arranged for their purchase.

[55]Alden, *op. cit.*, 299.

[56]Howard H. Peckham, "Military Papers in the Clements Library," *Military Affairs*, II (Fall 1938), 126-130; Charles L. Mowat, "Material Relating to British East Florida in the Gage Papers and Other Manuscript Collections in the William L. Clements Library," *Fla. Hist. Quar.*, XVIII (July 1939), 46-60.

deputy quartermaster at Montreal was responsible for provisioning the western posts, the correspondence with the officers filling that position is useful for the history of the posts and for shipbuilding, transportation, and communication on the lakes and in the adjacent country.[57] Numerous maps will enlighten the geographer as well as the historian.

During the 20 years that he served in America, General Gage wrote many letters to relatives and friends. Some of these and other documents relating to his military commands are still preserved at the Gage home at Firle.[58] Few papers of this character are found in the Gage papers in the William L. Clements Library; the mass of them once existing has still to be located.

While the Gage papers were still in England, photostatic reproductions of over 4,000 items were obtained by Dr. Carter for the Library of Congress.[59] Dr. Carter's published selections from Gage's correspondence with the British officials comprise the major portion of the general's reports to London and of the letters received from the British ministers.[60]

In the papers of a number of the correspondents of General Gage are preserved the original letters received by them and in some cases copies of letters written to the general. Both types as well as orders are represented in the Haldimand papers and in the papers of Colonel Henry Bouquet in the British Museum. Letters sent by Gage to Colonel John Bradstreet and Sir William Johnson were collected by William B. Sprague and presented to Harvard College Library.[61]

## General Haldimand

During nearly 30 years of service in North America, Frederick Haldimand systematically filed away his papers, forming a collection of great value for the history of the period. The general's grandnephew, William Haldimand, a member of Parliament, presented the papers to the British Museum in 1857. By that repository they were assigned the numbers 21631-21892 in the series of "additional manuscripts," and they are listed in detail in the museum's catalogue.[62] Inasmuch as General Haldimand served for only a year during 1773-1774 as British commander in chief, only a minor portion of his papers are devoted to that service. Besides correspondence, the papers include instructions, a cash account, a receipt book, warrants, and orders.

For earlier years the Haldimand papers form a useful supplement to the papers of the various British commanders in chief for data pertaining to military affairs. Haldimand had previously served in the campaigns of 1758-1760 for the conquest of Canada and subsequently at Montreal and Three Rivers, and from 1765 to 1773 in Florida. His papers include correspondence with Abercromby, Amherst, and Gage, with the officers in charge of the other military districts in Canada, viz., James Murray and Ralph Burton, with Indian superintendents William Johnson and John Stuart, with provincial governors, and with other officers and officials. Other types of documents in this ex-

---

[57]For appraisals of the Gage papers see Clarence E. Carter, "Notes on the Lord Gage Collection of Manuscripts," *Miss. Valley Hist. Rev.*, XV (March 1929), 511-519; Scott, *loc. cit.*; Peckham, *loc. cit.*; Mowat, *loc. cit.*

[58]Alden, *op. cit.*, 301. Enquiry by Mr. Alden has failed to disclose other personal letters.

[59]Griffin, *op. cit.*, 232-233.

[60]Carter, *The Correspondence of General Thomas Gage.*

[61]Winsor, *op. cit.*, V, 233, VIII, 463. A volume of transcripts of these letters was acquired by the Library of Congress in the Peter Force collection.

[62]British Museum, *Catalogue of Additions to the Manuscripts in the British Museum, in the Years MDCCCLIV-MDCCCLX* (London, 1875, 2 vols.), I, 494-554.

tensive collection include reports, account books, regimental returns, commissariat statistics, general orders, instructions, military rules and directions, journals, diaries, plans, bills of exchange, naval and military commissions, warrants, maps, invoices of cargoes, letters of appointment, statistics of trade, memorials, speeches, addresses, inventories, advertisements, and valuations.

One of the early tasks undertaken by the Archives Branch of the Canadian Government following its establishment in 1872 was the transcription of the Haldimand papers. The Dominion Archivist, Douglas Brymner, visited London in 1873 and before his departure arranged with the British Museum for copying both the Haldimand papers and the Bouquet papers.[63] A comprehensive calendar prepared by Dr. Brymner and published in his annual reports of 1884-1889 furnishes the scholar with a more useful finding aid than the list in the British Museum catalogue.[64] The Historical Society of Montreal also has some transcripts of Haldimand correspondence. A small number of copies from the Haldimand papers made by the Illinois Historical Survey are in the University of Illinois Library. The University of Chicago Library has some copies of the copies in Canada. Photostatic copies of extensive selections from the Haldimand papers have been procured by the Library of Congress.[65] Copies of the Haldimand transcripts in the Canadian Archives Branch were published not long after their procurement in the *Wisconsin State Historical Society Collections.*[66] These relate to the period of British domina-

tion in the Old Northwest from 1763 to 1814. A much larger quantity of Haldimand documents from the same depository was published in the *Michigan Historical Collections.*[67] Covering the British regime from 1762 to 1790, these contain a great amount of information regarding Indian relations, military affairs, and navigation on the lakes. Included in this compilation are letters from commanders at Detroit, Mackinac, and Fort Pitt.

## General Howe

Historians and biographers interested in William Howe have searched in vain for any considerable collection of his papers. Certain of his papers were transferred to his successor, Sir Henry Clinton, upon his departure from America in May 1778.[68] A further transfer brought the documents into the possession of Sir Guy Carleton. The collection is chiefly comprised of correspondence with British ministers, officials in the Floridas, and General Washington. The orderly books of General Howe have been brought to light at different times and are partly in print.[69] The Howe material in the Carleton papers

---

[63]Douglas Brymner, "Canadian Archives," *Amer. Hist. Asso. Pap.,* III (1899), 397-398; David W. Parker, *A Guide to the Documents in the Manuscript Room at the Public Archives of Canada* (Ottawa, 1914), 198.

[64]For Haldimand's correspondence as commander in chief see Canada, Archives, *Report on Canadian Archives,* 1885, 210-221.

[65]Griffin, *op. cit.,* 129-138.

[66]"Papers from the Canadian Archives," *Wis. State Hist. Soc. Colls.,* XI (1888), 97-212; XII (1892), 23-132.

[67]"The Haldimand Papers, Copies of Papers on File in the Dominion Archives at Ottawa, Canada," *Mich. Hist. Colls.,* IX (1908), 343-658; X (1908), 210-675; XI (1908), 319-656; XIX (1911), 296-700; XX (1912), 1-295.

[68]For information concerning these see Great Britain, Historical Manuscripts Commission, *Report on American Manuscripts in the Royal Institution of Great Britain* (London, 1904-1909, 4 vols.), I, vi, and index.

[69]*Ibid.,* I, ix, 41; Benjamin F. Stevens, ed., *General Sir William Howe's Orderly Book at Charlestown, Boston and Halifax June 17, 1775 to 1776 26 May* (London, 1890); M. V. Hay, "The Missing Howe Order Books, 1776-1777," *Americana,* XVIII (April 1924), 85-101; the order books of 1775-1778 are printed in Stephen Kemble, *The Kemble Papers* (N. Y. Hist. Soc. Colls.,* 1883, 1884), (New York, 1884-1885, 2 vols.), I, 251-603.

can be supplemented by his correspondence to be found in other collections of personal papers such as that of Haldimand. Since Clinton came to America at the same time as Howe, the early portion of his papers contains a great deal on Howe's command. In answer to a demand from the House of Commons General Howe prepared a defense of his command in America which was published.[70]

## General Henry Clinton

After Cornwallis's surrender Clinton waged a controversy with him over the responsibility for the failure of the campaign in the southern colonies. Six pamphlets that were published contained official correspondence or extracts thereof. When Clinton's library was sold in London in 1882 and 1884, Benjamin F. Stevens purchased Clinton's own copies of the pamphlets containing his manuscript notes and other books which had been annotated by the general. In searching for the complete text of the 183 documents printed in the pamphlets, Stevens located about 3,456 other papers constituting the official correspondence of Clinton and Cornwallis during 1780-1781. Stevens then published the six pamphlets, the complete texts of the documents found therein, Clinton's notes, extracts from the House of Lords journals, the correspondence of Lord George Germain, and a catalogue of the additional correspondence.[71] The depositories searched for correspondence included the British Museum, the Royal Institution, Public Record Office, various French archives, and private collections. These volumes, besides throwing

new light on the controversy, afforded in the catalogue a guide to much additional manuscript material.

Certain other items purchased by Stevens at the sale of the "library of the late Colonel Henry Clinton" in 1882, comprising some of the headquarters papers of Sir Henry Clinton, were resold by him in New York in the same year. At this sale the well-known collector, Thomas Addis Emmett, bought two small manuscript volumes, one recording private intelligence received by the British and the other information obtained from deserters and others. The secret private intelligence record, containing entries for January to July 1781, was soon afterwards published.[72] An atlas of maps relating to Clinton's campaign in New Jersey was obtained by the Library of Congress. Some letters from General Washington went to an historical scholar of New York. For some years longer, however, the bulk of Sir Henry Clinton's papers remained in the hands of the family.

The headquarters papers taken to England by Sir Henry Clinton in 1782 were purchased in 1926 by Mr. Clements from a great great granddaughter and later deposited in the Clements Library at Ann Arbor.[73] These papers begin in 1775, but they are most numerous for the years 1778 to 1782 when Clinton was commander in chief. The 260 volumes contain 18,500 pieces, including letters, orders, memoranda, war council minutes, military returns, intelligence reports, intercepted material, ledgers, warrants, and Clinton's own three-volume history of the war. Of great value for following the campaigns of the war is a group of 350 maps

---

[70]William Howe, *The Narrative of Lieut. Gen. Sir William Howe, in a Committee of the House of Commons, on the 29th of April, 1779, relative to His Conduct, during His Late Command of the King's Troops in North America* (London, 1780).

[71]Benjamin F. Stevens, *The Campaign in Virginia 1781; an Exact Reprint of Six Rare Pamphlets on the Clinton-Cornwallis Controversy* (London, 1888, 2 vols).

[72]Edward F. DeLancey, ed., and Thomas A. Emmett, contrib., "Sir Henry Clinton's Original Secret Record of Private Daily Intelligence," *Mag. Amer. Hist.*, X (Oct.-Dec. 1883), 327-342, 409-419, 497-507; XI (Jan.-June 1884), 53-70, 156-167, 247-257, 342-352, 433-444, 533-544; XII (July, Aug. 1884), 72-79, 162-175.

[73]Adams, "American Revolutionary Records," 235.

and sketches which are largely in manuscript.[74] Clinton correspondence is also to be found in the Carleton papers and in the Haldimand papers.[75]

## General Carleton

Sir Guy Carleton became Lord Dorchester in 1786 and hence his papers are called both the Carleton papers and the Dorchester papers. Because they also contain some of the papers of Gage, Howe, and Clinton, the Carleton papers are also referred to as the British Headquarters Papers. Carleton's secretary, Maurice Morgann, gave the papers in 1798 to John Symmons who in 1804 presented them to the Royal Institution of Great Britain in London.[76] A list of the collection prepared by an agent of the Canadian Archives Branch was published in one of its early reports.[77] An extensive calendar prepared by Benjamin F. Stevens and Henry J. Brown and published in 1904-1909 by the British Historical Manuscripts Commission affords the investigator an excellent finding aid to this important group of papers.[78]

Ownership of the Carleton papers was transferred in 1929 by purchase from the Royal Institution to Dr. A. S. W. Rosenbach, prominent Philadelphia dealer in rare books and manuscripts. John D. Rockefeller, Jr. acquired the collection in 1930 and deposited it in the New York Public Library. In 1935 he presented it to Colonial Williamsburg, Inc., and it was removed in the following year from New York to Williamsburg.[79]

At the time of their acquisition by Rockefeller, the Carleton papers were in worn bindings in 58 quarto and four folio volumes arranged according to subjects originally selected by Maurice Morgann. The New York Public Library broke up the volumes, rearranged the papers in chronological order according to the Stevens and Brown calendar, and rebound them with interleavings of rag paper in bindings of half red chrome leather and cream du Pont washable fabricoid. The motif of the new binding was the color scheme of the British redcoats' uniform. The rebinding produced 103 volumes, which are kept in solander cases, two special boxes, and two long cylinders. A bound photostat set has also been made.

The Carleton papers consist of 10,434 documents in 28,052 pages. The papers date from 1747 to 1783; one volume covers the years prior to 1776; 34 volumes cover 1776-1781, and for 1782-1783 there are 65 volumes. The collection is made up of correspondence, warrants, muster rolls, lists of officers, orders, inquisitions, record of negroes registered and certified, returns of clothing, provisions, prisoners, and Loyalists, affidavits, memorials, and petitions from Loyalists, commissary general accounts, and letters patent.

Transcripts had been obtained of some of the Carleton papers prior to their transfer to the United States. Jared Sparks located the Carleton papers during a visit to England in 1840 and made selections for copies. The Canadian Archives has copies of those documents relating to Canada. A smaller number of facsimiles was purchased by the Library of Congress from Benjamin F. Stevens.

[74]Randolph G. Adams, *British Headquarters Maps and Sketches Used by Sir Henry Clinton while in Command of the British Forces Operating in North America* ... (Ann Arbor, 1928).

[75]For a calendar of the Clinton-Haldimand correspondence see Canada, Archives, *Report on the Canadian Archives,* 1887, 536-563.

[76]Great Britain, Hist. MSS. Com., *op. cit.,* I, v.

[77]H. A. B. Verreau, "Report of Proceedings Connected with the Canadian Archives in Europe," Canada, Agriculture Department, *Report, 1874* (Ottawa, 1875), 184 ff.

[78]Great Britain, Hist. MSS. Com., *op. cit.*

[79]Letter from Lester J. Cappon, Archivist, Colonial Williamsburg, Inc., and accompanying report on the British Headquarters Papers, Jan. 25, 1949.

The personal papers of Lord Dorchester were burned by his widow following his death in 1808.[80]

### Other Sources

The activities of the British commanders in chief are documented not only in their own papers but also in a number of other classes of manuscripts and archives. Papers exist for subordinate officers, some of whom held important commands. More or less correspondence occurred between them and the commanders in chief, and hence letters of the latter are to be found in these officers' papers. No papers of Brigadier General John Forbes survived, but a collection derived from various archival and manuscript sources has been published.[81] This compilation concerns Forbes's successful campaign against Fort Duquesne in 1758. Brigadier General Robert Monckton came to America in 1752 and served in Canada, New York, and Pennsylvania during the next ten years. An extensive collection of Monckton papers presented to the Canadian Archives has been catalogued.[82] In the New York Public Library are two additional volumes of Monckton papers concerning the Pennsylvania frontier. By far the most important group of papers for Pennsylvania is that of Colonel Henry Bouquet, who served in that colony from 1756 to 1765. The original manuscripts are in the British Museum, but reproductions have been obtained by both the Canadian Archives and the Library of Congress. The Pennsylvania Historical and Museum Commission, which has already issued a mimeographed edition of most of the Bouquet papers, is planning to print them.[83] For two of Bouquet's predecessors in the Pennsylvania command, Brigadier Generals John Stanwix and Robert Monckton, Captain Horatio Gates served as brigade major or military secretary. English by birth, Captain Gates arrived in America in 1754 and continued in service there until 1761. He emigrated to a Virginia plantation in 1772 and fought throughout the War of Independence on the colonial side. After his death in 1806 his papers were carefully preserved by his wife and eventually came into the possession of the New York Historical Society.[84] In the period of the French and Indian War, one of his most frequent correspondents was General James Abercromby. Letters of Dinwiddie and Gage and of the later British commanders in chief are to be found in the manuscripts of George Washington. As superintendent of Indian affairs in the Northern Department from 1755 to 1774 and as a military officer during the French and Indian War, William Johnson had frequent occasion to correspond with the British commanders in chief.[85] The journal of Stephen Kemble, deputy adjutant general under Gage, Howe, and Clinton, is in print.[86] Extensive collections of the papers of Benjamin Franklin containing letters from Gage and Shirley and other officers are preserved in several depositories.[87] The published

---

[80]Arthur G. Bradley, *Lord Dorchester* (London, Toronto, 1926), xi.

[81]Alfred P. James, ed., *Writings of General Forbes Relating to His Service in North America* (Menasha, Wis., 1938).

[82]Canada, Archives. *The Northcliffe Collection* (Ottawa, 1926).

[83]Sylvester K. Stevens, et al., eds., *The Papers of Col. Henry Bouquet* (Harrisburg, 1940-1943). The *Report on Canadian Archives, 1899* contains an extensive calendar of the Bouquet papers, and in the British Museum's *Catalogue of Additions ...* (London, 1875), I, 476-494 is a descriptive catalogue.

[84]*N. Y. Hist. Soc. Proc.*, 1847, 60; Samuel W. Patterson, *Horatio Gates, Defender of American Liberties* (New York, 1941), 430.

[85]James Sullivan, et al., eds., *The Papers of Sir William Johnson* (Albany, 1921-1939, 9 vols.).

[86]Stephen Kemble, *The Kemble Papers* (*N. Y. Hist. Soc. Colls.*, 1883, 1884) (New York, 1884-1885, 2 vols.).

[87]Carl Becker, "Benjamin Franklin," *Dict. Amer. Biog.*, VI, 598.

colonial records of Pennsylvania, New York, Maryland, North Carolina, New Jersey, Rhode Island, Connecticut, and Virginia contain correspondence with the British commanders in chief and other material relating to their operations.

The commanders in chief in America carried on a voluminous correspondence with officials of the British Government in London. The records of the British ministries preserved in the Public Record Office and the papers of numerous officials preserved in the British Museum are, next to the papers of the commanders in chief, the most important sources for the history of the operations of the British Army in America. But these sources are too voluminous for consideration here, and they will eventually be treated elsewhere.

## Opportunities for Research

The exploitation of the papers of the British commanders in chief in North America by American historians and writers has hardly begun. Only a few biographies and monographs have been based upon them. While the various groups of papers were still in England, most of them were inaccessible and few were much used by historians. The collections in the original or in reproduction have become available in the United States largely during the present century. Students of the colonial period will find these papers fruitful sources not only for biographies of the generals and others, but also for numerous other topics. Too much of the writing on military affairs has been of battles and too little has been of military operations in other areas and of the far-flung activities of peace time. The administrative history of the British Army in North America in both war and peace is yet to be written. The history of Indian affairs is still incomplete, particularly in the Northern Department. There is still room for the study of Indian trade. Research can be done on communication and transportation by land, by river, and on the Great Lakes. Contributions to the cartography of the West by British officers were considerable and have never been presented in an integrated account. Regional and local historians can profitably delve into these collections. Editors of documentary compilations will find in them an extensive variety of material. These papers are exceedingly valuable acquisitions for the study of American life, and the institutions and individuals responsible for their availability in the United States have performed an outstanding service to American history.

# THE MEDICAL ADMINISTRATORS
# OF THE AMERICAN REVOLUTIONARY ARMY

By Howard Lewis Applegate*

WHEN the Continental Congress assumed control of the Massachusetts forces on June 14, 1775, no provision was made at that time for a Continental medical department. This can be explained partially by the fact that some congressmen assumed that the Massachusetts Hospital Department could care for all sick and wounded in that area. Others realized that a medical corps would have to be established in the future, but felt that for the time being the colonial establishment would have to be sufficient. Finally, a minority of legislators were unwilling to spend precious moneys on medical services for a war that they expected would not last more than several months.[1]

After the battle of Bunker Hill on June 19, 1775, however, when approximately 30 percent of the estimated 1500 Americans were either killed, wounded, or captured, Congress realized that a Continental Hospital would have to be created because the Massachusetts hospitals were inadequate for treating the wounded.[2] Therefore, on July 27, "The Act for the Establishment of the

Hospital for the Army" was passed. This "Hospital," which meant in contemporary terminology a medical department rather than merely a building for sick and wounded, was administered by a single officer called, "Chief Physician and Director General of the Army Hospital."[3] The act which was intended to provide centralized authority, was unsatisfactory. It was vague and lacked the specific character of legislation necessary for a truly centralized agency. Moreover, it did not take into account further expansion of the army and the medical department, probably because the legislators did not have any idea of the magnitude of the conflict facing them.

To provide expansion of and necessary centralization in the medical department, Congress, on April 7, 1777, abolished the Hospital which had been established in 1775, and called for the formation of a new Hospital, to be managed by a Director who was given many varied powers.[4] As the Director General assumed his responsibilities, he quite naturally added other duties and he became one of the most powerful men in the entire military establishment. His duties were varied and extensive. He examined all applicants for medical berths and appointed minor departmental officers. He established most hospitals, and saw to it that the sick were transported to them and that the recovered men were returned to their regiments. He enforced all departmental rules and regula-

*This study is a result of research on aspects of the American Revolution which the author conducted at Drew University and Syracuse University, New York, during the latter half of the 1950's.

[1]Worthington C. Ford, et. al., Journals of the Continental Congress (34 vols., Washington: Government Printing Office, 1904-1937), June 14, 15, 1775, II, 85-91; A Virginia Delegate to Congress to a constituent, June 15, 1775; Pennsylvania Delegates to Committee of Correspondence of Cumberland County, June 15, 1775; and John Adams to Abagail Adams, June 17,1775; Letters of the Members of the Continental Congress, ed., Edmund C. Burnett (8 vols., Washington, The Carnegie Institution, 1921-1936), I, 124, 125, 130-132.

[2]Christopher Ward, The War of the Revolution, (2 vols., New York: Macmillan, 1952), I, 96.

[3]Journ. Cont. Cong., July 19-27, 1775, II, 191-211.
[4]Ibid., April 7, 1777, VII, 231-237.

tions, supervised the professional methods and techniques of his surgeons, and was required to inspect all installations under his command. He controlled the purchase and distribution of departmental supplies and prepared Hospital budgets and vouchers for Congressional examination.[5]

Quite naturally, during the war period, the Directors General had many problems in the management of their department. Competent surgeons were difficult to obtain. There was intense competition between the four districts that the Hospital was divided into, and as a consequence the treatment of the sick and wounded sometimes suffered. Few of the buildings of colonial America were satisfactory for use as hospitals. Patients were sometimes unruly and the surgeons needed the aid of special detachments assigned to hospitals to enforce the rules. With most hospitals located in isolated areas and a general scarcity of wagons, the Director's task of getting the sick and wounded to the hospitals was made difficult. The scarcity of food, drugs, and supplies was another problem, which was often accentuated by meager departmental budgets. These were the typical problems facing the Directors General, those of a general nature which the medical administrators learned to expect. Yet, there were other difficulties encountered in Hospital administration, the unexpected and often unsurmountable problems peculiar to the Director General's tenure in office.

When General George Washington assumed control of the Continental forces in July, 1775, he inherited the Massachusetts medical department directed by Dr. Isaac Foster. The hospitals under its jurisdiction were informal and without a permanent staff. Washington "Made an inquiry with respect to the Establishment of the Hospital and

[found] it in a very unsettled condition."[6] Therefore, he began a needed reorganization of the Hospital. His action, made mandatory by the pressures of a large-scale war, was opposed by the regimental surgeons who were no longer allowed free use of medical supplies and who were now required to prepare weekly reports. Furthermore, most of the sick were transferred from regimental to general hospitals.[7]

This clash between the Commander-in-Chief and the regimental surgeons was the original problem to greet Dr. Benjamin Church, who was appointed the first Director General on July 27, 1775.[8] Using the British Medical Department as his model, he continued Washington's reorganization. Church examined all Hospital personnel to test their competence. He also advanced the idea that the regimental surgeons should treat only minor cases in the regimental hospitals, and that all severe cases should be sent immediately to the general hospital.[9]

The regimental medical men, determined to prevent the successful completion of Church's plans, constantly hindered his work. Sometimes they kept all of their sick in the regimental hospitals and simply refused to send the worst cases to the general hospital. On other occasions they would send their entire sick list including all trivial cases to the general hospital. Regimental surgeons demanded drugs from Church but refused to account for their use.[10]

The regimental surgeons were opposed to

[5]Ibid., April 7, 1777, September 30, 1780, November 30, 1781, and January 3, 1782, VII, 231-237, XVIII, 878-886, XXI, 1093-1094, and XXII, 4-7.

[6]Samuel F. Batchelder, Bits of Harvard History, (Cambridge: Harvard University Press, 1924), 164; and To President of Congress, July 20, 1775, George Washington, The Writings of George Washington, ed. John C. Fitzpatrick (41 vols: Washington, Government Printing Office, 1931-1932), III, 350-351.
[7]General Orders, July 7, 22, 24, and September 7, 1775, Wash. Writings, III, 315-317, 354, 363, 480-481.
[8]Journ. Cont. Cong., July 27, 1775, II, 211.
[9]Benjamin Church to Samuel Adams, August 22, 23, 1775, Adams Mss., New York Public Library; and General Orders, August 22, 1775, Wash. Writings, III, 440.
[10]Ibid.; and General Orders, September 7-28, 1775, Wash. Writings, III, 480-524.

the reorganization for several reasons. This controversy was based on conflicting interests between those upholding Continental authority and those who paid allegiance to local authorities. The first campaign of the struggle, which was reminiscent of the hostility between the eighteenth century colonial militiamen and their provincially appointed field officers, was a debate on the importance of regimental hospitals. The surgeons complained that they were not being allowed medicines for their sick and wounded. They were supported by their officers, who feared the invasion of centralized authority in their locally elected units. General John Sullivan reported that his sick would rather die under the care of friends than go to the general hospital where they would be placed in the hands of strangers.[11] Church replied that the regimental hospitals cost more than they were worth, that the care provided by the surgeons was less than satisfactory, and finally, that most of the waste of drugs and supplies had been traced to these medical installations.[12]

Washington agreed with Church's argument. To stop the controversy, however, courts of inquiry were slated to be held in each regiment, where the matter would be fully discussed.[13] These investigations were promoted by surgeons who were jealous of the Director's authority over them. Church realized that some men worked against him behind the scenes while currying favor for themselves.[14] Church had planned to resign upon the conclusion of the inquiries, but before the investigations were less than half

completed, he was arrested for treason and supervision of the medical department temporarily reverted to Dr. Foster.[15]

Despite popular suspicion of the department formerly managed by a man convicted of treason, there were four candidates for the vacant position of Director General: Isaac Foster, director of the Massachusetts hospitals; Edward Hand, a Continental Lieutenant Colonel and formerly a surgeon of the British 18th Royal Irish Regiment; Jonathan Potts, a Pennsylvania militia surgeon; and Dr. John Morgan, one of the founders of the Philadelphia Medical College. After several weeks delay, Morgan was selected on October 17, 1775.[16]

Unfortunately for Morgan, he immediately became involved in the controversy with the regimental surgeons, because he too insisted that the general hospital staff was superior to the regimental staff. Morgan's claim to a superior status was rejected by the regimental surgeons.[17] Morgan's efforts to

[11]To John Langdon and Josiah Bartlett, September 4, October 4, 1775, and Officers' Petition against Benjamin Church, September, 1775, John Sullivan, *Letters and Papers of Major General John Sullivan*, 1771-1777 (Concord; New Hampshire Historical Society, 1930), 81-85, 97-99).

[12]Benjamin Church to Samuel Adams, *op. cit.*

[13]General Orders, September 7-28, 1775, *Wash. Writings*, III, 480-524.

[14]Benjamin Church to John Sullivan, September 14, 1775, *American Archives*, ed. Peter Force (Fourth series, vols. 1-6; Fifth series, vols. 1-3, Washington: Clarke and Force, 1843-1856), 4, III, 712.

[15]Horatio Gates to Benjamin Church, September 24, 1775, Church to John Fleming [July, 1775], Henry Ward to Nathaniel Greene, September 26, 1775, 4 *Amer. Arch.* III, 780, 809, 958-960; *Jour. Cont. Cong.*, October 14, 1775, II, 294-295; Thacher, *A Military Journal of the American Revolution* (Hartford: Hurlbut, Williams and Co., 1862), 31-32; and to Church, September 24, 1775, to President of Congress, September 30, 1775, and General Orders, September 30, October 3, 1775, *Wash. Writings*, III, 517, 524-526, IV, 2, 9-11. Church was found guilty of conducting cipher correspondence with the British by both the Massachusetts House of Representatives and the Continental Congress. After nearly two years of prison and parole, Church was released in late 1777 and sailed to the British West Indies on a boat that was shipwrecked. He was never heard from again.

[16]*Journ. Cont. Cong.*, October 17, 1775, III, 297; and to President of Congress, October 12, 1775; to R. H. Lee, November 8, 1775, and to Joseph Reed, November 20, 1775, *Wash. Writings*, III, 297, IV, 23, 104-105. Washington was pleased that an appointment had been made although he preferred William Shippen, Jr. for the post.

[17]Morgan to Washington, December 16, 1775, quoted in Duncan, *Medical Men*, 80; to Washington, February, 1776 and February 1, 1777, to Samuel Adams, July, 1776, to Regimental Surgeons, July 1, 3, 1776, John Morgan, *A Vindication of His Public Character in the station of director general of the Military Hospitals and physician in chief to the American Army* (Boston: 1777), *passim*; and to President of Congress, September 24, 1776, and to Morgan, January 6, 1779, *Wash. Writings*, VI, 113, VIII, 481.

assert his authority were handicapped by his original commission, which was vague and left his powers and responsibilities undefined. Congress often ignored his pleas for advice, but then would disapprove of or interfere with his subsequent actions.[18] In July, 1776, Congress intervened in the controversy, because it felt that the constant fault-finding and back-biting were causing the medical staff to neglect the patients. Moreover, the controversy gave the Hospital and the army an unsavory reputation, which was said to be partially responsible for the decline in enlistments.[19]

During an investigation, Congressman found that the regimental hospitals, which were over-crowded, poorly ventilated, dirty, and lacking proper medical necessities, had a higher rate of disease contagion and death than did the general hospitals. As a result, a series of new regulations concerning the Hospital Department was passed by Congress. The staff of general hospitals was empowered to inspect all regimental hospitals and was given authority to transfer any or all patients. Regimental surgeons were prohibited from using general hospital stores and were required to keep elaborate records.[20] These acts of Congress, designed to lessen the conflict, in actuality proved to be unsatisfactory and only widened the gulf between the two groups as the new rules were particularly obnoxious to the regimental surgeons. This hostility abated slowly after Morgan's dismissal.

Morgan's position was subject to constant infringement. He assumed that he was "Director General and Physician in Chief." However, on September 14, 1775, Samuel Stringer had been appointed director of the Northern district hospitals, giving him one month's seniority over Morgan. Then, on May 10, 1776, Janathan Potts was named chief physician of the Northern district.[21] Washington warned Congress that it was not wise to have three prominent leaders in the medical department, but more logical to have only one administrator.[22] Morgan feared that Stringer and Potts were slowly replacing him, and he wanted Congress to reaffirm his superiority. To please the complaining Director, Congress declared, on August 20, 1776, that he was "Chief Physician and Director General of the American Hospital," and that Stringer was director of the Northern district hospitals with autonomous control in that area. While Morgan assumed that he was the departmental head, several Congressmen privately told Stringer that Morgan was not his superior.[23]

Morgan, with lofty ideas of the prerogatives of his office, then became involved in a jurisdictional dispute with Dr. William Shippen, Jr., who, on July 15, 1776, had been appointed chief physician of the Continental flying hospital in New Jersey. In October, Congress announced that Morgan was responsible for the hospitals east of the Hudson River and that Shippen was responsible

---

[18]Morgan to President of Congress, May 13, 1776, quoted in James Gibson, *Doctor Bodo Otto and the Medical Background of the American Revolution* (Baltimore: Thomas, 1937), 113; and Morgan, *Vindication*, passim.

[19]*Journ. Cont. Cong.*, July 17, 1776, V, 568-571; to Washington, July 25, 1776, February 1, 1777, Morgan, *Vindication*, 64-66.

[20]*Journ. Cont. Cong.*, July 17, 1776, V, 568-569; Regulations Proposed by the Director General, July, 1776, to Washington, July 25, 1776, February 2, 1777, Morgan, *Vindication*, 3, 64-66, 83, 98; and General Orders, July 3, 25, 1776, and to President of Congress, September 24, 1776, *Wash. Writings*, V, 213, 235, VI, 113.

[21]John Hancock to Washington, June 7, 1776, Jonathan Potts to Congress, April 29, 1776, 4 *Amer. Arch.*, V, 1118, VI, 746; Hancock to Philip Schuyler, October 9, 1776, *Letters of the Members of Cont. Cong.*, I, 222; and *Journ. Cont. Cong.*, September 14, 1775, May 10, June 6, 1776, II, 249, IV, 344, V, 424.

[22]To President of Congress, April 26, 1776, *Wash. Writings*, IV, 520-521.

[23]To Samuel Adams, June 25, 1776, Morgan, *Vindication*, 50-51; *Journ. Cont. Cong.*, August 20, 1776, V, 673; Morgan to President of Congress, 5 *Amer. Arch.*, I, 919; Samuel Stringer to Jonathan Potts, August 17, 1776, quoted in Gibson, *Doctor Bodo Otto*, 108-109; and Thomas Heyward to Morgan, September 4, 1776, *Letters of Members of Cont. Cong.*, II, 69.

for those west of the river.[24] Morgan and Washington interpreted this resolution as being a distinction only between armies, for which separate hospitals were to be established. On the other hand, Shippen claimed that he had exclusive jurisdiction over all medical facilities west of the Hudson River.[25] During the American evacuation of New York City, Washington ordered Morgan to establish hospitals in the suburbs and two of these were located in New Jersey. Shippen demanded control of them, but Morgan refused. Shippen was particularly interested in Morgan's supplies, which he said were being reserved for future use although they were urgently needed at this time. However, before Shippen could obtain these materials, the advancing British seized the warehouse in which they were stored.[26]

Morgan, lacking the political acumen possessed by his opponent, whose object was to become Director, was helpless against his attacks. Shippen felt that a controversy could be employed to force Morgan out of office and he exploited the hostility between Morgan and his regimental surgeons. In the hopes of getting supplies some surgeons unwittingly cooperated with Shippen by spreading falsehoods of the Director's atrocity and negligence. Others, jealous of Morgan's power and hoping that he would be censored or dismissed, spread rumors of his supposed inefficiency and inhumanity.[27]

Simultaneously Shippen publicly charged Morgan with: taking part of his subordinate's wages, employing ignorant youths as mates, withholding hospital stores, selling candles to the hospital at great personal profit, and keeping rations for his own use. Shippen also conducted a clever and secret plan to win Morgan's position for himself. In writing to his brother-in-law, Richard Henry Lee, Shippen noted, "I have my information [regarding Morgan] from the united voice of his own officers—methinks I hear you say 'Yet this is the man you had chosen'—but good God, did you or I believe he would be so damned a rogue?" Congress finally discharged Morgan on January 9, 1777.[28]

Morgan vociferously proclaimed his innocence, but his first appeals to Washington and Congress went unheeded. After collecting various documents and volumes of testimony, he published in late 1777, his *Vindication*, a defense of his conduct as Director General. Morgan's persistence induced Congress to investigate his dismissal. After extensive study, Congress admitted on June 12, 1779, that the "general clamor and critical state of military affairs" and not specific charges against Morgan had led to his discharge. Congress further stated that he had ably and faithfully performed his duties as Director of the military hospitals.[29]

24John Hancock to William Shippen, July 15, 1776, 5 *Amer. Arch.*, I, 346; and *Jour. Cont. Cong.*, July 15, October 9, November 28, 1776, V, 526, VI, 857, 989.
25Morgan, *Vindication*, XXII, XXV; Shippen to President of Congress, November 9, 1776, Shippen to Washington, December 5, 1776, 5 *Amer. Arch.*, III, 618, 1119; and to Shippen, November 3, 1776, *Wash. Writings*, VI, 239.
26Morgan, *Vindication*, XXI, XXII, XXIII, XXV, XXXVI; Shippen to President of Congress, November 9, 1776, Shippen to Washington, December 8, 1776, 5 *Amer. Arch.*, III, 618, 1119; and to Shippen, December 12, 1776, to Morgan, January 6, 1779, *Wash. Writings*, VI, 361-362, XIII, 481-482.
27John Hancock to Philip Schuyler, December 30, 1776, 5 *Amer. Arch.*, III, 1478; to Isaac Foster, January 22, 1777, *Wash. Writings*, VII, 86, and various letters of Congressmen, *Letters of the Members of Cont.*

*Cong.*, III, 158, 188, 211-212, 271.
28*Journ. Cont. Cong.*, January 9, 1777, VII, 24; Shippen to R. H. Lee, December 20, 1776, Richard Henry Lee, *The Letters of Richard Henry Lee* (2 vols., New York: 1911-1914), II, 171; Shippen to R. H. Lee, January 17, 1777 quoted in Gibson, *Doctor Bodo Otto*, 202; and Elbridge Gerry to Morgan, November 20, 1776, Morgan, *Vindication*, XXI, XXVI. In 1780 when Morgan pressed for Shippen's trial he accused Shippen of arranging his removal. This was denied. Shippen inquired of R. H. Lee if there was anything in the records to show that he was behind Morgan's discharge. Lee replied negatively, probably "forgetting" his brother-in-law's letters of 1776 and 1777. Actually, Shippen had submitted his new hospital plan before Morgan had been dismissed. See Lee-Shippen letters in Lee, *Letters*. I, 166-167, II, 168-169, *Letters of Members of Cont. Cong.*, V, 129, and Gibson, *Doctor Bodo Otto*, 254.
29John Fell Diary, June 12, 1779, Statement of Henry

After Morgan's dismissal, William Shippen fully expected to become the new Director General. He submitted a new Hospital Bill to Congress, which, after debate and some modification was passed on April 7, 1777.[30] Congress then had to choose a Director General from three candidates: Shippen, John Cochran, and Philip Turner, all of whom were department physicians. On the first ballot the latter was elected. Before Congress adjourned, however, a minority said that the author of the new Hospital Act should have first claim upon the office. Consequently, Congress invalidated the first election and Shippen obtained the coveted office.[31]

One might assume that after the first Director General was discharged when he was found guilty of treason and the second dismissed in disgrace, the third Director General would certainly have tried to keep his administration free from adverse publicity. Unfortunately, this was not the case and Shippen's tenure of office was constantly under the cloud of suspicion and scandal.

Congress also appointed Shippen's assistants, one of whom was Dr. Benjamin Rush, physician general of the Middle district.[32] Although Rush's previous demands for departmental reform had been ignored, once in office, he gathered evidence to show that the system was defective. Intense investigation revealed to Rush that Shippen was neglecting his duties. He wished to report this matter to Congress, but other medical officers, who feared Shippen's political influence, urged him to remain silent.[33] At first Rush crusaded for an inquiry in his personal correspondence with those Congressmen who were not political friends of Shippen. He noted that an investigation should be conducted by men not related to Shippen by blood, marriage, or political affiliation. When this method failed, he publicly charged Shippen with: waste of supplies, peculation in hospital stores, negligence, unnecessary support of supernumerary officers, and ignorance of true conditions in the hospitals, which Rush claimed were over-crowded, dirty, unguarded, and understaffed. He concluded: "The fault is both in the establishment and in the Director General. He is both *ignorant* and *negligent* of his duty. There is but *one* right system for a military hospital, and that is the one made use of by the British army."[34]

Rush's demands for a public hearing were presented to General Washington and Congress. He failed to convince the Commander-in-Chief of the urgency for an inquiry, but finally persuaded Congress to hold a hearing.[35] Rush and Shippen were ordered to tes-

Laurens, June 3, 1779, *Letters of Members of Cont. Cong.*, IV, 247, 259; *Journ. Cont. Cong.*, August 9, 1777, June 12, 1779, VIII, 627, XIV, 724; Morgan to President of Congress, June 15, 1779 quoted in Louis M. Duncan, *Medical Men in the Revolution 1775-1783*, (Carlisle, Penna.: Medical Field School 1931-1938), 291-292; Morgan, *Vindication*, XIV; and Nathaniel Greene to Morgan, January 10, 1779, *Pennsylvania Magazine of History and Biography* XLII (1919) 77-80. One document reprinted in the *Vindication* is signed by prominent doctors who remained in the service and attested to Morgan's competence and efficiency. That they supported a discharged officer against his known successor is worth noting.

30*Journ. Cont. Cong.*, April 7, 1777, VII, 231; R. H. Lee to Shippen, January 1, 1777, and Shippen to R. H. Lee, December 12, 1776, Lee, *Letters*, I, 166-167, II, 168-169; Shippen to R. H. Lee, January 17, 1777, and Shippen to Washington, January 25, 1777, quoted in Gibson, *Doctor Bodo Otto*, 202; and to Shippen, January 27, 1777, *Wash. Writings*, VII, 71-72.

31Harvey E. Brown, *The Medical Department of the United States Army, 1775-1783* (Washington: Surgeon General's Office, 1873), 39; *Journ. Cont. Cong.*, April 11, 1777, VII, 253-254; and to R. H. Lee, Benjamin Rush, *Letters of Benjamin Rush* (2 vols., Princeton: Princeton University Press, 1951), I, 129. Cochran was elected physician and surgeon general of the Middle district and Turner surgeon general of the Eastern district.

32*Journ. Cont. Cong.*, April 11, June 23, July 1, 1777, VII, 253-254, VIII, 490, 518; and Benjamin Rush, *Autobiography* (Princeton: Princeton University Press, 1948), 131.

33Rush, *Autobiography*, 131-133.

34To Washington, December 26, 1777, Rush, *Autobiography*, 134-136; to William Duer, December 8, 13, 1777, and to John Adams, October 1, 31, 1777, Rush, *Letters*, I, 156, 161, 165, 173, 176.

35Bernhard Knollenberg, *Washington and the Revolution* (New York: Macmillan, 1940), 65-77; Rush to Washington, December 26, 1777, Rush, *Autobiography*, 134-136; Rush, *Letters*, II, 1197-1208; to Rush, Janu-

tify before a special Congressional committee, but Shippen, who was reluctant to attend, tried to evade the proceedings by publicly stating that he did not want to neglect his medical duties. However, he finally appeared on January 28, 1778.[36]

It soon became obvious to most informed men in official circles that Rush's charges would be quickly dismissed. For one thing, the committee chairman, John Witherspoon, was one of Shippen's political associates. Shippen, conscious that Congress was terrified of anything which would reveal the desperate state of the army to the public, privately told Witherspoon that he would demand an open hearing unless Rush was discharged. Soon afterwards, the committee, ignoring the validity of Rush's criticism, declared that the departmental troubles were caused by a personal feud between two rivals. Richard Peters, Secretary of the Board of War, expressed the view of many when he wrote, "I fancy both were wrong at least in some degree." Rush resigned after being denied a medical position on a proposed expedition to Canada.[37]

Although Rush gained one objective, stripping the purveying powers from the Director General, temporary failure to have Shippen removed from office gave him greater determination to continue the prosecution. After extensive investigation during the remainder

of 1778, he accused Shippen of diluting hospital wines, using hospital provisions and liquors, and falsifying vouchers and reports. However, Congress refused to hold another inquiry. This setback discouraged Rush from any further serious attempts to have Shippen discharged.[38]

As Rush's enthusiasm abated, John Morgan became increasingly interested in his successor's conduct, and by June, 1779, he had replaced Rush as Shippen's chief accuser. As a matter of fact, on the day of his own vindication, Morgan charged Shippen with malpractice and misconduct in office and demanded a court-martial. After some delay, Congress ordered General Washington to begin the proceedings, but the Commander-in-Chief replied that the movements of the enemy made it impossible to try the Director General at that time. Upon hearing of this delay, Shippen publicly stated his desire for an immediate court-martial which would acquit him and disgrace his accuser.[39]

Morgan, convinced that the only way he could bring Shippen to trial was to show without a doubt the Director General's malpractice and misconduct, began to collect evidence. He soon found many were unwilling to testify. Some medical officers did not

ary 12, 1778, and to Patrick Henry, March 28, 1778, *Wash. Writings*, X, 297, XI, 169. Washington was not partial to Rush because of the latter's duplicity in the Conway Cabal and his unsigned letter sent to Henry in which Rush criticized the Commander.

[36] *Journ. Cont. Cong.*, January 6, 1778, X, 23; and Shippen to President of Congress, January 18, 1778, quoted in Gibson, *Doctor Bodo Otto*, 213.

[37] *Journ. Cont. Cong.*, January 27, 1778, X, 93; James Lovell to John Langdon, February 8, 1778, John Witherspoon to Rush, February 2, 1778, John Witherspoon to William C. Houston, January 27, 1778, and Richard Peters to Robert Morris, February 3, 1778, *Letters of Members of Cont. Cong.*, III, 59, 66-67, 67n, 77; to John Adams, January 22, February 8, 1778, to Morgan, June 1779, to Nathanial Greene, February 2, 1778, and to Shippen, February 2, 1778, Rush, *Letters*, I, 191, 195-197, 200, 228; and to Committee of Congress, January 29, 1778, *Wash. Writings*, X, 394-395.

[38] *Journ. Cont. Cong.*, February 6, April 3, June 4, 1778, X, 128-131, 303, XI, 569; James Lovell to John Langdon, February 8, 1778, and William H. Drayton, et. al., to Rush, April 7, 1778, *Letters of Members of Cont. Cong.*, III, 77, 157; to Shippen, November 18, 1780, to Washington, December 25, 1778, Petition of Bethlehem Medical Men dated February 19, 1778, and to Daniel Roberdeau, March 9, 1778, Rush, *Letters*, I, 201-205, 256-260; Shippen to Congress, January 11, 1778 and Shippen's depositions quoted in Gibson, *Doctor Bodo Otto*, 213, 227; and to President of Congress, March 21, 1778, *Wash. Writings*, XI, 125. Rush and Shippen ignored each other until late 1780 when they exchanged bitter letters in the *Pennsylvania Packet* (September 2, 1780 to January 1, 1781).

[39] *Journ. Cont. Cong.*, June 15, 1779, XIV, 733-734; Morgan to President of Congress, July 19, 1779, Shippen to President of Congress, July 28, 1779, quoted in Gibson, *Doctor Bodo Otto*, 243-244; Morgan to President of Congress, July 15, 1779 Quoted in Duncan, *Medical Men*, 291-292; to Morgan, June 1779, Rush, *Letters*, I, 228; and to Morgan, June 24, 1779, *Wash. Writings*, XV, 309-310. Rush warned Morgan of Shippen's political influence and wished him good luck.

want to undermine Congressional confidence in the department which could possibly jeopardize future appropriations, while other surgeons simply wanted to hide their own corrupt activities. Some very likely feared Shippen's political power.[40] After Morgan's constant complaining, Congress recommended thrat the states grant writs requiring persons whose testimony was needed to appear before the court-martial. All legal depositions had to be jointly witnessed by both the accused and the accuser.[41] Shippen, claiming his presence was needed in the hospitals, refused to cooperate. Incensed by Shippen's apparent defiance of their authority, Congress declared that if the accused failed to appear at a previously announced taking of depositions, the testimony would be legally valid.[42] Afterwards Morgan obtained the depositions alone, but when he introduced them into the record of the court-martial, Shippen loudly protested. To resolve this controversy, Congress decided that both parties in question and a member of the Judge Advocate's staff should gather all official testimony.[43]

The court-martial was delayed until after the final military campaign of 1779 and after preceding trials had been completed. The prosecution passed its case upon Morgan's charges, which were presented to the Judge Advocate in early 1780. Shippen was accused of: selling hospital stores fraudulently and transporting them at public expense, speculating in hospital supplies at a great personal profit, diluting hospital wines, falsifying hospital records and account books, refusing to pay honest debts, neglecting hospital duties, evading his trial, and behaving in a manner unbecoming a gentleman and an officer.[44] After several months of proceedings, Shippen was finally acquitted on July 15, 1780, of all charges except that of peculation, and his case was referred to Congress. After much debate, Congress resolved on August 18, "That the court martial having acquitted the said Doctor W. Shippen, ordered that he be discharged from arrest." However, a number of delegates felt that he was guilty of peculation.[45]

After this long period of scandal and adverse publicity, Congress reorganized the medical department. On October 6, 1780, Shippen was reappointed to the post of Director General, but by a close seven to six vote. However, by January, 1781, Shippen realized that he had lost the confidence and support of Congress and resigned.[46]

Despite the fact that the medical department had an unsavory reputation and that Congress had simply lost faith in the ability and honesty of many of the military medical men, there were several candidates for the directorship. The nominees were: John Cochran, William Brown, James Craik, and John Morgan. Congress had vindicated Morgan and even reluctantly allowed him to prosecute Shippen, but refused to grant him another term as Director General. The position was awarded to Cochran, who had more adminis-

[40]Morgan to President of Congress, July 19, 1779, quoted in Gibson, *Doctor Bodo Otto*, 244.

[41]*Journ. Cont. Cong.*, November 16, 1779, XII, 1278; and Morgan to President of Congress, October 22, 1779, quoted in Gibson, *Doctor Bodo Otto*, 245-246.

[42]*Journ. Cont. Cong.*, December 24, 1779, XV, 1409; and Shippen to R. H. Lee, April 16, 1780, quoted in Gibson, *Doctor Bodo Otto*, 253-254.

[43]Shippen to R. H. Lee, April 16, 1780, Morgan to President of Congress, March 28, 1780, quoted in Gibson, *Doctor Bodo Otto*, 252-254. Shippen sent an aide to visit those who originally testified for Morgan and he reported that 90% did not mean to injure Shippen's character, but were pressured by Morgan to testify.

[44]*Journ. Cont. Cong.*, January 1, 1780, XVI, 1-2; Morgan to President of Congress, November 22, 1779, quoted in Gibson, *Doctor Bodo Otto*, 246-249; and General Orders, December 17, 1779, *Wash. Writings*, XVII, 282.

[45]*Journ. Cont. Cong.*, July 18, August 16, 18, 1780, XVII, 646, 738, 745-746; to President of Congress, July 29, December 4, 1779, to John Laurence, December 2, 1779, General Orders, March 13, 1780, and to Colonel William Davies, April 20, 1780, *Wash. Writings*, XVI, 5-6, XVII, 214, 216, XVIII, 109-110, 289; and Shippen to President of Congress, August 18, 1780, quoted in Duncan, *Medical Men*, 297-298.

[46]*Journ. Cont. Cong.*, October 6, 1780, January 3, 1781, XVIII, 908, XIX, 15; and to Shippen, November 18, 1780, Rush, *Letters*, I, 256, 260.

trative experience than either Craik or Brown.[47] Cochran was one of the most popular officers in the service and had never become involved in departmental feuds. Moreover, he had not waged an active campaign to obtain the position. He wrote, "My appointment was unsolicited and a rank to which I never aspired, being perfectly happy where I was."[48]

Cochran had three important problems facing him. He had to put an end to departmental controversies, which were typical of the preceding administrations. Cochran wanted his assistants to be happy in their work and to cooperate with him in order that the hospitals could be managed efficiently.[49] There was a complete lack of medicines and supplies, most likely the result of Congressional indifference. Finally, there were numerous staff resignations caused by the nonpayment of wages, lack of tenure, and Congressional apathy.[50]

Cochran's administration was more efficient and better managed than those of his predecessors. He was fortunate to have a trustworthy assistant in James Craik, who was a sincere friend rather than a promotion seeker. Cochran reduced the number of staff resignations by persuading Congress to pay back wages and to institute plans for seniority and tenure. Congress, impressed with Cochran's administrative ability, moderately increased the medical budget, and the department was able to procure most of its necessi-

ties. During the last three years of the war, there were no controversies in the department. In 1783, after the signing of the peace treaty, Cochran retired from the medical department.[51]

Of the four men chosen by Congress to direct the medical department, three were poor choices. The first man, Benjamin Church, was a noted civilian doctor who had earned his way into the patriot councils of Boston. His delicate health, hopes for high political office, lack of administrative ability, controversy with the regimental surgeons, and constant highhandedness and lack of tact were handicaps preventing Church from managing his department competently and efficiently. There is no evidence to show that Church tried to destroy or weaken the hospital, even though there is sufficient testimony to conclusively prove his guilt as a traitor. Yet, his treason cast upon the medical staff an unwarranted suspicion by soldiers and officers, and Congressmen and their constituents.

The next director, John Morgan, was given his post by Congress, who rejected Washington's recommendation of William Shippen, a Philadelphia rival of Morgan. This deep seated conflict of personalities combined with Morgan's insistence on absolute authority were the basis for the Director General's later disgrace. Morgan was personally interested in the welfare of the sick and wounded, but his ultimate downfall was caused by Shippen's maneuverings and by circumstances beyond his control which caused sickness and death to increase rapidly; for example summer heat, newness of troops, lack of medicines and supplies, Congressional interferences, and constant army movements.

After Morgan's dismissal, Shippen's political friends secured the directorship for their candidate. This man of recognized talent

[47]*Journ. Cont. Cong.*, January 11, 14, 1781, XIX, 47-48, 56, 65.

[48]To James Craik, March 26, 1781, to Peter Turner, March 25, 1781, and to George Campbell, March 16, 1781, John Cochran, "Letters of John Cochran," *Pennsylvania Magazine of History and Biography* III (1879), 245-247.

[49]*Ibid.*, and to Thomas Morris, February 28, 1781, to George Stevenson, March 28, 1781, and to Barnabas Binney, March 25, 1781, Cochran, *op. cit.*, 245-246.

[50]To Jonathan Potts, March 18, 1781, to Thomas Bond, March 25, July 26, 1781, to Abraham Clark, February 28, 1781, to Samuel Huntington, May 24, 1781, to Thomas Morris, February 28, 1781, and to Malachi Treat, March 25, 1781, Cochran, *op. cit.*, 247-253.

[51]To James Craik, March 26, 1781, Cochran, *op. cit.*, 247.

had a perfect opportunity to prove his ability, but his shabby dealings before assuming office and his skullduggery in forcing Morgan out of the post were an indication of things to come. Simply stated, Shippen was a better politician than a medical administrator. His interests were personal profit and glory, rather than care of the sick and wounded. Only the faithful work of some of his subordinates kept the department from being completely corrupt.

Upon Shippen's resignation in 1780, the natural selection for the Director General's office was a devoted physician who had served the patriot cause since 1775 without due recognition. This man, John Cochran, was not a politician, but a practical administrator, whose success can be explained by several factors. The soldiers knew of his interest in their welfare and his fellow surgeons felt that he was working honestly to save lives and help to create a new nation. In the long run, Cochran's success can be attributed to his years of experience in military hospitals, and his ability to profit from the mistakes of others. He was the best Revolutionary War Director General of the American Hospital.

# THE BRITISH EXPEDITION TO CONCORD, MASSACHUSETTS, IN 1775

By Allen French

English historians commonly do not give much space to a study of the military expedition which, on the 19th of April, 1775, marched from Boston to Concord. While to an American it is of perennial importance as the beginning of the Revolutionary War, to an Englishman it is but one of many expeditions, almost indistinguishable in the tremendous sweep of his military history. As this story has, however, lately been illuminated by the discovery of several British manuscrips, I am, though an American, making an attempt to analyse it from the British point of view, endeavouring to give to army men details which until now have been obscure. But an article of this length must ignore everything but the essentials of the narrative. I will assume on the part of my readers a general knowledge of the previous conditions—the military methods of that day, and the strained situation in Massachusetts. The British Governor was General Thomas Gage, with headquarters in Boston. There was much political discontent in the colony, and considerable ill-feeling between the troops and the militia. Anticipating war, the Provincial Congress had assembled munitions, and had stored much of them in Concord. Informed that the Provincial Congress was about to assemble an "army of observation" under arms, Gage determined to send and destroy the stores.

The experiment was hazardous. Gage's army was small, not more than 4,000 privates, and he could not afford to lose the 700 that he planned to send out. Though early in 1774 Gage had been confident of subduing the Americans with but a few regiments, in November he had asked for 20,000 men, who, by the way, were denied him. He had had accurate information of the plans of the colonists, and had even been informed (by a letter which he sent to the Colonial Office) of the exact method which the provincial militia

would use in attacking his troops. It was the fashion of the day to call the Americans cowards; but Gage, who had seen the courage of the Virginians at Braddock's defeat, should not have believed that New Englanders would flinch. He knew enough, therefore, to have made every effort to secure success by means of a swift expedition which should succeed in its purpose and return without shedding blood. Perhaps he believed that the numbers which he sent would be enough to awe the provincials into quiet. But speed and secrecy were essential. The first he failed of because the commander whom he chose, Lieutenant-Colonel Francis Smith of the 10th Regiment, was sluggish and resentful of advice. Of secrecy Gage was robbed by the quickness of the Yankees.

Yet he tried to prevent news of his plans reaching Concord. On the afternoon of the 18th he sent out perhaps a dozen mounted officers to post themselves, early in the night, between Lexington and Concord, and stop the main road. These were under the command of Major Edward Mitchell of the 5th; and some of the members of the group were Captain the Hon. Charles Cochrane of the 4th, Captain Charles Lumm of the 38th, and Lieutenants Peregrine Francis Thorne of the 4th and Thomas Baker of the 5th. Travel between Lexington and Concord was very light after midnight, and for a time all the patrol stopped and held were a few harmless travellers, who could bring to Concord only the news that these officers were out.

The detachment under Smith was made up of the light infantry and grenadiers of the 4th, 5th, 10th, 23rd, 38th, 43rd, 47th, 52nd and 59th Regiments and of the Marine battalion, with the grenadiers of the 18th Regiment, whose light company was not in Boston. In other words these were the flank companies of all Gage's regiments, detached for this purpose. Frequent short practice marches

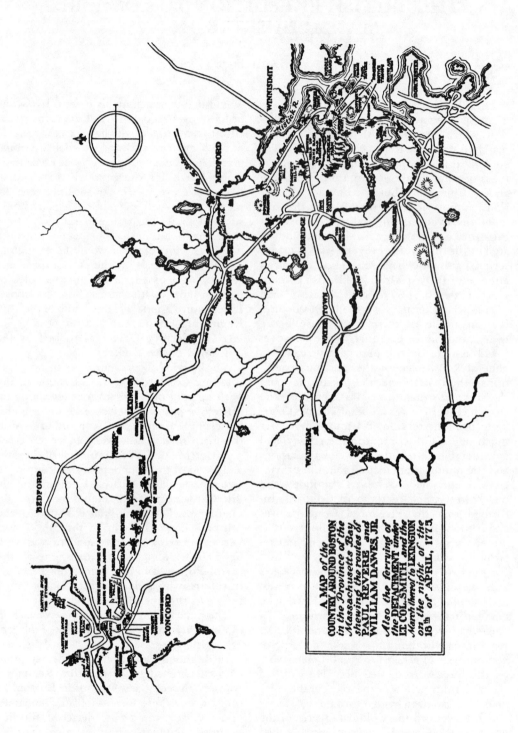

had put the whole little army in fair training for a push of this sort. As the distance was but seventeen and a half miles, a prompt start and a quick march should have brought the expedition to Concord by dawn.

Time was lost, however, at the very beginning. The detachment assembled at the waterfront, Smith arrived when the boats were all filled, and the first trip was made across the tidal Charles. A second trip had to be made before all the men were landed, probably about midnight, and then a wait of an hour followed, probably for rations. The march did not really begin, it would appear, until one o'clock, though some of the members of the expedition put the time as late as two.

Meanwhile the Boston Whigs had noted the departure, and sent out, by different routes, two messengers to alarm the country. One was Paul Revere, who, dodging two mounted officers who tried to stop him, brought his news safely to Lexington, where he warned Samuel Adams and John Hancock to put themselves in safety. The other was William Dawes, who reached Lexington soon after Revere. In company with a young Concord doctor, they started for Concord, only to be intercepted by Major Mitchell's patrol. Revere was taken, but Dawes turned back, and the young doctor, knowing the country, escaped through fields and brought his news to Concord. The captured Revere warned Mitchell that the expedition was delayed and that five hundred provincials would soon be in Lexington, an excellent piece of bluff that convinced Mitchell that he had best warn the approaching column.

Already Smith, at last under way with his detachment, had made his own discovery that the country was alarmed, for he heard the quiet of the night broken by church bells and signal guns. Disturbed by this, he sent a messenger to Gage asking for support, and also sent in advance his second-in-command, Major John Pitcairn of the Marines, with six light companies, to seize and hold the bridges at Concord. As Pitcairn's companies hurried on they were preceded by certain enterprising officers (Lieutenants William Sutherland of the 38th Regiment, Jesse Adair of the Marines, and William Grant of the Artillery) who, though on foot, captured, one by one, mounted scouts sent by the militia at Lexington. Daylight was approaching when the column was met by Major Mitchell and his patrol, with their warning. On this news the advance party halted, and Pitcairn, coming up from its rear, and hearing from Sutherland the additional report that a countryman had snapped his piece at him, ordered his men to load and move forward, "but on no account to fire, or even attempt it without orders."

Thus appears before us one of the most reprobated Englishmen in American Revolutionary history, long believed to have given the order to fire at Lexington. But Pitcairn was well liked by even his opponents among the Americans, and everything in his private life, as we now know it, goes to show that strongly as he blamed the "foolish bad" Provincial Congress, as he called them, he would keep within his orders. And Smith had given him the order not to fire unless attacked, which he, in his own way, passed on to his men. Of late years American historians have tried to do justice to Pitcairn, and fortunately his own report to Gage has at last appeared, by which to judge of what happened at Lexington.

On Lexington Green were assembling, just at sunrise, a part of the militia of the town. Alarmed much earlier by Revere, they had concluded, because their scouts did not return, that there was nothing to report, and had scattered to their homes or, for those who lived at a distance, to nearby taverns. But at last one scout, seeing and avoiding the British advance-guard, galloped into town with the warning, and such of the militia as were within sound of the drum hastily assembled, some seventy at most. The first of the British saw them standing on the green, apparently intending to let the regulars pass by at a distance of some sixty yards, if only they came and went in peace. Had Smith started earlier his men might not have seen the provincials in the dark; but as it was, the leading companies, perhaps taking their presence as a challenge, at once turned on to the green, the first of them, the 10th, spreading out to full company front. The rest followed, and Pitcairn, perceiving, galloped up to command them, followed by Mitchell's mounted officers.

shot was from gun or pistol, by British or American, by accident or design, is still in doubt, each side having always imputed it to the other. Its bullet seems to have gone wild. But the sound of it was enough. Without

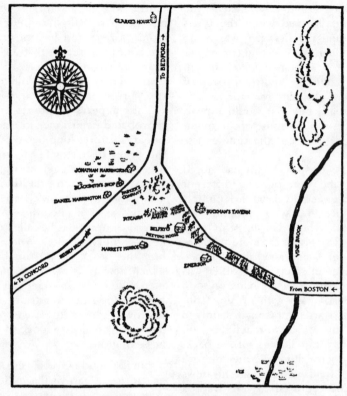

**LEXINGTON GREEN AT SUNRISE, APRIL 19th, 1775.**
**Showing the more important buildings and the approximate positions of the troops and minute-men.**

Recognizing their overwhelming force, the militia captain ordered his men to disperse. Some of them obeyed, but at least half of them doggedly remained. Pitcairn ordered them to lay down their arms; and when they did not obey, while some continued to depart, the leading company hurried to intercept them. On this Pitcairn shouted to his men not to fire, but to surround the provincials and disarm them.

Then someone fired a shot, a fateful action with momentous consequences. Whether the

orders the leading company, at closest range, at once fired a volley. I have ventured the suggestion, in one of my books, that as at Dettingen "the whole three ranks made a running fire of their own accord." On the accumulated evidence it seems a fair explanation, and a natural outcome of the strong feelings between troops and provincials. A feeble return fire was made, with no execution. Pitcairn's horse was grazed, and a private wounded in the hand. But the British killed eight of the provincials and wounded ten, in this first bloodshed of the Revolution. With difficulty Pitcairn, angrily gesticulating, controlled his men. Smith came upon the ground with his grenadiers, and after a short delay the whole marched on to Concord, uninterrupted in those next five miles.

But from the moment of the British departure from Lexington, American revenge was certain. The alarm already sent out, merely precautionary, now was seconded by another. Americans had been killed at Lexington: let every man now turn out. Long before noon hundreds of the militia, singly or in companies, were on the march. All winter their leaders had drilled into them the precept, they must not fire first. Now they were released.

As the British approached Concord, on a road that crossed a wide meadow, they saw in front of them a ridge which sloped down to this plain, and on its top another armed force, watching them. This consisted of the minuteman companies of Concord and Lincoln, who, on seeing that the British were too strong for them, turned and marched away, with music playing. The light infantry climbed up the ridge and followed them; the grenadiers kept to the road below*; and the provincials, gathering in their militia companies as they went, abandoned the centre of the town and took up a position north of it, near a bridge across which they could make a final retreat. As they were for the moment out of reach, Smith halted his troops in the town, and proceeded to execute his orders, which were to search for and destroy the military stores. Informed of their hiding-places, he set men to searching in the town, sent a detachment to hold the south bridge, and ordered six companies of light infantry to the north bridge,** three to hold it and three (later reinforced by a fourth) to march two miles beyond it, to hunt for stores at the farm of Colonel James Barrett. They were under the command of Captain Lawrence Parsons, of the 10th Regiment.

*See Sketch Map on p. 98.
**See maps on pages 94 and 103.

As this detachment marched out of the town they were seen by the provincials, who at once crossed the bridge, perhaps two hundred yards in front off the regulars. They marched up another hill beyond it, and out of sight. Captain Parsons, coming to the bridge, therefore had before him the following problem. The provincials, reinforced, might interfere with his return from the farm to which he must march, two miles beyond the bridge. He must protect both the bridge and his line of march. Consequently he left at the bridge the 5th and 43rd light companies, and posted on the hill beyond it the 4th and 10th, the first commanding his road toward the west, and the second in position to watch the provincials, who had retired to the north. With the 38th and 52nd light companies he marched to Barrett's farm. A little later Smith sent him the light company of the 23rd, and Parsons sent for the 5th to join him.

Thus he had four companies at the farm. They searched the place, and burnt what munitions they found, which were not many, for some they missed and the rest had been removed. They finished this work and marched back toward the town, not suspecting until they reached the bridge that anything had happened.

Meanwhile, at the bridge, Captain Walter Sloane Laurie, of the 43rd, was in command of his own company, and those of the 4th and 10th. His lieutenants were Edward Hull and Alexander Robertson. Of the company of the 4th, the captain is not named as present; the lieutenants were Edward Thoroton Gould, and John Barker, the diarist. The captain of the 10th Company was Parsons, who had marched on to the farm, leaving behind him Lieutenant Waldron Kelly in command. Lieutenant Hamilton, feigning illness, had not come, and was later cashiered for it; but as volunteer in his place was Ensign Jeremy Lister, whose narrative, lately discovered, tells us much. All three of these companies were on the farther side of the stream, for even the company of the 43rd had crossed the bridge. The other two were each perhaps a couple of hundred yards away.

With the expedition was Lieutenant Wil-

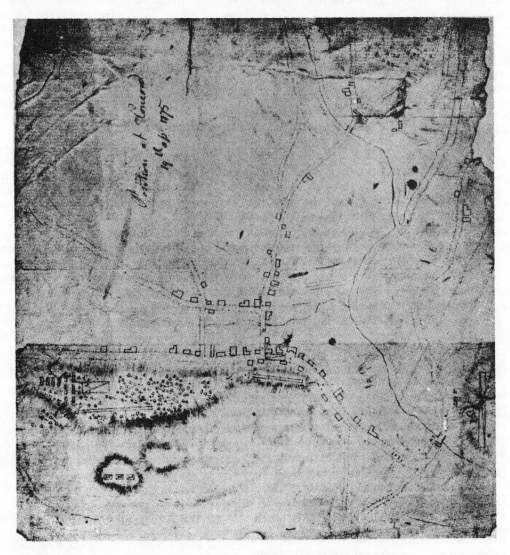

**CONTEMPORARY MAP OF THE POSITION AT CONCORD.**

(Drawn by Frederick Mackenzie, Lieutenant 23rd Regiment.)

liam Sutherland, already mentioned. Coming as a volunteer, attached to no company, he had made himself useful on the march to Lexington, and marching from Concord with Parsons' detachment he stayed with the 10th Company on the hill until to his disgust he learned that Parsons had gone on to the farm. Begging of Lieutenant Kelly two men to go with him, he was following after Parsons when one of the men said to him, "Sir, the company of the 4th are retiring." Looking for the reason, Sutherland saw "a large body" of provincials marching almost within pistol shot; and thinking that it "would be disgracefull to be taken by such Rascals" he hurried to the bridge. Meanwhile the companies of the 4th and 10th, seeing the approach of the provincials, marched down and put themselves under the command of Captain Laurie. Yet strangely, they still remained on the American side of the water, and for "a long time very near an hour" remained so, watching the provincials gathering and forming beyond a wall at the top of the low hill.

Captain Laurie did, it is true, send Lieutenant Robertson, probably on foot, to ask support from Smith. Reply was returned by Captain Lumm, mounted, that a reinforcement would come. Laurie sent him galloping back to hurry it. Smith, however, put himself at the head of a detachment of grenadiers, and (wrote Lieutenant Barker) "being a very fat heavy man he wou'd not have reached the Bridge in half an hour." And by that time it was too late.

For the Americans on the hilltop, growing restless as companies joined them from other towns, and as they saw smoke rising from the village, resolved "to march into the middle of the town for its defence, or die in the attempt." Possibly as many as four hundred and fifty in number, they went in double file against the hundred regulars at the bridge. Because of uncertainty whether men had been killed at Lexington, they were given the order not to fire first. By a byway they marched downhill to the main road. Then turning, they marched straight at the bridge. On seeing them in motion, Laurie did what he should have done long before, and with-

drew his three companies across the bridge. Once there, in great haste and with too little time, he attempted to form his men for a manoeuvre in which, it presently appeared, they had not been drilled. In addition, he complicated this one with another.

For years before this, and for years after, there used to be in British and American books of tactics a manoeuvre called Street-Firing, by which a column of men in platoons or squads could, though armed only with muskets, maintain a nearly continuous fire along a narrow way. The first unit having fired, it would divide right and left, march down the sides of the column to the rear, and forming again, load and wait its turn to fire once more. The successive units could fire from their own ground, or could advance to the position of the first or even beyond it for firing, thus making the column retreat, or hold the same position, or advance. Laurie, by his own account, planned to give ground as his "divisions" fired one by one. That at least one of the officers did not understand what he was about is evident from the comment of Lieutenant Barker in his Journal, though Lister named the scheme correctly.

Between the low stone walls that flanked the road, Laurie formed the companies of the 4th and 10th in column for Street Firing, the 4th nearest the bridge. But at the same time he tried to make the company of the 43rd line the bank to the right and left of the bridge, to fire upon the approaching provincials. This order does not seem to have been understood by even his own company, for only a few men crossed the left-hand wall, under the lead of Lieutenant Sutherland.

This enterprising officer had been consulting with Laurie since rejoining him; he had advised sending for support, and agreed that it was wise to retreat across the bridge. He was the last to cross, and on Lister's advice had tried to take up the planks—the proper means to destroy Parsons' detachment, had he succeeded. But the Americans approached so fast that after a few planks had been taken up the attempt was given over. Sutherland then crossed the wall, calling to the men of the 43rd to follow. There he was in position to fire on the flank of the American column. It was his opinion that the Americans fired first; but Laurie and Gould thought otherwise, and so did Smith, reporting. Americans claimed that the British fired warning shots and then a volley. Sutherland, in the field, fired his fusil.

The Americans had approached the bridge with Major John Buttrick, of the Concord minute-men, in the lead, the Action Company immediately behind, and the Concord companies following. Men were wounded by the first few shots, and then at sixty yards the volley killed the Acton captain and one of his men. "Their balls whisled well." Buttrick then gave the order to fire, and the provincials, some of them breaking from the column in order to see, responded. "A general popping," said Laurie. But Lister spoke with more respect of it. "The weight of their fire was such that we was oblidg'd to give way then run with the greatest precipitance." There is no doubt that the regulars broke. With a chance to give a good account of themselves, why should they not have stood 'for at least a few more volleys?

First, as there had been no fighting for more than fifteen years, all of the younger men there were green soldiers. Second, the whole were a haphazard group of companies from different regiments, unaccustomed to act together, and, except for the 43rd, unused to Laurie. Again, it is plain that Laurie's manoeuvre was not understood by all, so that the confusion at the head of the column, and the perplexity at its rear, were extreme. The retreat of the first squad, after firing, down the two sides of the column, perhaps in haste in order to reach the rear and load, may to many have seemed like flight. And next the American volley did fair execution. A private was killed and three wounded, two mortally. A sergeant was wounded, and beside him four lieutenants, Sutherland, Gould, Hull and Kelly, the last three of whom were in command of companies. Sutherland afterward wrote: "I called to Capt. Laurie I was wounded & made the best of my way leaving 2 of the men that turned out with me dead on the Spot & I myself retiring under a fire from the Enemy." With leaders thus disabled and quitting the field, with the head of the column

seeing the Americans still coming on, and the rear apparently seeing their own men in flight, here are reasons enough why the regulars broke, and why Concord Fight was over almost before it had well begun.

The Americans were quite as green soldiers as the British. Too many of them stopped to look after their few wounded. The rest did not pursue the regulars far, but seeing the column of grenadiers approaching, formed behind a wall on a hillside, and waited to see what would be done by Smith. Seemingly abandoning Parsons to his fate, he marched back to the village, and there stayed until noon, perhaps two hours. Parsons joined him unmolested, though his men were dismayed to see one of the wounded men, of the 4th Regiment, lying near the bridge with his head hacked. This was the deed of a young American, not a member of the militia, who coming alone to the empty battleground, struck the mortally wounded man. Parsons' men reported what they saw: "the Skin over His Eyes cut and also the Top part of His Ears cut off." This was not scalping; but word spread among the troops that he, and also others, had been scalped.

During the long wait of full two hours, Americans and British merely watched each other, though to Smith time was invaluable. The provincials were strengthened by more reinforcements, but never thought of blocking the road of Smith's retreat, by which means they could have captured his whole force.

As it was, he escaped narrowly enough. His little column, with the wounded in chaises, had gone but a mile before they were attacked in the rear. From that time on, rear and flanks were shot at by the provincials, fighting individually. Diarists and letter-writers among the troops complained that the Americans would not come into the open to be killed, and Smith stated that "they did not make one gallant attempt." But at the end of the day Lord Percy reported, "They knew too well what was proper, to do so." Using every cover, and often behind impenetrable stone walls, they came as close as they dared. Some did actually come too close, some were caught in houses, and others were surprised by Brit-

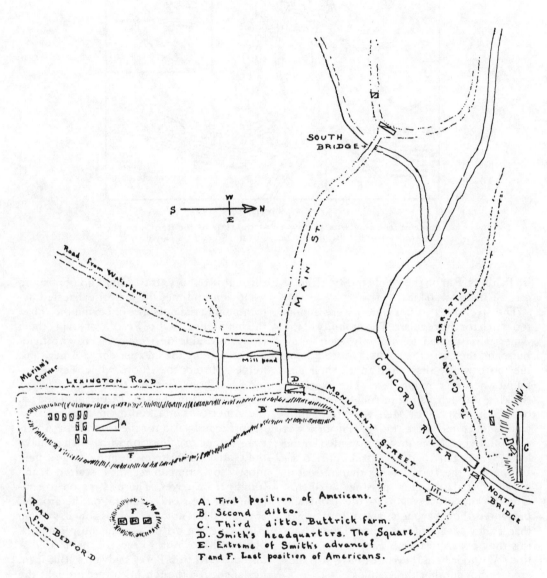

A. First position of Americans.
B. Second ditto.
C. Third ditto. Buttrick farm.
D. Smith's headquarters. The Square.
E. Extreme of Smith's advance?
F and F. Last position of Americans.

**SKETCH INTERPRETING MACKENZIE'S MAP.**

(Drawn by Allen French.)

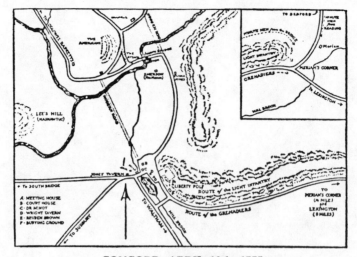

**CONCORD, APRIL 19th, 1775.**
Showing the roads as they were at the time of the fight, and the
more important buildings. (Inset: Meriam's Corner.)

ish flankers. But on the whole they took good care of their own skins.

The five miles to Lexington were almost too much for the regulars. The mobility of the Americans seemed to multiply their numbers, and the more the soldiers missed them, the more wildly they fired, until their ammunition was running low. The work of flanking was exhausting in rough country or over ploughed fields. Men were frequently wounded, some were killed, Pitcairn was dismounted, and Smith was wounded in the leg. "We began to run," wrote Ensign de Berniere of the 10th, "rather than retreat in order." At last, after passing Lexington Green, "the officers got to the front and presented their bayonets, and told the men that if they advanced they should die: Upon this they began to form under a very heavy fire." Without help they must have surrendered within another three miles.

Fortunately, though almost too late, support had been sent out. Gage had ordered out his first brigade (the battalion companies of the 4th, 23rd, 47th, and Marines, some eight hundred men) under command of Lord Percy, Colonel of the 5th, and Brigadier. Again the story of the start is one of long and unnecessary delays. But marching out at last

through Roxbury, they found no opposition whatever, and met the almost exhausted detachment in the outskirts of Lexington. "I had the happiness," wrote Percy, "of saving them from inevitable destruction." His two field-pieces, aweing the inexperienced Americans, helped protect the troops while they rested for a half-hour. For that time the provincials were quiet. But when the British marched on, the Americans attacked them again.

Fortunately also for the troops, the Americans had no organization with which to make their attack effective. Coming to the field mostly by companies, they scattered and fought from cover. There is reason to suppose that their only General on the ground, appointed but not yet commissioned, with no Aide to carry his orders and no regimental officers in position to receive them, tried at one place to stop Percy's advance. But if so, he failed; for though his effort brought the column to a halt, Percy's cannon, brought up from the rear, scattered the assailants. Except for this, the chief attack of the Americans was in flank or rear. The weary detachment, marching at the head of Percy's column, thus were mostly free of fighting. Yet the attack was ceaseless. Percy wrote of the "incessant fire, which like a moving circle surrounded

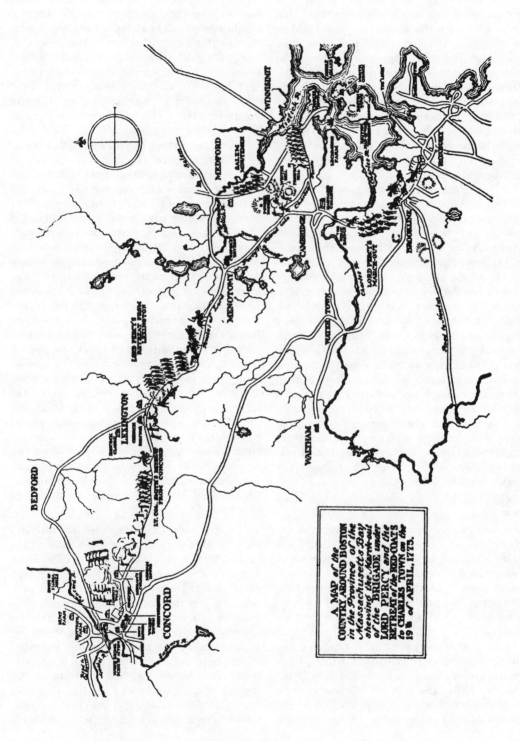

and followed us wherever we went." The Americans hung so close on the rear that again and again the weary rear-guard had to be changed, while from time to time they halted to unlimber the cannon. Then the wounded tumbled from the carriages, the cannon fired, the provincials scattered, and the wounded were lucky to perch on the limbers again, as the column started onward. Mile after mile the troops thus plodded on, their flankers exhausted by their efforts, their ammunition gradually growing less, their numbers slowly dwindling.

It is true that the dwindling was slow. The British killed were but 73, the wounded 174, the missing 26, a total of 273, less than one man in five. With four thousand Americans eventually in the fight, why were the casualties so few? Partly because of the clumsy firelocks, whose effective range was little more than a hundred yards, and whose best distance, for accuracy, was but sixty. And accuracy is a misleading term. There was not a rifle there, on either side; and the muskets, without rear sights, were used like fowling-pieces for blazing away. Few men, American or British, came to the field with more than thirty-six rounds; and when the provincial powder was gone the men could get no more, and were forced to give place to others. Nor were many of them marksmen, for they were not frontiersmen, nor even hunters. It was bad enough shooting indeed. Yet none of the regulars complained of it.

On their part, the troops killed but 49 of the Americans, and wounded 39, no great testimony to their own skill. Yet the military memoirs of the eighteenth century show many a famous battle with the proportion of casualties no worse than this. It was not until these same contestants met at Bunker Hill, some two months later, that they showed what they could do, at close range or with bayonet.

One trap was set for Percy, which he had pointed out himself. Leaving Boston by land, he had crossed the Charles River by the Great Bridge. Expecting him to follow the same route in returning, the Americans took up the planks of the bridge, and a strong force was waiting for him. And it was in order to force him to take the road to the bridge that the single attempt to head his column was made. But as if knowing what was in store for him, Percy forced his way to the road to Charlestown, where the warships' guns would protect his men, and their boats would ferry them to Boston. It was his salvation. Clinton wrote him later: "I have always thought and said that had not your Grace decided at Cambridge to move by Charles Town instead of Roxbury, there would have been an end that day of British Government in America." The statement is extreme; but had Gage lost that day this more than third of his little army, the rest would have been in great danger.

Much was said by early American historians against the "barbarity" of the regulars, in burning houses at Lexington, and in killing non-combatants on the retreat. In spite of the exasperations given them by the Yankees in previous months, at Concord the troops behaved with great restraint. In Lexington houses were burned because they would give shelter to men wishing to attack the resting troops. As for non-combatants on the retreat, it is a fair suspicion that some were not so innocent after all, while others suffered for lingering too near troops who were angry and afraid because their comrades had been reported scalped. Anyone found in a house from which snipers had fired, and which the regulars broke into, had to take his chance. First among modern American historians, Mr. Harold Murdock cleared the British of this blame.

Steadily marching, it was almost dusk before the British came in sight of Charlestown, and of Boston across the water. At about the same time militia of Essex county, perhaps half their regiment, came to the field in a body. It was the last American opportunity. Had Heath, the American general, thrown them across the British path, and stopped the regulars while the pursuers closed in, there would have been a struggle of heroic proportions. But Heath had had his taste of the British cannon, and asked the Essex colonel for a conference. Percy marched on into Charlestown, across a narrow neck which his rear-guard and his field-pieces could hold. Night was falling as the boats began ferrying the wearied troops to Boston, but the consequences of Gage's expedition had not ended. From as far as messages had been carried that day, the militia were on their way to besiege Boston, and the Revolutionary war had begun.

Gage's attempt to destroy the stores had failed in its main object, for most of the munitions had been concealed. Smith's waste of time, both in beginning his march, and in quitting Concord, was almost disastrous. Behind breastworks his regulars could hold in check treble their own numbers; but marching in the open they were at the mercy of an irregular force, particularly since they disdained to use Indian tactics. The efforts of the troops were exhausting; and the distances that they march, with little food or rest, were very great. Had they held the bridge at Concord better, the final result would have been the same. Only the coming of the brigade saved the detachment; and had Percy turned toward Roxbury, or had he had another few miles to march, he could scarcely have saved himself. The courage of the troops was admirable; but discretion would have prevented the experiment. As it was, Gage was fortunate in getting his men back at all, while the success of the provincials emboldened them to besiege his army in Boston, with the most meagre equipment, yet with eventual success. The war might have begun some other way, and probably would have,

sooner or later; but this way was a poor one. By teaching the Americans that the regulars were, after all, not so very formidable, Gage made a bad beginning of the war.

NOTE.—For lack of space, I have written this article without references. Those interested in the original documents will find them freely quoted in my *Day of Concord and Lexington,* and *General Gage's Informers.* Copies of these are in the British Museum. The chief British manuscript sources are: the reports of Smith and Percy to Gage, and Gage's own report, all in the Public Record Office (C.O.5/92); Pitcairn's and Laurie's reports to Gage, and Sutherland's letter, in two forms, all in the Clements' MSS.*; Barker's dairy (*The British in Boston*†), Lister's narrative (*Concord Fight*), and the Mackenzie Diary,‡ all published by the Harvard University Press.

* In the Clements' Library, Ann Arbor, Michigan.

† Reproduced in full in Volume VII of the *Journal of the Society for Army Historical Research,* London, 1928.

‡ The portion of this diary which deals with the Concord fight was edited by me and published by the Harvard University Press in 1926, under the title, "A British Fusilier in Revolutionary Boston." The contemporary "Mackenzie Map" accompanying this article, is reproduced by kind permission of the Harvard University Press.

(This article has been reprinted from Volume XV, Spring, 1936, of the *Journal of the Society for Army Historical Research* with the kind permission of this Society and of the author.)

# THE LOGISTICS OF ARNOLD'S MARCH TO QUEBEC

By James A. Huston*

WHEN the American colonies took up arms in revolt against Great Britain, it was to be expected that the military systems they would employ, including arrangements for logistical support, would be patterned after those with which they were familiar. The weaknesses in central control and direction that were characteristic of colonial military efforts would continue to plague the colonies as they battled for independent existence.

from headquarters at Fort Ticonderga.

Shortly after his arrival at Cambridge in July to assume command of the forces before Boston, General Washington found an occasion to exercise his bold imagination such as came to him all too infrequently during the long years of war that followed. Convinced by reports that Montreal and Quebec were lightly held, the Commander-in-Chief determined to support the proposed invasion of Canada by sending a detach-

*General Washington at Cambridge; from an old woodcut.*

After their capture of Fort Ticonderoga in May 1775, in the first American offensive action of the Revolutionary War, Ethan Allen and Benedict Arnold began to look toward Canada as a likely area for further offensive ventures. At first reluctant to encourage far-flung attacks in a war whose sole purpose seemed to be defensive, the Continental Congress soon persuaded itself that offense might be the best defense against invasion from Canada. In any case every effort should be made to win Quebec over as the fourteenth revolting colony. Congress appointed Major General Philip Schuyler of New York to command the

northern army, moving against Canada ment through the Maine wilderness to strike at Quebec, while Schuyler's forces marched on Montreal over the traditional Lake Champlain—Richelieu River route. By moving in from an unexpected quarter, the first column might capture Quebec, or at least draw British forces from Montreal, thus aiding Schuyler. Col. Benedict Arnold, fresh from disappointment with the Northern Army on Lake Champlain, was anxious to lead the detachment from Cambridge to Quebec, and Washington was persuaded that no better choice could be found for the command of such a hazardous undertaking as this promised to be.[1]

Arnold was to lead his force up the

*Dr. James Houston is Professor of History and International Relations, Lynchburg College.

Kennebec River, across the divide to Lake Megantic, and then down the Chaudière River to Quebec City. Though not a new plan, it had never been tried. In 1754 Governor Shirley of Massachusetts had appointed Capt. John Winslow to lead an expedition over this route, and under Jedediah Preble Winslow's force apparently had gone as far as the Great Carrying Place, between the Dead River (a branch of the Kennebec) and Lake Megantic, before turning back. Lt. John Montresor, a brilliant young officer who had come to America as chief engineer with Braddock's expedition, had explored the route from Quebec southward to the Great Carrying Place, and had left a map and a journal, upon which Washington and Arnold based their plans. Several weeks before Washington made his decision, Col. Jonathan Brewer had offered to lead a force up this route, if 500 men could be assigned to him. Brewer's suggestion had not been opportune, but perhaps his reasoning influenced Washington, who decided that he could spare 1,000 to 1,200 men for Arnold's northern expedition.[2]

Preparations had to be made hastily in order that the expedition might leave in time to reach Quebec before the worst of the winter. Already the season was late, and winter in the north woods was not many weeks away. On September 2 Washington charged Nathaniel Tracy with collecting vessels for transporting the expedition from Newburyport (northeast of Boston) to the Kennebec River.[3] The next day he approved an order on Reuben Colburn of Gardinerston, drawn up by Adjutant General Horatio Gates, for the construction of boats, arranging for supplies, and raising a company of twenty artificers, carpenters, and guides to accompany the expedition. The order called for 200 four-oared bateaux, equipped with two paddles and two setting poles. The price of forty shillings each was to cover all wages and materials. Colburn was authorized to buy 500 bushels of corn for the boatbuilders. For the supply of the expedition he was to speak for all the pork and flour that could be obtained from the inhabitants along the Kennebec, and for sixty 220-pound barrels of salted beef, which a commissary would shortly purchase for the army. Washington also directed Colburn to send scouts out along the proposed route to reconnoiter and report back to Arnold.[4]

Washington put a force of approximately 1,000 men at Arnold's disposal: Volunteers from the regiments formed ten companies of musketmen, and three companies of riflemen (two of Pennsylvanians and one of Virginians) were chosen by lot. After some delays owing to shortages of tents and other equipment, and the refusal of some of the men to march without a month's pay in advance, the detachment paraded on the common at Cambridge on September 11 under the supervision of Colonel Arnold and the adjutant general, and received equipment from the quartermaster general. The riflemen began moving northward that evening, and they camped within a mile of the Merrimac on the 13th. Capt. Daniel Morgan of the Virginia Riflemen, more by force of personality than anything else, made himself the senior captain of this element. Next came the five companies forming the battalion under the command of Lt. Col. Christopher Greene, with Maj. Timothy Bigelow second in command, which left Cambridge on the 13th and arrived at Newburyport late on the 15th. The five companies under Lt. Col. Roger Enos and Maj. Return J. Meigs left somewhat later on the 13th and arrived at Newburyport early on the 16th. Dr. Isaac Senter, surgeon for the expedition, accompanied Greene. The medical section also included a surgeon's mate and two assistants. Arnold's staff included two adjutants, two quartermasters, and a chaplain. In addition there were five volunteers acting as secretaries and aides, and two soldiers' wives.[5]

Washington instructed Arnold on the 14th to respect the property and the religious sensibilities of the French Canadians, as one of the principal objects of the whole enterprise was to persuade the Canadians to join the revolutionary cause; failing that, nothing was to be done that might cause them to abandon their neutral attitude and become actively hostile to their American neighbors. Arnold, therefore, was to be particularly careful to pay full value for all provisions or services which might be obtained, and he received a generous allotment of coin for this purpose. In no case were any of the Canadians or their farm animals to be impressed into service.[6]

Arnold himself left Cambridge on the morning of September 15. At Salem he received 270 blankets from the Committee of Safety on the order of the quartermaster general, he bought 200 pounds of ginger and various other small stores, and engaged a teamster to transport these things to Newburyport. In Newburyport Arnold lodged with Nathaniel Tracy, the wealthy merchant whom Washington had asked to assemble ships to transport the force to the Kennebec. The efficient Tracy had eleven schooners and sloops of various descriptions waiting, having advanced £700 to fit out the expedition.

The transports (except for one schooner, which ran aground) departed from Newburyport shortly after noon on the 19th, made the nearly 100 miles to Wood Island, near the mouth of the Kennebec, in about eleven hours, and were able to get upstream as far as the vicinity of Gardinerston by the night of September 22. Near this town Reuben Colburn had his shipyard, and by a tremendous effort he had completed the construction of the 200

bateaux ordered.[7] But Arnold was disappointed with the results. With sides and bottoms made of green pine, the boats were heavy but weak. Many of them appeared to be undersized, and Arnold ordered twenty more to be built within the next week in order to make up for the lost space. While at Gardinerston, Arnold received the report of the scouts whom Washington had ordered Colburn to send to reconnoiter the route (they had gone as far as the Dead River), and he picked up some rough maps which had been prepared by Samuel Goodwin.

Since Gardinerston was about as far up the Kennebec as the sailing vessels could go, supplies were transferred from the ships to the bateaux for the remaining nine or ten miles to Fort Western (Augusta), which was to be the final staging area for the expedition. Arnold assigned 100 men to row the boats up the river. A road between Gardinerston and Fort Western also made it possible for some of the supplies—probably some of those which had been delivered at Colburn's shipyard by Joseph Farnsworth, the commissary—to be moved over land. For some three days men and supplies were sent up to Fort Western, where supplies were stowed in the bateaux and the troops were reorganized for the wilderness march. Built in 1754 on the site of the old Cushnoc Trading Post, which the Pilgrims of Plymouth had used as a fur trading post with the Indians, Fort Western had not been in use for military purposes since 1759; but its sizable barracks (a squared-log house 100 feet long) provided good shelter for a number of troops and space for organizing supplies and equipment, and the parade ground was a good location for the tents or makeshift huts of other troops.

Total supplies and equipment for the expedition probably amounted to about 100 pounds per man. This included some 4,500 rations, each consisting of twelve ounces of biscuit or flour and twelve ounces of meat, plus some dried vegetables, sugar, salt, yeast, butter, and various extras. This total probably included, too, about 100 rounds of ammunition for each man, or a total of about four tons, and rifles and muskets contributed another five and one-half tons to the total load. Tents, blankets, and individual clothing and equipment probably accounted for another fifteen or sixteen tons, and shovels and axes and other tools, medical supplies, and utensils, another one or two tons. The boats alone weighed approximately 400 pounds each.

Shortly after his arrival at Fort Western, Arnold sent off parties to reconnoiter the route to Dead River (a northwest fork of the Kennebec) and Lake Megantic. By Monday morning, September 25, the expedition was ready to begin its movement up the Kennebec. Now the army was divided into four divisions. The first three—the rifle companies under Captain Morgan, three musket companies under Colonel Greene, and four companies under Major Meigs— left on successive days, beginning on the 25th. Each carried provisions for forty-five days, though the riflemen, as "light infantry," carried somewhat less equipment than the others. Each company generally manned twelve to sixteen boats, with three to five men in each boat, and the rest of the men marched along the river banks.

A series of falls and rapids extending up the river for half a mile beyond Fort Western presented an immediate obstacle to the units as they set out. But here, fortunately, a road connected Fort Western and Fort Halifax (about eighteen miles to the north, at the junction of the Sebasticook River and the Kennebec), and it is likely that local inhabitants made horses and wagons available to help get the heavily laden boats around the falls. Most elements reached Fort Halifax within two days after

their departure from Fort Western.

The fourth division, under Colonel Enos, including three musket companies plus Colburn's company of carpenters and artificers, was rather slower than the others in getting away. To these companies fell all the details common to bringing up the rear of a military column. Several men had to remain at Colburn's until the twenty additional boats that Arnold had ordered were ready. Moreover this division was to bring all the supplies that their bateaux would carry, and to forward all remaining supplies to Fort Halifax. Enos further had to round up the stragglers, arrange for the evacuation of some sick men and one or more criminals. Two companies of his command had departed by the 29th, though Enos himself and Colburn's company of artificers remained behind with the commissary for another day or two. Arnold remained at Fort Western until the leading companies of the fourth division had set out on the 29th, and then he embarked in a birch-bark canoe paddled by Indians to overtake the head of the column.

Beyond Fort Halifax (Winslow), Ticonic Falls made necessary the first major portage. Already the inexperienced boatmen had found it difficult going to row or pole their bulky craft up the rocky stream, but that was as nothing compared to the work required to get the boats and supplies around such obstacles as this. Still the expedition was not completely out of touch with civilization, and horses of local inhabitants, as well as a few oxen that were accompanying the expedition, may have provided some help in the arduous task of portaging the heavy boats and supplies. For such a distance as this the boats had to be unloaded, the supplies carried to the next launching site, and the boats themselves carried or dragged over the same path. As each boat came to the bank, near the falls, the men would climb out into the water and unload the supplies and equipment; then, passing handspikes under the bottom, four men would carry the bulky craft up the bank and around the falls. For shorter distances, and where the banks were not too steep, it was possible to carry the fully laden boat around obstacles without losing time unloading and reloading.

Ticonic Falls proved to be only the first of the many falls and rapids where hand-carries were necessary. And between those falls that had to be detoured, other, smaller ones joined with boulders and swift current to put up an almost continuous battle against the green boats and the green crews. Not far above Ticonic Falls they had to push against the "Five Mile Ripples," then carry around Skowhegan Falls, and then move along the river again for several miles of boulders and rapids to the difficult portage at Norridgewock Falls. Unfortunately, the boats were not built for such rough handling. Within four or five days their seams began to open, and with each new leak the men cursed the boatbuilders more violently. Attempts to stop the leaks by caulking were only partially and temporarily successful, so that by the time the boats reached Norridgewock Falls, many of the supplies had been ruined, and major overhaul and rebuilding jobs were necessary before many of the craft could proceed any further.

Casks of dried peas and biscuit had taken on water and burst. Water had washed away the salt from the fish which had been stowed loosely in the boats, and most of it had to be thrown away. Moreover, the salt beef, prepared during the hot summer, was found to be almost wholly spoiled, whether water-soaked or not. Much of the pork was damaged too, although some was still good. About the only food left now was flour and salt pork. There was little prospect of replenishing supplies before reaching the Canadian settlements, for only two or three families of settlers lived near Norridgewock Falls, and beyond there was nothing but wilderness. Sometimes one of the soldiers was able to bring in a moose, or to catch some fish, but little game stayed near the route of an advancing army.

Delays at Norridgewock made a bottleneck which permitted the column to close up. Arnold reached the falls on October 2, just as the first division was completing its carry. The second division arrived the same day, the third two days later, and the fourth two days after that. Arnold remained for a week to supervise the activities.

As repair of the boats went on, the great advantage of canoes must have become obvious to everyone. Why canoes were not used on an expedition up a river so full of rapids and falls is not clear, but it seems probable that the number of canoes needed could not have been obtained in time.

By October 11 all the elements had somehow arrived at the "Great Carrying Place" between the Kennebec and the Dead Rivers. Some distance to the north of this point the Dead River empties into the Kennebec, but these rivers were not navigable for most of that distance, and it was simpler to make use of a series of three ponds which lay between the Kennebec and the upper Dead River than to follow the Kennebec further upstream.

While Morgan and his riflemen continued on ahead to cut crude roadways along the portage routes between the streams and ponds, Arnold looked to further logistical activities. Wet weather, poor shelter, and exhausting work had begun to weaken some of the men so that they could not continue, though Arnold reported on October 14 that he still had 950 effectives. At any rate the commander ordered the construction of a log hospital on the second portage, where the first division had already put up a small hut for its sick men. As soon as the new hospital building was completed, eight or ten sick men moved in, and others arrived later. At the same time Arnold ordered Enos to put a bateau on each of the ponds to ferry across sick men who were returning to the rear.

In addition to the hospital, Arnold had another log house built, this one on the first portage, to serve as a supply depot; and he sent word to Farnsworth, the commissary, to hire some men to send up to this place the approximately 100 barrels of provisions that had been left behind. These were to provide a source for resupply if food ran short before the troops reached the Canadian settlements, or in case the army had to retreat without reaching them; but apparently the instructions never were carried out, and the provisions never got beyond Fort Halifax. The only resupply that could be counted upon now was in whatever extra provisions the fourth division might be carrying. At this time Arnold ordered Enos to send forward a yoke of oxen to be slaughtered, and he ordered Meigs to furnish a detail of forty men from his third division to improve the roads for the fourth division.

The fourth portage on the Great Carrying Place—a distance of approximately three miles from the third or "West Carry" pond to Bog Brook—presented the worst obstacle so far encountered. Beyond a hill near its beginning, this route appeared to be inviting enough—a relatively flat grassland. Carrying the heavy bateaux and supplies for nearly three miles would have been no small task even over smooth meadows, but here the appearance was deceptive. The grassland turned out to be tangled undergrowth, moss and marsh. While the riflemen labored to make some kind of a passable road, the men of Greene's first division completed the seven or eight trips necessary to get their boats and supplies across, and then they passed through the rifle companies and took the lead in launching their boats down Bog Creek the mile or so to Dead River, and then up Dead River. At

first this river was deep and smooth, though the current was strong, but soon rapids again began to force portages.

Now food supplies began to run short. Some companies had been able to shoot some moose, and some had caught good quantities of fish in the ponds at the Great Carrying Place, and the yoke of oxen that Enos had sent forward now had been butchered. But all this only helped to postpone the inevitable consequences of the spoilage and losses that had occured, and quite probably the careless use of what earlier had appeared to be abundant supplies. On October 15 Arnold fixed the ration strictly at twelve ounces each of flour and salt pork. When he arrived at Greene's camp on the Dead River the next day, Arnold found that the supply shortage was becoming serious. The companies here had gone on half rations on the 16th. The next morning Arnold directed Major Bigelow, second in command of this division, to take a detail of three officers, six noncommissioned officers, and eighty-seven men, with twelve boats, back to the rear division under Colonel Enos to get more provisions, but Bigelow returned four days later with but one or two barrels of flour. In the meantime the supply situation in Greene's division had worsened, for the rifle companies had passed through to resume the lead on October 17, and its appears that in doing so the riflemen resorted to some "moonlight requisitions" against Greene's stores to replenish their own supplies.

By October 20 Arnold's army was strung out along the Dead River. But now for two days rainstorms had been adding serious difficulties to those already encountered in the forests and rapids. Violent winds and heavy rains—possibly a hurricane which had moved up from the West Indies— struck, and men encamped near the river found themselves driven from their beds by flood waters which had risen eight feet or more in nine hours. It was nearly impossible the next morning to move at all, either by land or by water, and worst of all was the further loss of boats and provisions that resulted. Trying to move upstream against the swollen river, six or seven of the bateaux upset, with the loss of all of their contents.

With provisions now becoming desperately short, and no word yet from Canada, Arnold called a council of war to decide what should be done. It was questionable whether they should try to continue at all. The officers present agreed that the expedition should by all means continue, but they recognized that some special steps would have to be taken in order to supply the army as it pressed further into the wilderness. Arnold sent Capt. Oliver Hanchet of Meig's division with a company of fifty picked men to hasten forward to the first French settlements at the Chaudière to obtain fresh provisions. At the same time all sick men, and men who could not be supplied during the time before the army could be expected to reach the Chaudière, were to be sent home. These men received three rations each, and Arnold instructed the commissary to give them additional supplies when they reached his position. He sent a message to Enos which ordered him to proceed with as many of his men as he could furnish with fifteen days' provision, and to send the remainder back to the commissary. Similar instructions went to Greene.

On receiving these orders, the commanders of the two rear divisions found themselves in something of a dilemma. What were they supposed to do if already their provisions were so low that they could not supply anybody with rations for fifteen days? The officers of the fourth division now decided that this was their predicament, and their solution was to turn about and take the whole division home.

Quite understandably Arnold was surprised when he learned that Enos and his entire division, had abandoned the march. When he arrived back at Cambridge, Enos was court-martialed for returning without orders, but after a trial in which only his own officers, who had returned with him, were available for witnesses he was acquitted with honor.[8]

All of Enos' officers testified that they had forwarded all remaining supplies to the other divisions and had only three days' supplies for themselves when they turned about. From this it would appear that they had no other choice. Yet a closer examination of the supply situation suggests that the fourth division was at least as well off as some of those who continued forward, and if the ultimate test of a military decision is the extent to which it contributes toward accomplishing the assigned mission, it is difficult to see how any decision of a subordinate commander to turn back with his entire command without the knowledge of the commander of the expedition could be justified. If it was true, as Enos and his officers contended, that the division had only three days' provisions when it turned back, then of course it would have been quite impossible to comply strictly with Arnold's order. However, if it was true, as internal evidence of the journals indicates, that Enos had at the very least six days' supplies for all the 400 men assigned or attached to his command, then it would have been possible for him to send back 328 men—including 178 of his own and the 150 others who were only attached—with four days' provisions each, and still to send seventy-two men forward with fifteen days' supplies. Or, if Enos had given the returning men three days' supplies, as Arnold had done, he could have gone forward with 100 men, carrying rations for fifteen days, and sent back 300 men. On an expedition of this kind 100 men and fifteen days' food supplies could have made a really significant difference.

When the supply crisis developed, Greene at first had gone forward to confer with Arnold about what should be done, but the leader was now so far ahead of the column that Greene could not overtake him. On returning to his own troops, he found that Enos and the officers of the fourth division had come up to discuss the question of continuing in view of the serious shortage of food supplies. On the part of Green's officers there was no doubt; the thought apparently did not occur to them that everybody should turn back; they insisted that only the weak and unfit should be sent home. But the officers of the fourth division held that the only alternative was to give up the expedition. In a formal vote the officers were evenly divided until Enos, presiding, had cast the deciding vote in favor of proceeding forward. Then in spite of his vote, he yielded to the demands of his own officers for his division to turn back, and early that same afternoon he gave the order to that effect.

Enos, bringing up the rear, was supposedly carrying extra supplies on which the forward units could draw when they ran short. But when, after the conference, Greene sent a captain and a boat back down the river to pick up supplies from the fourth division, no flour or pork appeared to be available. Enos indicated that the men had gotten out of control and would not give up any of their supplies. Finally one of the captains did turn over two barrels of flour to Greene's emissary, but that was all. Now it is practically certain that the supply situation in Enos' division was at least as good as, if not substantially better than, that in Greene's division; yet Greene's men pressed on while Enos' did not. Perhaps the severe hardships which subsequently fell to the other divisions demonstrated the wisdom of Enos' decision in some measure

particularly in the eyes of his own troops. But from the broader viewpoint of the requirements of military service, it was an action which could only weaken the expedition, and possibly jeopardize the accomplishment of its mission.[9]

During the following week Arnold's little army, tramping through the wilderness, moving from one to the next of the "Chain of Ponds," carrying heavy boats—sometimes virtually wearing the shoulders of men through to the bone—over the rolling ground of the divide separating the tributaries of the Kennebec from those of the St. Lawrence, was on the verge of starvation. As supplies ran out, the men seized upon anything at hand that would help sustain them until relief could be obtained.

Where was the place of the commander in this kind of critical situation? Should he remain with the main body of troops to urge the men on, or should he push ahead to see about getting supplies. For Arnold the answer was clear. He hastened on with all possible speed to the first French Canadian settlements to buy what food he could to send back to the near-starving soldiers. On October 27 Arnold and the advance detachment reached Lake Megantic. Here a messenger whom he had sent ahead to the Canadian settlements returned to say that the inhabitants would be pleased to furnish supplies, and that they would welcome the arrival of the American expedition. The next morning Arnold sent back a guide and instructions to direct the companies around the swamps ahead of them to the lake. In the interest of greater speed, he advised them not to try to carry the boats over the height of land but to march on without them. This done, Arnold set out with four bateaux and a birchbark canoe and fifteen men to go on ahead as rapidly as possible to arrange for the vital food supplies.

After entering the outlet of Lake Megantic, the Chaudière River, Arnold's advance party for a time was able to hold its own in the rushing waters of that boulder-filled stream. But fifteen miles down the stream the water became so violent that all the boats went out of control and capsized. Two of them were destroyed against the rocks, and three others were damaged. Several men lost all their weapons, ammunition, equipment, and food supplies, but all were able to escape with their lives. They had no more than embarked again after repairing the damage as well as they could when a man who was up forward shouted that there were falls. This warning very likely saved the whole party. The next day the canoe had to be abandoned, but the party continued on with the two bateaux that remained. At last, late on October 30, Arnold arrived at the first French Canadian settlement, St. Georges (referred to by Arnold and his men as "Sartigan"). His first thought was to get supplies back to his army; a single day's delay now might mean the difference between survival and starvation for many men. The next day he sent a lieutenant and a party of eight or nine Frenchmen to the rear with supplies of flour, and soon thereafter a second party, apparently, started for the rear with cattle, sheep, oatmeal, and other provisions.

In the meantime, the army had been going through the most severe ordeal of its entire march. On the day that Arnold and his party had sailed down Lake Megantic and into the Chaudière River, all remaining elements of the army, had assembled in the meadows along the Arnold River south of Lake Megantic. Now most of the men learned for the first time that Colonel Enos and his fourth division had turned back. Bitter resentment arose against the men who, bringing up the rear, had had the easiest time of it and had then turned back with an important part of the ammunition and other supplies upon which the expedi-

tion depended. Here the officers brought together all remaining food supplies, and probably ammunition too, and distributed them among the men, so that it would be clear to all just what supplies they had. Each soldier received four or five pints of flour, and some of the more fortunate ones received two to four ounces of pork. That was all. Arnold's message, arriving after the distribution had been completed, stated that he hoped to have supplies half-way up the Chaudière River to meet the troops in six days. That meant that the men would have to exist on rations of less than a pint of flour a day. Many actually had less than that. Some interpreted Arnold's message— that he hoped to reach the first settlements within three days, and have provisions back within another three—to mean that food would be available within three days, and carelessly they consumed all their rations very quickly. Loss, misfortune, and poor supply discipline brought some of the men to the very brink of starvation during the next few days.

Now followed the nearly disastrous march of the army as it attempted to find its way to Lake Megantic. Morgan's men had brought their serviceable boats all this way —across the height of land and across the long portages near the Canadian boundary— so that they could now be used in getting down the streams and across the swamps to the lake. But the others had to march. Arnold had warned them strictly against following the river, lest they be led into swamps, and he had sent a man to guide them. But the guide lost his way, and most of the companies did get into the swamps, became confused among the false mouths of the Arnold River, and then apparently marched all the way around the east side of Spider Lake before finally coming down to the eastern shore of Lake Megantic. The weather had turned cold; snow was upon the ground, and ice was forming in some of the streams that had to be waded. Most of the boats that remained were lost in the Chaudière River in the same rapids where Arnold had lost his, and the whole force was reduced to walking before it had gone far down that stream.

By November 1 some of the men were desperate, turning to anything they could find for nourishment. The game and fish upon which the advance party had been able to depend to some extent were not to be found when the rest of the army came along. Cartridge cases, leather moccasins, rawhide thongs—all went into stock for soup, as did three or four pet dogs.

Then on November 2—exactly six days after Arnold had sent his message expressing hope that he could have provisions back within that length of time—the relief parties sent back from St. Georges met the column. With the first, Arnold sent instructions that each company was to take only enough provisions to permit it to reach the falls, where further supplies could be expected; the remainder should be passed on to the rear. Soon other food began to appear. As horses carrying sacks of flour and cattle and sheep came into sight, the men cheered as wildly as their feeble condition would permit. They butchered the cattle, and each man had a pound or more of fresh meat. Against the warnings of their officers, some gorged themselves until they were sick. One man who ate ravenously of boiled beef, hot bread, and potatoes died two days later. Now Arnold also sent instructions to Major Meigs, with whom he had entrusted a part of the money for the expedition, to give twenty or thirty dollars to each of the captains so that they could make local purchases of their own for themselves and their men.

As the column continued northward toward Quebec, Arnold arranged to have beef and potatoes ready every ten or twelve miles, though some of the men preferred to rely on milk, butter, eggs, and bread when they could be obtained from local inhabitants. The Canadians were apprehensive, but on the whole friendly, as the American force, "Les Bostonnais," marched through their country. Their attitude seemed to be one of neutrality between Great Britain and the rebelling colonies, and they were willing to sell supplies to whoever had the money. It was possible at times for some of the men to get food at taverns along the way as well as from the farmers.

At St. Marie, about twenty-five miles south of Quebec, Arnold's force closed up, and the men were able to find comfortable shelter in houses. As the column resumed its march, Arnold sent out a detail of three officers to try to hire or purchase enough canoes so that ninety-six sick men could be carried down the Chaudière River, and to provide transportation for the army across the St. Lawrence.

On the night of November 8 Arnold's expedition reached the St. Lawrence River opposite Quebec, and the energetic commander began taking the necessary steps for crossing the river. A dissident Englishmen made available some precious supplies of wheat and flour stored at a local mill, and then offered his services in giving advice and guidance for making the crossing. Unfortunately for Arnold, the British in Quebec had learned of his coming, and nearly all the boats and canoes along the south shore of the St. Lawrence had been moved away or destroyed. Moreover, two British gunboats had arrived on the scene to try to prevent a crossing. Then to make matters worse, high winds blew for the next three days, so that it was impossible to venture out on the river in a small boat or canoe. While Arnold chafed at the delay, he also continued his preparations, collecting thirty-five or forty canoes of various kinds and adding to his stocks of food supplies.

At about eleven o'clock on the night of November 13 the crossing began. By four o'clock the canoes had made three round trips in the quiet darkness, carrying some 500 men across the mile-wide river. The rest of the force, excepting sixty men who remained on the south bank as a rear guard, followed the next night or two. Of the approximately 1,050 officers and men who had left Cambridge, approximately 675 had arrived at the St. Lawrence River and the gates of Quebec. If 300 men turned back with Enos, there were only about seventy-five casualties and stragglers who failed to come through the whole ordeal.

In the meantime the other American column, under Brigadier General Richard Montgomery, had been advancing on Canada from Fort Ticonderoga. On the 13th, the same day that Arnold began crossing the St. Lawrence, Montgomery marched into Montreal—evacuated by the small British garrison two nights earlier—and took possession. The Americans then took Sorel and sailed on down the St. Lawrence toward Quebec.

Arnold was anxious to attack at once before enemy reinforcements could arrive, but in an inspection of the arms and ammunition of his men on the Plains of Abraham he found that many of the cartridges that had been prepared during the march were useless. Only about five rounds of ammunition per man could be found, and in view of this situation Arnold deemed it more prudent to withdraw some distance from Quebec. If he had been but a few days sooner, he might have been immediately successful in taking the city, for the inhabitants were disposed to capitulate without a struggle to this army which had suddenly come upon them out of the wilderness. But Col. Allan Maclean had been able to slip into the city a day and a half before the Americans formed outside the walls, and he organized resistance which now made

necessary either a siege or an assault. Arnold moved his forces some twenty-five miles westward to Point aux Trembles to await the arrival of Montgomery.

During the two months since the departure of the expedition from Cambridge there had been no opportunity for any resupply of clothing. The men were facing winter with only the protection of such rags as remained after the weeks of struggle along the wilderness trails and streams. Arnold took advantage of the pause now to send to Montreal for clothing. In a memorandum to General Montgomery on November 20 Arnold stated his requirements: 600 pairs of coarse stockings, 500 yards of coarse woolen for breeches, 1,000 yards of flannel or baize for shirts, 300 milled caps, 300 pairs of mittens or gloves, 300 blankets, powder and ball, a barrel of rum, and a barrel of sugar.[10] At the same time Arnold reported to Montgomery that his cash was nearly exhausted. So far his expenditures had amounted to about £392, sterling, and he felt that it would not be expedient to offer paper to the Canadians for the further purchases which he now required. Nevertheless he did count on his own good credit to cover the procurement of some clothing for his army from a firm of Montreal merchants. He sent Capt. Matthias Odgen with a letter to Prince and Haywood, Merchants, asking that, if the captain had insufficient funds to cover his purchases, the goods be charged to Arnold's account.

Leaving a garrison at Montreal, Montgomery marched with about 300 men to Arnold's camp at Point aux Trembles, arriving on December 3; he brought supplies, including British clothing captured from the 7th and 26th British Regiments, to the relief of Arnold's haggard band. Lacking the resources for a long siege, and troubled by the knowledge that several hundred enlistments would expire at the end of the year, Montgomery resolved on assault. Taking advantage of a blinding snow storm, the Americans attacked in the pre-dawn hours of December 31. But Montgomery was killed and Arnold severely wounded, and the attack narrowly missed success.

Arnold now assumed command of the total force. He had no thought of giving up the effort. For weeks from his sick bed he directed the disposition of his men to maintain a siege against the city of Quebec then garrisoned by a force twice the size of his own. He obtained assurances from a French Canadian foundryman at Three Rivers that artillery shells in whatever size and number required could be cast between the first of January and the first of April. He raised a force of Canadian volunteers to join his cause, and sent to General David Wooster, who had arrived at Montreal to take command, for weapons and equipment for them, as well as for other supplies for the army. Once again Arnold's cash was running low; his expenditures for the expedition now amounted to about £868 sterling. He expressed the hope that Congress would see fit to send eight to ten thousand men to reinforce his army, and to send to him all the heavy mortars and howitzers from Ticonderoga, Ft. George, and Crown Point, so that in the spring he would have a force capable of carrying Quebec and winning Canada for the United Colonies. But retreat, not attack, was to be the fate of the remaining elements of Arnold's army.

About April 1, 1776, General Wooster arrived at Arnold's camp near Quebec to take active command there, and almost immediately Arnold asked leave to go to Montreal, where, on arrival, he took command of the garrison. Shortly thereafter a commission appointed by the Continental Congress to visit Canada arrived in Montreal. Made up of Benjamin Franklin, Samuel Chase, and Charles Carroll of Carrollton, and accompanied by the latter's brother, the Rev. John Carroll, a prominent Catholic clergyman, the commission had as its principal objective the persuasion of the Canadians to join the rebellion; but inevitably its attention was drawn to the condition of the army now in Canada. What the commissioners found was far from reassuring, for as time had gone on the supply situation had become progressively more difficult. Too far removed from home bases to expect effective support from them, the Americans in Canada found the sources of local procurement drying up as hard money became scarce and the fortunes of war turned against them. The commissioners reported to Congress:

> The Army is in a distressed condition, and is in want of the most necessary articles—meat, bread, tents, shoes, stockings, shirts, etc. . . . Such is our extreme want of flour that we were yesterday obliged to seize by force fifteen barrels to supply this garrison with bread. . . . Nothing but the most urgent necessity can justify such harsh measures; but men with arms in their hands will not starve when provisions can be obtained by force. . . . We cannot find words strong enough to describe our miserable situation; you will have a faint idea of it if you figure to yourself an Army broken and disheartened, half of it under inoculation, or other diseases; soldiers without pay, without discipline, and altogether reduced to live from hand to mouth, depending on the scanty and precarious supplies of a few half-starved cattle and trifling quantities of flour, which have hitherto been picked up in different parts of the country.
>
> Your soldiers grumble for their pay; if they receive it they will not be benefited, as it will not procure them the necessaries they stand in need of. Your military chest contains but eleven thousand paper dollars. You are indebted to your troops treble that sum; and to the inhabitants above fifteen thousand dollars.[11]

The resort to seizures of supplies—a course against which Washington had cautioned in his original instructions, but now so clearly necessary that the commissioners who had been sent by Congress to woo the Canadians apparently recommended it—was bound to alienate the Canadians, and so immediately to work against the accomplishment of the mission of the whole enterprise. But the alternative seemed to be complete loss of an army.

By June even Arnold was convinced that retreat had become necessary. He acted hastily to get stores deposited to secure the retreat. Buying when he could, resorting to seizure when he had to, Arnold reported that he himself had to act as commissary, quartermaster, and contractor to obtain supplies of ammunition, clothing, and food, and get them moved to Chambly and St. Johns, on the Richelieu River. Here further difficulties arose when the commander at Chambly, Col. Moses Hazen, refused to accept or store the supplies when they arrived. Heaped in piles on the bank of the river, boxes were broken open, and many of the supplies plundered. The whole affair resulted in a court martial of Hazen, counter-charges against Arnold, and an altogether unsavory situation which did little for the support of the retreating Army.

At Quebec, American reinforcements arrived, but too late and too few in number to turn the outcome of the Canadian venture: British reinforcements had come over in far greater numbers. Largely because of the dissatisfaction of the congressional commission with his work, General Wooster was replaced on May 1 by Major General John Thomas. A quick inspection of the army and of the defenses convinced the new commander of the prudence of retreat at the earliest opportunity, but even then he was unable to depart before the newly arrived British reinforcements struck. Abandoning most of their supplies, equipment, and cannon, the ill-prepared Americans fled westward in panic. General Thomas himself had to leave his warm dinner to be enjoyed by the British commander, Sir Guy Carleton. After pulling back further to Sorel, Thomas succumbed to the epidemic of smallpox that had been raging among the troops, and in the first week in June Major General John Sullivan arrived to replace him.

Sullivan sent an ill-fated attack against Three Rivers on June 7, and a week later he evacuated Sorel just ahead of the oncoming British vanguard under Lieutenant General John Burgoyne. Sullivan led his troops southward along the Richelieu River, destroyed fortifications, boats, and supplies at Chambly that could not be carried, and moved on to St. Johns, where he met Arnold, who had simultaneously led his 300 remaining troops across the flat land from Montreal. The British were still in pursuit, and at St. Johns, after a council of war, the quartermasters assembled boats and began transporting troops to Isle-aux-Noix. Here, surrounded by water, they were at last safe from the British, but not from smallpox, malaria, and dysentery, which proved to be more deadly than the British ever were.

Disease perhaps as much as anything else broke the army which had braved the wilderness, stormed Quebec, and suffered from lack of food and clothing. Almost no medical preparations had been made in the Northern Department when the invasion of Canada began. As has been noted, Arnold did have a surgeon and assistants, and some medical stores, but resupply was impossible through the Maine wilderness, and little in the way of medical stores arrived with General Montgomery by the Lake Champlain route. Medicines and other medical supplies had indeed been ordered, but they had never reached Lake Champlain. Arnold's men had come through the hardship of the wilderness march in remarkably good health, considering the deficiency of food, but smallpox broke out among the troops before Quebec and raged throughout the retreat until the troops were reconcentrated at Ticonderoga in July, 1776. Although forbidden by general orders, the soldiers almost universally resorted to self-inoculation, and this probably did more to spread the disease than to control it.

The attempt against Canada had ended in complete failure—after victory had seemed so near. But soon Arnold's expedition was being compared with the anabasis of Xenophon and the 10,000 Greeks, and with Hannibal's crossing of the Alps. If it were not for Arnold's later treachery, his expedition doubtless would have readily gained the lasting reputation which it deserves. Here logistics was the crucial element—principally of supply and transportation and, to some extent, hospitalization and evacuation. The only enemies encountered until the crossing of the St. Lawrence were those of wilderness and treacherous streams, rain, cold, exposure, and hunger. When it became impractical to depend upon additional supplies from the rear, Arnold hastened forward personally to arrange for resupply by local procurement, shifting the impetus of supply from the rear

to the front! Arnold was taking a risk to depend on buying the things needed in a possibly hostile country, but boldness and hard cash paid off—as they are likely to do in most similar situations. At the end, when seizure had to be resorted to, the objective was already lost, and it had become a question of saving the army. Perhaps the greatest mistake in Arnold's expedition was the use of the heavy bateaux instead of light canoes, which could have been carried easily across the portages and maneuvered more surely in the rapids of the rivers. But it appears that this was less a mistake than a necessity: Not only would it probably have been impossible to obtain the materials and build the required number of canoes in the time available, but doubtless few of the men in the expedition had had any canoeing experience. Indeed the shortage of skilled boatmen was unquestionably a principal reason for the unsatisfactory results obtained with the bateaux.

Yet in spite of all difficulties, and in spite of the tragic ending, Arnold's march to Quebec remains one of the most remarkable feats of its kind in American annals.

## REFERENCES

1. For accounts of the expedition see especially the journals of the members of Arnold's expedition printed in Kenneth Roberts, *March to Quebec* (Garden City, N.Y., 1953); information from these journals used in this paper will not be identified specifically. A second important source is Justin H. Smith, *Arnold's March from Cambridge to Quebec* (New York, 1903); see also John Richard Alden, *The American Revolution, 1775-1783* (New York, 1954); Isaac N. Arnold, *The Life of Benedict Arnold: His Patriotism and His Treason* (Chicago, 1888); James Thomas Flexner, *The Traitor and the Spy* (New York, 1953); John C. Miller, *Triumph of Freedom* (Boston, 1948); Lynn Montross, *Rag, Tag, and Bobtail: The Story of the Continental Army, 1775-1783* (New York, 1952); Willard M. Wallace, *Appeal to Arms: A Military History of the Revolution* (New York, 1951); Wallace, *Traitorous Hero: The Life and Fortunes of Benedict Arnold* (New York, 1954); Christopher Ward,

*The War of the Revolution* (New York, 1952), Vol. I. For interesting and informative fictionalized accounts of the expedition see F. J. Stimson, *My Story: Being the Memoirs of Benedict Arnold, Late Major-General in the Continental Army and Brigadier-General in That of His Britannic Majesty* (New York, 1917); and Kenneth Roberts, *Arundel* (New York, 1933).

2. Douglas Southall Freeman, *George Washington* (New York, 1948—), III, 532; Letter, Washington to Maj. Gen. Philip Schuyler, 20 August 1775, John C. Fitzpatrick (ed.), *Writings of Washington* (Washington, D.C., 1931-41), III, 437-38.

3. Letter, Washington to Nathaniel Tracy, 2 September 1775, *ibid.*, III, 470-71; see Washington to Gov. Jonathan Trumbull, 2 September 1775, *ibid.*, III, 470.

4. Orders to Reuben Colburn, 3 September 1775, *ibid.*, III, 471.

5. Smith, *Arnold's March*, pp. 57-61; Wallace,

*Traitorous Hero,* p. 60.

6. Instructions to Arnold (drafted by Thomas Mifflin), Fitzpatrick, *Writings of Washington,* III, 492-96.

7. Though Washington's order had specified that the price of 40 shillings was to be for each boat complete with paddles and other equipment, Colburn added paddles, oars, setting poles, and pikes to his bills as separate items. He apparently never was paid in full. Washington had made payments of £17 for earlier services, and Arnold paid about £100 for the bateaux, but for these and other items the Continental Congress still owed, according to Colburn, about £368. In 1818, General Henry Dearborn, who served as a captain on Arnold's expedition, and later became Secretary of War and then General in Chief of the Army, testified to the justice of a claim on this account which Colburn made at that time (Smith, *Arnold's March,* pp. 293-97, n. 6). Final action on Colburn's claim did not come until March 1824, when Congress refused to approve payment—largely on the ground that the lapse of so much time, and the loss of public records, made the justice of the claim doubtful! *Annals of Congress,* 12 March 1824, p. 338, and 15 March 1824, pp. 342-43.

8. Proceedings of a General Court-Martial of the Line . . . Dec. 1, 1775, *American Archives,* 4th Series, III, 1709-11.

9. For a defense of Colonel Enos see Horace E. Hayden, "General Roger Enos," *Magazine of American History,* XIII (1885), 463-76.

10. The wording was slightly different in Arnold's letter to Washington of November 20: "600 blankets, 600 thick clothes, 600 shirts, woolen, 600 milled caps, 600 do. gloves, 600 do. hose, 600 thick woolen breeches lined with wool or leather" (in Roberts, *March to Quebec,* pp. 93-94).

11. *American Archives,* 4th Series, VI, 589-90.

# EQUIPMENT FOR THE MILITIA OF THE MIDDLE STATES, 1775-1781

## By Hugh Jameson

MUCH has been written concerning the unprepared condition of the American colonies in 1775 and the dearth of military equipment of every kind during the early years of the war, but most of the writers have considered the subject in terms of its effects on the Continental army.[1] Little has been done with the problem as it bore directly on the effectiveness of the militia.[2] The Continental army was a permanently embodied force raised by the united efforts of the states, and nominally under the control of the Continental Congress. It was not blessed with an abundance of equipment at any time during the war, but as Van Tyne has shown, the work of Beaumarchais and Silas Deane kept it in the field during the critical year of 1777, and thereafter it was tolerably well armed and reasonably well equipped. The militia was the local defensive force of each individual state, theoretically composed of the entire adult male population. It was not a permanently embodied force, but rather one which, in theory at least, could be mobilized rapidly in any emergency and disbanded quickly when the danger was past.

At the outset the revolutionary government had no intention of using the militia for any purpose other than purely local defence, but circumstances shortly forced them to change their plans, if not their ideas, as to the type of service for which militia might be properly called.[3] The initial refusal of Congress to recruit a standing army, or to authorize long term enlistments, and the subsequent failure of the states to raise their quotas for the Continental army made it necessary to call increasing numbers of militia into active service to augment the army which never attained its authorized strength. Militia were the poorest and most unwilling of troops, but they did serve throughout the war as replacements in the Continental lines of their respective states and as militia units attached to the army on a temporary basis. In their various localities they were called repeatedly to render services which ranged from turning out on any sudden alarm, to guarding prisoners, apprehending deserters, building fortifications, and protecting cattle. They contributed much to the many failures of the period and shared in the successes. In whatever capacity they served, however, they retained their identity as militia and they emerged in 1781 as destitute of arms and equipment as they were in 1775; a condition which this paper attempts to account for.[4]

In 1775 every adult male in the colonies, excepting only the inhabitants of Pennsylvania, was supposed to have in his possession

[1]Among the foremost studies are: L.C. Hatch, *The Administration of the American Revolutionary Army;* O.W. Stephenson, *The Supplies for the American Revolutionary Army.* (MSS thesis Univ. of Mich. Library); O.W. Stephenson, "The Supply of Gunpowder in 1776" *Am. Hist. Rev.,* XXX, 271; C. H. Van Tyne, *The War of Independence;* E. Upton, *The Military Policy of the United States.*

[2]A beginning has been made by Allen French, *The First Year of the American Revolution* (Boston, 1934).

[3]One of the best illustrations of the prevailing ideas of militia service in 1775-1776 is found in the reply which Washington received from the Committee of Safety of New York, April 25, 1776. Washington wanted to know how long it would take to embody 2,500 or 3,000 New York militia and what plans had been made to collect them in a hurry. *Writings,* (Ford ed.) IV, 33. The Committee replied that they had no idea how long it would take, and that since they foresaw no such emergency they had not considered any method of mobilization. *Jour. of the Prov. Cong. of N.Y.,* I, 420.

[4]In one sense, perhaps, militia lost their identity as such while serving as replacements in the army, but they were recruited from the militia for that special service. They retained all the characteristics of militia during their brief term of service and returned to the militia when their tour of duty was done.

a full complement of arms and equipment. Colonial militia laws were precise and detailed on this subject. Every man was expected to furnish himself with a musket, flints, knapsack, powder, and shot. Periodic inspection of these articles was prescribed and penalties imposed for delinquency with respect to any and all of them.[5] Despite the laws, however, few men possessed the requisite equipment for the very simple reason that the laws had been indifferently observed, or altogether ignored. They remained on the statute books but it was common practice, throughout the colonial period, to permit them to pass into abeyance between wars; which practice had been faithfully observed after 1763.[6] The situation as it was on the eve of the war is perhaps best seen in the replies of the colonial governors to Lord Dartmouth's questionnaire of 1773.

As Secretary of State for the Colonies, Lord Dartmouth attempted a survey of the state of the colonies. To this end the governors were questioned for information on a great variety of subjects, among them the number of militia and the general state of colonial defence. Governor Wentworth of New Hampshire said, in his reply, that the regulations as to arms and equipment were so little observed that he was sure there was not four ounces of powder per man, or one musket to every four men and, he feared, "still less of the other requisites." The governor of Massachusetts did not know either the number of the militia, or the condition of their equipment, because many of the regiments had been without officers for years and there were no returns upon which to base even an estimate. The replies of other governors were in similar vein. They were forced either to plead ignorance as to the state of the militia, or to state frankly that the laws were openly disobeyed.[7] On the whole it was

a most distressing picture but the accuracy of it was amply attested by the development of 1775.

The middle colonies were slow in catching the military fever in 1775. There was little in the way of preparation for armed resistance prior to Lexington, and that little was entirely local and unsystematic.[8] Except in Maryland where a provincial congress adopted a few half-hearted resolutions it was neither authorized, nor sanctioned by the most radical of revolutionary leaders.[9] Immediately after Lexington, however, a vast volunteer militia began to form under the guidance of local committees and when this happened the lack of military accessories of every kind became abundantly evident. Petitions urgently requesting guns, powder and lead, poured in upon the committees and conventions from every quarter. Some localities had a few muskets but no powder, some had powder but no flints, some could boast small amounts of everything, but none, apparently, had a sufficient store of any essential item.[10] The local committees could do nothing but make recommendations which had the effect of throwing the problem back on the volunteers, but the provincial congresses and conventions, when they assembled some weeks after Lexington, incorporated the volunteers as part of the militia and took steps to arm and equip them.

In the matter of military equipment, as in all things pertaining to militia, the provisional governments of 1775 followed the practices and traditions of the colonial period, requiring the militia, first by recommendation and later by law, to purchase their own arms and

---

[5]For examples of colonial militia laws see: *Arch. of Md.*, I, 77; W. Hening, *Statutes at Large of Va.*, I, 528.

[6]H. L. Osgood, *The American Colonies During the Eighteenth Century*, I, 500.

[7]The Dartmouth Papers containing the questions and answers are in manuscript form in the William L. Clements Library, Ann Arbor, Mich.

[8]A. C. Flick, *Loyalism in New York*, p. 23- W. C. Abbott, *New York in the American Revolution*, Ch. V; *Minutes of the Provincial Congress and Committee of Safety of New Jersey. 1774-1776*, pp. 1-19; C. H. Lincoln, *The Revolutionary Movements in Pennsylvania*, pp. 40-52.

[9]*Proceedings of the Conventions of Maryland, 1774-1775*, p. 8.

[10]*Min. of the Prov. Cong. of N.J.*, 1774-1776, p. 165; *Jour. of the Prov. Cong. of N.Y.*, I, 527, II, 286, 313; *Arch. of Md.*, XII, 80, passim; *Arch. of Pa.*, V, 114; *Col. Rec. of Pa.*, X, 322; *Statutes at Large of Pa.*, IX 529, 557; Force, *Am. Arch.*, (4th ser.), II, 469, 485, 516, 542, 548.

*The Continental line was not blessed with an abundance of equipment. Drawing by Count J. Onfroy de Breville ("Job") in Frederick T. Hill, Washington, Man of Action.*

accoutrements.[11] Additional measures were passed, however, to provide a supply of public arms which could be loaned to the militia if and when they should be called into active service. The Convention of Maryland authorized the Council of Safety "to contract for, purchase, and provide 5,000 stand of arms," to remain the property of the province available for the use of the militia in time of need.[12] A commission was appointed in New Jersey to provide 3,000 stand of arms, and the Pennsylvania Council of Safety urged the county authorities to procure immediately "a proper number of good new firelocks, with bayonets fitted to them, cartridge boxes with twenty-three rounds in every box and knapsacks," a "proper number" being 4,500.[13] Under directions from the Provincial Congress the City Committee of New York ordered the arms belonging to the city to be equipped with steel ramrods and announced that it was prepared to purchase arms from any person who had them to sell.[14]

It was undoubtedly the intention of the various revolutionary governments, in the early summer of 1775, to use whatever military supplies their measures produced to arm and equip their militia, and there is nothing in the record of their proceedings to indicate that they contemplated any diversion to other purposes. Unfortunately for their intentions, however, very little of the equipment ever found its way into the hands of the militia, and that little did not remain long, because the appearance of new and more urgent problems shortly forced a change in their plans.

On May 25, 1775, Congress asked New York to raise 3,000 men to garrison the fortifications at Kings Bridge and other places along the Hudson.[15] In June, Congress requested six companies of riflemen from Pennsylvania, and two from Maryland.[16] In

October, New Jersey was asked to raise two battalions and Pennsylvania one battalion for the army.[17] Congress agreed to assume the cost of arming and equipping such troops, but asked the several governments to find the necessary articles and place them in their hands.[18] In view of the scarcity this was a real problem and one which increased in difficulty as Congress called for an ever increasing number of troops.

There was no certainty in 1775 that the militia of the middle states would ever be called for active service. It was in fact generally hoped that they would not be.[19] It was, however, imperative that troops raised for immediate field service be armed as speedily as possible, and the available supplies were consequently diverted to that end. By September 2, the Provincial Congress of New York had collected 4,500 pounds of powder and an order was issued for its distribution to the militia, but before the order could be executed it was cancelled and the powder was sent to General Schuyler.[20] On December 30, the Pennsylvania militia were ordered to return all the firearms belonging to the province, that they might be employed in arming the boats for the defense of the Delaware.[21] The Maryland Council of Safety, March 6, 1776, ordered the militia officers to deliver all the arms, then in the hands of their companies, to Continental officers, because the public service required the arming of the regular troops.[22] By March 13, it was reported on good authority that the arming of two battalions for the Continental service had drained New Jersey of its best arms.[23] Measures of this sort soon took most of the "public arms" out of the hands of the militia, but the needs of the army were yet so great that those

[11]*Jour. of the Prov. Cong. of N.Y.*, I, 114; *Min. of the Prov. Cong. of N.J.*, 1775-1776, p. 239; *Statutes at Large of Pa.*, VIII, 502-528.

[12]*Arch. of Md.*, XI, 30.

[13]*Statutes at Large of Pa.*, VIII, 488.

[14]Force, *Am. Arch.*, (4th ser.), II, 530, 531.

[15]*Jour. of the Cont. Cong.*, II, 59-60.

[16]*Ibid.*, p. 89.

[17]*Ibid.*, III, 285, 291.

[18]*Ibid.*, III, 441, IV, 415.

[19]The issues were not clearly drawn. War-like preparations were mixed with peaceful petitions, a long war was not contemplated and Independence was not seriously thought of.

[20]*Jour. of the Prov. Cong. of N.Y.*, I, 135, 168.

[21]*Arch. of Pa.* IV, 694.

[22]*Arch. of Md.*, XI, 203.

[23]Duer, *Life of Sterling*, p. 140; *Min. of the Prov. Cong. of N.J.*, 1774-1776, p. 341.

privates who owned arms were urged to sell them to agents appointed for that purpose, which also depleted the privately owned stock.[24]

On March 14, 1776, Congress adopted a resolution, calling upon the states to disarm the loyalists and recommending that the confiscated arms be applied, in the first place to arming the Continental troops, in the next place to arming such provincial troops as each state might raise for its own defense, and the residue to the militia.[25] This resolution, adopted in substance by all of the provisional governments, is perhaps the best statement of the policy pursued during the rest of the war.[26] The wisdom of it is scarcely open to question. In the light of existing conditions it was much wiser to arm the troops in the field than to leave arms in the hands of a civilian militia who might or might not be called upon to use them, but the fact remains that there was very little "residue" for the militia.

Occasionally thereafter, small dribbles of powder and shot were issued to "well affected militia" with the admonition that they were "not to depend on any further supplies at the public expense,"[27] but for the most part their repeated appeals were answered by regretful refusals on the ground that there were not enough arms to supply the regular troops.[28] The militia were thus left very largely to secure their own military effects by purchase in the midst of an appalling shortage.

The policy of requiring the militia to purchase their own equipment was a failure from first to last. For one thing, the cost of a complete outfit was prohibitive in a great many cases. The list of articles necessary to equip a militia man, as specified by Congress, included ten separate items.[29] It has not been

but "a good musket with a bayonet attached thereto" was undoubtedly the most expensive item. In the summer of 1775, a reasonably good musket could be had for four pounds ten shillings.[30] By the end of the year, however, the shortage had forced the price up. The Provincial Congress of New Jersey was forced to remove the price limit in February, 1776, and contract for firearms "upon the best terms in their power without any limitation, or restriction."[31] In May, Mr. Stephen West, a gun broker in Maryland, was holding out for a price of six pounds, twelve shillings and six pence.[32] By August 1777, gunsmiths in Philadelphia were demanding upwards of nine pounds, and a year later twenty rifles sold in Pennsylvania for thirty pounds each.[33] Cartridge boxes rose from nine to twelve shillings and knapsacks, flints, tomahawks, powder and shot advanced in proportion.[34] A complete outfit must, there-

---

[24]*Ibid.*, p. 342; *Jour. of the Prov. Cong. of N.Y.*, II, 309-310.

[25]*Jour. of the Cont. Cong.*, IV, 205.

[26]*Proc. of the Conv. of Md.*, p. 75; *Min. of the Prov. Cong. of N.J. 1774-1776*, p. 486; *Jour. of the Prov. Cong. of N.Y.*, I, 528; *Statutes at Large of Pa.*, VIII, 560.

[27]*Jour. of the Prov. Cong. of N.Y.*, I, 244.

[28]*Arch. of Md.*, XI, 276.

[29]A good musket that will carry an ounce ball, with a bayonet, steel ramrod, worm, priming wire and brush, a cutting sword or tomahawk, a cartridge box to hold twenty-three rounds, twelve flints, and a knapsack. *Jour.*

[30]*Min. of the Prov. Cong. of N.J.*, 1774-1776, p. 247; *Arch. of Md.*, XI, 26; *Col. Rec. of Pa.*, X, 711.

[31]*Min. of the Prov. Cong. of N.J.*, 1774-1776, p. 358.

[32]Mr. West's price is of interest since he submitted an itemized list of the materials and labor necessary to produce a musket, with the cost of each; *Arch. of Md.*, XI, 407-408.

| | | |
|---|---:|---:|
| Barrel | £ 1, | 15 |
| Loop for sling swivels | 2 | |
| A screw and nut for the butt | 1 | |
| Fixing loops and sights to barrel | 3 | |
| A set of brass mountings which must be polished and filed | 15 | |
| A stock | 15 | |
| A lock | 15 | |
| A rammer | 5 | |
| Screw and pins for butt, guards, and loops | 5 | |
| A spring for the rammer | 1 | |
| Polishing the barrel | 5 | |
| Two slings swivels and screws | 5 | |
| A Bayonet scabbard hook and fixings | 4 | 6 |
| A good bayonet | 12 | 6 |
| To a workman putting all parts together, fixing lock, brasses, loops, swivel and fitting in the lock to the stock | 5 | |
| A woolen case for gun including thread and making | 2 | 6 |

£ 6, 12s, 6d

[33]*Arch. of Pa.*, V, 520, VI, 467.

[34]*Min. of the Prov. Cong. of N.J.*, 1774-1776, p. 247.

fore, have demanded a cash outlay of from ten to fifteen pounds. There were many men who could not afford such an expenditure, and there were also many who could have purchased equipment but who were not in sympathy with the cause to spend money for that purpose.[35] The prohibitive cost of arms and disaffection were not, however, the only causes of the failure.

The incomplete returns of the period indicate that considerably numbers of men possessed arms in 1775 and that others did purchase them during the first wave of enthusiasm following Lexington. But such arms were invariably regarded as private property. The owners were loath to take them into service where they might be lost or injured and they would seldom lend them even when promised compensation.[36] This reluctance increased as the war progressed because governments were ever quick to make promises but very slow in paying for lost or damaged arms.[37] The practice of hiding arms to avoid

taking them into service became so general during the final years of the war that it was made the subject of legislation imposing penalties.[38] It does not appear from the records, however, that the laws served as any material check, most men would not purchase arms and powder and donate them to the public.[39]

All hopes that the militia would be left at home for occasional local needs were abruptly ended June 3, 1776, when Congress called for 16,750 militia from the middle states to augment the army, and expressly requested that this number be armed and equipped by the states.[40] Obviously no adequate store of arms and equipment was in the possession of any of the state governments and no sufficient quantity was ever accumulated during the campaign. By July 19, the Maryland militia were flocking into Annapolis every day, "but many of them without arms, blankets, or any other necessaries."[41]

The Militia of Ulster County, New York marched without ammunition because there was none to give them, and there was in general among all regiments an "abysmal lack of guns, cartridge boxes, and every other accoutrement of war."[42] Everywhere it was the same story. By January 9, 1777, there were upwards of 2,200 militia in Philadelphia waiting for arms.[43] Companies and regiments were started for camp "half armed and totally devoid of blankets, tents, and camp utensils."[44] Some detachments were halted on the march because their arms were out of repair and unfit for service, but many were sent on with only a vague hope that they would find equipment some where on the

[35] The extent of disaffection was much greater than is frequently supposed. In such areas as Somerset, Sussex and Worcester Counties in Maryland, Bergen and Burlington, New Jersey, Lancester and York in Pennsylvania and Kings, Queens, Richmond, Suffolk and Westchester, New York, there were so many tories as to render the militia organization relatively ineffective.

[36] *Arch. of Md.*, XII, 32, 56, 80, 106, 112, 143; *Arch., of Pa.*, V, 570.

[37] General Potter, commanding a detachment of Pennsylvania militia at Wilmington in 1777, was amazed at the unarmed condition of the men. After investigating the cause he reported as follows: "One reason why the militia came so ill armed is that they are afraid if they lose their arms in battle they will not be paid for, as proof of their fears they give an instance of the arms lost at Ft. Washington. There are great numbers who have arms but they will not bring them into the field." *Arch. of Pa.*, V, 570.

The Executive Council, September 4, 1777, promised that the state would pay for any privately owned equipment which was lost in battle, or captured. *Col. Rec. of Pa.*, XI, 291. In May 1778, however, the people were still complaining about arms which had been lost for over two years and for which no payment had been made. *Arch. of Pa.*, VI, 547-548. In Nov. 1779, no payment had been made, and Richard McCalister, a county lieutenant protested to the Council that the law was so poorly worded that no official had any responsibility in the matter. "It has soured the minds of many" he wrote, "the people tease me daily for their pay and I am at a loss what answer to give." *Arch. of Pa.*, VIII, 16. See also *Arch. of Md.*, XVI. 346-348. XLV, 403.

[38] *Arch. of Pa.*, VI, 547-548; *Laws of the State of Maryland.*, 1781. Chap. X; *Journal and Proceedings of the Legislative Council of the State of New Jersey.*, 1780. Chap. XXXI.

[39] It was generally futile to levy fines on militia, since there was very little prospect that they would be collected.

[40] *Jour. of the Cont. Cong.*, IV, 410-412.

[41] *Arch. of Md.*, XII, 80, 190-191.

[42] *Jour. of the Prov. Cong. of N.Y.*, II, 286, 304, 313.

[43] *Arch. of Pa.*, V, 178.

[44] *Ibid.;Arch. of Md.*, XII, 238, 246, 258; *Jour. of the Prov. Cong. of N.Y.*, I, 527; *Col. Rec. of Pa.*, X, 665.

march, or obtain it at camp when they arrived.[45] It is, in fact, impossible to discover a fully furnished militia regiment in the records of the campaign of 1776. Despite the distressing aspects of the picture, however, considerable numbers were armed and equipped in a manner, and the important fact to be noted is that the vast majority of these did not carry their own arms but drew their supplies from public stores furnished in part by their own governments and in part by the Continental Congress.[46]

It was apparent from the beginning of the campaign that militia troops were exceedingly hard on equipment of all kinds. Being virtually without training they did not know how to use arms, or care for them, and they were notoriously careless as to the fate of public equipment, and even private property if it did not happen to belong to them. Moreover, many were not above stealing public arms and selling them. According to the universal testimony of the officers who tried to command them, they often left in a "scandalous manner without returning the ammunition and other public stores."[47] Notwithstanding the most positive orders" they carried away the public arms "and in many cases exchanged them for an inferior sort."[48] Such arms as they did return were frequently found to be "exceedingly out of repair owing in many instances to the shameful neglect and abuse of the persons in whose hands they have been."[49] Washington complained bitterly to Congress of the great consumption and waste of arms by the militia. "Many of these,"

he said, "threw their arms away, some lost them, whilst others deserted and took them away."[50] Towards the end of the campaign he apprehended the "most fatal consequences" unless some check could be speedily applied to the general wastefulness and destructive propensities of the militia. "The mischief " he said "is not confined to desertion alone. They stay until they are properly equipped to render essential service, and by that means plunder the public of the necessaries that were at first otherwise intended and would be better applied."[51]

The campaign of 1776 taught both Continental and state authorities that it was extremely unwise to arm militia until the moment they entered service, and thereafter, throughout the rest of the war, the most positive orders were given that arms and equipment were to be doled out at the last possible minute and collected immediately after the term of service expired.[52] The idea that the militia could or would purchase their own arms and accoutrements was given over by Maryland and Pennsylvania. In those states the militia acts of 1777 provided that arms and equipment sufficient for two classes in each company should be provided at the expense of the state. Such arms were not to be issued to the militia but to remain in the custody of the county lieutenants who were to issue them only to militia going into active service.[53] The legislature of New Jersey continued in its militia regulation to give lip service to the principle of private purchase, but at the same time made provision for a partial supply at public expense.[54] In New

---

[45]Arch. of Md., XII, 258; Washington, Writings, (Ford ed.), V, 119, passim.

[46]Urged repeatedly by the states and prodded by Washington, Congress did what it could. Twenty thousand dollars was appropriated to arm the militia intended for the Flying Camp. Some old arms belonging to Congress were sent to Pennsylvania, and the secret committee was directed to deliver arms to Maryland troops. Journal, V, 558, 566, 627, 706; Washington, Writings, (Ford ed.), IV, 244.

[47]George Clinton to the New York Convention, Public Papers of Geo. Clinton, I, 441.

[48]General McDougall to the New York Convention, Jour. of the Prov. Cong. of N.Y., I, 781.

[49]Arch. of Pa., V, 558.

[50]Washington, Writings, (Ford ed.), V, 119.

[51]Ibid., 186.

[52]Jour. of the Prov. Cong. of N.Y., I, 720; Arch. of Md., XXI 102, 105; Public Papers of Geo. Clinton, V, 333; Arch. of Pa., IX, 365; Washington, Writings, (Ford ed.), VII, 190.

[53]Laws of the State of Md., 1777, Chap. XVII, Sec. XVI; Statutes at Large of Pa., IX, 84. According to statutes the militia were divided into eight classes, which classes were to take their tour of duty in rotation. Arms sufficient for two classes meant, therefore, arms for one fourth of the militia.

[54]Acts of the State of N.J., 1777, Chap. XX, Sec. I; Ibid., 1778, Chap. XXII, Sec. 6.

York the requirement was maintained under the theory, as Governor Clinton said, that "the militia must be induced, if possible, to provide the means of defence . . . for they waste with a lavish hand all of the supplies furnished them by the public."[55] But Clinton admitted on many occasions that it never worked.[56]

The policy of issuing equipment only to that portion of the militia going into immediate service at the last minute and collecting it at the first possible moment when they were discharged may have saved some public supplies, but it did not materially improve the situation, because it could not stop the misuse and destruction of supplies while they remained in the hands of the militia during their tour of duty, and because the militia-man never developed the habit of waiting to be disarmed when his term of service expired.

The militia records for the years 1771-1781 are fragmentary and incomplete, but they present convincing evidence that the waste, destruction, and thievery of public equipment continued throughout the war.[57] On October 8, 1777, General Armstrong, who commanded the brigade of Pennsylvania militia then in service, wrote to the Executive council:

> I can give you but a faint idea of our many perplexities, among which is the villainous practice of theiving Guns, Gunlocks, and Ammunition, more especially on hasty and night movements which I could not have imagined the militia capable of.[58]

Early in May, 1778, ammunition was released by the Board of War to General Roberdeau for distribution to the frontier militia. He issued it to them on the occasion of an alarm which proved to be abortive, but a few days later when the Indians did appear "there was scarcely a cartridge to be found among them."[59] In September 1779, President Reed complained to William Henry, city lieutenant of Philadelphia, that the state was continually under heavy expense for the repair of arms delivered to the militia. "Sometimes," he said, "being out only a few days they return the Arms in such condition as to take considerable time to repair them."[60] Washington estimated August 20, 1780, that "the consumption of Provisions, arms, accoutrements, and stores of every kind" had been doubled during the war by reason of the "carelessness and licentiousness incident to militia and irregular troops," and he cried out a month later: "no magazines can be equal to the demands of an army of militia, and none ever needed economy more than ours."[61]

There was no improvement in 1781. In fact the situation was, if possible worse than it had ever been. Governor Clinton, who knew the militia well, found the whole state of New York miserably wanting in arms and ammunition. Great quantities had from time to time been issued to them but he could not supply more from a depleted store because it would only be wasted.[62] When the Maryland militia were called in August 1781, the arms, which had been repaired and cleaned a few months past were found to be "rendered useless by rust."[63] The Council could not arm a fraction of the militia called for service. Arms were issued in lots of twenty-five and fifty to supply the needs of entire counties, and when a county lieutenant had received his meagre share he could get no more.[64] The situation in Pennsylvania was so bad that President Reed, after numerous appeals for arms had reached him, wanted to know "whether every time the militia go out they expect to be supplied with new arms; if they do" said he, "it is the most extraordinary establishment in the World."[65] It was indeed "a most extraordinary establishment," for it was only necessary to place arms in the hands of the militia to have them disappear or be

---

[55]*Public Papers of Geo. Clinton*, VI, 765.

[56]*Ibid.*, 766, V, 104, 733.

[57]The illustrative material which follows in the above paragraph has been taken at random from a great mass of documentary material, all of which tells the same story.

[58]*Arch. of Pa.*, V, 655; see also *Public Papers of Geo. Clinton III*, 123.

[59]*Arch. of Pa.*, VI, 587; *Arch. of Md.*, XXI, 396.

[60]*Arch. of Pa.*, VII, 711.

[61]Washington, *Writings*, (Ford ed.), VIII, 395, 441.

[62]*Public Papers of Geo. Clinton*, VI, 765-766.

[63]*Arch. of Md.*, XLV, 52.

[64]*Ibid.*, 389, 390, 392, 394, passim.

[65]*Arch. of Pa.*, IX, 271.

returned almost useless.

The public arms carried away by the militia were seldom recovered, because they were frequently hidden "and few cared to give information to the magistrates."[66] Even when such arms were located "the offenders offered defiance on the presumption that the state must offer proof and prove the property" and since many of the arms were unmarked, such proof was hard to obtain.[67] Powder and shot, with no possible means of identification, simply vanished.

It is extremely doubtful whether any measures within the power of the revolutionary state governments could have stopped the continuous waste of equipment, but conditions might not have been quite so bad if the militia officers had done their duty even passably well. It was their duty to inspect and check the equipment of their men at stated periods, and to take charge of all public accoutrements and keep them in good order. Above all they were enjoined to keep the executive department fully informed as to the state of their troops by means of frequent returns. In such matters, however, as in most others, they were negligent and remiss.[68] Despite repeated appeals they made returns but seldom, and such as they did make were likely to be incomplete by reason of their incompetence and lack of knowledge.[69] Because of such negligence on the part of officers, the various state executives, who were nominally commanders-in-chief of the militia, were frequently kept in ignorance as to

the state of the militia for more than a year at a time.[70] During the greater part of the war they could not have improved bad situations had they known of them, but there were occasions when some military stores were available which could have been sent to areas most in need of them.[71] There were, of course, some officers who made returns with reasonable regularity and from such reports it is clear that the shortage was chronic,[72] but for the most part the average militia officer inspected the arms and equipment of his men and looked to the condition of the magazine after the militia were called for immediate service, at which time he discovered that any ammunition previously issued had been wasted and that muskets were either non existent or badly out of repair.

It is clear from the factors considered that the militia of the middle states were never equipped to render much in the way of effective field service. The original shortage of war-like equipment and the early diversion of the available supply to the Continental army got them off to a very bad start in 1776. Thereafter a combination of regulations which were never enforced, official incompetence and their own wastefulness and "lack of public virtue," kept them in a chronically unarmed condition. Tradition pictures the

---

[66] loc. cit.

[67] Arch. of Pa., VIII, 96.

[68] Arch. of Md., XI, 90, 127, 128, 145, 214, 474, 522, XII. 261, 472, XXI, 258, 296; Arch. of Pa., VI, 486; Force, Am. Arch., (5th ser.), II, 366; Jour. of the Prov. Cong. of N.Y., I, 800, II, 203; Public Papers of Geo. Clinton, II, 365, III, 522, 524, IV, 123, 211, 391; T. Sedgwick, Life of Wm. Livingston, pp. 197-198.

[69] Militia officers needed no qualifications except the ability to get elected. Between the periods of active service they were civilians engaged in the business of making a living and they were not expected to drop their private pursuits on accepting a commission. Moreover, they received no pay for performing their duties, except when in active service.

[70] Governor Clinton sent one of his numerous requests for a return of the militia, January 9, 1778. The commanding officer of Albany County, reported as follows February 5: "I am sorry that I am not able to send your Excellency a return of my brigade . . . I have had no returns made me from my colonels since July, 1776. I can furnish your Excellency with this but am well convinced that great alterations have taken place since that time." Public Papers of Geo. Clinton, II, 741. see also Arch. of Md., XXI, 80; T. Sedgwick, Life of Wm. Livingston, p. 283.

[71] Arch. of Md., XLV, 256, 360; Public Papers of Geo. Clinton, IV, 123-125, 211, 391, VI, 95, 704.

[72] Colonel Samuel Drake of Westchester County, New York, made frequent reports which were complete and informative. On August 5, 1780, he had a total of 446 men in his regiment and their equipment consisted of 212 guns, 146 bayonets, 167 cartridge boxes, no powder and no lead. Public Papers of Geo. Clinton, VI, 104. Joseph Beall, lieutenant of Prince George County, Maryland, reported July 3, 1780, that he could find only one piece belonging to the public and "but 246 pieces fit to fire in the whole county." Arch. of Md., XLV, 4.

militia as being mustered and trained in their various localities between periods of active service and as showing a steady improvement during the course of the war,[73] but the tradition is not in accord with the facts. Laws prescribing periodic musters were on the statute books as an essential feature of all militia codes, but they were not observed. In all of the records pertaining to the militia, there are only a few scattered references to musters and training, and it is quite obvious that one of the primary reasons for the failure was that

[73]The foundation for the tradition was laid during the War of Independence. In April, 1777, the Executive Council of Pennsylvania issued a statement to the effect that Philadelphia had been saved during the previous winter "by the vigorous and manly efforts of a few brave associators who generally stept forward in defence of their country." William Livingston spoke in September 1777 of "the real bravery of our militia and the terror with which they have frequently struck the enemy," and the *New Jersey Gazette,* a Livingston press, carried articles praising the progress of the militia in the art of war with frequent references to the numerous occasions upon which they had filled the enemy with awe. President Reed of Pennsylvania stated publicly in 1779, "that the history of all countries, our own experience, and the testimony of our enemies, all concur to prove that a well regulated militia . . . is the best defence against an invading enemy and the surest safeguard of public liberty." The Maryland council claimed in August 1781, that the militia had acquired a confidence which would "stimulate them to conduct which would not disgrace regulars." In view of the records it is difficult to escape the conclusion reached by Washington that the virtues of the militia system were extolled by men "whose credulity easily swallowed every vague story in support of a favorite hypothesis."

the militia had few or no arms and little ammunition with which to train. Moreover the efforts of both Continental and state authorities were directed, from 1776 to 1781, towards arming whatever portion of the militia were to take the field, not to arm and equip the vaster numbers who made up the reserve force at home. Whenever militia in service could be caught in time their arms were taken away, so that many went home as empty handed as they had come. If they escaped with the equipment, they possessed stolen property which they took pains to conceal, along with any arms and powder which they may have acquired by purchase.

In August 1780, William Livingston said "our militia through five years of war are become inured to arms."[74] As a piece of war-time propaganda uttered for public consumption such a statement is understandable, but Livingston knew better, for he had had experience with the militia both as an officer in the field and as a governor of New Jersey. On previous occasions he had said many things not so complimentary, and he would have been more accurate on this occasion if he had stated from his knowledge and experience that through five years of war the average militia man seldom had a gun in his hand except during his brief tour of duty, and that the spectacle of a fully accoutered militia man was indeed a rarity.

[74]*Selections from the Revolutionary Correspondence of the Executive of New Jersey,* p. 250.

# IRREGULAR BUT EFFECTIVE: PARTIZAN WEAPONS TACTICS IN THE AMERICAN REVOLUTION, SOUTHERN THEATRE*

## By Jac Weller**

MUCH of the Revolutionary fighting in the South was quite different from that in the North. More than 80 per cent of the actions in the war were in the Southern Theatre.[1] It would seem likely that more men were killed and wounded south of the Dan than north of it. The serious fighting in the North ended at Monmouth on 28 June 1778. North Carolina Patriots and Tories were butchering each other even after 1782.[2]

The type of warfare in any conflict is dependent upon the participants, local geography, political situations, transportation facilities, weapons available, and other factors. In the South, many of these differed from their Northern counterparts. There were, of course, many similarities in the Revolutionary fighting in both sections; however, the Southern partizans employed weapons tactics unknown in the North. To one

acquainted with the fighting around Boston in 1775, in New York and New Jersey in 1776 through 1778, and around Philadephia and Saratoga in 1777, King's Mountain, Cowpens, and Guilford seem like a different war. The dissimilarity is even more pronounced in the hundreds of smaller partizan actions so important to the final American victory in the South.

## EUROPEAN AND AMERICAN FORMAL WEAPONS TACTICS

Let us look briefly at the way the British and Hessian professional soldiers and American Continentals fought. In Europe battles were decided by a combination of musket- and bayonet-armed infantry, sabre-armed (and sometimes lightly-armored) cavalry, and n u m e r o u s, medium-weight field-artillery pieces. This is to some extent an over-simplification: The infantry also had a variety of edged and pole weapons and auxiliary firearms; the cavalry had pistols, carbines, and sometimes lances; the artillerymen were equipped for individual combat. The European commanders relied upon the iron discipline of seasoned infantry in close order, firing precise volleys before closing with the bayonet. They also employed the smashing power of well-ordered sabre-armed cavalry charging on heavy horses shoulder to shoulder. Relatively heavy and numerous artillery pieces were sometimes a vital factor.

During the Revolution, the fighting in the North generally followed the basic European pattern; but there were two considerable differences, along with a shift of em-

*The Southern Theatre as commanded by Nathaniel Greene comprised Georgia, the Carolinas, Virginia, Delaware, and Maryland. However, for the purposes of this article, only the fighting in Georgia and the Carolinas will be considered; most of the serious fighting in Virginia was done by the main Continental Army under Washington and generals immediately under his command. The partizan actions were mainly south of the Dan.

**Jac Weller is a military historian and authority on firearms.

[1]Edward McCrady, *The History of South Carolina in the Revolution* (2 vols.; New York, 1901). Volume I, p. 852, lists 36 identified actions in South Carolina in 1780 alone. There were 23 more identified actions in the same state in the first three and a half months of 1781, not counting Continental battles. Fanning, the Tory, fought 40 actions; David Fanning, *Colonel Fanning's Narrative* (Toronto, 1906), *passim.*

[2]Robert O. DeMond, *The Loyalists in North Carolina during the Revolution* (Durham, 1940), pp. 118 and *passim.*

phasis in one particular. First, cavalry in the European sense just did not work in America. Geographical conditions were against shock tactics. As late as 1776, Washington thought so little of cavalry that he sent home the only mounted unit in his army.[3] Only two of the 24 cavalry regiments of the British army fought in America during the Revolution, whereas some 52 of the 70 infantry regiments fought here at one time or another.[4] Even when cavalry was present in the North, it served for reconnaissance, screening, outpost fighting, and pursuit; it was of no importance for actual battlefield combat.

Second, field artillery even in the North was smaller and sometimes less numerous than in Europe. Heavy pieces and their greater weight of ammunition and auxiliary equipment could not negotiate the American roads, trails, and distances.[5] The lighter pieces nevertheless were of extreme importance in some actions in the North.[6]

Finally, even in the North, there was a distinct tendency from the first to emphasize light infantry tactics and open-order skirmishing. Both British and American commanders understood this type of fighting. It was used more here than in Europe; however, its employment in the North was neither so extensive nor so successful as is sometimes believed.[7]

Many of the same British and Continental infantry units served first in the North and then in the South.[8] Those fought in approximately the same manner in both theatres. The field artillery was also basically the same, although the pieces were even fewer and smaller in the South.[9] Line infantry armed with muskets and bayonets was the principal reliance of both sides in the pitched battles where British regulars faced American Continentals. Just the same, if the British and Tories had had only the Continental regulars to contend with, they would have won a complete victory in the summer of 1780. The Southern Patriot militia or partizan forces, acting alone or in combination with Continentals, were the salvation of the American cause. These irregular forces had neither the arms nor the weapons training and discipline for formal tactics; but they could fight in their own way very well indeed.

Let use look carefully at the weapons tactics of the Southern volunteer militia. We will discuss the fighting of the Patriot (or Whig) partizans, for the Southern Tories used the same patterns. In the South, even the British regulars adopted in some measure the weapons and tactics of the American partizans opposing them.[10]

## Factors Influencing Partizan Weapons Tactics

The fighting of the irregular forces was based to a very large extent upon four fac-

[3] John C. Fitzpatrick, ed., *The Writings of George Washington* (39 vols.; Washington, 1932), V, 286. For Washington's opinion of cavalry at this time, July 1776, see *ibid.*, pp. 240-242.

[4] Edward E. Curtis, *The Organization of the British Army in the American Revolution* (New Haven, 1926), p. 151.

[5] Hoffman Nickerson, *The Turning Point of the Revolution* (New York, 1928), p. 359, passes on the statement of Major Williams of Burgoyne's artillery "that once a 12-pounder was taken from the artillery park and moved into the American Wilderness" it was lost.

[6] Jac Weller, "Guns of Destiny," *Military Affairs* Vol. XX (Spring 1956).

[7] The early rifle companies raised by the Continental Congress were not a complete success, as will be seen.

[8] All British and Hessian units serving in the South were at least stationed for a time in the North; most fought in both theatres. Many Continental regiments from North Carolina, Virginia, Maryland, and Delaware also fought in both theatres.

[9] In the North it was usually 6-pounders and 12-pounders, in the South 3-pounders and 6-pounders.

[10] Parts at least of several British Infantry regiments were mounted. The infantry Brown Bess musket was shortened for more convenient use. British and Tory riflemen were quite effective in the later stages of the war.

tors. First, the Southerner of this period was usually an Indian fighter and hunter; he was trained in using his weapons as required in these activities. Second, in general, the partizans had only their personal arms plus whatever they were able to capture that was largely similar to their own.[11] Third, the militia of the South were inseparable from their horses; neither the British nor American commanders were able to get these men to march long distances on foot,[12] although serious fighting was usually done dismounted. Fourth, the country over which the war was fought in the South was by Northern and European standards still largely wilderness. We will discuss each of these factors at some length.

## INDIAN FIGHTING

Several of the Continental commanders and all the Patriot partizan leaders in the South had experience fighting Indians. Dan Morgan was with Braddock in 1756, and at many another more successful Indian action.[13] William Moultrie, Francis Marion, Isaac Huger, and Andrew Pickens were officers in the victorious campaigns against the Cherokees in 1761.[14] Pickens, Richardson, and Rutherford, even during the Revolution, were often fighting the Indian allies of Brit-

ain. Sumter's early life was partly spent in the British army fighting Indians and partly in guiding a group of their chiefs to London; he accompanied them home as an Indian trader.[15] The lesser and younger leaders of the Carolinas almost all served in the Snow campaign of the winter of 1775 and the late summer campaign in 1776 against the Cherokees.

This early experience was not confined to leaders only. The Hill Country of the Carolinas, settled hardly a quarter century at the beginning of the Revolution, was still subject to murderous attack from stealthy parties of Cherokees and exasperating larceny by Catawbas.[16] Boys who grew up in these areas learned early to take care of their hair and their property. Even the Low Country around Charleston could remember the deadly peril of the Yamassee war of 1715. A trader was scalped by Indians near the gates of the city as late as 1752.[17] Georgia was even closer to potential savagery.

Southerners knew how to fight in the Indian fashion. Further, they had confidence in their ability to beat Indians at their own game. Early in the 18th Century, a Cherokee or Yamassee was a match for a white man, sometimes more than a match for him.[18] The tide suddenly turned; the whites learned to take cover, move almost as silently, shoot far more accurately, effect surprises and ambushes, and, most importantly of all, develop the loose teamwork so necessary in all successful irregular fighting. These abilities were still available when British regulars and Tories replaced the Indians as primary enemies.

---

[11]One of the most effective measures for suppressing the numerous Tories was their systematic disarming by home search and confiscation. The partizans also took weapons from the British regulars and sometimes stole them from the Continentals. Chalmers G. Davidson, *Piedmont Partizan* (1951), p. 69.

[12]George Washington Greene, *The Life of Nathaniel Greene* (New York, 1871), p. 225, quotes Greene as being "sorely troubled by their insisting upon the wasteful custom of going into service on horseback." Many other similar complaints were made by commanders on both sides.

[13]James Graham, *The Life of General Daniel Morgan* (New York, 1859), *passim*.

[14]William Dobein James, *A Sketch of the Life of Brigadier General Francis Marion* (Charleston, 1824), p. 17. This was reproduced in Marietta, Georgia, 1948. Also see Benson J. Lossing, *Pictorial Field-Book of the Revolution* (2 vols.; New York, 1855), II, 140.

[15]Anne King Gregorie, *Thomas Sumter* (Columbia, 1931), *passim*.

[16]Davidson, *op. cit.*, p. 7.

[17]David Ramsey, *History of South Carolina* (Newberry, S. C., 1858), p. 94.

[18]Douglas Southall Freeman, *George Washington* (6 vols.; New York, 1948-1954) I, *passim*. The Indians had an ascendency psychologically until about 1758.

## WEAPONS

The arms of the Southern partizan were as important to his way of fighting as his experience against the Indians. These were mainly the weapons with which each family lived their usual lives. Artillery was seldom used by the irregular partizan forces of the South. Although Caswell employed three small pieces at Moore's Creek,[19] his command at that battle resembled Continentals more than true volunteer militia. Marion had two field pieces with him for a short time in the fall of 1780.[20] These were abandoned in the retreat to the Downing (sometimes Drowning) Creek section of North Carolina and were never replaced. Marion preferred to be free from the burden of even the lightest field guns.

Occasionally an effort would be made by an irregular commander to utilize a captured piece of artillery. General Thomas Sumter captured one at Hanging Rock, but had no one who knew how to load and fire it.[21] Colonel Elijah Clark took one at Augusta, but had his only gunner shot a few moments later by a Tory rifleman.[22] Frequently, in the latter days of the mopping-up operations in South Carolina and Georgia, a field gun and its crew of Continental artillerymen would be placed under the command of one of the irregular leaders,[23] but such an assignment was only temporary.

Pole arms such as spears and pikes, though of some importance in Continental forces, were seldom used by the Southern partizans.[24] The limited pistol supply was used when available. Range and reliability also were not great.

As already noted, the Continental and British regular infantry relied upon the bayonet. The Southern partizan sometimes considered the weapon better for roasting a fowl than for carrying either mounted on his musket or in an expensive and clumsy sheath at his side. Besides, many militia "firelocks" were not adapted to take bayonets. There were cases of individual partizans fighting with bayonets, sometimes in most irregular ways,[25] but in general, they did not have either the weapons themselves nor the close-order discipline necessary for their effective use.

The sword, during the Revolution, was almost completely abandoned by the British and Continental infantry save for officers and sergeants. Sabres were, however, the most effective weapon for cavalry. The partizan leaders in the South were quick to realize this after Banastre Tarleton's successes at Monck's Corner, Lenud's Ferry, the Waxhaws, and Fishing Creek.

Good swords were rare in the South, even among officers.[26] There had been little use for them against the Indians.[27] Every family, no matter how humble economically, had firearms, but swords of all types were luxuries. Militia laws in all Colonies required

---

[19]C. Steadman, *The History of the . . . American War* (2 vols.; London, 1794) I, 181. Here "one 2-pounder (probably mounted in a Galloper carriage) and two swivels" are referred to. One of each of these is at Moore's Creek National Military Park.

[20]W. Gilmore Simms, *The Life of Francis Marion* (New York, 1846), p. 133.

[21]Gregorie, *op. cit.,* p. 93.

[22]Lossing, *op. cit.,* II, 510.

[23]Captain Samuel Finley's 6-pounder particularly. Henry Lee, *Memoirs of the War in the Southern Department* (2d ed; New York, 1869), *passim.*

[24]Catawba Indians fighting on the American side used spears. DeMond, *op. cit.,* p. 136. For use of polearms in Continental Forces, see Harold L. Peterson, *Arms and Armor in Colonial America* (Harrisburg, 1956), p. 287.

[25]Simms, *op. cit.,* p. 207. Marion's Sergeant McDonald stuck his bayonet in Tory Major Gainey's back while both were mounted and galloping in the same direction. The bayonet came loose from the musket, but remained fixed in the back; Gainey escaped and lived.

[26]Colonel John Donaldson to General Harrington, 30 December 1780, as quoted in Alexander Gregg, *History of the Old Cheraws* (Columbia, 1925), p. 349: "I am in great want of a good sword."

[27]Pickens did make some effort to "add swords to weapons used against the Indians." Lee, *op. cit.,* p. 527.

an able-bodied man to provide and maintain for himself a useable "firelock" and a side-arm. The latter could be a sword, a bayonet, or a hatchet. Apparently, if this provision were observed at all in the South, the sidearm was usually a hatchet.

If enough sabres were to be obtained, they had to be manufactured. Sumter, Davie, and Marion, as well as minor leaders, went to extreme lengths to provide at least a portion of their forces with sabres.[28] Country blacksmiths were set to reshaping pit or mill saws and other suitable civilian tools into crude but effective broadswords.[29]

The main reliance of Southern partizan forces was in their "firelocks" which inflicted most of the enemy casualties. There was little uniformity in the weapons themselves. These Southern shoulder weapons were in some instances quite different from those used by Northern militia. The rifle in the North had some early propaganda value and was effective in a few isolated instances, but fell finally to such low estem that it was largely replaced by muskets.[30] It took too long to load, fired too few shots before cleaning was necessary, and did not take a bayonet. Conditions in the South, however, were almost ideal for rifles. King's Mountain was only one of literally dozens of actions determined by accurate fire from rifles.

The rifle was difficult to produce and cost a great deal of money, hence, there were relatively few of them. Original and authoritative secondary sources probably refer to "rifles" when the actual arms so designated included both rifles and smoothbores.[31]

[28]Ibid., pp. 175 and 196; Gregorie, op. cit., p. 79.
[29]James, op. cit., p. 92; Simms, op. cit., p. 171; Davidson, op. cit., pp. 72, 104.
[30]Peterson, op. cit., p. 197; Fritz Kredel and Frederick P. Todd, Soldiers of the American Army, 1775-1954 (Chicago, 1954), text opp. Pl. II.
[31]Many surviving "Kentucky"- or "Pennsylvania"-type "rifles" are smoothbores. The often-repeated excuse that they were bored out for shot late in their active lives just doesn't seem credible for any large part of them.

The American partizans kept every rifle they had in service as long as possible, but the smoothbores were probably always in the majority. Anyway, a carefully-loaded medium-size smoothbore gun with a tightly-fitted bullet would shoot in the hands of a hunter accustomed to it infinitely better at 100 yards than would the Brown Bess, with its small bullet and no rear sight in the hands of an Irishman in the British infantry who had never had any instruction in marksmanship, even if the latter were firing at a range of 35 yards.

The most common muskets used by Southern partizans were probably standard British Brown Besses, which were the most common of all weapons throughout the Colonies before the war began. Large quantities of them, newly arrived from Britain, fell into the hands of the Patriots both by capture and by desertion of supposed Tories recently supplied with them.[32] French muskets in the Southern Theatre were predominantly in the hands of the Continental infantry.

Enough rifles and British muskets could not be obtained and anything that would shoot was undoubtedly used in emergencies. Most partizans fought with their own arms. A volunteer was likely to take with him the best weapon that he could procure at home, even though it were a long-barreled fowling piece of the Queen Anne type or a militia musket of the century before. There was no uniformity in bore size, lock type, or anything else. This was not as important, however, as it may seem to us today. There were few paper cartridges in partizan organizations and smoothbores were often loaded with buckshot only. Professional armorers with sup-

[32]Ferguson's command had about 1500, which were all captured at King's Mountain (Lee, op. cit., p. 173). Lieutenant Colonel Lisle led almost his entire Tory regiment into the Whig camp in the summer of 1780 immediately after they had been armed and equipped with new British muskets and other material.

plies of spare parts for field maintenance were unknown;[33] each man probably maintained his own weapon as he did at home and the more obsolete or worn weapons were exchanged for better ones when possible.

### THE HORSES OF THE PARTIZANS

The irregular warfare in the South took on a distinctive character because the Southern partizans were almost always mounted. Initially, most men brought their own animals, for horses were plentiful in the South at first. If a man lost his horse, he expected his leader to provide another; if this were not done, the man went home.[34]

These horses were usually neither powerful nor particularly fleet.[35] They were too light for shock cavalry tactics, but they were quite capable of carrying a militiaman and his arms for relatively long distances through the summer heat or winter mud. Once arrived upon the scene, Marion, as well as other partizan commanders, dismounted most of his men, but kept the animals close for pursuit or flight.[36] Marion's sabre-armed men, who fought mounted, although not numerous, were important. These as well as McCall's mounted Georgians who fought at Cowpens probably had larger and stronger-than-average horses.

Although the Patriot partizan preferred to fight seriously on foot and use his horse for transportation only, he could and often did fight on horseback, particularly when surprised. There were not enough sabres and pistols to go around, but many muskets were shortened for mounted use in emergencies.[37] A long column of mounted men charging down a narrow country road, even on Low Country horses, was dangerous, even if unarmed.

### THE TYPOGRAPHY OF THE PARTIZANS' COUNTRY

The Carolinas and Georgia were unbelievably wild at the time of the Revolution; save for a few stretches near the towns which the Patriot partizans generally avoided, the wilderness was never more than a musket shot away. In the Low Country, it was in the form of swamps and cyprus-bordered, sluggish streams. The Hill Country was still covered by long stretches of impenetrable woods between the small clearings. The mountains precluded all formal battlefield tactics of that period.

Tactics had to be fitted to the surroundings, if they were to be successful. No one could depend on good roads, or even safe navigable rivers; there weren't any of either. Distances were great; most of the country was sparsely populated and could not support heavy concentrations of men and horses, save for short periods. In each locality, the leaders who were ultimately victorious took into consideration the country. Those who lost often did not. Perhaps Marion was most outstanding in this respect. His personal sense of direction and minute knowledge of the Low Country were phenomenal. His trails survived for years, some becoming roads.[38]

### HOW THE PARTIZANS FOUGHT

Neither the partizans nor their leaders were ready in 1775 to adopt immediately a new and different mode of warfare; their tactics were in part developed during the war. The

[33]Even Greene's Continentals didn't "have a common armorer . . . nor the means of making the slightest repairs" (Greene, op. cit., p. 264).

[34]Francis Marion, usually a model lieutenant, offered his resignation to Greene over a quarrel about horses. In order to keep his men, Marion had to supply them with replacement mounts from the captured animals; there were none left for Greene. Almost overnight 75% of Marion's men left him when it was rumored that their horses were to be taken from them and given to the Continentals.

[35]Lossing, op. cit., II, 401, gives a very good resumé of what Lee, Greene, Tarleton, James, and others wrote of these animals.

[36]Lee, op. cit., p. 175.

[37]The British also followed this procedure; they shortened their Brown Besses to about a 34-inch barrel length and refitted the bayonet.

[38]James, op. cit., p. 70.

militia organizations in all the Colonies before the Revolution required a certain amount of close-order drill. The Southern militia leaders who had served under Middleton, Montgomery, and Grant against the Cherokees in 1759-1761 had a considerable respect for formal British infantry tactics. They had seen British regulars perform precisely their complicated evolutions and deliver the type of fire that won for Britain most of her 18th Century wars and was eventually to defeat Napoleon.

Tidewater militia, in part under Caswell, Ashe, and Harnett, all later Patriot leaders, although outnumbered almost two to one, beat the Regulators on the Alamance on 16 May 1771. They won a complete victory largely because of better organization, discipline, and arms. The tactics employed were local approximations of those specified for musket- and bayonet-armed infantry in the manuals of the times. Even early in the Revolution, formal tactics were in favor. At Moore's Creek on 26 February 1776, Colonels Caswell and Lillington with tidewater Patriot forces, aided by some field fortifications, defeated a considerably larger Royalist army of Highlanders and Regulators who made a disorganized and extremely imprudent attack over a partially dismantled bridge across a small but deep stream. The Patriots were following more closely than their antagonists the approved weapons tactics of the 18th Century.

Respect for and confidence in formal tactics fell almost to zero among the partizans as defeat followed defeat for the Continentals. A British force under Campbell took Savannah and Prevost threatened Charleston and defeated the Franco-American attack on Savannah. Clinton took Charleston with almost all the Continental troops in the Southern Theatre on 12 May 1780. Cornwallis beat Gates at Camden on 16 August 1780. Organized American forces, both Continental and militia, were driven from Georgia and South Carolina.

Meanwhile, however, a completely new opposition to the British cause in the South was being born. Some of these men knew little and cared less about the original political principles of the Revolution.[39] They felt strongly enough, however, once the fighting arrived at their doorsteps, to serve without pay and without hope of compensation even in the event of disabling injury. They could think and did so freely on many occasions.[40] They would serve only under leaders of their own choice and they fought best in their own most unusual manner.

Analysis of the weapons tactics of these volunteer militia forces will repay the effort. First, they could shoot. Second, both the arms and composition of these forces fitted them particularly well for surprising their enemies. Third, these commands were particularly able at both defensive and harassing operations. Fourth, they were masters of improvisation and subterfuge.

### AIMED FIRE

Aimed fire is said to be traditionally American. One hears frequently that the rifle won the Revolution. Yet almost the whole basis of this popular argument is Tim Murphy's shooting of British General Frazer at Freeman's Farm, a bit of target shooting at Boston, and the Battle of King's Mountain. In the North, as we have seen, rifles were not really practicable. In the South, however, they

---

[39]Particularly true of the Hill Country Presbyterian Scotch-Irish who until the actual British invasion of the South had little knowledge of nor interest in the arguments between the tidewater political groups and the faraway British Ministery.

[40]The Hill Country partizans as well as the Over-Mountain men usually made major decisions in open meetings in which every man had a voice; even General Daniel Morgan gave at least lip service to this principle. These strategic-decision meetings waned in the spring of 1781 when civil government and authority was to some extent restored.

were of extreme importance to the partizans. King's Mountain is the best example of aimed fire winning against musketry and bayonets in all history.

British Colonel Patrick Ferguson, himself a noted rifleman and inventor, but commanding mostly musket-armed Tory militia, was brought to bay on top of a small mountain. Ferguson had about 1,100 men; various Patriot leaders had slightly fewer Over Mountain and Hill Country militia, mostly riflemen. The Americans surrounded Ferguson and closed in, shooting from behind trees and rocks. Ferguson's men charged with fixed bayonets several times. The partizans gave in front, but closed in on the flanks of each attack, ceaselessly shooting individual enemy soldiers. The British and Tory force was annihilated and Ferguson killed.

The fight at Musgrove's Mills was smaller, but along the same lines. Some 150 partizan riflemen engaged a British Tory force of more than 450 men and utterly defeated them, inflicting 223 casualties at a cost of about a dozen of their own.[41] The British initially attacked the Patriots who were behind quickly erected breastworks and trees. Aimed fire against targets in the open did great damage. The Patriots followed up their advantage and forced the British to recross the Pacelot within point-blank range of the deadly rifles.

Cornwallis' occupation of Charlotte in the fall of 1780 was extremely unpleasant and costly for the British. The accurate fire of the Mecklenberg and Rowan riflemen kept the Royal army in a perpetual state of alarm. Foraging parties were cut off and messages failed to arrive. Even large detachments were fired at from points of vantage in the woods. Partizan marksmen picked off sentries and anyone else straying from the main camp. The British called Charlotte the "Hornet's

Nest" and abandoned it after a short stay.[42] During their time there they received almost no intelligence from the rest of the Southern Theatre.

The Low Country also possessed skillful riflemen, although not so much has been written about them. Marion had a group of them under Captains William McCottry and Gavin Witherspoon. When British Colonel Watson attacked Marion along the Black River, these Patriot riflemen initially prevented the British from crossing the river. McCottry himself is credited with killing a British officer at a range of 300 yards.[43] They caused a temporary abandonment of pieces of British artillery which had been placed at a sufficient distance from the American positions to insure comparative safety from muskets. Watson suffered so severely during several days of almost continuous long-range fighting that he had to abandon the contest. He was lucky to get away into Georgetown and lost a large portion of his force and all his baggage. Throughout this whole series of actions between Watson and Marion, aimed fire from the Low Country riflemen was extremely important.

## SURPRISE

The advantages of unexpected attack have been known as long as man has fought man individually, in small groups, or in large armies. Surprises of one type or another have been of value to able commanders in every war ever fought. However, there was a distinct tendency in the 17th and 18th Centuries in Europe towards formal fighting in which the

[41]McCrady, op. cit., pp. 689, 853.

[42]Brigadier General William Lee Davidson, in command of this area for the Patriots, did a superb job of directing and coordinating these activities. See Davidson, op. cit., passim. Charlotte may have had a rifle factory (ibid., p. 72). Davidson wanted all good rifles, even going so far as advocating that fellow commanders in other parts of Carolina take them from inhabitants regardless of political feelings (ibid., p. 83).

[43]James, op. cit., p. 101. Sergeant McDonald shot British Lieutenant Torriano at long range (ibid., p. 103).

[44]Ibid., p. 71.

unexpected was of relatively small importance. In the Revolution in the North, British flank maneuvers at Long Island and Brandywine aided greatly in giving them their victories. Washington won at Trenton and Princeton by unexpected maneuvers. Three of these four actions were surprises as to exact point of attack only. Complete surprises in the North were relatively rare. In the Southern Theatre, they were frequent. An analysis of the 65 main actions in the South shows that 23 were complete surprises. The proportion in the smaller actions was even higher.

The great master of partizan surprise was Francis Marion. Few men in any war anywhere have been his equal at this type of strategy. Marion sometimes rode as much as 60 miles along the swamp paths and marsh traces that he knew so well in order to take a British or Tory force completely by surprise.[44] They would not realize that an armed enemy force was within many miles when Marion's men struck, usually at night or at dawn. Marion's tactics aimed at inflicting maximum casualties quickly at short range. A part only of his force would actually fight mounted and with sabres;[45] the main portion would use firearms.

Marion, as well as other partizan leaders, favored multiple-pellet loads for their smoothbore weapons. There was always the chance of hitting several men with a single discharge. Marion's forces employed either about a dozen buckshot or a musket ball and three or four buckshot.[46] The loading of a musket entirely with buckshot or gooseshot seems to have been widespread throughout the Low Country of the Carolinas and Georgia.[47] There is also some evidence that one or two musket balls might be cut with a knife

so that they would come apart in flight.[48] This whole multiple-projectile idea was, of course, to inflict quickly the maximum damage at close range.

A typical example of one of Marion's surprises occurred at Tarcote in the forks of the Black a little after midnight on or about 25 September 1780. Marion with about 400 men surrounded and attacked a Tory camp commanded by Colonel Tynes with about the same number recently equipped with "new English muskets and bayonets, broadswords, and pistols."[49] The inital discharge of multi-projectile weapons was so disastrous as to lead to the immediate panicking of the Tories into the swamps nearby without inflicting a single Patriot casualty in return.

The second form of surprise common in the South was to decoy an enemy force into a trap or ambush, or to lead them into the same situation with false information. Marion frequently employed a ruse as old as war; it undoubtedly was used to a considerable extent in the actions against the Cherokees and other Indians. He would send a small mounted force toward the enemy. This force would deliberately attack, and then apparently retreat in panic. It was natural for the enemy to pursue. They were then lured within point-blank range of an ambush.

In the fall of 1781, Marion was doing very well in his section of the Low Country on both sides of the Santee. However, the British and Tories were too much for Colonel Hardin some 80 miles further south. Unknown to the enemy, Marion suddenly joined Hardin. Marion, in over-all command, devised a plan by which apparently Hardin's whole force attacked, found out they were outnumbered, and retreated in extreme disorder. The British and Tories pur-

[45]*Ibid.*, p. 59.
[46]*Ibid.*, p. 128.
[47]Gregg, *op. cit.*, p. 328.

[48]Peterson, *op. cit.*, p. 228. This specific reference is to New York City excavations; however, Southerners are known to have used this expedient in hunting before the Revolution.
[49]Simms, *op. cit.*, p. 142.

sued to within a score of yards of the main body of concealed American partizans and were badly mauled by accurate rifle fire and multi-projectile discharges from their muskets and fowling pieces.[50]

Guile was responsible for the slaughter of Pyle's Tories by Light Horse Harry Lee's Legion on 18 February 1781 in central North Carolina. Lee and his men intentionally impersonated Tarleton and Tarleton's British legion. The Tories were asked to allow the Legion to pass them on a narrow road; they, the Tories, were armed only with muskets, rifles, and the like which they had on their shoulders. Lee's men had their sabres drawn. The Americans attacked the unprepared Tories and killed and wounded more than 50 per cent of them. The rest dispersed to their homes not to rise again.[51]

## GUERILLA OPERATIONS

Surprise, although of great importance strategically and tactically in the larger sense, was also used in the more limited sense of individual sniping and strategic defensive operations now known as guerilla warfare. Two instances of this type of warfare have already been given in connection with aimed fire: Davidson's isolation of Charlotte and Marion's long running fight with Watson. There were many others. The successful partizan leaders managed to develop a peculiar knack of "hit and run" and shooting from cover. Marion in the early days of his partizan activities would assemble his men, strike a blow, and disperse his entire command so as to make British or Tory pursuit impossible.[52] Sumter also tended to have his maximum force available only for decisive action. Davie and Pickens were extremely

able in harassing cavalry operations in the Hill Country. On two occasions Davie gave crippling blows to British detachments within sight of greatly superior enemy forces.[53] Had he not finally accepted the post of Commissary General in December 1780, he might have earned a reputation second only to that of Marion as a partizan leader.[54]

Sometimes the ability of the partizans to take cover and shoot accurately was employed to surround an enemy force and maintain a fluid tactical defensive. Strategically, since the British force could be totally destroyed in this manner, this was definitely an offensive maneuver. King's Mountain and Marion's long fight with Watson were of this type; there were many more.

About the middle of February, 1781, British Major McLeroth (or McIlwroth) with a strong detachment and a convoy of wagons was surrounded by Marion. Each command consisted of between 300 and 400 men,[55] but the Americans soon had the upper hand. The tidewater swamps and thick woods concealed; the rifles gave opportunity to injure at a distance. A British close-quarters attack would be met by Patriot buckshot. Actions of this type sometimes went on for days. Partizans who could not stand in the open and fight regulars were more than a match for them in such circumstances. McLeroth lost his wagons and heavy casualties, but got away finally.

## IMPROVISATION AND IMPOSITION

Many of the Southern partizans were farmers and mechanics; they were used to doing things for themselves, often without

[50]*Ibid.*, p. 267.

[51]Lossing, *op. cit.*, II, 387, a neutral account of a rather controversial action.

[52]Banastre Tarleton, *A History of the Campaigns . . . in the Southern Provinces . . .* (London, 1787), p. 171.

[53]Action near Hanging Rock, 1 August 1780, and at Wahab's Plantation, 20 September 1780.

[54]William Richardson Davie, a Princeton graduate of the class of 1776, was a remarkable soldier, administrator, and diplomat. He was at his best in personal combat, but undertook to perform at one and the same time the functions of Commissary General of the Continental forces, the North Carolina State forces, and the South Carolina State forces.

[55]McCrady, *op. cit.*, II, 101.

proper tools, materials, and equipment. When need arose in their warfare, they came up with some novel ideas which often worked. Perhaps the best known is the Maham Tower. When Marion and Henry Lee were besieging the small British Fort Watson, they were unable to make any headway at all until Maham, one of Marion's officers, proposed building in a single night a high, rectangular, box-like tower of green logs notched at their ends so that riflemen mounted on a platform on top and protected by a wooden breastwork could command the inside of the British fort.[56] Surrender now came quickly.

The idea was so successful that in most later sieges there was at least one Maham tower; sometimes both sides used them.[57] Sometimes they were made strong enough to support one or more pieces of artillery. Finley's American 6-pounder was so placed at the siege of Augusta. Tory Colonel John Harris Cruger placed all three of his guns on a single tower at Ninety-Six.

Fire in some form or other was often used, since most of the fortified structures were in part built of wood. Frequently, a small force would take refuge in a house or barn; if the enemy could set it afire surrender or a suicidal sortie was almost certain. The same tactics were used in larger sieges also; Sumter endeavored to fire the three houses within the British fortified post at Rocky Mount, 30 July 1780, but was foiled by a rainstorm.[58] Fort Motte was taken by Marion and Lee by setting the roof of the main building within the earthworks afire.[59]

Although the Southern irregulars seldom used real artillery, they employed fake, or "Quaker," guns very well indeed on two occasions. Tory Colonel William Henry Mills was proceeding with a Tory militia command down the Pedee by boats about 1 August 1780 when at Hunt's Bluff they suddenly found themselves under the guns of a newly-raised Patriot battery on shore.[60] Most of the force immediately surrendered, even though the battery contained only fake artillery pieces. Colonel William Washington with a small force of Continental cavalry and mounted partizan militia forced Colonel Rowland Rugeley to surrender a strongly fortified post called Rugeley's Mills by showing at a distance a tree-trunk mounted on a pair of wagon wheels.[61]

An old trick used many times during the war by the partizans often worked superbly: A small force would pretend to be a larger one to force surrender or panic in an enemy. Perhaps the most disproportionate example of this was the capture on 1 October 1779 of 40 men and five moderate-size vessels, one mounting 14 guns, by Colonel John White and four soldiers.[62] This occurred at the Ogeechee river some 25 miles below Savannah.

## TACTICS AT COWPENS

We have discussed the way the Southern partizans fought when they were operating substantially on their own; however, they fought often in combination with Continental regulars. Militia in the North and in the early battles in the South were expected to fight as regulars did. Rarely did they do

[56]The various references to the actual construction of the tower are somewhat at variance, but it seems that all logs were horizontal.

[57]At Augusta and Ninety-Six.

[58]Gregorie, op. cit., p. 92; and Lossing, op. cit., II, 454. Flaming pine knots were thrown first; then, according to Lossing, a wagon filled with combustibles was rolled down upon the post.

[59]There is confusion as to actual means employed. Christopher Ward, The War of the Revolution (2 vols.;

New York, 1952), II, 818, says fire arrows were shot from muskets. Simms, op. cit., p. 235, and Lee, op. cit., p. 347, say that an East Indian bow and fire arrows were used while James, op. cit., p. 120, says that balls of flaming resin were slung onto the roof "by Nathan Savage, a private in Marion's brigade." Perhaps all three methods were used; one at least was successful.

[60]Gregg, op. cit., p. 316.

[61]Ward, op. cit., II, 745.

[62]Lee, op. cit., p. 144.

this. Howe lost at Savannah, Gates lost at Camden, and Ashe lost at Briar Creek when their militia broke without giving even one effective fire. However, when partizans were allowed and encouraged to fight in their own way, they were very formidable. The first man to combine successfully a force composed of Continentals and militia was Daniel Morgan, a giant Virginian, and a great soldier.[63] He used the considerable ability of the Southern partizans in tactical defensive situations based upon aimed fire, taking cover, and agility backed by the solidarity and the bayonet-wielding discipline of the Continental infantry. At Cowpens on 17 January 1781 his command achieved one of the greatest victories in American military history. This battle was not only imitated by American and British commanders later in the Revolution, but has been imitated very often since. Modern concepts of tactical defense in depth can be said to be in essence an adaptation of the same principles so brilliantly applied by the unlettered former Virginia teamster.

The British commanders attributed all their later failings and their ultimate defeat in the Southern Theatre to the battle of Cowpens. The very flower of their army, their "Light Troops," were either killed, captured, or utterly and hopelessly routed by an American army smaller in size than theirs and composed of more than 50 per cent partizan militia who had been almost useless for battlefield service before this battle. Morgan has been criticized for his choice of position and his gambling courage in meeting Tarleton in a place where defeat would have meant complete annihilation for the American forces,[64] but no one has ever criticized

either his weapons tactics or the careful preparation and organization of his weapons team. Morgan had considerable experience with riflemen and with irregular militia. He knew their strengths and their weaknesses. Furthermore, he understood their thinking better than any other Continental general. He did not ask them to do things alien to their nature, their discipline, and their training.

Morgan's plan at Cowpens was simple.[65] He deployed his forces in three lines in open woods and pasture. The first line was composed of 150 riflemen chosen for their ability to shoot, active strong fellows armed with the personal rifles they knew so well. These men were about half from Georgia under Major John Cunningham and half from North Carolina under Major Charles McDowell. Morgan had these two commands competing with each other. Their leaders urged them to take advantage of trees for cover and to steady their forearms and hands in taking aim. Each man chose his position in a most irregular line.

Morgan's second line, some 200 yards to the rear, was composed of General Andrew Picken's militia, about 300 of them mostly from the South Carolina Hill Country. These men were in a thicker line, but had been carefully coached; each knew exactly what was expected of him. They were to wait until the British regulars were within easy shot and then to fire deliberately two rounds. They were then free to retire by their left flank around Morgan's third line, which, some 150 yards further to the rear on a small hill, was composed of about 450 Continental infantry. Behind them there was the cavalry reserve of 80 Continentals and 45 Georgia partizans mounted and armed with sabres under Colonels William Wash-

[63]Morgan combined tremendous physical strength with great bravery and true loyalty to Washington when it was needed most; he was also a natural soldier of a high order.

[64]Morgan's own defense of this criticism is quoted in Ward, op. cit., II, 756, and elsewhere.

[65]Many references both original and secondary from both sides agree more closely than is usual for accounts of Revolutionary battles.

ington and James McCall.

Tarleton displayed more impetuosity and courage than military ability in this battle. He had artillery, but used it poorly and late. He smashed blindly into what he believed to be an army of poor fighting ability. His mounted vanguard of dragoons charged the first irregular line of partizan riflemen. These Georgians and North Carolinians fired but a single round each. This stopped the dragoons in their tracks, emptying a number of saddles. The ultimate value to the American cause of this single fire cannot be measured, however, in the number of casualties inflicted at this time. The dragoons in the vanguard as well as the rest—Tarleton's force was almost 50 per cent dragoons—were badly shaken by the accuracy of this first irregular volley.

The riflemen from Morgan's first line now retired and joined the South Carolina militia under Pickens in the second. It is probable that there were more smoothbores than rifles in this second line. However, as already mentioned, a militiaman with a musket he knew well and loaded carefully with a bore-fitting ball could deliver accurate fire, if the range was not too long.

Tarleton admonished his repulsed dragoons and sent forward immediately his regular infantry against the American second line. Militia had never stood in the open against British regulars. The British 7th Foot, their Light Infantry, and the Infantry of the British Legion were truly fine soldiers; they came on superbly in their bright uniforms. At a range of less than 100 yards the American line exploded in an irregular volley. This fire was directed at Morgan's insistence at "the men with the epaulets," the commissioned and non-commissioned officers. Some of the militiamen fired a second round; others did not.[66] The whole now took to

their heels by the left flank as they had been instructed to do and as the Continentals in the rear knew that they would do.

The sudden and precipitous flight of the American second line was wrongly interpreted by the British. They pursued exultantly, but in very poor order. Their loss in officers and non-commissioned officers was probably fatal to their chances of winning the battle. A disproportionate number of these men fell, mainly at the first fire of Picken's militia.[67] Due to a confusion of orders, Morgan's Continentals of the third line retired behind a low hill to their rear, but faced about and met the disordered British regulars with a devastating volley and with bayonets. The British broke.

There were a few moments of confused fighting. Tarleton had ordered forward his Highlanders, the first battalion of the 71st Foot, to the left of his first line and his dragoons to the right just before the crisis. However, Picken's partizans, after traveling around the Continentals, fired again into the British, this time from the American right with the Highlanders as their principal target. Washington's part-militia cavalry charged home, even though Tarleton's dragoons now refused close action. The British, with few officers remaining, went into uncontrollable panic. The defeat was complete; only a part of the British dragoons got away in an organized body. Out of a British force of about 1,100, Morgan captured, wounded and unwounded, more than 800 and killed about 100. He took all the British artillery, baggage, supplies, and arms.

Morgan's victory was due essentially to his employing militia to fight the way they wanted to fight and fought best, to a simple well-understood plan, and to the intangibles of true natural leadership. He and his com-

[66]Probably not many rifles were loaded for a second fire, for the careful loading of them took too long.

[67]According to Ward, *op. cit.*, II, 762, "the British lost 100 killed, among them 39 officers."

mand made hardly a mistake; their weapons tactics from the initial rifle fire, through the militia volleys and Continental bayonet wielding, to the final charge of sabre-armed cavalry were superb.

## THE COWPENS WEAPONS TACTICS EMPLOYED ELSEWHERE

The tactics of Cowpens were employed by Greene at Guilford Court House on 15 March 1781, where the fire of the riflemen and militia in the first two lines was largely responsible for the extremely heavy and disproportionate British losses. The Continentals in the third line were for a time successful in breaking the British infantry. Had Morgan commanded instead of Greene, complete disaster might have overtaken the British again.[68] The final outcome was that the British "won" the battlefield, but lost almost a third of their force compared to an American loss of about 8 per cent. Cornwallis was unable to face Greene's army in battle ten days later.[69]

Lord Rowdon employed Tory riflemen specifically to shoot at American officers in his victory at Hobkirks Hill on 25 April 1781.[70] The loss of two Continental officers at a critical time in this battle because of aimed fire probably turned the tide against the Americans. The Maryland Continentals, up to this time the best regulars in the American army, unaccountably panicked.

Many times in the 19th and 20th Centuries United States and foreign commanders have used aimed fire from a thinly held first line, a numerous second line of troops more able to produce enemy casualties than to defeat them at close quarters, and a third line of their best disciplined and most reliable soldiers.[71] Sometimes the numbers engaged have been more than 100 times what the "Old Wagoner" had to deploy.

## CONCLUSIONS

We should not forget in admiration of Morgan and the combined American forces at Cowpens and Guilford that we usually lost the larger pitched battles and formal sieges in the South. The greater value of the partizan militia was in the many independent actions. For each King's Mountain and Musgrove's Mills, there were scores of little known, or even nameless, fights which tipped the scales toward a Patriot victory in the South.

The Whigs were not more numerous than the Tories in 1775. The Carolinas and Georgia received less aid from the Colonies to the north than they might have reasonably expected, certainly very little indeed compared to the British regulars, equipment, arms, and money which were sent against them. The war fought in the South was long and bloody. The Patriots ultimately won very largely because of their superior weapons tactics. The Patriot partizans and their leaders could shoot, use the advantages of surprise, exert pressure defensively and in harassing operations, and improvise. The names of Marion, Morgan, Pickens, Sumter, Davie, Davidson, and other shine. Their blood and that of their nameless followers, true amateur soldiers, was shed freely, although thoughtfully. Let us remember to fight the way they fought, to take advantage of every favorable factor, and to win.

---

[68]No adverse criticism of General Greene is intended; his very great value to his country was based upon his ability to keep his army "in being" in his theatre. A gamble at Guilford could also have lost the South for the Patriots, if the superb small British army had won a complete victory.

[69]See particularly, William Johnson, *Sketches of the Life and Corespondence of Nathaniel Greene* (Charleston, 1822), *passim.*

[70]Ward, *op. cit.,* II, 804.

[71]The idea of a skirmish line to annoy and disorganize an attacking force is as old as formal war; Morgan's innovation was to get real fighting from his first and second lines. His aimed fire wasn't supposed just to annoy and disorganize, but to kill the most important of the enemy personnel before the crucial test with the third line.

# FIRST BLOOD FOR THE INFANTRY—1776

By Lincoln Diamant

SOMETIME DURING the summer of 1876, the New York Historical Society decided that a large outdoor ceremony would be the proper way to celebrate the approaching centenary of the Revolutionary Battle of Harlem Heights. The Society planned a huge public picnic on the actual battle site, with several prominent speakers to address the gathering. It was a year after the Revolutionary celebrations at Lexington and Concord, and the six-year centenary period was getting into full stride.

Although only a few thousand men had been involved on both sides, the military engagement on the Heights (whose name has successively been Vanderwater, Harlem, Bloomingdale, and finally Morningside) had considerable importance, for it ended in the first clear-cut victory for the strategy and fighting ability of the Continental Army. Coming when it did after the disastrous rout on Long Island and the subsequent defeat along the East River, the victory did much to restore the shattered confidence of the patriots in their own ability to stand up against seasoned veterans of the Crown.

The action itself was simple. An early morning scouting party left the American positions on the heights north of the "Hollow Way," a deep east-west valley splitting the high ground that parallels the Hudson River on upper Manhattan Island. The scouts worked their way onto the southern heights and then further south until they encountered a British picket near what is now 108th Street. After a skirmish, they retreated, and arrived back at the Hollow Way with two regiments of British Light Infantry in hot pursuit. When Washington realized these British had overextended themselves, he successfully decoyed them down into the Hollow Way, sent a flanking column around toward their rear, and joined battle.

The American attack on the British front was *too* strong. Instead of arriving on the enemy rear, the American circling column struck what retreat had turned into a strong British flank, and in the initial shock, Colonel Thomas Knowlton (heading America's first "commando" group, the Connecticut Rangers) was mortally wounded. His men deployed successfully, however, and reuniting with the Americans on the front, soon drove the British up into a barley-field at the crest of the southern heights. It was in this field and in a small orchard to the immediate south that the day's heavy fighting took place.

Washington and Lord Howe, content with feeling each other out, fed small groups of fresh troops into the conflict. The Americans, however, never lost their initial edge, and by late afternoon, the beaten and disheveled British Regulars had broken and were fleeing to the safety of their main lines. The tried but victorious patriot troops were called from the chase by their Commander, who wished to avoid a major encounter at that time. The men who rested around the American campfires that evening had been treated to their first taste of victory since the militia engagements at Lexington and Concord, and were imbued with new courage and determination.

This was the victory whose centenary the good people of New York City would gather to commemorate on September 16, 1876, and the members of the New York Historical Society made extensive preparation for the celebration. "The ground was carefully studied by the committee charged with the details: all known maps, records and deeds relating to the locality were examined and compared, and all the documents and letters, printed and in manuscript, known to exist, were collected and collated."[1] The center of the battleground was finally determined to be near the eastern edge of Morningside Heights at 117th Street, and it was on that spot that the speaker's pavilion was erected.

In reviewing the committee's reasons for choosing this location, it must be noted that there were no contemporary maps available to the committee which indisputably marked the location of the battleground. The Americans had abandoned New York City entirely soon after the battle and hence had no occasion to map the site, which was in a "no-man's land." And the British always disregarded the engagement as an "unfortunate skirmish." So the spot remained unmarked (so far as the 1876 Committee knew), except for a sketch map drawn by Sloss Hobart, who participated in the battle. This map had been unearthed in the diary of Ezra Stiles, D.D., along with the following note:

Oct 18-1776—When I was at Fairfield I saw Sloss Hobart Esq a sensible Gent. & a member of the New York Conven-

tion. He gave me the following draft of the Action of 16 Sept which began near the 14 m stone & ended at the 8 m stone. Unfortunately, these mileage figures were wrong and contributed much to the later confusion. But the sketch map, despite its crudity, easily fitted the battle onto Morningside Heights.

Selections from two contemporary letters served to corroborate this choice of Morningside. One is from a letter which General George Clinton of the American Army wrote to his wife a few days after the battle:

Our Army, at least one division of it, lay at Colo. Morris's[2] & so southward to near the Hollow Way, which runs across from Harlem Flats to the North River at Matje Davit's Fly.[3]

This apparently identified the "Hollow Way" as the valley of present day 125th Street, for no other comparable topographic feature exists on upper Manhattan. And in a letter dated the 18th of September, Lewis Morris, one of the signers of the Declaration of Independence, wrote of the battle:

. . . the enemy advanced to the top of the hill, which was opposite to that which lies before Dayes door.

The Day Tavern was located near what is now 126th Street on the road that led to the King's Bridge over Spuyten Duyvil. Directly across the road from the tavern lay the steep slope leading up Point of Rocks, the southernmost tip of the high ground on which the American Army was encamped. It was from Point of Rocks that Washington directed the course of the battle.

With these few but apparently conclusive bits of direct evidence before them, the Committe unhesitatingly placed the engagement at the Morningside Heights spot previously mentioned. The celebration was held on a

---

[1]From the main Centennial speech by John Jay, grandson of the Chief Justice, and U. S. Minister to Austria.

[2]Now the Jumel Mansion.
[3]A swampy meadow.

2

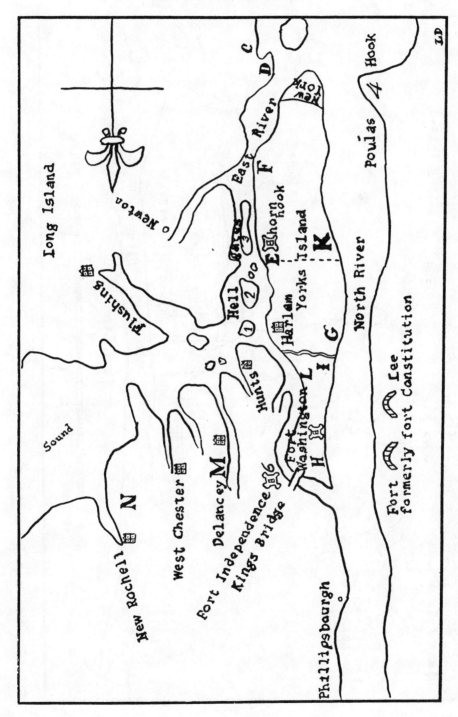

FIGURE I. MAJOR ANDRÉ MAP

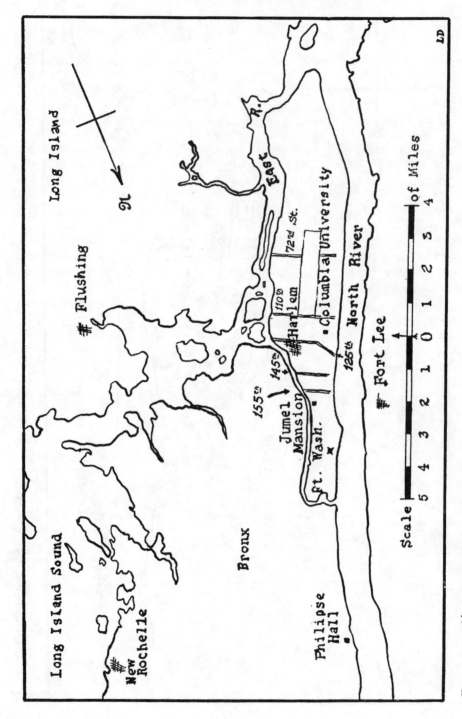

FIGURE II. NEW YORK CITY TODAY

beautiful Saturday afternoon, and was considered a great patriotic success. The Historical Society was proud of its work, and closing the book, considered they had done an excellent job of research and preparation.

But just a year and a half later at their regular spring meeting in February, 1878, grave doubts arose in the minds of some members when no less an historical authority than the Chancellor of the University of the State of New York, Erastus C. Benedict, delivered a paper wherein he charged the celebration Committee with gross negligence and misinterpretation in locating the battlefield site on Morningside Heights. Actually, Benedict claimed, the engagement was fought two miles to the direct north, in the vicinity of what is now Audubon Park.

A heated argument followed, with Benedict, a thoroughly accredited historian, ranged against all the other members of the Society. Despite his convincing re-interpretation of the available evidence, he could rally no support. Already in his late seventies, Benedict died two years later, but the dispute was continued following the publication of Martha Lamb's famous *History of New York*. Therein it was apparent that Benedict had finally succeeded in convincing Mrs. Lamb (formerly a supporter of the Morningside site), for she located the Hollow Way as being "the ravine, now Audubon Park (153rd to 158th Streets),"[4] and reiterated all of Benedict's arguments with a few additional interpretations of her own.

A surprising fact was that the source material with which Benedict and Lamb were repudiating the selection of the Morningside location was practically identical with that already presented *in its support*. The Stiles-Hobart sketch map (with its disturbing milestones) was one exhibit. Another was some

[4]*History of New York*, Vol. II, No. 3.

additional material from the Clinton letter. A third, newly introduced, was a brief account by a British Army Captain; and the final argument was that cannon balls had been recently uncovered in excavations in the vicinity of Audubon Park.

If one were to accept the Hobart milestones, the battle *did* take place on lower Washington Heights, and the crossed swords on his sketch (indicating the Point of Rocks command post) were interpreted by Mrs. Lamb to indicate the Jumel Mansion, Washington's general headquarters, located (fittingly) at 160th Street.

General Clinton's complete letter had contained a short account of the entire battle, and he estimated the various distances traversed during the day. His estimates total two and a half miles, which means that if the battle had begun at Morningside, it would have ended at 75th Street, or a mile and a half within the main British lines, which is ridiculous. So to make any sense out of Clinton's total, the high-water mark of the British Light Infantry pursuit must be moved two and a half miles north from the British outposts to the ravine at 158th Street. This fits the Lamb theory perfectly.

The British Captain was George Harris of the Fifth British Regiment, and he wrote an account of the battle to his uncle:

> The 16th of September we were ordered to stand to our arms at eleven A.M. and were instantly trotted about three miles (without a halt to draw breath), to support a battalion of light infantry which had imprudently advanced so far without support as to be in danger of being cut off.

His estimate of a three-mile trot north matches the Clinton estimate of the distance covered by the Americans going south.

It was on these sources that Benedict and Lamb based their theory that the Battle of

Harlem Heights was fought, not on Morningside, but on the lower section of Washington Heights (which section, through the irony of fate and local nomenclature, had by 1880 itself come to be known as "Harlem Heights").

The stage was now set for a researcher's battle-royal. In the May, 1880, issue of the New York Historical Society's *Magazine of American History*, John Austin Stevens, founder of the magazine, replied sharply to the Lamb-Benedict theory in his review of the Lamb *History of New York*. Stevens outlined in print for the first time the source material on which the 1876 Committee's choice of location was based. Apologizing for the circumstantial nature of the material, he nevertheless insisted that the final selection was correct, and the Harris-Clinton distance estimates nothing more than natural exaggerations. The cannon balls near Audubon Park were ascribed to the British assault on Fort Washington, which took place two months to the day after the Battle of Harlem Heights.

Stevens then struck a devastating blow at the Lamb interpretation. He cited the original order-of-the-day for the 16th of September, which began by ordering out the scouting party that precipitated the battle, and concluded by instructing General Silliman to take his brigade and throw up entrenchments along a line roughly paralleling present-day 147th Street. Stevens continued by quoting from a soldier's journal to the effect that the Silliman brigade had been kept busy at this task all day, despite "heavy firing below us." In other words, the fighting never even came near 147th Street, which exploded the 158th Street Audubon Park theory. Mrs. Lamb realized its demise, and though she did not recant, showed no further interest in the controversy.

January, 1881, however, saw the publica-

tion of a pamphlet by Erastus Benedict's nephew, containing his uncle's original 1878 paper plus some added recriminations against Mr. Stevens by the younger Mr. Benedict. To which Stevens replied in April:

> . . . of itself it needs no notice or comment, the author having attained no reputation as an historian which gives weight to his individual opinion, when it conflicts with well-known facts, established by authority in accord with tradition; and the subject would not receive further attention in this column but for the prefix and appendix which accompany it. In both of these Mr. Benedict (younger) charges the writer with unworthy personal motives in the review of Mrs. Lamb, and the condemnation of the new version which she adopted on his authority. And secondly, of perverting facts and of "garbling authorities and cooking maps," to use his own inelegant but characteristic words.[5]

There was no reply (in print) by Mr. Benedict (younger) to this expressive review of his work, and the matter rested for another sixteen years unresolved, for although Stevens had successfully destroyed the Audubon Park theory, he had uncovered no further substantiating evidence for the Morningside site.

In the fall of 1897, Columbia University became an interested party to the proceedings, for it moved in October from its cramped quarters on Madison Avenue downtown to the proclaimed Revolutionary battlefield on Bloomingdale Heights (whose name was soon altered again, to the present "Morningside"). Inspired by its new location, the Columbia University Press in the winter of 1897 brought out what is still the most authoritative and well-documented work on

[5]*Magazine of American History*, Vol. VI, No. 7.

2 ★

the Harlem Heights engagement. Its author was Henry P. Johnston, Professor of History at the College of the City of New York, long interested in the excited discussion raging over the proper location of the battlefield.

In *The Battle of Harlem Heights*, Johnston supported the majority view that placed the battle on Morningside, but he located it farther west on 117th Street, at Broadway rather than Morningside Drive. He justified this shift on purely logical grounds, supported adequately by photographs he had made of the few remaining contemporary landmarks on Morningside. His primary exhibit was the location of Bloomingdale Road, the only road running through the district in 1776, and around which most of this battle of advance and retreat must of necessity have centered. Bloomingdale Road ran to the west of present Broadway, but crossed over at about 118th Street.

Johnston also argued that Knowlton's flank attack would never have attempted to climb the sheer rockface of Morningside Park. Instead, he claimed, it actually ascended the rocky ridge (no longer visible) just west of Amsterdam Avenue and 124th Street. Johnston also disclosed for the first time that the 1876 Committee had discarded still another candidate for the battlefield site, for in 1860, Benson J. Lossing's *Field Book of the Revolution* had more or less arbitrarily placed the action on the flats (or "Plains") of Harlem around McGowan's Pass, near the northeastern end of what is now Central Park. (In consequence the battle was often referred to as the "Battle of Harlem Plains.")

Although the Lamb-Benedict theory could now be considered buried, Johnston officially staked it into its grave:

> Their version represents that four hundred light infantrymen, chasing Knowlton's Rangers, actually penetrated the American lines for more than a mile without being observed by other troops; that they blew their defiant bugle notes[6] in the rear of our main encampment; that Washington found it necessary to order out a flanking party to hem them in when there were ten American brigades already below them. . . . In a word we are given to understand that a mere detachment of the British army pushed through Washington's lines, fought, at times, within four short blocks of his headquarters, made the circuit of his strong position, and then returned to Morningside Heights, carrying all the guns and wounded with them, and losing but fourteen men killed. A proud day that, for the enemy!

Noting the order-of-the-day to General Silliman's brigade regarding the digging of entrenchments, Johnston concludes:

> . . . they present us with the singular spectacle of an army fortifying itself against an enemy . . . engaged in a "bloody battle" immediately in its rear.

He then added one final touch. A member of the American burial party on the night of the battle had written that "the British had already removed their own dead when we arrived." This, Johnston pointed out, would have entailed a double crossing of the American lines by the British. Finally feeling that he had satisfactorily disposed of the Lamb-Benedict theory, Johnston ended his discussion. But he too failed to supply any new evidence that indisputably placed the battlefield on Morningside.

This time it was nine years before argument was resumed. Then, in the fall 1906

---

[6]The notes of the fox-chase, represented by some chroniclers as having irritated Washington into giving battle.

[7]"The Battle of Harlem Heights," *Magazine of History*, Vol. IV, No. 3.

issue of the (retitled) *Magazine of History*, an article[7] appeared over the signature of Thomas Addis Emmet, M.D., in which he repudiated Johnston's carefully documented work. Basing most of his assertions on boyhood reminiscences, Emmet endeavored to prove that the battle was fought north of 125th Street, and took the following swipe at Columbia along the way:

> ... beyond the fact that the present site of Columbia University must necessarily be nearer the locality where the battle was fought, it has no greater claim, I believe, to that honor than has Union Square. ... I simply wish to offer a protest, in consequence of my knowledge that the history of our country is being constantly perverted and misstated.

This article naturally caused considerable agitation among those members of the Historical Society who imagined that the problem of the Morningside site had been accepted as settled.

In a blistering attack[8] on Dr. Emmet in their January, 1907, issue, two editors of the *Magazine of History*, Reginald P. Bolton and Edward Hagaman Hall, took it for granted that the Doctor was resurrecting the old Audubon Park theory, and immediately proceeded to pounce upon him with all the proper arguments. To which the instigator of the uproar could only reply weakly that he didn't believe the Lamb-Benedict theory either, and that:

> The battle was, in my judgment, fought below the site of the present Convent of the Sacred Heart, at the Point of Rocks and along the irregular line of high ground to the north of the plain to the east of Manhattanville.[9]

All these anti-climactical fireworks were in one respect fortunate. The Bolton-Hall research unearthed a paragraph from Moore's *Diary of the Revolution* which cleared up the oldest problem of all, proving the inaccuracy of the milestones on the Hobart sketch map, and showing that the mileages given by Captain Harris and General Clinton *were* exaggerated. The Moore entry ran:

> 16 Sept. 1776
>
> Our army is now between the nine and ten-mile stones, where they are strongly fortified and intrenched. The enemy's lines are about one mile and a half below them.

Contemporary maps show the tenth milestone at what is now 153rd Street, the ninth at 133rd Street. A mile and a half below would be 103rd Street, which fits our picture of a British picket at 108th Street exactly.

Since 1907, the controversy has rested without presentation of new material for either side. The Sons of the American Revolution of the State of New York imbedded a bronze plaque marking the (preferred) battlefield site in the west wall of Columbia University's School of Engineering, soon after the building's erection, and thereby added to the University's pride in its Revolutionary War heritage.

The present author's interest in this long chain of events beginning in the dim morning light of the 16th of September, 1776, was first generated by a study of the inscription on this tablet, while still an undergraduate at Columbia College. He became also interested in the obvious modification of the Morningside terrain from 1776 to the present day, as part of a great city grew up upon it, and conceived the idea of a large map depicting the battle area as it must have appeared in 1776, with an overlay showing the contemporary culture of the area. After several years, sufficient time presented itself and the cartographic job was begun and finished.

[8]"The Battle of Harlem Heights Again," *Magazine of History*, Vol. V, No. 1.
[9]A small village existing later in the Hollow Way.

But it was in the research of preparing a proper 1776 base-map of Morningside Heights that a most startling discovery was made. Thumbing through a catalogue list of maps contained in the Clinton Collection of the Clements Library at the University of Michigan, the author was arrested by a description of Map No. 143, a map of Manhattan Island and vicinity, drawn during the winter of 1776 by the sadly famous Major John André (then of His Majesty's Royal Engineers).

Located by block letters on the map (the description said) were a number of important places — one of them keyed as follows:

"G Noltens Battle Sept. 16"

—so clearly and delightfully a misspelling of Knowlton, who had died heroically at the head of the flanking column.

So a map definitely locating the battle site —and one made soon after the battle—actually existed! A piece of paper that Stevens and Johnston and Bolton and Hall would have moved worlds to learn about, and all the while it lay quietly and undiscovered along with the rest of the Sir Henry Clinton papers in the bottom of an old trunk until almost twenty years after the last shot in the great literary Battle of Harlem Heights had been fired.

The seventy-five-year-old controversy can now be resolved. Further investigation has shown the André map to be of sufficient scale to prove the location of the battle site beyond any further doubt. *Figure I* accompanying this article is a rigidly accurate pen tracing of the original André map now at the University of Michigan, with superfluous details omitted in the interests of clarity. *Figure II* is a pen tracing of a modern topographic survey map of New York City, reduced to exactly the same scale as that of the André original, and also relocating several important points shown on that copy.

The letter "G" — the key letter — superimposes precisely on the site of Columbia University, on Morningside Heights.

Thus the long-held (but circumstantial) view is effectively vindicated, the element of doubt completely removed. Columbia University rests upon a height whose rocky soil was splashed with the blood of free men fighting bravely to defend precious ideals of liberty — Colonial infantrymen giving the newly-formed American nation its very first taste of military victory.

# REVOLUTIONARY WEST POINT: "THE KEY TO THE CONTINENT"[1]

By Gerald C. Stowe and Jac Weller*

THE SIGNIFICANCE OF THE HIGHLANDS

West Point was the center of "the almost infinitely important posts in the Highlands"[2] of the Hudson during the Revolution. These defensive positions were the base on which Washington pivoted his entire strategy from the fall of 1776 until the end of the war seven years later. It was by far the most important American fortification during the war, as well as the main armory and ordnance depot of the new country in the peace that followed. Our entire standing army of less than 700 was stationed there on 3 January 1784.[3]

West Point continued to be of importance as a fortification well into the 19th century.

The United States Military Academy, which started a continuous existence in 1802, has, by virtue of its location there, added greatly to the popular appreciation of the name.[4] This monograph is devoted to the defenses of the Highlands, centering finally at West Point, during the period from 1775 to 1783, and particular attention is given to Washington's strategic use of this bastion.

The strategic importance of the position stemmed from its situation. The Colonies were naturally divided by a line which ran from British Canada south through Lake Champlain and its tributaries, and down the Hudson to British New York. Because of Britain's Navy, and her well-disciplined in-

*(Editorial Note: The authors of this study base their observations not merely on an analysis and reinterpretation of secondary and a few primary sources and old maps, but also, and perhaps more importantly, on exhaustive personal tactical reconnaissance of the entire Highlands area. Gerald C. Stowe is a veteran of WWII whose great interest in weapons brought him to the West Point Museum of which he has been the curator for several years. Readers will recall Jac Weller as the Author of "The Logistics of Nathan Bedford Forrest," in *Military Affairs*, XVII, 4 (Winter, 1953). In addition to the works specifically cited in the footnotes, the following best known secondary sources proved the most useful in the preparation of the article:

Douglas Southall Freeman, *George Washington*, 5 vol. completed (New York, 1948-1952), hereafter cited as Freeman; Christopher Ward, *The War of the Revolution* (New York, 1952), hereafter, Ward; George O. Trevelyan, *The American Revolution*, 4 vol. (London, 1909-1914); William W. Fortescue *A History of the British Army*, 20 vol. (London, 1911-1935), hereafter, Fortescue; Benson J. Lossing, *The Pictorial Field-Book of the Revolution*, 2 vol. (New York, 1855), hereafter, Lossing; Charles Stedman, *The History of the American War*, 2 vol. (London, 1794), hereafter, Stedman.)

[1] Washington Irving, *Life of George Washington*, 5 vol. (New York, 1855-1859) vol. III, p. 497; also General Huntington as quoted by Boynton, p. 178, with slight change.

[2] Knox to his brother, 7 May 1779, in Francis S. Drake, *Life and Correspondence of Henry Knox*. (Boston, 1873) p. 61; hereafter, Drake.

[3] Noah Brooks, *A Soldier of the Revolution* (New York, 1900) p. 186; hereafter, Brooks.

[4] The earliest recorded ideas for a military academy were embodied in Knox's "Hints for the Improvement of the Artillery" submitted to a committee of the Continental Congress 27 September 1776; similar plans were proposed from time to time by others, particularly Washington and Hamilton: Elward C. Boynton, *History of West Point* (New York, 1871) p. 177; hereafter, Boynton. Knox also established a military or artillery academy of sorts at his headquarters at Pluckemin in the winter and spring of 1779: *Philadelphia Packet*, 6 March 1779 as quoted by Brooks, p. 118. The rank of cadet was created in 1794 and classes of a sort conducted at West Point during 1796: Sidney Forman, *West Point: A History of the United States Military Academy* (New York, 1950) pp. 14-15; hereafter, Forman.

fantry, superbly effective in formal open battles, this entire line was extremely vulnerable to capture. It could be defended effectively only in the rugged mountains where the Hudson flows in almost a gorge. Below these Highlands, the British Navy was supreme; once through this barrier, small ships of war could interrupt all save desultory communications to well above Albany. On two occasions during the Revolution, the British came extremely close to achieving complete control of this whole line. They would have cut the Colonies in two and probably, at least temporarily, defeated the independence movement in America.

Continental communications are so good today that we seldom think of them at all. Boston is six hours from San Francisco by air. Only three days are required for the trip by rail; a private citizen in his passenger automobile can do it in a week easily regardless of weather and season. The different sections of the country are now united into a homogeneous whole by superb communications. During the Revolution, an express message took days to go from Georgia to Massachusetts; an ordinary traveler would take weeks to go the same distance over land. After the sea lanes were closed by the British Navy, goods and materials just didn't move at all over such long distances although, throughout the Revolution, important supplies continued to move across the Hudson in both directions. The economy of the new country was to a considerable extent dependent upon this exchange.

Men were the most precious freight carried across the Hudson. Washington had the advantage of interior lines of land communications so long as he held the Highlands; they were slow, but they were as reliable as those of the enemy which were dependent upon sailing vessels. Massachusetts furnished more than twice as many troops

to the Continental Army than any other state; Connecticut was second.[5] After 1776, few of these troops fought actively in New England, save in the relatively small actions around Newport in Rhode Island. Washington's communications system, poor at best because of 18th century roads, would have practically ceased between New England and the South if the British had been able to take and hold the Highlands. The mere physical interruption of the free flow of information, troops, and supplies perhaps would have been fatal; in addition there was another source of danger.

In 1775, there were two different groups of Colonies. It is hard to realize today the extreme division of interest between New England and the South. The latter term had, in the Revolution, a different meaning than its Civil War connotation. In the earlier conflict, it meant not only Virginia and her southerly neighbors but also Maryland, Delaware, Pennsylvania, and New Jersey. In fact, the Deep South was so far away that its people were not well known in New England. Not so Pennsylvanians and their neighbors; these were sometimes actively hated. Two definitely different ways of thought, action, and life extended along the seaboard on either side of the former Dutch colony of New York, through which the riparian line ran. Early in the Revolution it was sometimes necessary to encamp troops from these two sections of the Colonies in two separate areas with what amounted to a neutral strip between them.[6] Sometimes their feelings for each other were slightly less bitter than those they had for the British. There was seldom a more obvious opportunity to divide and conquer.

[5]Henry B. Carrington, *Battles of the American Revolution* (New York, 1876) p. 653; hereafter, Carrington,
[6]Major General William Heath, *Memoirs* (New York, 1901) p. 80.

### EARLY EFFORTS IN THE HIGHLANDS

The geographical and political situation of the Lake Champlain-Hudson River line was fully appreciated by both sides. The military leaders of Great Britain realized its importance before Burgoyne's effort to reach and maintain himself at Albany in 1777. Indeed, the original seizure of New York from the Dutch stemmed from the desire of the British to unite their two groups of Colonies. The importance of the Hudson River and Lake Champlain was appreciated during the entire period of the wars with France.[7] That was why Ticonderoga was one of the three or four most powerful fortifications in the new world. The British were actively planning to seize and fortify the Highlands as early as the fall of 1775.[8]

Washington, as well as other Continental leaders, realized from the start of hostilities the great advantage to the maritime enemy given by the many navigable rivers of coastal America. Washington, as a member of the Continental Congress from Virginia, served with the Congressional Committee which drew up and proposed on 25 May 1775 the fortifications of the Highlands.[9] But the first positive action was undertaken by the Provincial Congress of New York in a resolution for actual building, passed 18 August 1775; construction began 11 days later.[10] In order to understand the fortifications and their significance, let's take a closer look at the entire terrain of the lower Hud-Hudson Valley.

In Revolutionary times, the river was navigable for heavy shipping as far as Albany, about 160 miles. The river is tidal throughout most of this stretch; the water is brackish

in the Highlands most of the year. The river runs roughly north and south; for 50 miles from its mouth, any river-closing fortifications erected by the Continentals could be taken from the rear easily, or out flanked. At this point, however, a mountain range about twelve miles wide, running roughly northeast and southwest, intersects the river. The range extends too far in either direction for strategic flanking by another line of communications. Even tactical flanking would be impossible against a vigilant commander with sufficient defensive troops. This range, which has several names, is anchored at either end in the Vermont-New Hampshire and the Pennsylvania-New Jersey mountains. "The Highlands" means in this specific case only the mountainous country close to the Hudson River.

On the west side of the Hudson, there are three principal mountains with rugged country between. These are Dunderburg on the south, Bear Mountain in the middle, and Storm King on the north, to give them their present names. On the east of the Hudson, the mountains are not quite so well defined, although rugged country extends from around Peekskill north to Breakneck Ridge which is a continuation of Storm King on the east side of the Hudson. Anthony's Nose, opposite Bear Mountain in the middle Highlands, was of extreme military importance. In the river, there are a series of points and bends of various types as well as rocky islands; navigation was reasonably difficult, although there was sufficient water so that the largest ships then able to get into New York Harbor could sail well past the Highlands.

Stony Point juts out into the river at the southern edge of the west side of the Highlands. Verplanck's Point is on the east side. The little town of Peekskill is slightly above and to the east of Verplanck's Point. On the west side of the Hudson just above Bear

---

[7]Freeman, vol. II, p. 24.

[8]Peter Force, editor, *American Archives* (Washington, 1837-1853) Ser. 4, vol. III, p. 927; hereafter, Force.

[9]*Journals of the Continental Congress, 1774-1789* (Washington, 1904-1922) vol. II, p. 60; also Boynton, p. 16.

[10]Forman, pp. 7-8; he cites several original references in this sequence of events.

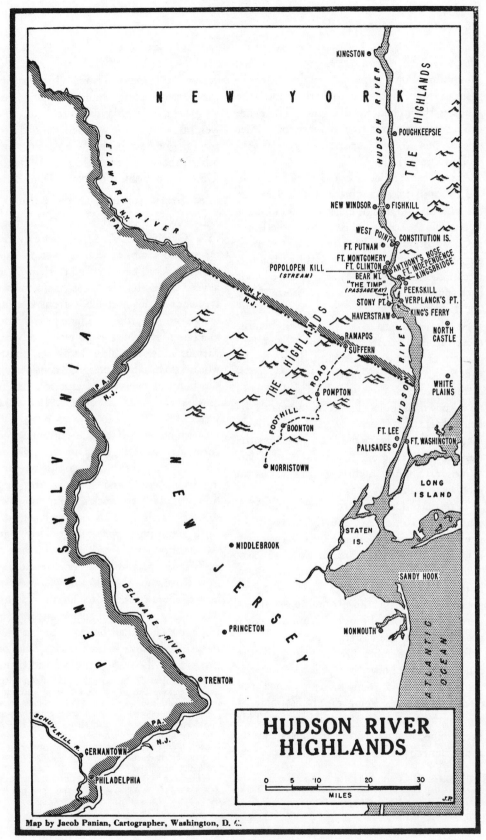

# HUDSON RIVER HIGHLANDS

Map by Jacob Panian, Cartographer, Washington, D. C.

Mountain, Popolopen Kill makes a deep gash in the Highlands and runs into the Hudson through a steep ravine. There are two excellent points for defense on either side of this stream. Across the river is Anthony's Nose.

About four miles above Popolopen Kill, the Hudson takes a ninety degree bend to the west around a high mass of rock. This is West Point. Across the river from the Point is Constitution Island, again using the modern name. Both are eminently suited for fortification. Above West Point, the river bends back north and runs between Storm King and Breakneck Ridge.

At the northern end of the Highlands, there begins a stretch of 90 miles of rolling country extending past Albany. Close to the east bank of the river and just to the north of the mountains there is a small rocky island now known as Polopel's or Bannerman's Island. Here the river is wide, but relatively shallow. Across from the island, and on the western shore, stood the village of New Windsor. Slightly higher up on the eastern shore was Fishkill.

Transportation across the river in the 18th century was, of course, entirely by boat. In reading old accounts of life on the river one is impressed with the maritime skills of New York State people; they seemed to use a boat in place of a wagon, or coach, wherever possible. Early in the Revolution frigates were built at Poughkeepsie, 20 miles further up the river on the eastern shore.[11]

Probably the most used crossing of the Hudson above New York City during the Revolution was at King's Ferry which ran from Verplanck's Point to Stony Point at the southern end of the Highlands. This Ferry joined a main road from Massachusetts and Connecticut to one extending to New Jersey and Pennsylvania. Interruption of the ferry crossing would do little harm so long as the Highlands were held, as there were at least two more well defined crossing places: one just below West Point, and the other above Storm King and Breakneck Ridge from Fishkill to New Windsor.

FIRST SYSTEM OF HIGHLAND FORTIFICATIONS

During the period from 29 August 1775 to 7 October 1777, a group of forts, batteries, and camps as well as river obstructions took shape. These cost more than $250,000, a very large sum for those days, as well as tremendous physical labor from Continental troops and militia.[12] There was confusion, bickering, improper engineering advice, and various other troubles. However, these first works eventually emerged, considering the shortages of everything, especially of "know how" and brains, as quite a fair defensive system.

Without regard to the chronology of its construction, and going up the river in the direction that the enemy would take advancing from New York City, the first fortification was at Verplanck's Point on the east side of the river. This was an inconsiderable work mounting, apparently, only two guns.[13] About three and a half miles farther north, at "Continental Village" on the old Albany Post Road, was the customary station of the largest Continental force in the Highlands. The early American commanders in the Highlands had their headquarters in or about Peekskill. Above Peekskill Bay, and on the east side of the river, was Fort Independence.

---

[11]William H. Carr and Richard J. Koke, *Twin Forts of the Popolopen, Bear Mountain* (New York, 1937) p. 20; hereafter, Carr and Koke.

[12]Boynton, p. 47. This is the usual figure given, but seems too low. According to the same authority, iron for the chain and boom cost $440 per ton; since more than 100 tons were required, the entire expenditure would have been used for this alone. Albert H. Heusser, *The Forgotten General: Robert Erskine* (Paterson, New Jersey, 1928) p. 141, estimates that the Fort Montgomery, or first chain, alone cost £70,000, or about $350,000; hereafter, Heusser.

[13]Hoffman Nickerson, *The Turning Point of the Revolution*, (New York, 1925) p. 342; one was lost and the other saved; hereafter, Nickerson.

This work was situated on a small promontory below Anthony's Nose which put it completely at the mercy of an enemy who controlled the river.[14]

Two miles farther north, where the majestic summit of Anthony's Nose—the present eastern terminus of Bear Mountain Bridge—rises almost sheer from the river to a height of almost 900 feet, the Americans had their principal fortifications and obstructions. There were inconsiderable works on the face of Anthony's Nose, probably of the nature of rifle pits. Across the river, where Popolopen Creek or Kill enters the Hudson at right angles through a full sized chasm, there were forts on the high ground, to the north, Fort Montgomery, and to the south, Fort Clinton. These two forts were connected by short stretches of road and a bridge across the Popolopen, probably of a floating type.

The Hudson was obstructed here by a chain, a boom of logs, and one or more rope hawsers stretched from Fort Montgomery to Anthony's Nose. These effectively closed the river so long as the 60 guns in the two forts prevented the British from working on the obstructions.

Above the twin forts of the Popolopen, there was little save the badly planned and costly fortifications of Constitution Island across from West Point. The Point was not at that time occupied, although the original plans proposed in the Continental Congress seem to have included the fortifications of the site.

At the northern end of the Highlands level with Polopel's Island was a line of marine chevaux-de-frise—iron pointed tree trunks sunk below the surface of the river set in cribs of timber and stone.[15] There was originally a battery on the west bank controlling this line of submerged obstructions.

## THE CAMPAIGNS OF 1776 AND 1777

It will be recalled that the Continental Army under Washington drove the British from Boston early in 1776. The British retreated to Halifax and then, in accordance with Washington's expectations, returned to Staten Island with the obvious intention of trying to wrest Long Island and Manhattan Island from the Americans. During the early summer, both the British and American armies were concentrated around New York. The Hudson was closed by American batteries on lower Manhattan and by Forts Washington and Lee, with a line of chevaux-de-frise 12 miles farther north. The lower batteries proved worthless; Knox lost more men by his old guns bursting than were hurt aboard the British ships that ran the gauntlet on 12 July 1776.[16] The upper forts and chevaux-de-frise were passed on 14 September 1776 without serious loss. The line of chevaux-de-frise inspired respect, but the submerged iron-pointed stakes were not thick enough to stop vessels proceeding cautiously.[17]

The early battles went badly for Washington and the Continental army; both were destined to profit by experience. First, they lost Long Island, and then Manhattan Island save for Fort Washington, which remained but was isolated. Sir William Howe, a skillful commander, won again in a series of maneuvers which caused Washington's re-

---

[14]Fort Independence has sometimes been differently located; this is based on Captain Thomas Machin's Map of 1778 now in the Cornell University Library. This map shows, however, several variations from usually accepted works including a "third" boom or chain and fortification not mentioned elsewhere.

[15]Heusser, pp. 116-20, gives a well documented account of Erskine's original idea of this marine chevaux-de-frise; however, the originally proposed "tetrahedrons" were probably too complicated. Those used in Polopel's Island were certainly of the simpler crib-anchored type. The point of one is preserved in the Newburgh Museum.

[16]Knox to Mrs. Knox, 13 July 1776, as quoted by Drake, p. 28.

[17]Henry P. Johnson, *The Campaign of 1776 Around New York and Brooklyn* (Brooklyn, 1878) pp. 99-100.

tirement to White Plains. A battle was fought and, after an interval, the Continental army retreated to North Castle, which is almost three-quarters of the distance from New York City to the Highlands. The British considered the American position here to be unassailable.

Thus far, Washington had been fighting and maneuvering to the east of the Hudson; New England had been more or less the base of his operations. The retreating Continental army, however had moved north rather than east. They had retreated towards the Highlands. So long as Washington remained at North Castle, the whole line of communications from the Highlands east to New England was secure.

When the British army failed to attack at North Castle and moved back south early in November, 1776, there were other considerations. The Continental army, probably because of political pressure, still held Fort Washington on upper Manhattan Island; Fort Lee on top of the Palisades on the Jersey side was also strongly held. New Jersey and Philadelphia were, of course, vulnerable now that the British were firmly established in and around New York. Washington left General Charles Lee in command of a strong Continental force at North Castle and crossed the Hudson into New Jersey with about half his army. This move was necessary both to support the two garrisons and to oppose British occupation of New Jersey and eastern Pennsylvania. It was also the beginning of the great importance of the western line of communications with the Highlands.

The isolation of Fort Washington and the exposed position of Fort Lee were fundamental weaknesses. Washington and the Continental army, although in New Jersey, could not really support either. The British capitalized on these conditions. Fort Washington fell by assault on 16 November 1776.

Fort Lee was hastily abandoned to the enemy on 20 November 1776. Washington and his shrinking army were driven across New Jersey and into Pennsylvania. Nevertheless, he held fast to the Highlands. General Heath was in command at Peekskill with about 3,000 men, which was almost as many men as Washington retained under his own command.[18]

General Charles Lee (no relation to Confederate General Robert E. Lee) with culpable intentions, treated his command on the east side of the Hudson as independent of Washington's orders. He delayed for days complying with positive instructions to cross the Hudson with his force and reinforce the commander-in-chief in Pennsylvania. When he finally started he proceeded so slowly that he was captured at Basking Ridge in New Jersey; Sullivan, his second in command, quickly completed the rest of the march to join Washington.

Washington fought the tremendously important actions of Trenton and Princeton partly in order to restore the western lines to the Highlands. As will be explained later, the geography of the region made these lines far stronger now that Forts Washington and Lee were gone. At Morristown, early in January, 1777, he took up for the first time the ultimately victorious strategic line from Philadelphia to the Highlands. Washington took full advantage of his interior lines of communication. Morristown itself was shielded by a respectable small range of mountains making the field fortifications at Middlebrook extremely formidable and behind these he was able to move freely.

The British grand strategy of Burgoyne's attack from Canada was well known. Carlton had opposed Arnold in the Lake Champlain region in the summer and fall of '76. Washington was prepared to oppose strength to strength. Although he was not entirely

[18]Force, vol. III, p. 543.

responsible for the American dispositions, as the Continental Congress continued to meddle in command affairs, the general counter strategy was his, nevertheless.

A strong northern Continental force under Schuyler, and later Gates, was centered on the upper Hudson. Old, brave, and illiterate Israel Putnam was now in command of the Highlands. During the entire spring, Washington held his forces in positions between Philadelphia and the Highlands, with his main concentration at Middlebrook and Morristown. The attack from Canada was begun early. Washington anticipated that Howe would go up the river for a junction with Burgoyne at Albany, as this was obviously the sound move for the British commander to make.[19] Instead, Howe feinted overland through New Jersey towards Philadelphia. Washington had his army well in hand behind the Middlebrook fortifications. The British could not march off southwest and leave him on their flank and rear, and they were unwilling to attack the Continental army in its field defenses. Howe therefore pulled back to his ships. Washington anticipated the logical advance up the Hudson. Although the Highlands were already powerfully held, with supports at Pompton, more reinforcements were sent north. A large part of the infantry at Middlebrook was in motion along the valley and foothills roads, to be described later.

The British fleet, however, moved south, leaving only a garrison force in New York City. This move was inexplicable to Washington; but he had to oppose strength with strength. So he took his army across the Delaware to defend Philadelphia as soon as he was positive that Howe was committed to an attack on the seat of the Continental Congress. If Howe had attacked the Highlands in full force, Washington would, of course, have been there. Such a hypothetical move would have changed the war considerably.[20]

In the move to Philadelphia, Washington concentrated the army under his personal command—the Southern Army—at the lower end of the Highlands-Philadelphia line. As the Northern Continental army was above Albany, Howe had successfully spread the American defense,[21] won the battle of Brandywine and taken Philadelphia. Washington weakened the army defending the Highlands in order to get sorely needed reinforcements. Some withdrawals had already been made from the forces in the Highlands to strengthen the Northern army. In the words of another age, this was a calculated risk. Washington shrewdly figured that, at this time at least, decisive actions in the Highlands were unlikely. Sir Henry Clinton, the British commander in New York City, had neither the force nor the temperament to attack in strength. The fate of the new nation was at stake at Philadelphia and high up the Hudson. The fresh reinforcements enabled Washington to fight the tremendously important, drawn battle of Germantown.[22] Morgan's riflemen, in the Highlands during the summer, were sent north and helped immeasurably towards Burgoyne's defeat.

Both sides were straining for victory above Albany and at Philadelphia. Sir Henry Clinton in New York City had only about 4,500

[19]It is emphasized, however, that the decision was Howe's to make. His orders from Britain, although delayed, were advisory only, and not mandatory; see Fortescue, vol. 3, pp. 209-10. Sir Henry Clinton in his manuscript notes on Stedman (Nickerson, p. 339) certainly had no doubts that Howe should have gone; perhaps this was wisdom after the event.

[20]In the opinion of the authors, an attack up the Hudson by Howe would have been of most doubtful success. Washington with his whole force would have been in the Highlands.

[21]If the whole Continental Army had been united on the upper Hudson, Washington would have been in command personally. In preventing this, Howe could conceivably have considerably extended the war in point of time, since he and his army might otherwise have shared Burgoyne's fate.

[22]The use of "drawn" may be open to question; even the immediate results were favorable to the Continental cause: Freeman, vol. IV, pp. 516-19.

men; Putnam at the Highlands had even less. However, on or about this date, the British commander received about 3,000 men direct from England. With skill and dexterity, he moved up the Hudson. This attack was not intended to be more than a diversion. Clinton had neither the force nor the intention of cutting his way through to relieve Burgoyne, and he didn't even know of the British Northern army's perilous situation.[23]

In order to understand fully the fighting in the Highlands in early October, 1777, a knowledge of what went on elsewhere in the early months of the Revolution is important. We learned several things the hard way; so did the British. As already referred to, Knox found that batteries alone were useless where ranges were excessive. Probably about 600 yards would be the limit for positive closing of a channel by even the largest guns in daylight.[24] Accurate fire at night was next to impossible. Token installations, or installations with passages purposely left open, of chevaux-de-frise were not proof against the British Navy either in the Hudson between Forts Washington and Lee, or in the Delaware below Philadelphia.[25] Chains and booms of logs stretching continuously from bank to bank were rightly considered the only positive obstructions to a channel.[26]

[23]Sir Henry Clinton to Burgoyne from Montgomery, 7 October 1777, as quoted in Carr and Koke, p. 42.

[24]Even this is questionable; the old wooden fighting ships would absorb a great many solid shot without being totally destroyed. Lighter faster vessels moving with advantageous wind and tide were hard to hit. The whole is, of course, dependent also upon the size of guns as well as the skill of their crews. Other things being equal, the larger the gun the more accurate and destructive it was. On 1 June 1776, the largest guns in the Highlands were 15 9-pounders: Stirling-Putnam-Sargent report as quoted in Boynton, p. 28. In September 1780, there was one 24-pounder and 18 18-pounders: see reference No. 4 above. Knox's report of 24 August 1781 shows three 24-pounders and 20 18-pounders: Brooks, p. 142.

[25]For lower Hudson obstructions, see reference No. 15 above; also Ward, p. 269. For Delaware below Philadelphia, see Archibald Robertson, *Diaries and Sketches in America*, (New York, 1930) p. 151.

On the other hand, the glorious defense of Sullivan's Island against attack by the British fleet in Sir Henry Clinton's unsuccessful effort to take Charleston in 1776 taught the British not to attack our forts with ships alone. Forts Washington and Lee were taken from their land sides. Fort Mercer on the Delaware was evacuated in the face of a strong force of British and Hessians approaching overland. Fort Mifflin, on an island in the Delaware at the same point, was blasted into nothingness mainly by batteries of British naval guns landed on the Pennsylvania shore.

SIR HENRY CLINTON'S BREAKTHROUGH

Sir Henry Clinton arrived below Stony Point with 4,000 men on 5 October 1777. The American defenders in the Highlands numbered a total of only about 2,000, many of whom were militia. Major General Putnam, who had probably passed his period of greatest efficiency, was in general command with his headquarters at Peekskill on the east side of the river. A rather unusual condition existed on the west side. Brigadier General George Clinton who was also the governor of the State of New York was in a somewhat ambiguous general command. Though he was brave and capable he shifted from Governor to General and back again, probably without changing his hat. He was technically on leave of absence from the army at the state capitol at Esopus, or Kingston, but hastened down to the Highlands to assume command of the fortifications on the west side.[27]

It will be recalled that there were two main fortifications on this side: Fort Clinton to the south of Popolopen Kill and Fort Montgomery to the north. Brigadier Gen-

[26]These obstructions in the lengths required to close the Hudson were new; they were never attacked by ships during the war. What a frigate, or small ship-of-the-line, would have done to them with the wind and tide behind her remains in the realm of conjecture.

[27]*Quarterly Journal* of the New York State Historical Association, April, 1931, p. 168.

eral James Clinton, the brother of the governor, was in command of Fort Montgomery. There was an abundance of people and places by the name of Clinton; towards the end of the Revolution, there was to be another and quite different Fort Clinton in the Highlands.[28]

Sir Henry Clinton[29] the British commander, landed first on the east side of the river at Verplanck's Point and took a minor work there, convincing Putnam that the attack was to be on him at Peekskill. Putnam actually sent across the river to the two American Generals Clinton for reinforcements, weakening the forces on the west side.[30] The main British attack, however, was to be on the west side. On the morning of 6 October 1777 before dawn, an expeditionary force was landed at Stony Point and marched inland through extremely difficult terrain south of Dunderburg. There were points in the route over which they advanced where a determined corporal's guard could have held them up for hours,[31] but they were completely unopposed.

This passage from Stony Point across the back of Dunderberg culminates in a position known locally as "The Timp." A part of this trail remains today very much as it was then; it's a tough climb for an active man unencumbered with 60 or 80 pounds of equipment. Even the British did not attempt to take artillery. Apparently, Washington was the only Continental commander who suggested that The Timp be garrisoned,[32] yet neither of the American Clintons saw fit

to even post scouts there.

After arriving at the hamlet of Doodletown, one half of the British force turned off to the right to attack Fort Clinton from the land side. The other half continued behind Bear Mountain and came down on the northern side of Popolopen Kill to attack Fort Montgomery. These two forces, beautifully coordinated as to time, brushed aside American forces sent out to impede their progress. They delivered their assaults with precision and bravery. They were both completely successful, although the American garrisons fought bravely and well, causing heavy losses to the assailants, and some of the defenders made good their escape.[33]

Sir Henry Clinton had failed at Charleston against fortifications by attacking from the sea. He succeeded in the Highlands from the land. The chain stretched between Fort Montgomery and Anthony's Nose on the other side of the Hudson, and the boom of logs which was actually a series of rough hewn tree trunks bound with iron hoops and links like the rungs of a ladder were now useless.[34] These things are of value only when the whole ensemble is protected by powerful batteries. These obstructions, along with rope hawsers, were easily severed by the British the following day.[35]

Perhaps the most disappointing blow of all was the fate of several Continental ships-of-war, including the frigates *Montgomery*

[28]Fort Arnold at the tip of the high land at West Point was renamed Fort Clinton after Arnold's treachery; the original Fort Clinton was not rebuilt after it was torn down by the British about 26 October 1777.

[29]Probably a cousin of the New York Clinton's; Sir Henry was at one time in the New York Provincial Militia while his father was Royal Governor.

[30]A total reduction of 260 men according to Henry B. Carrington, *Battles of the American Revolution* (New York, ca. 1876) p. 360.

[31]Charles Stedman, *History of the American War*, London, 1794, vol. I, pp. 400-01.

[32]Nickerson, p. 347.

[33]A well documented and clear account of this is in Carr and Koke, pp. 31-39.

[34]Apparently the original idea was to use "four or five booms of logs," such as are used in lumbering where water transportation to a mill is required; these would extend all the way across the river, if secured together with suitable chains. However, an entirely different idea was actually used. The best reference for this is the segment of the actual boom, probably that from West Point, preserved in the Newburgh museum.

[35]*Year Book*, Dutchess County Historical Society, 1935, says "cut off by British artificers"; hereafter Dutchess County. A diagram in Boynton, p. 70, of the West Point chain would indicate that cutting was necessary. However, clevises, which could be opened easily, were included in the West Point chain at least; Boynton, p. 57.

and *Constitution*. They had moved down the river in accordance with General Putnam's orders, even though undermanned and poorly equipped. The wind was strong from the north; the crews hadn't the skill to sail up the river, nor the strength to pull their vessels to safety with their boats.[36] The *Montgomery* was set on fire by her crew and eventually blew up as she lay helpless close to the chain; several smaller vessels were similarly destroyed within a few hundred yards. The *Constitution* went aground and was burned by her crew considerably farther north.[37]

The Highlands were then practically defenseless above Fort Montgomery. The rather elaborate defense installations on Constitution Island were burned and abandoned by the few defenders, without a fight. The line of chevaux-de-frise opposite Polopel's Island was useless, since there were no manned batteries to defend it.[38] The British Navy found the great iron-shod trunks secured in their boxes of stone on the river bottom and pulled them out.[39]

The British, as already pointed out, had no intention of joining Burgoyne farther up the river. Sir Henry was a cautious commander and was understandably anxious about New York City, which was his primary responsibility. The temporary capitol of New York State was then at Esopus, also called Kingston. The British burned this place and a few other things in this general vicinity. Light vessels of the British Navy

penetrated as far north as Saugerties on 17 October 1777, the day Burgoyne surrendered 45 miles farther north at Saratoga, but Sir Henry Clinton was already returning to New York City as early as 10 October 1777.[40] Fort Montgomery was demolished,[41] and a temporary garrison was left at Fort Clinton, but this was withdrawn about 27 October 1777, after the news of Burgoyne's surrender had been confirmed. The victorious Northern Continental army of nearly 20,000 men was far too strong for Sir Henry Clinton to risk a part of his relatively small command defending an incomplete work 50 miles north of his main position.

The Highlands were once more back in American hands, but the original fortifications were almost valueless. The British had taken or destroyed more than 100 guns, the chain, the boom, and all American naval vessels built or building in the Hudson. In addition to the river fortifications, the Continental Village above Peekskill had been destroyed. This was perhaps the best winter quarters for American troops in the country. The damage was very extensive indeed.

### FINAL SYSTEM OF HIGHLAND FORTIFICATIONS

Clinton's breakthrough and destructions were probably blessings in disguise. They did no permanent harm, since he held the Highlands only 20 days. As often happens in war, the second system of works was far stronger than the first due to the experience gained in losing the first. There was now time, because of Burgoyne's surrender, for Washington and his staff to carefully plan proper fortifications in the light of experience in the recent past both here and elsewhere. The combination of a chain and a

[36]Many references; Stedman, vol. I, pp. 405-06, is most picturesque.
[37]Clinton Papers, vol. II, p. 394.
[38]Dutchess County, p. 98.
[39]There is a tradition that this line of obstructions was built in part with impressed Tory labor, and that one of these Tories showed the British where they were. This is unlikely: Force, vol. III, pp, 324, 860; Clinton Papers, vol. I, pp. 571, 617. Machin's battery near New Windsor was originally constructed to command the river here, but was not defended. Remains of this battery are still clear, but the river is too wide here to be effectively controlled by even the largest guns of that day.

[40]Nickerson, p. 391.
[41]Apparently, the British never intended to keep Montgomery and may have begun their systematic destruction of it earlier than that of Fort Clinton, where the remains of the works are more in evidence today.

boom of logs with water batteries at both ends could be relied upon to close the river, but these water batteries must be secure from land assault. So another careful study was made of the entire area and a new system was evolved.

West Point and the island opposite were the key to this system. Washington himself designated this location.[42] It involved a completely different arrangement of fortifications. This new plan was not only far stronger, but more adapted to Washington's use of the Highlands. Communications on the west side of the river were now more important militarily, although those with New England were still the primary consideration in holding the new country together politically and economically. A new chain and boom were now placed here.[43] All efforts to close the river were concentrated at this single point. A single defense community was set up which was strong from any angle of approach. The water batteries at other points were weak and actually for other purposes.[44] Mere outposts were established at the entrance to the Highlands.

The landside defenses were now far more important than formerly. Fortunately, Constitution Island was almost perfectly situated for Washington's use. It was separated from the eastern mainland by only a small stretch of water, but by a wide and fairly easily defended marshland. There was no possibility

of large vessels passing between the island and the eastern mainland. It would be very difficult for soldiers to attack the island from the mainland.[45] In other words, only the island need be held on the east; it could be supplied, reinforced, and controlled easily from West Point on the other side of the river. This fitted perfectly into Washington's strategic plan, as his communications with West Point from his positions farther south in New Jersey were to the west of the river.

It should not be inferred, however, that this shift of emphasis from the east to the west side was either complete, or without fluctuations. The only good road paralleling the Hudson was to the east—the old Albany Post Road. Two or three important batteries were maintained on the long hill across from West Point—now called Fort Hill. The Beverly Robinson House, situated between these points and the river was frequently used as the Headquarters of the Continental Commander in the Highlands. During the joint action with the French against Newport, Washington transferred a portion of his main force from west of the river to the east.

West Point and Constitution Island were nevertheless the basic defenses, and these were independent of communications to the east. The actual fortifications consisted of water batteries at either end of the chain and boom, and other water batteries both at the Point and on Constitution Island covering the open stretch of water before the river bends sharply around the Point. High above the river on the Point there was an enclosed

[42]Washington to Major General Putnam, 2 December 1777, as quoted by Forman, p. 9.

[43]Heusser, p. 141.

[44]Mainly to prevent the interruption of King's Ferry by small naval forces of the enemy. The breakdown of artillery given to André by Arnold and quoted in Lossing, vol. I, p. 722, shows three pieces at both Stony Point (one iron 18-pounder and two iron 12-pounders) and Verplanck's Point (three small mortars). Colonel Rufus Putnam built a small open battery on the site of Fort Montgomery in August 1779, according to Carr and Koke, p. 52. Samuel Richards, "Personal Narrative of an Officer in the Revolutionary War," *United Service Magazine*, Series 3, vol. IV, p. 80, under date of 3 June 1778, refers to "cannon brought back after being used to drive ships away from King's Ferry;" hereafter, Richards.

[45]At the time of the Revolution, this was a tidal swamp with a small creek through it, and is little better today. Richards, p. 55, states it to have been on 21 March 1778, "half leg deep in mud and water, and could not get across . . . ." However, a battery was "to be erected . . . to hinder the enemy from getting in the upper river by way of the creek with small armed boats.": Lieutenant Colonel Gouvion's report on the State of the Works at West Point, 2 November 1780, in West Point Library.

fort named at first Arnold and, after his defection, Clinton.

On the plain beside Fort Arnold, there were barracks and warehouses. About a half mile on a rugged hill stood Fort Putnam; around it at a rough radius of about a mile were other works called redoubts and batteries connected by semi-fortified trails situated in good natural positions overlooking streams, small fields and roads. The whole was very strong indeed, and Knox was voicing the feelings of the army when as early as 7 May 1779[46] he said he did not fear for the post.

The fortification of West Point was begun in January, 1778, at first under the direction of a French engineer, Lt. Col. Louis Dashaiy de la Radière. Later a Pole in our service, Col. Thaddeus Kosciuszko, was of great value. The basic structure discussed above slowly grew under the hands of thousands of men; minor changes and additions were made constantly. Perhaps the whole reached its ultimate strength under Knox, who became commander on 29 August 1782,[47] after the danger of attack had passed.

Even more important than the main fortifications at West Point were the ten to twelve miles of rugged country extending to the south end of the Highlands.[48] Surprise was impossible so long as outposts were vigilant. An advance through these mountains, then mainly roadless, would be extremely hazardous in the face of a strong enemy.[49] In order to retain this situation, Washington refused to occupy the British fort at Stony Point after Wayne took it in 1779. After all usable

cannon and supplies had been removed it was razed and abandoned.[50]

To the east of the Hudson, there is rolling country between Manhattan Island and the Highlands. There is little continuous rugged country. This is not true of the land to the west of the river; in fact, the Palisades, when first examined, seem extremely defensible. These verticle masses of igneous rock, rising to heights of 400 feet above the river and only about a quarter mile wide, are most unusual.

This long narrow formation extends almost to the Highlands. At its northern end, the range broadens out into small mountains with steep faces. Yet the military strength of this territory is limited. To the west, there is a belt of low, in part swampy, country unfit for defense but good for surprise and encirclement. After Cornwallis so nearly cut off General Nathaniel Green and his garrison in Fort Lee, Washington made no attempt to hold any part of the Palisades and used the low country behind as a kind of neutral zone into which he sent patrols frequently.[51]

Since the range of mountains forming the Highlands—locally called the Ramapos—intersects the river at an angle, the low country between this range and the Palisades is roughly triangular. There were two main roads in this area leading north. The valley road lay roughly in the middle of this area and ended at Haverstraw at the end of the Palisades. The foothill road lay further to the west in the hills in front of the Ramapo Mountains. Both routes were, therefore, somewhat exposed to the British attacking across the neutral ground. The danger became greater as the roads drew closer to the river. The British Navy gave the enemy freedom to attack where and when they liked.

[46]Drake, p. 61.

[47]Brooks, p. 167.

[48]Several roads crossed the Highlands west of the river: Boynton (Map), opposite p. 44.

[49]There was only one "usable" road across the Highlands on the west side of the river within reach of a force using the river for their line of supply. This crosses Dunderberg through "the Timp." It was probably improved somewhat after the British used it in October of 1777, but was still extremely steep in places. It remains but a difficult trail today.

[50]Freeman, vol. V, p. 115 with his usual complete references.

[51]This neutral ground extended all round the British New York defenses; Freeman, vol. V, pp. 125-30.

Throughout the Revolution, this country was frequently the scene of British activity, and at various times they held several points on the western shore.

The main road from New England crossed the river at King's Ferry at the southern end of the Highlands and then joined one or the other at these roads. The valley road through Scotch Plains, Springfield, Orange, Bloomfield, Acquackanonek and Paramus (now Ridgewood) has largely lost its identity in the growth of highways and the suburban metropolitan area. However, the foothill road is now in part United States Route 202 through Suffern, Pompton and Boonton to Morristown. Morristown was well protected behind the defenses at Middlebrook, but the northern part of even the foothill road was exposed.

When the British occupied Stony Point, King's Ferry was closed to Continental use, and the valley road was seriously affected. However, these things were not disastrous. A simple detour up the Albany Post Road on the east to Fishkill and across the river to New Windsor solved this problem. The trip could be continued behind the mountains to the Ramapo Gap, or by crossing the Highlands near the river and using the foothill road. In either case, however, the foothill road from Suffern to about Pompton was somewhat exposed.[52] Washington did not like this situation; his communications with West Point were almost as important as the Post itself. He opened, therefore, a military road that ran from Morristown behind the Ramapo Range to the gap,[53] which was fortified.[54] He was able to communicate, if need be, entirely behind the mountains from Mor-

ristown to New Windsor and then over Storm King Mountain to West Point.[55] This second road system was well removed from British interference. The ultra-modern Route 17 from New York City now passes through Ramapo Gap and continues north behind the mountains for some miles very much as the old roads did in 1778.

## THE CAMPAIGNS OF 1778-1780

With the above general conditions in mind, let's return to actual operations. The new system of defenses was surprisingly quickly put in a state to repel an attack.

Heavy guns arrived at West Point on 25 May 1778.[56] A stronger chain had been stretched across a month before,[57] and the boom followed a short time later. In addition to obstructing the river, both of these served as emergency bridges, as men could cross the river dry shod on either.[58]

In the Spring, Sir Henry Clinton succeeded Sir William Howe in command of the British armies in America. The British immediately abandoned Philadelphia and returned overland across New Jersey to New York, fighting on the way the drawn battle of Monmouth. The strategic situation was now very much as it had been the two years before. Again Washington's army lay mainly around Morristown. He made full use of his line of communications stretching from West Point to Philadelphia. The Delaware River, since it was impassable to all forms of fighting ships above Trenton, presented no problem.

In the meantime, however, one completely new factor emerged. A French fleet and army

---

[52]Ward, p. 587; Carrington's Map opposite p. 302.

[53]The remains of a portion of this cordoroy road were revealed by the draining of Lake Wee-wah near Tuxedo Park, New York, in 1954, as an indirect result of the building of a new super-highway.

[54]The remains of Fort Sidman near Hillburn, New Jersey, at the southeast entrance to the Ramapo defile are still extant.

[55]This road is still traceable; the new Storm King Highway—not that blasted out of the river face of the mountain, but the newer super-highway over the mountain—coincides with the old Continental road in part. It should be remembered, however, that during the Revolution transportation by water was used whenever possible.

[56]Richards, p. 77.

[57]Heusser, p. 138.

[58]Boynton, p. 77.

arrived off Sandy Hook, but as the large French ships-of-the-line drew too much water to enter the New York harbor area, it was decided to attack Newport in Rhode Island instead. Again the Continental troops went north in front of the Ramapos; a large part of them crossed at King's Ferry or further down the river at Haverstraw.[59] In August, Washington again occupied White Plains, so after two years of fighting he was back almost where he started, while the British were cooped up in New York City and its tributary islands.

But the attack on Newport was doomed to failure. Sullivan, the Continental commander, had at one time 10,000 men including two Continental brigades from Washington's main force under LaFayette, as well as militia. In part due to friction between the allies, and in part the appearance of a British relieving fleet and a severe storm, nothing was accomplished.

In the early fall, heavy forces of British and Hessians from New York City moved north overland on both sides of the Hudson. These were in reality little more than foraging expeditions, although Cornwallis on the west side had 5,000 men and Knyphauser to the east had 3,000. These moved through the country below the Highlands cutting all roads against light opposition and, as Washington kept his main forces well back from the relatively open areas, there was no full scale clash between the opposing forces.

The winter of 1778-1779 was spent by the Continental army on both sides of the Hudson. The weather was comparatively mild, and as both the British and American forces remained long in their winter quarters, a great deal of work was done on the West Point defenses during this period.

Finally, on 28 May 1779, Sir Henry Clinton moved up the Hudson with 6,000 men and landed on both sides of the river just below the Highlands. There was an uncompleted Continental work on the west side at Stony Point which was abandoned without a fight. On Verplanck's Point to the east, there stood a small completed fortification known as Fort LaFayette, which was surrendered after being surrounded, and some 70 North Carolina Continentals were made prisoners.[60]

Washington had West Point strongly garrisoned. In addition he moved his main army up the west side of the river and interposed it between the British at Stony Point and the fortifications around the Point. Sir Henry Clinton completed the Stony Point defenses but as he could do no more, he left a garrison here and at Varplanck's Point and retired down the river.

Washington planned an attack on both these posts. Wayne carried out the attack on Stony Point successfully on 16 July 1779. The British lost almost 700 in killed, wounded, and prisoners as well as the fort and all it contained. The attack against Verplanck's Point failed. After an inspection and careful consideration, as already pointed out, Washington, because of its exposed position, decided against the occupation of Stony Point.[61] The works were burned, or otherwise gutted.[62]

In the spring of 1780 in the north, things had to some extent reached a crisis. The Continental Army and many civilians were discouraged by internal conditions. On the other hand, Washington's strategic position from the Highlands to Philadelphia was even more trying on the enemy. Sir Henry Clinton felt that he could not attack the Highlands,

[59]As usual when no enemy offensive activity was expected, these forces used the "valley road" which was presumably better, but more exposed to attack from the Palisades; Ward, p. 587.

[60]Stedman, vol. II, p. 149.

[61]Freeman, vol. V, p. 115.

[62]Most fortifications in the Highlands were composite affairs of stone and masonry base walls with timber and fascines above. See particularly Arnold's report taken from André and reproduced by Lossing, vol. I, notes pp. 722-23.

or Washington's somewhat flexible positions to the south and west. Washington could concentrate his forces easily, and relatively quickly, at any threatened point. Ample warning was assured by the nature of the country which had to be crossed. Beacon fires or signal cannon announced any maritime advance up the Hudson.[63] Assuredly, the British felt hemmed in. They had only the islands around New York Harbor, and the "neutral ground" which surrounded them outside these was most unfriendly.[64]

Actually, the British force in New York was relatively weak; a large part of their army had been sent to the south where the British southern campaign was now in full swing. The British feared, and to some extent the Continentals planned, an attack on New York.[65] Meanwhile, however, the Highlands were in extreme peril. All through the summer, Benedict Arnold, who managed to be made Continental commander in the Highlands, was planning to sell out to the enemy. By this time, The British were well aware of the tremendous value to them of this position.[66]

The André-Arnold meeting, papers taken from the former, the flight of the latter, and the final complete failure of the whole con- spiracy are well known.[67] But the actual mechanics of the plan to give West Point to the enemy are usually not clear. One shudders to think how easily it could have succeeded. It depended upon four factors and one vital condition that was not fulfilled: first, André had to get back to Sir Henry Clinton with the details of the plan and set the British ships in motion up the river; second, the mobile Continental forces, which would have undoubtedly moved north, had to stop between Stony Point and the Highlands proper;[68] third, Arnold had to manage to dissipate most of his garrison by sending it south, east, and west, as if to meet the enemy at the edge of the Highlands, and he also had to weaken the chain and boom by removing some clevis pins, or links, so that British ships could get through the river;[69] fourth, Arnold had to mismanage the river defenses with his reduced force so that British soldiers and sailors could get ashore and give Arnold a tangible excuse for a quick surrender. The British, already thoroughly briefed in the land side defenses by means of plans and descriptions,[70] would then quickly take over the whole West Point defense system, and, with Arnold's aid, try to beat the inevitable Continental counter- attack.

The one vital condition for all this was the absence of Washington himself from the area. He passed through Peekskill on his way to a conference with French officers at Hart- ford on 18 September; he was not scheduled to return for several days. The surrender of West Point was to have taken place during Washington's absence, if André had not been

[63] Arrangements were made at various times for quick notification of the garrison at West Point of an attack up the Hudson; beacon fires and the firing of cannon were to give the alarm. Sentries placed on the South Bastion of Fort Arnold were cautioned to be particularly alert for the firing of the beacon behind the battery on the site of Fort Montgomery; Orderly Book of Conti- nental Army—12 Fabruary 1779 to 8 July 1779 (copy in West Point Library), entry, Headquarters West Point 1 July 1779. After Arnold's treachery, a gun- boat was stationed at Anthony's Nose for the same purpose; Carr and Koke, p. 52.

[64] This neutral ground on both sides of the Hudson was unfriendly to both sides; bands of criminals masquer- ading as Cowboys (Tories) and Skinners (Whigs) preyed on both sides almost equally. They seldom fought, but robbed the weak indiscriminately. Boynton, p. 135.

[65] Carl Van Doren, *Secret History of the American Revolution* (New York, 1941) p. 322; hereafter, Van Doren.

[66] Nickerson, p. 207.

[67] Van Doren; this work is extremely good in con- nection with this whole regrettable series of events.

[68] They had done so in 1779, and again in May 1780, when Clinton had moved up the river to occupy Stony Point and Verplanck's Point temporarily: Nickerson, p. 206.

[69] Lossing, vol. I, p. 720.

[70] Some of these were already in British hands; others were in André's boot when he was captured; Lossing, vol. I, p. 721.

captured. Washington returned to Arnold's headquarters on 25 September, and might easily have thwarted the whole plan, even if it were proceeding according to schedule.

Actually, André's capture on 22 September ended the real danger. The British could not proceed without the information he was carrying back both in documents and in his head. Three days elapsed before Arnold heard of his capture which meant, of course, his own (Arnold's) incrimination. While Arnold was escaping down the river, Washington quickly put the fortifications in a state of defense, and the British did not attack.

The winter of 1780-1781 was unpleasant in every way, yet the Continental army occupied posts from Middlebrook to the Highlands and into Connecticut still strangling the British in New York. Although the long war was sapping the energies of both sides, Washington was winning by strategy, despite his usual inferiority in forces. His advantage in handling positions and transportation was making up for his shortages of disciplined efficient soldiers. So long as he held West Point, there was little the British could do in the north.

### The Concluding Phase

The actual fighting of the final and greatest of Washington's campaigns opened with a dubious attack on New York, probably a feint down the east side of the Hudson early in July, 1781. Washington had about 5,000 men. Rochambeau with about the same number of French Allies had recently arrived from Newport. It seems unlikely that a real attack could have been seriously planned against Sir Henry Clinton who had 14,000 behind rivers and fortifications, but the effort was certainly useful in keeping the initiative in Washington's hands.

Clinton with the main British army was in New York, and Cornwallis with a smaller but more active force was in Virginia. Washington now decided to attack the latter with the aid of the French Army and Navy. In a superbly executed strategic move to his right flank late in August, he and the French marched to the head of Chesapeake Bay, where they were ferried down the bay by the French fleet to the peninsula above Yorktown. Heath, the original commander in the Highlands, in 1776, was again left in charge with perhaps 2,500 to hold West Point against Clinton who now had about 17,000.

Clinton was deceived by the first attack on him in New York near Kingsbridge. The French, who crossed the Hudson just below the Highlands appeared to make preparations to attack Staten Island from New Jersey, but then secretly marched south. Somehow everything went well for the Allies. Cornwallis with his entire force was surrounded, besieged and captured. In the meantime, Heath seems to have convincingly concealed his weakness until he was again reinforced.

The fighting war was now virtually over. New York and Charleston remained in British hands for two more years, but no battles were fought in 1782 and 1783. Throughout the new nation, people turned to peaceful pursuits, as if a full treaty of peace had been concluded. Yet some sort of an army had to be kept in the field.

West Point and the Highlands were the scene of many troubles during the two years between Yorktown and final demobilization. During the winter of 1781-1782 Heath and his subordinate McDougall indulged in an official exchange of words and name calling. The final winter saw the dreadful troubles in the Continental Army encamped between Newburgh and West Point, which could have had very serious and upsetting consequences but for Washington's great capacity to deal with men.

Major General Henry Knox was chief of

artillery under Washington. He was also perhaps the foremost military engineer in the Continental Army. He laid out some of the fortifications outside Boston in 1775. He advocated the Arsenal at Springfield in 1777 and had the first American military academy at his headquarters at Pluckemin in New Jersey in the winter of '78-79. He established his headquarters near West Point in November 1781 and busied himself writing a report on the fortifications. On 29 August 1782, he was invested with the command of all the forces in the Highlands, and under him, West Point became the center of the Army, and also the main depository of arms from the disbanded Continental forces.

The importance of the West Point fortifications dwindled with the passage of years; but even during the Civil War the post was still defensible. New model Columbiads were installed in water batteries to control the Hudson at this point. Some of these guns and fortifications remain; now useful only for decorative effect. It is unlikely that the Hudson, except for New York Harbor, will ever again play a significant part in military campaigns.

Although Knox undoubtedly continued his lectures and classes at West Point during his period of residence there—he was perhaps the earliest advocate of a military academy[71] —the present United States Military Academy was not officially established until 1802. Professionally, in its production of solidly grounded military men, many of them of the highest order of leadership, West Point continues to symbolize the power of Washington's original bastion on the Hudson.

[71]Boynton, p. 177.

# THE EARLY DAYS OF THE QUEEN'S RANGERS
## AUGUST 1776—FEBRUARY 1777

By John R. Cuneo*

RAISED for service in the American Revolution,[1] the unit known to history as "Queen's Rangers" — but originally called the "Queen's American Rangers"—began its history with an incident in the life of one individual.

Seventeen hundred and seventy-six. A small boat bobbled alongside the H.M.S. *Eagle* as it swung at anchor off Sandy Hook in the warm mid-July sun. A tall, middle-aged man wearily clambered aboard. Word soon spread through the swarm of tall-masted vessels surrounding the *Eagle:* "Major Robert Rogers has escaped from the rebels!"[2]

All knew "Major Rogers of the Rangers."[3] Newspapers had spread his fame on two continents. A brilliant career in the Old French War had been followed by his supposed treason at the far western post of Michilimackinac. He had been acquitted by a court martial but the dark cloud hovered around him as he frantically sought government aid in London, only to spend almost two years in debtors' prison. A famous civil action against General Gage had brought down on Rogers' head the condemnation of the army's high command and King George forbade his being given *any* command.[4] It was widely believed that he returned to America to enlist in the

rebel cause: rumor had made the Major American "Commander in Chief of the Indians."[5]

Actually, Rogers had returned to America with the hope of recouping his personal fortunes, since London's doors had been shut firmly in his face. He had little comprehension of the rebellion under way on these shores, and treated it as a surface manifestation which would probably soon disappear. When he finally realized that he must choose sides, he sought a commission from the Americans. But it was too late. Orders from General Washington caused his arrest while en route to Philadelphia, where he purposed to lay his recommendations before the Continental Congress. Imprisoned on "violent suspicion" (to quote Thomas Jefferson)[6] of being involved in the famous conspiracy against Washington (which existed principally in the inflamed minds of the patriots), he was refused an opportunity to serve with the Continentals or even to return to England via the West Indies. Facing trial, when niceties of proof meant little to revolutionary judges,[7] Rogers had little choice. The result was as his legend would have had it: he escaped from the Philadelphia prison and made his way to the British.

---

*The writer is a practicing attorney in South Norwalk, Conn., who authored *Winged Mars*, a history of military air developments in Germany, 1870-1914.

[1]The Queen's Rangers of the American Revolution had no connection with Robert Rogers' earlier ranging units or with detachments as the "Queen's Rangers" which fought at Detroit in 1763 during Pontiac's siege.

[2]See e.g. entry of 18 July 1776, *Thomas Moffat's Diary*, MS, Library of Congress; Serle to Dartmouth, 25 July 1776, *B. F. Stevens's Facsimiles of Manuscripts in European Archives Relating to America 1773-1783 with Descriptions, Editorial Notes, Collations, References, and Translations*, Vol. XXIV (London, Nov. 1895), 2040.

[3]A biography of this title is being prepared by the writer for publication.

[4]Memorandum of King George, 1 Apr. 1775, Sir

John Fortescue, ed., *The Correspondence of King George the Third*. Vol. III. *July 1773—December 1777* (London, 1928), 195-196.

[5]See e.g. letter of 6 July 1776 in Margaret Wheeler Willard, ed., *Letters on the American Revolution 1774-1776* (Boston & N. Y., 1925), 325. Such rumors were printed in the newspapers and were the source of the title on the famous fictitious portrait of Rogers issued by Thomas Hart in London on 1 Oct. 1776 and copied in both France and Germany.

[6]Jefferson to Fleming, 1 July 1776, photograph of MS, M. Lincoln Schuster, ed., *A Treasury of the World's Great Letters* (N. Y., 1940), opp. 170.

[7]For a contemporary admission that there was no proof of any guilt on Rogers' part see Bartlett to Landon, 15 July 1776, Peter Force, ed., *American Archives. Fifth Series*. Vol. I (Wash., 1848), 348.

Here he found welcome — possibly unexpected. With the news (actually false) that the rebels were trying to induce Rogers to join them, the King had changed his mind and General Howe had been given permission to make an offer to Rogers.[8] The latter can scarcely be blamed for some desire for revenge: he was now receptive to the British overtures.[9] On August 6, General Howe reported to Lord Germain: "Major Rogers, having escaped to us from Philadelphia, is empowered to raise a battalion of Rangers, which, I hope, may be useful in the course of the campaign."[10]

Loyalists had been flocking to the British, hoping to help end the uprising in a hurry. Recruiting progressed rapidly. Some of the new soldiers were men of principle, who had refused to abandon their loyalty to Great Britain and were now anticipating the joy of avenging the losses, insults and beatings enduring at the hands of the Sons of Liberty. Others were adventurers, looking toward gain when the obviously stronger side surely would prevail, or mere scoundrels interested in the loot of war. It was a weird combination, with one common denominator: few had any experience as soldiers.

When Rogers surveyed these recruits of '76, farmers and townspeople who scarcely knew one end of a gun from the other, he must have despairingly recalled the experienced and sturdy New Hampshire men of '56 in his first ranger unit. These men, now facing him in ragged line, were not "rangers"

—yet inevitaly they carried the once proud title of "Rogers' Rangers."

British officers looked askance at the outfit. During the previous war, the regulars had been forced to accept the rangers because the battlefields were in the forests of northern New York. Here in southern New York the wilderness had disappeared. Conditions were not unlike European battlefields. Townspeople and farmers had no special qualities or training to stand in line with British regulars.

Something else had developed in the British mind: a tendency to "look down" on all Americans.[11] Shortly before he left London in 1755, Franklin told of the reflections cast "on American courage, religion, understanding, etc., in which we were treated with the utmost contempt, as the lowest of mankind, and almost of a different species from the English of Britain. . . ."[12] An English writer in 1776 described American troops as being "effeminate, new raised soldiers, commanded by officers without knowledge or experience."[13]

What particularly rankled the British officers was the fact that the officers of Rogers' unit were not even "gentlemen." In British regiments commissions were bought and sold within a rather restricted group. Therefore any purchaser was, in the current mind, prima-facie a "gentleman." Rogers carried on the colonial system of awarding commissions to any man who could enlist a certain number of men. This had its obvious faults which soon appeared in tory and rebel units alike.

A report on Rogers' unit presented the British officers' point of view:

". . . Many of those officers were Men of mean extraction without any degree of education suffi-

[8]Germaine to Howe, 5 Jan. 1776, Peter Force, ed., *American Archives. Fourth Series.* Vol. IV (Wash., 1843), 575.

[9]Rogers was approached by General Clinton when the latter put into New York harbor on 4 Feb. 1776 while en route to Charleston. Rogers refused on the basis that he had given his parole to the Americans not to bear arms against the colonies. Memorandum by Clinton, *Journal of an Expedition to the Southern Colonies under the Command of Maj'r Gen'l Clinton*, MS, *Clinton Papers*, William L. Clements Library. This contradicts the accepted historical view that Rogers at this time was guilty of duplicity towards the Americans.

[10]Howe to Germain, 6 Aug. 1776, *Force*, I, 789.

[11]See e.g. Ralph N. Miller "American Nationalism as a Theory of Nature," *The William and Mary Quarterly*, XII (Jan. 1955), 74-95.

[12]Quoted in *ibid.*, 82.

[13]*Idem.*

cient to quality them to bear His Majesty's Commission and . . . he (Gen'l Howe) had been deceived by Lt. Col'o Rogers who recommended those men for commissions in the Queens Rangers —in direct violation of a General Order of October, 76—by which Commanding Officers of Provincial Corps were ordered to be particularly careful to inform themselves of such persons as they intended should bear Commissions in the Corps . . . and to Recommend none but such as were Strictly "unexceptionable it can nevertheless be positively proved that many of those officers recommended by Lieu't Col'o Rogers had been bred Mechanecks others had kept Publik Houses, and One or Two had even kept Bawdy Houses in the City of New York . . . Mr. Brandon both during the time of his being an Officer in the Queens Rangers kept a Tavern and eating house in New York . . . Captain Griffiths kept a dram Shop in the Fly Market New York . . . Captain Eagles was still more illeterate and low bred than Fraser . . . Welsh was the last [least?] exceptionable of them all he had been a petty constable in the City of New York . . ."[14]

Yet something might be said on behalf of Rogers' officers. Daniel Frazer had served for twenty-three years in the regular army. He was wounded at Ticonderoga in '58 and had been recommended to Rogers by a British general for a lieutenancy.[15] John Brandon, who had been a New York resident since the end of the Old French War, in which he had served, was forced in May of '75 to flee to Boston. Here he became first lieutenant in the Loyal Irish Volunteers raised under General Gage. He went to Halifax with the British army when Boston was evacuated and followed it to New York.[16] Patrick Walsh had served fifteen years in the 35th Foot, four years as lieutenant and adjutant

in a Connecticut provincial regiment, and four years in the same rank in a New York unit.[17] John Eagles and John Griffiths had no military experience yet had demonstrated their loyalty as well as some qualifications and leadership by the then American standards. The former had raised a force of fifty-two loyalists in Westchester County at his own expense. He delivered them to Governor Tryon and was sent to Halifax. When the British army arrived, he and his men joined it. Back in New York he raised a company for the Queen's Rangers and also carried dispatches from New York to Quebec.[18] Griffiths' only claim to leadership was that he had allegedly raised a force of almost five hundred men for a projected raid to rescue some tories imprisoned in Albany.[19]

Rogers' unit, as raised originally, included a few captains who were accepted by the British officer class. In particular, there were Gymes and Armstrong, who had been former members of Lord Dunmore's Virginia unit of the same name.[20]

The contempt and coolness of the British officers. who made no effort to conceal their feelings, came as a shock to the loyalists who expected, or at least hoped for, a warmer welcome. Ill-bred or not, tory officers had risked a great deal in raising men for the unit. Take the case of William Lounsbury in Westchester County as described by a witness:

"William Lounsbury, a bold determined man. By General Howe's proclamation if anyone enlisted sixty men he should have a Captain's commission. A counter proclamation from the American Congress, decreed death to anyone caught enlisting for the enemy. Lounsbury was 50 or 60 years old, I believe, and bald. He came from below and a sloop was to wait for his men below

---

[14]Statement by Major Armstrong et al [no date], enclosed in Innes to Clinton, 9 Nov. 1779, MS, *Clinton Papers.* Here accusations of heinous crimes are joined with complaints about the low social standing of the officers "purged" in March 1777. It is difficult to tell whether the writers were more indignant about the criminal activity of the officers or their low origins and occupations.

[15]Memorial of Captain Daniel Frazer, 26 Jan. 1778 and memorial of same, 1 Dec. 1778, MSS, *ibid.*

[16]Memorial of Captain John Brandon, 1 Dec. 1778, MS, *ibid.*

[17]Petition of Captain Patrick Walsh Jan. 13, 1778, MS, *ibid.*

[18]Petition of Captain John Eagles, 11 Jan., 1779, MS, *ibid.*

[19]Petition of Captain John Griffiths, 12 Jan. 1779, MS, *ibid.*

[20]Innes to Clinton, 9 Nov. 1779, MS, *ibid.*

Delancey's Neck and take them over to Long Island. Lounsbury told his wife to send for Joseph Purdy and tell him he was among the rocks of Great Lot . . . [Purdy came and Lounsbury sent him to such loyalists as he thought could be induced to join with him.] Purdy told the men where Lounsbury was and he persuaded them to enlist. Purdy proved a traitor and informed the principal Whigs of M[amaroneck] vizt: Colonel Gilbert Budd, Gilbert Horton, and Captain Samuel Townsend commanded the party composed of the American Store Guard and the militial company of the vicinity. They marched to the Great Lots before Townsend let them know where or for what they were going. — Surrounding the fastnesses where Lounsbury was concealed, they called upon him and his party to surrender,—they being unarmed. His men attempted to escape but were fired upon and then surrendered. Lounsbury refused to surrender though called upon repeatedly and defended himself with a club. Orders came from the commander to bayonet him, and he was killed with seven bayonets, refusing to the last to yield. They found his enlisting orders in his pockets, and a roll of men whom they secured."[21]

This incident seems to have been the first news received by the rebels concerning Rogers' unit. The local Committee of Safety reported to Washington "That in his [Lounsbury's] Pocket book was found a Commission signed by Genl How to Major Rogers empowering him to raise a Battalion of Rangers with the Rank of Lieut Col Commandant. That annexed to this was a Warrant to this Lounsberry signed by Rogers appointing him Captain of one of these Companies & a Muster Roll of the Men already enlisted."[22]

Washington issued warnings about Rogers' unit in order to kindle patriot fires. On 30 September he wrote Governor Trumbull of Connecticut, that unless the enemy measures

were counteracted, the British would raise an army "of our own people."[23] On 4th October the President of the Continental Congress was told by Washington of the necessity of raising men and of offering a suit of clothes as well as pay and bounty. The general added: ". . . I question whether that will do, as the enemy, from the information of one John Nash, who with six others were taken by our guards, are giving ten pounds bounty for recruiting and have got a battalion under Major Rogers nearly completed, upon Long Island."[24]

Connecticut, meanwhile, worried about Rogers' position, just across the narrow ribbon of Long Island Sound. Governor Trumbull told Washington (13 October) that many of Rogers' men "have lately stole over to join him, and who are perfectly acquainted with every inlet and avenue into the towns of Greenwich, Stamford and Norwalk, where are considerable quantities of Continental stores. The design of Rogers, as far as we can learn, is from Huntington to make a sudden descent in the night more especially on the town of Norwalk, not only to take the stores there, but to burn, and destroy all before them." Trumbull did not expect much from the local militia. "The towns mentioned are much alarmed, especially Norwalk, who have taken an active part in bringing off inhabitants, stock, and stores from Long-Island, and are particularly threatened with reprisals being made on them."[25]

Although Trumbull admitted "the most particular account of Rogers' intentions were from a friendly woman of good character . . .", he enclosed two letters supposedly confirming the proposed raid. To us, today, the letters now appear more interesting as a reve-

---

[21]Testimony of Nelson Schofield, Nov. 1846, MS, *McDonald Papers*, Vol. III (1845-6), Hufeland Memorial Library, New Rochelle, N. Y.

[22]Committee of Safety to Washington, 30 Aug. 1776, *Calendar of Historical Manuscripts Relating to the War of the Revolution, in the Office of the Secretary of State*, Albany, N. Y. (Albany 1868), Vol. I, 465. (Hereafter ciated as "*Cal. N. Y. Hist Ms.*") See also Duerr to Washington, 30 Aug. 1776, *Force*, I, 1236.

[23]Washington to Turnbull 30 Sept. 1776, Peter Force, ed., *American Archives. Fifth Series*. Vol. II (Wash., 1851), 610.

[24]Washington to President of Congress, 4 Oct. 1776, *ibid.*, 868.

[25]*Ibid.*, 1028-1029.

lation of the thoughts of the writers than of the fears read into them by the patriots. The first[26] was addressed to a friend by a man who had suddenly stolen away from Norwalk. ". . . I had a good passage over to the island [Long Island] . . . I am under Captain Fairchild, in Colonel Rogers's battalion of Rangers, and as to news of the Rebel side I find it as false as ever. I have not heard from home since I came away, and should be exceeding glad if you should send me word. As to my coming away, I must own that my wife as well as all others was ignorant of my coming away, which makes me the more anxious of hearing from home." Almost every other sentence mentions his wife: "I should write my wife above all others, but be kind enough to let her know that I am well . . . Be good enough to remember my love to my wife and child, and if she has any desire to see this, let her." The patriots were alarmed by the sentences: "And you may tell her from me that the British troops will never give over until they have gained the victory. And furthermore tell her if she regards her own safety not to forsake her own house when the troops come through the country . . ." The other letter[27] is similar: "My love to my wife . . . Let her know that I am well and expect soon to see her."

The mention of Rogers' name undoubtedly increased the apprehension of the Connecticut patriots. Every reference to him repeated that he was "a famous partisan or ranger in the last war." His name conjured up visions of silent, grim giants suddenly apearing from nowhere, swooping down, Indian fashion, on a town under cover of darkness. Patriots tried to damn his name: he was, by now, "the infamous Major," but it did not quell the fears of the citizens along the shore.

At first, Rogers apparently established headquarters at Flushing on the north shore of Long Island. A sloop was used to pick up recruits waiting on the New York and Connecticut shores. During this time (22 September) a celebrated incident occurred about which there has been much speculation. Yet nothing more substantial is known than the brief entry in the diary of Captain William Bamford of the 40th Foot:

"Nathan Hale, a Cap't in ye Rebel Army, & a spy was taken by Maj'r Rogers & this m'g hang'd . . ."[28]

There are no records which would show the strength of the Queen's Rangers or tell what uniform they wore at the time that General Howe finally moved his forces (12 October) in pursuit of Washington. There do not seem to have been more than ten companies in Rogers' force, or a strength of about five hundred men. It had been decided to clothe the provincial units in green coats, (lined with white baize), white waistcoats and breeches, and dark brown leggings. The facings were to be white, green or blue. Uniforms and material for the provincials were sent to Howe from Great Britain during 1776 but whether these were received prior to his move into Westchester County cannot be determined.[29]

On 18th October the British army finally began to move on the mainland, having disembarked on Pelham Point. On the 19th it took a position facing East Chester with the right wing stretching towards New Rochelle. Rogers' corps—missing at least seventy-two men, detached on the 17th for work with the artillery—was on this wing. Captain John Eagles later claimed the honor of being the first to enter New Rochelle.[30] (He said he

[26]J. Cable to Hezekiel Jarvis, 27 Sept. 1776, *ibid.*, 1029-1030.
[27]Stephen Fountain to Darius Olmstead, 28 Sept. 1776, *ibid.*, 1030.

[28]"Bamford's Diary," *Maryland Historical Magazine*, XXVIII (1938), 10. For a speculative reconstruction of the incident see Morton Pennypacker, *General Washington's Spies on Long Island and In New York*, Vol. II East Hampton, 1948), 8-15.
[29]Charles M. Lefferts, *Uniforms of the American, British, French, and German Armies in the War of the American Revolution 1775-1783* (N. Y., 1926), 222,230.
[30]Eagles' Petition of 11 Jan. 1779, *cit. supra.*

was publicly thanked in the army orders—but this was derided: there is evidence that there had been no opposition.[31] Certainly there is no record of any skirmish at this point.)

On the evening of 20 October, Rogers was ordered to take possession of the village of Mamaroneck. At sunrise the next morning—while the remainder of the British army only shifted its position slightly — his battalion swung into action. The Queen's Rangers attacked and (to quote a contemporary American letter) "took possession of Mamaroneck, which our militia abandoned with the utmost precipitation,—As usual." There had been considerable military stores deposited there for the Americans, but allegedly they were all moved "except some Onions, so that I think they have made a loosing voyage."[32]

The Queen's Rangers then camped on Heathcote Hill near the village. The men bivouacked around fires made from neighboring fences. Rogers used a nearby schoolhouse as headquarters and one of the scholars, dismissed for an unexpected holiday, recalled the Colonel many years later as "a very rough looking red eyed man."[33] As night came on, strong outposts were set to the north and east but only a weak one to the west, the direction of the British army.

Meanwhile the Americans were watching the British. Informed of Rogers' position,[34] Lord Stirling (who had been exchanged after being captured during the battle of Long Island) decided to execute a coup, to revive lagging American morale. Seven hundred and fifty men, of whom six hundred were from Delaware and Maryland, and the remainder from Virginia, were placed under the command of Colonel Haslet of Delaware. They, the cream of the Americans under one of the ablest field commanders, were to attack Rogers under cover of darkness.

Local guides led the Americans around so that they approached the tory unit from the southwest. Then, nearing the unsuspecting loyalists, the guides swung the Americans cross-country, to make the surprise complete. A single outpost — a young Indian — was easily dispatched with a sword, and the Americans pushed on to complete the coup.

Meanwile Rogers had become dissatisfied with the positions taken by his unit and had ordered Captain Eagles' company of about sixty men to be stationed on the southwest (Eagles was later accused of being absent at this important moment.[35]). This move was not known to the American guides and when the vanguard composed of Virginians under Major Green attacked the post, the Americans thought they were striking the main body of the loyalists. Surprise as well as overwhelming strength gave the Americans an initial advantage and they expected to sweep all before them. While some tories quickly surrendered, others took advantage of the confused fighting in the dark at close-quarters and by shouting imprecations against Rogers and his crew, managed to withdraw to the main camp.

Rogers had been aroused at his headquarters by the melee and hurried to join the main body of his troops standing under arms on Heathcote Hill. Exhilarated by their easy victory and expecting only scattered resistance, the Americans pressed on, only to be met by heavy gunfire. Over the din was

[31] Affidavit of William Washburn et al, 5 Nov. 1779, MS, *Clinton Papers.*

[32] Tilghman to Duerr, 22 Oct. 1776, Peter Force, ed., *American Archives, Fifth Series.* Vol. II (Wash., 1851), 576. According to some evidence the Queen's Rangers destroyed large quantities of goods, principally rum, molasses, flour and pork.

[33] Interview with Stephen Hall, 5 Nov. 1846, *McDonald Papers.*

[34] Apparently by Rufus Putnam who had made a one-man reconnaissance. Rowene Buell, comp., *The Memoirs of Rufus Putnam and Certain Official Papers and Correspondence* (Boston & N. Y., 1903), 61-63.

[35] Affidavit of Washburn et al.

heard Rogers' hoarse voice: "Steady, boys, steady! Fire! Fire!" In the confusion the Americans' guides disappeared. Colonel Haslet decided to withdraw, content with the accomplishments of his initial surprise: thirty-six prisoners, along with a variety of trophies and spoil.[36]

The Americans whipped themselves into delirium over their "victory"—which in sober fact had but the proportions of an outpost overrun and repulse by a numerically inferior band of men.[37] But the Americans did not discuss these details. Instead, Colonel Haslet spread the canard thicker: "the late worthless Major; on the first Fire he skulked off in the dark. . . ."[38] This refrain was taken up and eagerly repeated throughout the colonies—"Major Rogers . . . it is said, was the first that run off. . . ."[39] The newspapers, of course, printed it.[40] Amerians gleefully assured one another: "This blow will ruin the Major's Rangers."[41] Lord Stirling, publicly, on parade, thanked the officers and men of the detachment. How he completed the celebration is described in a soldier's diary: "Tuesday 22 [September] . . . there was a gallos ordered by Genl Starling to hang three of the prisoners at 12 o'clock."[42]

Dr. James Tilton, the Delaware regimental surgeon, while thinking the outpost Rogers' main force—"little or nothing inferior to us in numbers"—admitted: "Though we were successful, I must confess this the most terrible instance of War I have seen; so much is the horror of terrible business increased by darkness."[43] The only really frank statement made by the Americans is contained in the report by Colonel Robert H. Harrison, Washington's secretary, to the President of the Continental Congress: "By some accident or other the expedition did not succeed so well as I could have wished. However, our advanced party led on by Major Greene, of the first Virginia Regiment, fell in with their out-guards, and brought up thirty-six prisoners, sixty muskets, and some blankets. . . ."[44]

General Howe reported the engagement to Lord Germain on 30 November. The initial loss was blamed on the fact that "the carelessness of his centries exposed him [Rogers] to a surprise from a large body of ye enemy by w'h he lost a few men killed or taken; nevertheless by a spirited exertion he obliged them to retreat, leaving behind them some prisoners & several killed or wounded."[45]

When Americans, returning from behind the British lines under a flag of truce, later reported Rogers the object of open scorn and insult by British officers, patriots were convinced that their propaganda was true. How exaggerated these reports were is difficult to say but there may have been at least an element of truth. An American wrote his father on 1 November:

---

[36]"List of Prisoners Taken 21st October [1776]," *Force*, II, 1230.

[37]Hall estimated the rangers at 400. Interview of 5 Nov. 1846. I can find no evidence of more than ten companies in the unit and the full strength would be approximately 500. Seventy-two men were detached on the 17th to assist the artillery and not ordered back in time for the battle. There were also 120 detached to the engineers; it cannot be determined if they returned prior to the engagement. Entries for 17, 20 and 22 Oct. 1776 *Orderly Book of Sir William Howe, Jan. 27, 1776-May 1, 1778*, MS, Clements Library.

[38]Haslet to Rodney, 28 Oct. 1776, *Force*, II, 1270.

[39]"Extract of a Letter of a General Officer dated 23 October 1776," *Force*, II, 1203. Rogers . . . is disgraced." Trumbull to Cooke, *ibid.*, 1077.

[40]See e.g. *Connecticut Gazette* quoted in Franklin B. Hough, ed., *Journals of Major Robert Rogers* (Albany, 1883), 277; *New Hampshire Gazette*, 5 Nov. 1776.

[41]Extract of a letter . . . dated 23 Oct. 1776.

[42]Charles Carleton Coffin, ed., "Diary of Capt. Peter Kimball, 1776," *The Granite Monthly*, V (1881) 233.

[43]Tilton to Rodney, 20 Nov. 1776, quoted in Christopher L. Ward, *The Delaware Continentals 1776-1783* (Wilmington, 1941), 81.

[44]Harrison to President of Congress, 25 Oct. 1776, Hough, *Rogers Journals*, 275-276.

[45]Howe to Germain, 30 Nov. 1776, *Force*, III, 922. Most of the details of the encounter given in the text are from the testimonies of Nelson Schofield, 10 Oct. 1844, MS, *McDonald Papers* I, and 10 Nov. 1846; of Stephen Hall 18 Nov. 1846, and of William Griffin, 5 Nov. 1846, MS, *McDonald Papers*, III. Although obviously suspect because of the date when made, these affidavits are supported by contemporary documents to an amazing extent.

". . . Roger who command the Rangers in the british service is Disgraced—A flag which went in two days ago to the Enemy were (by being oblig'd to wait an answer) Spectators of a Scene which is pleasing—The Persons who went in with the flag, were sitting in Company with a Col'o McDonald & some other Officers & in comes Rogers, with his hatt on, says, how do you do Gentlemen (meaning our flag of truce) but no reply was made, except by Col'o McDonald, who says, you Dam'd Rascal, why do you Presume to wear your hatt, among Gentlemen—if you are not out of the house immediately I will kick you out, accordingly he went out, Col'o McDonald was heard to say, that you are an Insolent Rascal & if you ever come into Gentlemens Company again, Where I am I will cane you as long as I can feel you—Rogers Reg't is taken from him & given to another officer . . ."[46]

Contrary to patriot propaganda and hopes, Rogers continued to devote his efforts to the corps. Frederick Mackenzie, a British officer, noted in his diary for 26 October:

"Major Rogers, with some of his corps, made an excursion lately as far as Bedford in Connecticut, where he released and brought off 6 or 8 officers and men of the Navy who were prisoners there. He was joined in these two days by a Company of 120 men, raised secretly in Connecticut by one of his old Captains."[47]

Loyalists, too, continued to risk their lives to seek recruits for the Queen's Rangers. Daniel Strong was captured near Peekskill in January 1777 with a commission in his pocket dated 30 December, 1776, authorizing him to recruit for the unit.[48] Strong met his end on Monday, 27th January. Seth Pomeroy recorded in his journal how "the Rev. Mr. Sackett of Cram Pond stood on the cart and prayed and preached an excellent sermon from these words 'Prepare to meet thy God, O Israel.' The whole army paraded in a circle. Gen. McDougal on horseback, the colonel on horseback, the whole army in a circle round the gallows to hear the sermon and behold the melancholy spectacle."[49]

The American leaders knew Rogers was still in command and tried in vain to destroy the hated corps. In mid-November, while retreating across New Jersey, Washington badly needed the troops he had left with General Charles Lee on the eastern bank of the Hudson. Lee, however, informed him (24 November): "I shou'd march this day with Glovers Brigade but have just received intelligence that Rogers's Corps, a part of the Light Horse, and another Brigade lye in so exposed a situation as to present us the fairest opportunity of carry'g 'em off—if we succeed it will have a great effect, and amply compensate for two days delay." Washington immediately agreed, believing a smashing defeat of Rogers' unit essential. But Lee failed. His excuse is amusing; he blamed "the timidity or caution of the enemy, who contracted themselves into a compact body very suddenly."[50]

In January, the Queen's Rangers were a part of the garrison in Fort Knyphausen (formerly Fort Independence). On the morning of the 18th, an American force under General Wooster suddenly appeared and demanded the fort's surrender. The Hessians in the fort were offered the best terms but the loyalist units were "to surrender at discretion. . . ." The demand was rejected and the Americans soon retired.[51]

Noncombatants in Westchester County, regardless of sympathies, began to suffer from pillaging. Troops on both sides as well as the criminal element present among civil-

[46]Eb Huntington to Jabez Huntington, 1 Nov. 1776, *Letters Written by Ebenezer Huntington During the American Revolution* (N. Y., 1915 ?).

[47]Entry for 26 Oct. 1776, *Diary of Frederick Mackenzie*, Vol. I (Cambridge, 1930).

[48]Commission quoted in Hough, *Rogers' Journals*, 277-278. It revealed that rumors of Rogers' removal were false.

[49]Louis Effingham De Forest, ed., *The Journals and Papers of Seth Pomeroy* (New Haven, 1926), 169.

[50]For correspondence between Lee and Washington see *The Lee Papers. Vol. II 1776-1778 (Collections of the New York Historical Society for the Year 1872)*, (N. Y., 1873).

[51][Stephen Kemble], *The Kemble Papers. Vol. I. 1773-1789 (Collections of the New York Historical Society for the Year 1883)*, (N. Y., 1884), 108.

ians were responsible. Undoubtedly men from Rogers' unit participated.[52] But all marauders soon saw how civilians abandoned all resistance at the dread words "Rogers' Rangers!" Soon all were loudly proclaiming their membership in that unit: thus suspicion was directed to a unit the Americans and even some British were happy to condemn.

A typical incident is described in a contemporary affidavit. About one o'clock in the morning of January 13, 1777, Henry Williams, asleep in a house in Bedford, was rudely roused by muskets smashing in the doors. Grabbing a sword, he was barely out of bed when his room became crowded with seven or eight men. Leveling pistols and muskets at him, they "compelled him to surrender a Sword he had in his hand Threatening him with immediate death, or to take said Williams prisoner to Rogers's Rangers declaring themselves to belong to said Core [Corps] and to be King Georges soldiers and they had express orders from said Rogers to bring down to him said Williams dead or live, they endeavoured to force said Williams (without Coat waistcoat or breeches) out of the house. They then broak open some and demanded all the Draws, Desk, and Packages to be opened and with many imprecations and threats continuing Fire Arms at his breast confined [him] to stand sit still, while they robbed and plundered all his premises often repeating with Oathes their violence they took from him and carried away the following particulars and sundry other articles not yet particularized." If the list of articles in the affidavit is accurate, Mr. Williams was a wealthy man! The victim added details of a picture worthy of Hogarth's brush: "The person who they called Captain put on and wore away said Gown and Surtoute, a good bever hatt with Crope hatt band, sword and one of the pistols, one man put one of the scarlet waistcoat, an other took a worn bever hatt a tall man black hair high Eyebrows took a large old white Bever hat, they put them on their old hatts. . . ."[53]

Similar incidents became a common experience in Westchester County and the inhabitants constantly appealed for protection. In December 1776 they petitioned the New York Provincial Congress, complaining that they were "in continual danger of being made prisoners, and . . . plundered by Robert Rogers' party . . . who daily make excursions in divers parts of said County, and taking with them by Force of arms many of its good inhabitants, also their stock, grain, and every thing etc. . . . laying waste and destroying all they cannot take with them." Patriot troops "instead of protecting its inhabitants from the enemy, did plunder and distress them more than the very enemy themselves, taking off with them our stock, household Furniture, and even our Farming utensils. . . ."[54] In May 1777 the Committee of Safety in Bedford told General Clinton that their town had become a frontier, "there being a Sartain Company of Robers, otherwise Called Rogers Rangers, that keep Consealed in Parts of North Castle & Cortlandt Manor. Hardly a Night Passes but there is Some Roberies Committed or Some of our good men Captivated and Draged in a most Barberous maner to the Enemy. . . ."[55]

[52]The strongest accusations against the unit are contained in the statement of Major Armstrong et al, cit. supra. I query if discipline had broken down the British army to the extent that such crimes as described in the statement would have gone unpunished. None of the accused officers were ever officially charged with any crime. If they were guilty and ample proof was available (as Armstrong et al claimed), Innes and Howe spurned an easy and certain way to end their careers which would have left no opportunity for later complaints. In fact the five "purged" officers who later presented memorials to the home government, based their plea largely on the fact that they were not removed by action of any court martial.

[53]Cal. N. Y. Hist. Ms, I, 591-592.
[54]Petition of Inhabitants of Westchester County, 23 Dec. 1776, ibid., 563-564. See also Force, II, 371-372.
[55]Committee of Safety to Clinton, 9 May 1777, Public Papers of George Clinton, First Governor of New York, 1777-1795—1801-1804. Military. Vol. I (N. Y., 1899), 801-802.

By this time, May 1777, Robert Rogers was no longer in charge of the Queen's American Rangers. In January 1777 Alexander Innes was appointed Inspector-General of the Provincial Forces in the British army. He shared the regulars' feeling that most of the provincial officers were not proper persons to hold commissions and objected even to the ranks including "Negroes, Indians, Mulattos, Sailors and Rebel Prisoners. . . ."[56]

Innes leveled charges against Rogers' unit. "Mr. Rogers had introduced into this Corps a number of persons very improper to hold any Commission and their conduct in a Thousand instances was so flagrant that I could not hesitate to tell the General, that untill a thorough reformation took place, he could expect no service from that Battalion which in the course of the winter had been reduced to one fifth of its original strength principally by desertion. . . ."

"On this representation the General determine dthat Lieut Col'o Rogers should retire on his pay and give the Command of the Corps to Lieut Col'o French then Major of the 22nd Regiment. . . ."[57] Rogers quietly stepped aside without protest.[58]

With the advent of Major French, the original Queen's American Rangers was—as Innes later pointed out—"to all intents & purposes dissolved and a new one formed. . . ."

The transition period before the appointment of Simcoe, under whom the unit became famous, may be briefly sketched. French had accepted his new position "on the express condition of being permitted to new-model the Regiment and to recommend such Officers only as were deserving of that honor."[58] In March, Captains Brandon, Sanford, Griffiths, McGinnis, Frazer, Fairchild, Gerow and Eagles were dropped.[59] As a palliative they were given three months' full pay and assured that they might apply "for such Commissions as they were qualified for when vacancies happened. . . ."[60] (Later in 1779 five officially protested to higher authorities but without avail.[61]) Two retained their positions: Major Grymes and Captain Armstrong. (The latter continued to serve in the unit throughout the war and became second in command.)

Major French soon resigned and was succeeded by Captain James Wemyss of the 40th. He, too, lasted only a short time. On October 15, 1777, the command was given to Colonel James Graves Simcoe. Although it continued to be considered a provincial unit, the influx of both officers and men, who were not native-born, changed its complexion. It was from this date no more a loyalist group than many of the regular British regiments.

[56]Innes to Clinton, 9 Nov. 1779.

[57]Idem.

[57]There were rumors that "Collonel Rogers has been broke for fraud." Affidavit of Henry G. Livingston, 15 Feb. 1777, Cal. N. Y. Hist. Ms, I, 671. An extensive search of available records failed to substantiate this charge. The nearest is a statement in a letter from Simcoe to Evan Nepean in Mar. 1783: "The Queen's Rangers were originally raised by Colonel Rogers to do the duty which their name implies, and his commission expressed. Sir Wm. Howe saw the necessity of such a corps, and Rogers and many of his officers being accused of mal practices, they were placed upon the half-pay list. . . ." P.R.O., C.O. 42/15. Simcoe was obviously referring to the replacement of officers in March 1777 at the time when French commanded the unit. Actually the charges of fraud were made against various officers but none against Rogers. The true story is given by Innes. Rogers continued to recruit. See e.g. Washington to Turnbull, 12 Apr. 1777, John C. Fitzgerald, ed., The Writings of George Washington from the Original Manuscript Sources 1745-1799, Vol. VII (Wash., 1933), 402-403 at 403; Washingotn to Clinton, 12 Apr. 1777, ibid., 409-410.

[58]Innes to Clinton, 9 Nov. 1779.

[59]"Copy of the Orders of Col'o Innis [sic], the Inspector Gen'l respect'g the Officers of the Queens American Rangers" [Mar. 30, 1779], MS, Clinton Papers. Brandon states that twenty-three officers were replaced in the unit. Memorial of John Brandon, 1 Dec. 1778.

[60]Innes to Clinton, 9 Nov. 1779.

[61]See besides the various documents in the Clinton Papers cited supra, the following: Thos. de Grey to Howe, 10 July 1779, MS, P.R.O., C.O. 5/156, f.283; Howe to Thos. de Grey, 13 July 1779, MS, ibid., f.329; Germain to Clinton, 2 Aug. 1779, C.O. 5/244, f.43; Germain to Howe, 11 Feb. 1780, C.O. 5/157, f.75.

# LEGACY OF CONTROVERSY: GATES, SCHUYLER, AND ARNOLD AT SARATOGA, 1777

By Paul David Nelson*

A MOMENTOUS event in the history of America's Revolutionary War against Great Britain occurred on the crisp autumn afternoon of 17 October 1777 at Saratoga, New York. On that day, Major General Horatio Gates, a former English officer leading troops in rebellion against the king, presided over ceremonies marking the capitulation of Lieutenant General John Burgoyne and an Anglo-German army. Supporters of Gates and Major Generals Philip Schuyler and Benedict Arnold almost immediately began quarreling over who should be credited with the victory. Today the issue is by no means settled.

The pro-Arnold, pro-Schuyler view of Saratoga has been stated by Christopher Ward, who maintained that Gates was "the (so-called) victor at Saratoga, about whose head shone the (spurious) glory of that success (due to the previous operations of Schuyler and the skill and bravery of Arnold and [Daniel] Morgan)."[1] John Richard Alden, on the other hand, has contended that "To do Gates justice, . . . unlike Schuyler, he did not anticipate defeat. It must be added, to his credit, that he understood Burgoyne. He

knew that the British general would attack, even under unfavorable circumstances." Moreover, when Burgoyne attempted to lure Gates into offensive action, the American officer "shrewdly and prudently declined to leave his entrenchments." Hence, Gates must be given credit for the outcome of the campaign, although factors such as terrain, a growing Patriot army started by his predecessor, Schuyler, and brilliant subordinate officers like Arnold and Morgan contributed to his victory.[2]

While neither Ward nor Alden examined the problem in great depth, it would appear that Alden's view is more valid than Ward's. Schuyler, an aristocratic and imposing figure, certainly deserves credit for slowing the Anglo-German advance after Fort Ticonderoga fell in July, 1777, but it seems clear that his exertions before Gates took command were not decisive. Once Burgoyne faced the Americans on the Saratoga battlefields, his army, although weakened, obviously was as

*Paul David Nelson, assistant professor of history at Berea College, Berea, Kentucky, is a specialist in American Colonial and Revolutionary history and has published articles in several journals. He wishes to thank Berea College for financial assistance in writing this article.

[1]Christopher Ward, *The Delaware Continentals, 1776-1783* (Wilmington, Delaware, 1941), p. 334. Similar interpretations may be found in Samuel Eliot Morison, *The Oxford History of the American People* (New York, 1965), pp. 248-49; George O. Trevelyan, *The American Revolution* (6 vols.; Boston, 1892), I, 327-28; Sir John W. Fortescue, *A History of the British Army* (13 vols.; London, 1899-1930), III, 234-44; Henry Cabot Lodge, *The Story of the Revolution* (2 vols.; New York, 1898, I,

250-55; William Addleman Ganoe, *The History of the United States Army* (revised edition, Ashton, Maryland, 1964), p. 47; Christopher Ward, *The War of the Revolution*, John Richard Alden, ed. (New York, 1952), II, 512; James Phinney Baxter, ed., *The British Invasion from the North . . . The Journal of Lieut. William Digby* (Albany, 1887), p. 170.

[2]John R. Alden, *A History of the American Revolution* (New York, 1969), pp. 322-323. Similar interpretations can be found in Robert Don Higginbotham, *Daniel Morgan, Revolutionary Rifleman* (Chapel Hill, 1961), pp. 75-76; Edward Channing, *History of the United States* (6 vols.; New york, 1905-1925), III, 278; Samuel White Patterson, *Horatio Gates, Defender of American Liberties* (New York, 1941), pp. 153-55, 171-72; Hoffman Nickerson, *The Turning Point of the Revolution, or Burgoyne in America* (Boston, 1928), pp. 331-32; George A. Billias, "Horatio Gates: Professional Soldier," George A. Billias, ed., *George Washington's Generals* (New York, 1964), pp. 90-96.

dangerous as a cornered tiger. Arnold, who contributed to Burgoyne's entrapment, was a bold and popular military leader, but he seemed capable of thinking only in terms of offensive action—regardless of circumstances. Unlike either of his subordinates, Gates was anything but an impressive military figure. Short, pudgy, ruddy faced, bespectacled, and mild mannered, he was, from the only surviving description left of him by a soldier, "an 'old granny' looking fellow."[3] His greatest ability lay in army administration and organization. Yet when called upon in 1777 he turned out to be a respectable strategist. At Saratoga his overriding concern was for caution in meeting an enemy in face to face confrontation. While at New York in April, 1776, he had stated the strategic principle that would guide him in the early years of the war: "Our Business is to Defend the main Chance; to Attack only by Detail; and when a precious advantage offers."[4] The evidence would seem to indicate that Gates' plan was far more prudent and perceptive than Arnold's, that nothing could have been gained and much lost, had the commander given in to his subordinate's plea to march boldly against Burgoyne's army.

In attempting to place Gates' role at Saratoga in better perspective, this writer has tried not to overlook certain considerations that somewhat qualify his thesis. First, he admits that Gates may have been overly cautious at times, and consequently may have missed chances to strike a final blow at Burgoyne and prolonged the possibility that he might lose his "prey."[5] Second, he believes that at Saratoga, as at every battle in history, chance played a major part in the final outcome. Third, he admits that perhaps Burgoyne was more responsible for his defeat than any American officer. For by September,

ber, 1777, the British general had gotten himself into such monumental difficulties that his capitulation resulted as much from his own rashness as Patriot opposition. Yet this last point should not be overemphasized, for British armies previously had cancelled the mistakes of generals by simple force of arms. With these provisos stated, the story of Saratoga can be retold.

In June, 1777, upper New York state lay under imminent threat of an invasion from Canada by General Burgoyne's Anglo-German forces. Having replaced Sir Guy Carleton as commander of English troops in Canada after that officer's abortive drive against Fort Ticonderoga in 1776, Burgoyne confidently expected to destroy American resistance and spend the winter in Albany. He had devised a strategy which called for a main expedition up Lake Champlain, under his personal command, which would eliminate Patriot opposition at Fort Ticonderoga and lay open a line of march to Albany. At the same time a second army of regulars, Canadians, and Indians, under Lt. Col. Barry St. Leger, would divert American strength by marching down the Mohawk Valley. Burboyne's orders from London were to get to Albany and put his army under the command of General Sir William Howe, who supposedly by then would have broken through the American fortifications in the Hudson Highlands and linked up with the armies out of Canada.[6]

To oppose these forces, Schuyler was trying to build up Patriot troop strength in the upper Hudson Valley, especially at Ticonderoga. His attention had been diverted by an altercation in the spring of 1777 with Gates and the Continental Congress over his right to command, which had forced him to spend costly months arguing his case in Philadelphia. However, Gates, as Schuyler's subordinate, had taken temporary charge of the Northern Department during his comman-

---

[3]Quoted in Charles K. Bolton, *The Private Soldier under Washington* (New York, 1902), pp. 243-44.

[4]Gates to John Adams, 23 April 1776, in Bernhard Knollenberg, ed., "Correspondence of John Adams and Horatio Gates," *Proceedings of the Masachusetts Historical Society, October, 1941-May 1944* (Boston, 1945). LXVII, 140-41.

[5]John C. Miller, *Triumph of Freedom, 1775-1783* (Boston, 1948), p. 212.

[6]John Burgoyne, *A State of the Expedition from Canada . . .* (Second edition, London, 1780), 5 and Appendix III, v-vi; Troyer Steele Anderson, *The Command of the Howe Brothers in the American Revolution* (New York, 1936), p. 253.

der's absence and had done as much as possible to put Ticonderoga into shape to ward off Burgoyne's thrust. When Schuyler secured from Congress unquestioned command of his department and returned to Albany in early June, he discovered that "as much as possible" was little enough. General Arthur St. Clair, placed in control of Ticonderoga after Gates had hurried angrily off to Congress upon Schuyler's triumphant return, reported to his superior on 13 June that, "I assure you, sir we are very ill prepared to meet [the enemy]." Only 1,500 Continentals were on hand, which along with five regiments of New England militia composed a total of less than 2,000 men.[7] Schuyler visited St. Clair a week later and decided the outlook was not totally bleak. But St. Clair warned him on 25 June. "I cannot . . . see the least prospect of our being able to defend the post, unless the militia come in."[8]

Although Schuyler attempted to recruit New Englanders into his ranks, he had little success, for by 1777 the Yankees despised him on a number of counts. He had lost their respect in earlier campaigns because of what they viewed as his haughty imperiousness toward Eastern troops. Moreover, before the war he had championed New York's claim to territory, later encompassed by Vermont, against the claim of New Hampshire. Hence the militia did not come in, and when on 1 July Burgoyne attacked Ticonderoga it quickly fell. The British had occupied an undefended eminence south of the fort named Mount Defiance, presenting St. Clair with the choice of surrendering or withdrawing. On 5 July he chose the latter course of action. Both Gates and Schuyler had seen the danger of leaving Mount Defiance unprotected, but had lacked the manpower to fortify it.

The British army, "flushed with victory," as Schuyler put it, "plentifully provided with provisions, cannon, and every warlike store,"[9] pursued the American army southward from Ticonderoga into the forests and quickly trounced it again at Hubbardton. The American general now began to send a series of despondent letters to Washington, which were immediately forwarded to Congress. These messages shook many congressmen's faith in their appointee; especially chagrined were those members who all along had supported their favorite, Gates. On 9 July, Schuyler wrote, "I have not been able to learn what is become of General St. Clair and the enemy. . . ." Five days later, he reported, "Desertion prevails, and disease gains ground . . . ."[10] By 11 August, Samuel Adams, an ardent Gates supporter in Congress, was arguing, "Schuyler has written a series of weak & contemptible *things* which . . . is sufficient for the removal of him from that command."[11] A week before, on 4 August, Congress had done precisely that by replacing Schuyler with General Gates.

Curiously, regardless of what he was *writing,* Schuyler had been *doing* as well as any American commander could have under the circumstances. As he retreated, he had his men fell trees across paths the enemy might use, wreck numerous bridges, and dam Wood Creek. He ordered his troops to destroy crops and to hide cattle that Burgoyne's men could seize for food.[12] While he strictly instructed his officers to avoid a pitched battle, he allowed militia forces to harass the enemy advance parties with all the strength they could muster. As a consequence, he slowed

[7]St. Clair to Schuyler, 13 June, 1776, William H. Smith, ed., *The St. Clair Papers* (2 vols.; Cincinnati, 1882), I, 399. Twelve days later Anthony Wayne, on the scene at Ticonderoga, wrote Gates that the entire garrison was less than 1,900 men, *one-fourth* of whom were unarmed. *Horatio Gates Papers,* box 6, New York Historical Society (hereafter cited as *Gates Papers,* NYHS).

[8]Jared Sparks, ed., *Correspondence of the American Revolution* (4 vols., Boston, 1853), II, 511.

[9]Schuyler to General Washington, July 7, 1777, Sparks, ed., *Correspondence,* I, 394.

[10]Schuyler to Washington, 7, 9, 14, 28, July, 4, 19, August 1777, *Ibid., 393-99, 415-16, 419-20, 425-26.* See Bernhard Knollenberg, *Washington and the Revolution, a Reappraisal: Gates, Conway, and the Continental Congress* (New York, 1940), 12-20.

[11]Samuel Adams to Roger Sherman, 11 August 1777, Harry Alonzo Cushing, ed., *The Writings of Samuel Adams* (4 vols.; New York, 1904-1908), III, 404-05.

[12]James M. Hadden, *A Journal Kept in Canada and Upon Burgoyne's Campaign,* Horatio Rogers, ed. (Albany, 1884), p. 94.

General Burgoyne's advance to a crawl. The British army, encumbered by enormous amounts of superfluous baggage and 52 cannons, took 20 days to advance 20 miles from Skenesborough, at the mouth of Wood Creek, to a position on the east side of the Hudson River, south of Fort Edward. Finally, Schuyler fell back with his main army to Van Schaick's Island, at the mouth of the Mohawk River, about 10 miles above Albany.

Even there he was not idle. Before Gates joined the Americans on 19 August, two very important blows had been struck against Burgoyne's forces. On 15 August Schuyler had sent out Benedict Arnold, whom General Washington had ordered north, to relieve a siege laid by Barry St. Leger against Fort Stanwix in the Mohawk Valley. Although Arnold did not repel St. Leger until 21 August, that vital blow to Burgoyne's plans could be attributed only to Schuyler. Another enemy defeat to the east, a Patriot victory by Brigadier General John Stark at Bennington on 15 and 16 August, was less Schuyler's doing. In two pitched battles, Stark's militia killed 200 Germans, captured 700 others, and mortally wounded Lt. Col. Friedrich Baum, one of Burgoyne's valuable officers. The British commander had lost a tenth of his army and had accomplished absolutely nothing.

Hence, by the time Gates assumed command in upstate New York, conditions were much improved over those days before. But this would hardly seem to justify the argument of some scholars that Schuyler's activities already had practically won the campaign before Gates arrived.[13] Doubtless Burboyne's army was weakened by his loss at Bennington. The elimination of St. Leger's threat west of Albany was also a severe blow. But the Anglo-German army was still powerful, and Burgoyne continued to believe he could accomplish his orders by defeating Gates. On 20 August, the British general declared to Lord George Germain that he would retreat, if his instructions did not absolutely require him to push on to Al-

bany.[14] Doubtless, however, he intended this letter as an apology in case of failure. Neither he nor Germain would have exposed his army to certain defeat, regardless of his orders. Clearly, Burgoyne still believed he could reach Albany before winter.

Moreover, General Gates had assumed command of an army that was still demoralized by defeat, suspicious of its previous commander, uncertain of its ability or strength. It was, in short, sadly in need of enlargement and reorganization to accomplish anything decisive. Perhaps it is useless to speculate on "ifs" in history, but one wonders whether the outcome at Saratoga would have been the same under Schuyler as it was under Gates. Would the New England militia have begun flocking to an army led by Schuyler, a man who, justly or unjustly, they felt by his own admission to be "a traitor?"[15] They did flock to Gates after he managed to whip the Yankees into a fever by a number of propaganda ploys against Burgoyne's mishandling of his Indian auxiliaries.[16] Thus by the time the campaign was over, Gates personally commanded more than 11,000 troops and another 9,000 were cooperating closely with him under other officers.

Would Schuyler have been able to raise the deadened spirits of his men after leading them only in retreat for more than a month? Gates did, if the statements of his subordinate officers are to be believed. On 6 August, General John Glover declared, "If we are not reinforced speedily we might as well give up the matter and [go] home." Yet two weeks after Gates arrived, Glover was writing happily, "I have not the least doubt of beating or compelling Mr. Burgoyne to return back to Ticonderoga, if not to Canada."[17] From a

[13]See, for example, Baxter (ed.), *Digby's Journal*, 170n.

[14]Burgoyne, *State of the Expedition*, xiii.

[15]Schuyler to Washington, 28 July, 1777, Sparks (ed.), *Correspondence*, I, 416.

[16]For example, in advertising the murder of Jane McCrea, a young girl killed by Indians while waiting in the woods for her lover, Gates accused Burgoyne of paying for American scalps (letter of 2 September 1777, *Gates Papers*, box 19, NYHS).

[17]Glover to James Warren, 6 August 1777, and to Jonathan Glover and Azor Orne, 5 September 1777, cited in George A. Billias, *General John Glover and his Marblehead Mariners* (New York, 1960), pp. 138-39.

"miserable state of despondency and terror," wrote Udney Hay, "Gates' arrival raised us, as if by magic. We began to hope and then to act."[18]

Would Schuyler have been able to reorganize the shattered Patriot army after it had suffered losses at Ticonderoga, Hubbardton, and in numerous other smaller skirmishes? Gates did, for he put to use his remarkable ability in matters of supply and organization, learned from years of experience as a former British officer, to reform the American troops into efficient fighting units. General Burgoyne, who inspected the American army after his capture, reported back to England that "the standing corps [Continentals] which I have seen are disciplined. I do not hazard the term, but apply it to the great fundamental points of military institution, sobriety, subordination, regularity, and courage."[19] Admittedly Burgoyne might have had reason for wanting to emphasize the Patriots' best points, but his remarks still have validity. Apparently Gates's assumption of command did much to change the outlook and organization of the troops formerly led by Schuyler.

His army renewed and full of spirit, on 8 September Gates decided to turn around and march toward the enemy. Out of the American camp moved 7,000 troops, the majority of them Continentals, but a growing number consisted of New England and New York militia. By then Arnold had returned to the American encampment from the Mohawk Valley, and Daniel Morgan, ordered northward by Washington, joined the American commander with a contingent of Virginia riflemen. Sending the young engineer, Thaddeus Kosciuszko, forward to reconnoiter for a defensive site, Gates indicated the tactics he would employ against Burgoyne. After marching for four days, the American army occupied the location which Kosciuszko had chosen, high ground named Bemis Heights, on the west side of the Hudson River, a bottleneck in Burgoyne's path of advance. To the right of this naturally defensive position ran the river, and on the left rose rugged, wooded bluffs. In front lay marshy, rolling, treecovered terrain, unbroken but for a few scattered clearings and wagon roads. While General Benjamin Lincoln, on the east side of the Hudson with a militia force, harassed the British army's advance, Kosciuszko laid out a plan of fortification and Gates's men began digging entrenchments. Finally, the left wing of the American position extended to another hill, three-fourths of a mile farther north, and the rear was covered by an abatis of felled trees, the sharpened branches of which pointed outward to fend off an attacker. These strong lines dominated the surrounding countryside and left the British no high ground within range for their many cannons.[20]

Gates now settled down to wait for Burgoyne's advance, leaving his enemy the choice of battering strong entrenchments, trying a flanking movement to the American left in dense, roadless woods, or retreat. "A few days, perhaps hours," Gates wrote on 10 September to John Hancock, president of Congress, "will Determine whether General Burgoyne will risque a Battle or retire to Tyconderoga. For I cannot think he will stay long inactive in his present position."[21] To Lincoln, who had been ordered to remain on the east side of the Hudson River, Gates noted on 13 September that Burgoyne was collecting his entire force at Stillwater by crossing the river on bridges. It appeared that the enemy was cutting his communications with Ticonderoga, but Gates was not sure.

[18]Hay to Governor Clinton, 13 August 1777, H.A. Washington, ed., *Writings of Thomas Jefferson* (9 vols.; Washington, 1853-1854), VIII, 496.

[19]Burgoyne, *State of the Expedition,* xcvi-xcvii.

[20]Gates to president of Congress, and to Lincoln, September 15, 1777, *Gates Papers,* box 19, NYHS. Professor Samuel Eliot Morison was factually confused when he remarked, in *Oxford History of the American People,* 248, that "Gates almost lost the campaign . . . by refusing to budge" from his entrenchments, "even when it became evident that Burgoyne was about to occupy a hill commanding his position." See Willard M. Wallace, *Traitorous Hero: The Life and Fortunes of Benedict Arnold* (New York, 1954), p. 154, and Higginbotham, *Morgan,* p. 71, for a refutation of Morison's belief that such high ground existed.

[21]Gates to president of Congress, September 15, 1777, *Gates Papers,* box 19, NYHS.

"Whether it is Genl. Burgoynes Intention to attack this Army . . . remains to be determined . . . [B]e constantly upon your Guard," he warned.[22]

By 15 September Gates was certain that his opponent intended to "risque a Battle," and he ordered Lincoln to strike at "that Part of the Enemy's Force, yet upon the East Side of the River." Lincoln already had seized the initiative, and since Burgoyne had evacuated Skenesborough, Fort George, and Fort Edward, nothing kept a Patriot militia detachment led by Col. John Brown from marching easily to Ticonderoga and carrying out an harassing attack against the fort that resulted in the capture of some prisoners. Burgoyne had seen a small example of the ease with which American militia could encircle him and cut off his route of retreat.

Having severed his lines of communication with Canada, the British general now intended to advance boldly against the Patriot army. Gates had assessed his enemy correctly Burgoyne was striking out on a rash line of action that could easily end in defeat but could hardly achieve more than a partial victory. On 15 September, the Anglo-German army began marching toward Bemis Heights with drums beating and colors flying, a spectacle that reminded one eyewitness "of a grand parade in the midst of peace."[23] Two days later the British army encamped near Sword's House, only four miles from the American lines. For all the show, however, Burgoyne was ignorant of the disposition of Gates' army and had no clear idea of the nature of the terrain he had to cover. The sniping of Colonel Morgan's sharpshooters, troops ordered by Gates to harass the enemy advance, had driven Burgoyne's scouts back into his lines. ". . . [We] did not know the nature of the country, nor the position of the enemy's left wing," General Friedrich, Baron Von Riedesel, commander of German troops, commented later.[24]

There was skirmishing between the two armies on 18 September. Gates ordered out Arnold at the head of 1,500 men to probe Burgoyne's strength. After a minor clash with British pickets Arnold returned to the American camp confirmed in an idea he had been mulling for days. The Patriots, he declared to Gates, should attack the enemy rather than wait for an assault on their own lines. Why, he asked, allow the British to move at will in front of the American position, perhaps use their heavy artillery advantageously against Patriot defenses?[25] But Gates refused to be shaken from his belief that the best course of action lay in awaiting Burgoyne's first move. He knew that attack was more costly than defense, and he was especially concerned about the quality of his troops if forced into linear formation against steeled British and German regulars. Especially problematical were Morgan's sharpshooting riflemen, who were deadly effective when sniping from concealed positions, but in open battle would lose every advantage they possessed.

Hence, it would appear that wisdom favored Gates' decision to bide his time, even if events during the battle of Freeman's Farm on 19 September indicated that he may have been overly cautious. Apparently, aside from delegating commands, he had made no overall plans for this conflict with Burgoyne. He decided that Arnold would lead the army's left wing, which rested on a hill about a mile from the Hudson River, and he placed Brigadier General Ebenezer Learned in charge of the center on a fortified plateau near Neilson's Barn. Gates himself took immediate command of the right wing, situated on a bluff overlooking the river. Probably the commander intended initially to await Burgoyne's assault on his fortifications. But he finally yielded to Arnold's arguments that the enemy would flank the American position on

[22]Gates to Lincoln, September 15, *ibid.*

[23]Cited in W. L. Stone, *The Campaign of Lieutenant General John Burgoyne* (Albany, 1877), p. 18.

[24]Baron Von Riedesel, "Abstract from a Military Memoir, Concerning the Campaign of 1777," in Friederike Charlotte, Madame de Riedesel, *Letters and Memoirs Relating to the War of the American Independence . . . (Albany, 1827)*, p. 146.

[25]Wallace, *Arnold,* 146-47; James Wilkinson, *Memoirs of My Own Times* (3 vols.; Philadelphia, 1816), I, 235; Arnold to Gates, 1 October 1777, *Gates Papers,* box 8, NYHS.

the left unless engaged outside the Patriot defenses. Hence, Gates decided to send Morgan's corps and a newly-organized contingent of riflemen under Henry Dearborn into the dense woods north of his line to oppose the British advance; Arnold would reinforce the riflemen if they got into trouble. In a way, Gates' action was a slight compromise between his own defensive strategy and Arnold's wish to advance. That he ordered the riflemen to bear the brunt of battle indicated his faith in both their leader, Morgan, and their particular battle skills.

On the morning of 19 September, Burgoyne attacked the American army. In a letter to Hancock, Gates told the story: "Friday morning I was informed by my Reconnoitering Parties that the Enemy had struck their Camp, and were moving towards our left. I immediately started Col. Morgan's Corps consisting of the Rifle Regiment & the Eighth Infantry of the army [under Dearborn] to observe their Direction & harrass their advance. This Party, at half after twelve, fell in with a Picquet of the Enemy, which they immediately drove." But Morgan's men had lost formation, and "the Enemy being Reinforced," Morgan was "in turn obliged to retire."[26] By midafternoon the battle was raging warmingly, and both Arnold and Burgoyne fed reinforcements into the line. The Americans, especially Morgan's men, fighting from concealment, hammered at a weak spot in the enemy line between the center, commanded by Burgoyne, and General Simon Fraser's right wing. Had Gates yielded to Arnold's pleading for enough reinforcements to exploit this weakness, perhaps the British defenses would have been crushed and the campaign terminated then and there. But Gates might have been afraid of an enemy blow on his right and feared weakening his position overlooking the Hudson River. In any case, he had indicated from the first day he took command that his sole intention was to hold Burgoyne and allow his impetuous enemy to destroy himself. Late in the afternoon he did send Learned's brigade

into battle, but his decision had been delayed too long to have much effect. By then, General Riedesel had rushed to Burgoyne's rescue. As it turned out, if Gates's army had not eliminated the enemy, it still emerged victorious in battle. Only 3,000 Americans took part at Freeman's Farm against about 3,500 British and German troops, but Burgoyne suffered 600 casualties, the Patriots only 320. More importantly, the Americans had sought only to maintain their position, while the British had attempted a breakthrough to Albany, so Burgoyne—although he denied it— clearly had been bested.

Since the conclusion of the battle of Freeman's Farm, both contemporaries and later scholars have argued whether Arnold actually was on the field that day.[27] Probably his part in the battle never will be fully known, for the sources are too contradictory; certainly the tired arguments pro and con need not be repeated here. Of all the statements on Arnold's role on 19 September, perhaps the most valid was made by the general's biographer, Willard M. Wallace, who declared: "In the last analysis, apart from the fact that it is practically impossible to conceive of an officer with a battle record and a fiery nature like Benedict Arnold's taking no role in the four to five hours of furious fighting that hot afternoon, it is an aspersion on Gates's own leadership to assume that he would deprive the army all that time of Arnold's abilities. . ."[28]

The whole question of Arnold's participation in the battle, one suspects, would be irrelevant except that some scholars have used that issue to "prove" Arnold should be given credit for Burgoyne's surrender. This writer believes that even if the general were on the field on 19 September—as he doubtless was— he hardly could be credited with halting the British drive southward. If Gates allowed his subordinates, Arnold and Morgan, some free rein to try their own tactics on

[26]Gates to president of Congress, 22 September 1777, *Gates Papers,* box 19, NYHS.

[27]See essays on this question by Christopher Ward, *War of the Revolution,* II, 941-42; Channing, *History of the United States,* III, 276-78; Nickerson, *Turning Point,* 473-77; and Wallace, *Arnold,* 326-32.

[28]Wallace, *Arnold,* 331.

the battlefield, if he struck no imposing stance as a leader of men in battle (he remained in his headquarters a mile from battle on the 19th), still he was in active control of his army and correctly had deduced the intentions of his enemy. It appears that he was wise to act a defensive part. These observations in no way detract from the brilliant battlefield leadership of Arnold and Morgan. As Professor Higginbotham has remarked, "None of the three [Gates, Arnold, Morgan] should be excluded from a fair share of the credit."[29]

After the battle, Arnold was furious with his commander because the latter had not taken his advice on a general advance against Burgoyne and because he felt he had been prevented from destroying the enemy.[30] But his final humiliation was Gates' refusal to mention him in the official letter to Congress on 22 September. Although the commander had what he considered sufficient reason for leaving Arnold's name off his "praise list," the slight cut Arnold to the bone. Soon the two officers were in a furious and unbecoming altercation, which culminated on 1 October when Arnold was relieved of all command. Historians who credit Arnold with victory at Saratoga generally look on this episode as an attempt by Gates to get rid of his rival for glory. It is more likely that Arnold, by his stubborn insistence on having his way, exhausted Gates' patience after a season and brought about his own humiliation.

The commander's quarrel with Arnold did not divert his attention from Burgoyne. On 22 September, he wrote his wife a letter. "One week more," he declared, "will determine the great Business of This Campaign; in that Time, The Enemy will either Retire, or by one Violent push, endeavour to recover the almost ruin'd State of their affairs."[31] As it turned out, Burgoyne did not resume action until two weeks later, but he was becoming desperate. On 3 October he put his army on half rations, and his officers and men were

discouraged. He had learned on 21 September that a British army under the leadership of Sir Henry Clinton, commander of New York in the absence of Howe (who was campaigning in Pennsylvania), would soon lead an army of 2,000 men up the Hudson River. But as time passed, Burgoyne became less and less certain of succor from that quarter. In fact, Clinton never promised him a breakthrough to Albany. Finally, Burgoyne decided to attempt on 7 October a "reconnaisance in force" against the American left flank, a desperate enough measure at best. His aim was to throw the Patriots off guard and extricate himself from an increasingly-dangerous situation.

Gates was not about to play the game by the Briton's rules. Just before the battle of Bems Heights (or the second battle of Freeman's Farm), the American commander learned that on 3 October Clinton had begun his advance upriver. Sir Henry hoped to force Gates to diivide his army; but the scheme did not work. Rather than panicking, Gates remained calm and self-possessed. Depending on Forts Montgomery and Clinton in the Highlands north of New York City to halt Sir Henry's drive, he refused to detach any of his troops to garrison Albany. Instead he ordered troops from Fort Stanwix in the Mohawk Valley to march eastward to that town. He continued to fortify his lines, to augment his forces by the acquisition of thousands of New England and New York militia, and to lay in supplies that Schuyler diligently sent him from Albany. Shrewdly reading his antagonist, on 4 October he wrote Governor George Clinton of New York, "Perhaps [Burgoyne's] Despair may Dictate to him, to risque all upon one Throw; he is an old gamester & in his time has seen all chances."[32] No more penetrating remark could have been spoken of "Gentleman Johnny" at that moment in the campaign. For Gates the obvious policy now was to continue the program he had followed all along: in effect, to give Burgoyne enough rope to hang himself.

Essentially the British commander, a some-

[29]Higginbotham, *Morgan*, 75-76.
[30]Arnold to Gates, 1 October 1777, *Gates Papers*, box 8, NYHS.
[31]Gates to Elizabeth Gates, 22 September 1777, *Gates Papers*, box 19, NYHS.

[32]*Gates Papers*, box 19, NYHS.

time playwright, followed his script well. On 7 October he led 1,500 regulars and 600 Loyalists and Indians out of his entrenched camp, built after the first battle, southwestward towards Freeman's Farm. Totally ignorant of both the terrain and Gates's arrangements to stop his flanking movement, he went in search of nonexistent high ground for his cannon. Pausing in a wheat field, he sent out scouts to examine the left wing of the Patriot army. American spyglasses picked out these skirmishers, and Gates, personally commanding the left wing after Arnold's removal, issued a command: "Order on Morgan to begin the game."[33]

The battle started, said the American commander in a letter to Congress on 12 October, "About the same Hour of the day & near the same spot of ground" as the previous struggle. Morgan, on the patriot left, moved on the British right wing led by Lord Balcarres; Learned advanced against the enemy center; and Brigadier General Enoch Poor attacked on the American right. Soon "the Conflict was very warm & Bloody" all along the front. While Poor's men were assaulting the British near the Hudson, Morgan, who made a wide circuit around the enemy's right to get into the woods on the flank and rear of Balcarres' troops, poured a deadly fire into the ranks of the disorganized royal soldiers and forced them to retreat into their fortifications. Arnold, without Gate's approbation and hardly under self control, now seized command of Learned's corps and dashed into the fight. Leading two charges against the enemy lines, he finally forced Lieutenant Colonel Henrich Von Breymann from a key redoubt and was wounded in his leg. When Gates heard of his subordinate's exploits, he swallowed his anger and on 12 October lauded "the gallant Major General Arnold" in his report to Congress. He also declared, "too much Praise cannot be given the Corps commanded by Col. Morgan."[34]

Burgoyne's position no longer was tenable

after the battle of Bemis Heights. While the Americans suffered only 150 casualties, the British had lost 700 killed, captured and wounded. Desertion was becoming rampant, especially among the Germans, who, said Gates, were coming over to the Patriots "in Shoals." At midnight on 9 October, Burgoyne began withdrawing toward Saratoga. Two days later he had taken post on high ground overlooking Saratoga Creek. Gates, pushing his army towards the retreating enemy, came upon the new British lines and ordered General Nixon to probe them. When Nixon discovered that Burgoyne's entire army faced him, he notified Gates, who immediately ordered the Patriots to disengage. The British commander, suffering from this "adverse" stroke of fortune, decided on 12 October to retreat once more; but he had dallied too long and his line of march was cut off. By then Gates had moved American militia into position on the opposite bank of the Hudson River, thus preventing the Anglo-German army from crossing.

Even now, Burgoyne was not ready to concede defeat. The British general had one more card to play: he would attempt again to frighten his opponent with the threat of Sir Henry Clinton's advance up the Hudson, even if he knew he could expect no assistance from that direction. On 13 October he opened negotiations with Gates for terms of surrender and then began to vacillate in hopes that the American commander would be stampeded into some hasty action because of imminent danger to his rear. At the very least, the Briton might secure a mitigation of the terms of capitulation. While Gates continued in his calm refusal to divide his army, he did begin to yield to Burgoyne on surrender terms. At first he had demanded a unconditional British capitulation. But in the early evening of 15 October he received word from American intelligence that the enemy drive up the Hudson, stalled for five days after capture of the Highland forts, had recommenced under the leadership of General John Vaughan and threatened his base of supply. When Burgoyne heard the same news, he quickly notified Gates that he would

[33]Wilkinson, *Memoirs*, I, 268; Wallace, *Arnold*, 154.
[34]Gates to president of Congress 12 October 1777, *Gates Papers*, box 19, NYHS.

accept only the conditional terms that his army be allowed to return to England and agree never to serve again in America. General Gates doubtless realized the furor such a capitulation might raise in Congress, for even if Burgoyne's troops were used elsewhere they still would free other soldiers for service in the "colonies." But, not knowing as his opponent did that the British push out of New York City was merely a feint and not intended to capture Albany, he felt compelled to accept Burgoyne's demands in order to free his army to march southward and secure that town.

Hence, Gates agreed to the Briton's proposals and in the process left himself open to what this writer believes were unfair charges by both contemporaries and later scholars that he had once again evinced a pattern of weakness and bungling. As James Truslow Adams put it, "Gates, who had held the British army at his mercy . . . had made absurd terms and thrown away the fruits of victory." Or as Henry Laurens, newly elected president of congress, said, perhaps Gates "was too polite to make the Lieut. General and his troops prisoners of discretion" owing to his being "a little captivated by the flattery" of a British officer. Yet General Washington himself, upon hearing of Burgoyne's capitulation, remarked that "the critical situation in which Genl. Gates was likely to be thrown" by the enemy advance up the Hudson, would not allow him to insist upon a more perfect surrender." Regarding the commander-in-chief's statement, Bernhard Knollenberg, an astute scholar, asked, "Could any impartial historian, giving weight to all the pertinent facts, reach a different conclusion?"[35] In any case, on 17 October 1777, Burgoyne's army surrendered, and the Saratoga campaign ended in triumph for the Americans.

To recapitulate this historian's thesis, it would appear that many scholars, in evaluating Saratoga, sometimes have unjustly com-

[35]Adams and Washington quoted in Knollenberg, *Washington*, pp. 21, 29; Laurens quoted in David Duncan Wallace, *The Life of Henry Laurens* (New York, 1915), p. 247.

pared Gates' role to the parts Schuyler and Arnold played. Due credit should be given to General Schuyler for his remarkable exertions against Burgoyne before he was relieved of command. Moreover, his role as a supplier of Gates' army, after he had been superseded by that officer, always will redound to his favor. Yet for all his contributions, it hardly seems possible to argue that he deserves the laurels for Burgoyne's capitulation. Two months after Schuyler had lost command of the Patriots the Anglo-German

army remained in the field, and any American who had predicted in August, 1777, that Burgoyne would capitulate in October probably would have been suspected by his countrymen of more verve than intelligence. British soldiers had been in worse situations before and had managed to extricate themselves.

As for Arnold's part at Saratoga, he, along with Morgan, deserves great credit for his tactical contributions and his remarkable ability to infuse his men with valor and boldness. This writer would not detract from General Arnold's deserved glory. But he questions the assertion that he merited fame as the "conqueror of Burgoyne." While he was doubtless a better tactician than mild, "Granny" Gates, he showed at Saratoga a strategic weakness that, had he gotten his way, might have resulted in a Patriot disaster. What would bold, offensive operations against Burgoyne have gained? Would they have strengthened the Americans, or would they have played directly into "Gentleman Johnny's" hands? Another look at the facts of the situation at Saratoga seems to answer these questions. Burgoyne, bold, impetuous, at times rash, had thrashed southward from his easy victory at Ticonderoga with too much baggage and too many guns. After expending a great deal of effort merely to reach the Hudson River, after losing a tenth of his army at Bennington, he still decided to cut his communications with Canada and push forward in a do-or-die maneuver. Gates, persistently recognizing his antagonist's impulsive, gambler's nature, led Burgoyne into a defensive trap. Time was on the Americans' side, for as the early winter of upstate New York drew closer, Burgoyne grew weaker. The farther south he moved, the tighter Gates drew American troops around the British army and its line of retreat.

Terrain also favored defensive, rather than offensive, strategy. The land over which Burgoyne had to march to reach Albany, gave every advantage to the defender and forced the opponent into pushing against strong, defensive positions. Bemis Heights presented high ground that commanded all surrounding countryside; the land was broken by precipices and ravines; all roads towards Albany were cut and the enemy had to maneuver through dense woods if he intended to attack or try a flanking movement. With relative ease Gates could keep Burgoyne under constant surveillance from his defended heights while the British officer had to exert himself mightily to gather information about his antagonist.

The nature of the opposing troops also led Gates to think in terms of defense. Burboyne was at the head of well-trained British and German regulars, whose main strength lay in their ability to use massed firepower and the bayonet in linear formation on open ground. The Americans, on the other hand, less trained (even the Continentals) than England's troops, less skilled in the use of the bayonet—in fact, generally unequipped with it— would suffer great disadvantages in open battle. As for Morgan's contingent of riflemen, had Gates used them in linear formation he would have wasted their power. The rifleman's greatest asset was his individual marksmanship with a weapon designed for accuracy, rather than rapidity, of fire. There was no way to attach a bayonet to the type of rifle Morgan's men carried, even if such weapons had been available for use. This consideration alone made riflemen practically worthless in linear tactics against troops skilled in employing the terror of a bayonet

charge. By disposing Morgan's men under cover at the wooded fringe of clearings used by the British for their close-order battlefield maneuvering, the American commander placed them in the best position to make them most effective.

Gates' caution during battle also fitted well into his scheme for reducing his enemy. He fed only enough men into the struggle on the 19th to halt Burgoyne's drive—all that he wanted to do. Perhaps Arnold was correct in believing the Patriots could have smashed the enemy had Gates unleashed enough men to do the job. But what purpose, the American commander prudently asked, would such a scheme serve? There seemed no need to risk even a remote possibility that the Patriots would be attacked on their right after weakening their lines on Bemis Heights. Burgoyne had been stopped in his tracks, had he not? What did it matter whether he was destroyed that day, or a week or a month later? It was true, of course, that delay might give the British in New York City time to organize an attack against Albany, but Gates felt that the Highland forts, just north of the city, could contain the enemy thrust. As it turned out, he was incorrect, but in fairness he could hardly be held responsible for knowing beforehand that the Highland defenses would crumble so readily. Other Patriot officers had placed undue trust in fortresses to halt a British drive, only to see their faith destroyed when the enemy struck. Once the British did threaten him from the southward, the American commander responded with coolness and refused to overestimate the danger.

The bulk of evidence on the Saratoga campaign indicates that Gates should be credited with victory over Burgoyne. He was not, it appears, a "(so called) Victor," as Ward argued, but an actual victor. While Gates' subordinates, Benedict Arnold and Daniel Morgan, deserve praise for their battlefield exploits, and while Philip Schuyler contributed greatly to the outcome of the campaign, still Gates deserves the greatest share of the laurels for his strategic contributions. Professor Don Higginbotham summed up the argument well when he said of Gates at Saratoga, "Few, if any, of Washington's generals could have surpassed his performance against Burgoyne."[36]

[36]Higginbotham, *Morgan,* 63.
More complete footnotes are available from the author.

# THE FRENCH CONNECTION

# CONTRABAND FROM LORIENT

By Henry Pleasants, Jr.

**B**RITISH and American bombers are roaring over the little seacoast of Lorient, in Brittany, France, and are dropping tons of bombs. Their objective is the great Nazi submarine base that has sprung into being since the Panzer divisions swept through from the east in 1940. So long as Lorient remains a spawning ground and hospital for the gangsters of the Atlantic, our transports loaded to the gunwales with troops and equipment will be in danger.

Few tourists have ever visited Lorient. It straggles along the Scorff River, about half way between the larger ports of Brest and St. Nazaire; and it is well off the beaten track of sight-seers. Karl Baedeker, whose guide books were always Bibles to summer visitors in foreign lands, gave little encouragement to any one who considered making the tedious journey thither from Paris. In fact, he spoke so disparagingly regarding the possible points of interest in this insignificant town that tourist trade probably languished as a result. No doubt, this was by no means resented by the French authorities, however, for Lorient was an important naval base as far back as 1827; and it was increasing steadily in its activity year by year prior to the First World War. From an official standpoint, the fewer strangers nosing around the quays, with cameras slung over their shoulders, the better.

Baedeker commented somewhat caustically upon the reticence and lack of hospitality on the part of the inhabitants. In 1909, he stated that the population of Lorient was 46,403. He added, "The town is well built, but uninteresting." He did, however, call attention to the bronze statue of Bisson, a young naval lieutenant, who blew up his ship to prevent its falling into the hands of Greek pirates.

There is more to the romantic background of Lorient than Karl Baedeker knew. In the earliest days of the American Revolution, l'Orient, as it was then called, was the scene of one of the earliest and certainly one of the cleverest and most daring smuggling exploits that history has recorded. The success or failure of the cause of the insurgent American Colonies depended almost entirely upon the importation of a supply of arms and ammunition for Washington's ragged troops holding the British at bay in Boston. The mission was entrusted to Captain Thomas Mason, of Philadelphia.

A word about Mason: He was born in Poole, Dorsetshire, England, about 1730. His father was a successful merchant of that town, highly respected, and a staunch adherent to the tenets of the Church of England, who steadfastly refused to take any part in the illicit trade that had made Poole notorious. Smuggling was to Poole as moonshine distilling is to the Tennessee mountain districts. Thomas Mason listened to the rare tales told by the grizzled sea-dogs on the quays, and caught the fever of adventure. When his stern parent thrashed him soundly for idling with the "riff-raff o' th' port on th' Lord's Day," he ran away to sea, shipping as a cabin-boy on a brig bound for Philadelphia.

He was then but thirteen years old. He never returned to Poole. Instead, he set himself steadfastly to the serious business of becoming a mariner the hard way. From able seaman, he rose steadily and rapidly to captain of the brig *Prince of Wales* and the *Charlestown Packet*, both of which vessels carried freight and passengers between Philadelphia and Charleston, South Carolina. Later, he became associated in the mercantile marine trade with Thomas Shirley, a wealthy Englishman, who was sojourning for his health in the South, and expanded his activities in trade to the West Indies, Bermuda, France, Portugal and Spain. His shrewd business ability brought wealth and many friends in the highest social and financial positions in the Colonies. He bought a comfortable home at 13 Vine Street, Philadelphia, and married his childhood sweetheart, a charming Quaker lass, Priscilla Sisom, in Christ Church, October 12, 1766. Even the members of the strict Society of Friends seem to have borne no resentment against Priscilla for marrying "out of Meeting."

With such a reputation in the mercantile marine trade as Thomas Mason had made by the year 1775, it is not surprising that General Horatio Gates, Adjutant-General of the American Army, should have approached him with the view to obtaining help for Washington. The actual story of the first interview with the Commander-in-Chief is best told by the young mariner himself in the pages of his personal record of his expedition:

1775 the 10th of July—being a Stagnation of all kind of business my Curiosity lead me to proceed with General Gates to Cambridge, and on my arrival there I was politely introduced by that Gentleman to General Washington, who in a Few Hours Became Acquainted with my Abilities as a Seaman, a man of propperty & capable of Exicuting any plan of a Voyage, that may be proposed Either in the Services of the States or Otherwise. General Washington acquainted me with the State of the Army in Respect to Ammunition, and Requested on my Return to Philadelphia that I would use my interest with other Gentlemen & proceed on a voyage to Europe for a Cargoe, to which I gave him my promise after coming from the Camp of Cambridge and finding their Distress was so greate for want of Ammunition . . . I concluded, in Case a Number of Gentlemen would join me—so as to make up a Capital of £4000 Sterling, that I would take the Hazardous Task on myself to Accomplish it—& Leaving a Sufficient Reale Estate Behind me as a Security. . . .

The details of the scheme are interesting from every angle: Mason evidently had much more difficulty in securing the necessary finacial assistance than he had anticipated. Only an extremely wealthy man would be willing to stake his reputation and fortune on a plan to provide munitions for the insurgents; for, if the expedition failed, the loss would be total. Even if successful insofar as the importation of arms was concerned, the possible discovery by the British of the connection of any merchant with such a venture would be met with disciplinary measures of the severest type. Withdrawal of trading license would be the least that could be expected. Imprisonment and fine would be likely; and even

capital punishment, such as hanging for treason was possible. No one but the most intrepid adventurer could possibly be expected to take such a chance.

Mason met with many rebuffs. Even some of his best friends declined to help him. Finally, he appealed to Robert Morris. The great financier was impressed. He agreed to become a partner in the scheme. This was highly satisfactory, as Morris commanded unlimited credit not only in the ports of Spain, France, and Portugal, but also in England, even at this period of colonial insurrection. Mason himself had some financial resources in England through his friend, Thomas Shirley. Morris insisted that his associate, Jacob Winey of Reading, Pennsylvania, be included as a third partner; but he stipulated that no other additions to the partnership be made. The final agreement between the three men was that each would advance 800 pounds Sterling; Mason would supply the vessel and command her, and Morris and Winey would load her with flour to be sold upon arrival at some foreign port, the proceeds of the sale to be added to the capital to be used later for the purchase of munitions. Mason set sail in the schooner *Charming Polly* on August 12th, 1775.

The voyage across the frigate-patrolled, pirate-infested Atlantic is described by the hard-bitten colonial mariner in just thirty-six words:

—The Next Day following Being the 12th I sett Saile & after a Passage of 34 day—with the Usual Occurences of a Voyage I had the Agreable Satisfaction to Arrive in Ferole [Spain] the 14th of September. . . .

Difficulties began to be encountered immediately. Mason had no trouble in disposing of his flour, and was able to get an advance of 500 pounds against its sale, the balance to be credited to Morris' account when the transaction was completed by the agent, but the purchase of arms and ammunition seemed out of the question. As Mason put it:

While the Vessel was Discharging—no steps was Left undone to make myself acquainted with their Laws & Customs of Trade & in particular, for the Cargoe I came for, which Sufficiently appears in my Querys, from some of the most Iminent Merchants in that place, with their answers amongst my papers, and I could not Discover the Least Shaddow of hopes in Obtaining arms or Ammunition.

Disappointed, but not discouraged, Thomas Mason decided to try his luck elsewhere. On the 27th of September, he dropped anchor in Port Lorient, after a passage of five days. Here, he says, "I made every Necessary Inquiry Respecting my outward bound cargo & Nearly found myself in Like Situation, as in Spain. . . ." The real obstructive element was, of course, the fact that all of the European nations were unwilling to enter into any trade negotiations for arms with representatives of the insurgent colonies for fear of incurring the wrath of England.

The young mariner found some light on the subject among his friends in Lorient: It would be possible to ship saltpeter, used in the manufacture of gunpowder, to Holland "in any Bottom, But American." It would also be possible to ship arms from the port of Nantes to the coast of Guinea. From there, it would be easy to transfer the shipment to America. Mason hesitated, however, stating in his report, "But in this case it is not complying with the Tenor of my orders—and in Case of Accident perhaps it may Involve me in a Law Suit." Sailing orders to captains were very strict in those days; and even though he was actually a partner in the venture, he was, nevertheless, an agent under orders of Morris and Winey.

His discomfiture was suddenly icreased when, "—after 2 days thus Reflecting, I concluded on the 29th of September to purchase the Saltpeter, but to my surprise no person would take my Bills, a report prevailing that all American Creddit was at an End in England."

Uppermost in the mind of Thomas Mason was the securing of arms and ammunition for the colonies. He had been given specific instructions verbally by Robert Morris to extend his credit beyond the notes and bills of exchange in his possession, if he thought wise. In those days, international credit was comparatively informal. Large amounts of gold or silver were seldom shipped to foreign ports unless it was to establish the credit of a new and comparatively unknown concern. Mason was actually in possession of 3900 pounds Sterling, ready for immediate investment. This was a persuasive form of argument with French merchants; and he used it immediately to the best advantage. He says:

In this situation I put my Bills of Exchange into the Hands of Berard Brothers to Forward them to London for Acceptance, which in Common takes 22 Days Before you have advice of Their Fate—But I prevailed on them Gentlemen to Load the Schooner & in case all my Bills came Back protested, the Vessel should be Dispatched with her cargoe & myself Stay as Hostage untill payment came from America, or security obtained for the amount from my Connections in England.

This was an adroit piece of business. In other words, in the very face of reports of failure of American credit in England, he persuaded an established mercantile firm of France to load his vessel with war supplies, and stand ready to ship it to America, holding him personally as hostage for ultimate reimbursement.

A new phase of the situation now appeared: the Continental Congress had at last been galvanized into action by the appeals of Washington, and had sent Captain Charles Biddle to France with cash for the purchase of war munitions. He arrived in Port Lorient in the brig *Chance* while Mason's negotiations were still pending, and the schooner *Charming Polly* was being cleaned preparatory to taking on her cargo. Everything, consequently, where the French were concerned, took on a new aspect. Thomas Mason had come as an individual; Captain Biddle as representative of the new government. Mason offered payment through somewhat questionable credit under the circumstances; Biddle was ready to offer hard cash and substantial security. Moreover, it was now apparent that the American Colonies intended to push their defiance of the Crown to great lengths. If successful, a valuable market for munitions would be opened. Mason instantly anticipated the reaction:

As he was a Stranger I introduced him to Messrs Berard Brothers, with a request to give them Gentlemen every satisfactory acct. of myself & those I were Concerned with—that in Case the Bills should come Back protested, they will still be safe in any amount I may contract with them. This being don and the Gentlemen perfectly satisfyed the 15th of October I began to Load & by the 20th everything Compleated & nothing to prevent my sailing but the Fate of the Bills—as I then was at Leasure Capain Biddle & myself had several consultations with Messrs Berard Brothers, Respecting the Loading of a French ship, & eventually agreed in Case I would proceed in her myself, they would advance me £1200 Sterling on acct of Thomas Mason & Co by the Thirds—.

Here we can see the development of a new plan to charter a French vessel in addition to the *Chance* and the *Polly*. It was evident that Mason intended to squeeze out of France every pound of ammunition he could while Berard Brothers were in a favorable mood. All seemed to be going smoothly.

A sudden crisis rose without warning. Word came from London that all the bills of Morris and Winey were accepted. The financial stability of Mason's expedition was unquestionable; on the other hand, by the same post that had brought news of the acceptance, an order arrived from the Prime Minister of France to the Commandant of the Port to seize Captain Mason's vessel and discharge her cargo. The French government would not chance the displeasure of England by allowing munitions to be shipped from France to America.

Action was necessary at once. By good fortune, the post had arrived in the evening. The schooner could not be seized until the following morning. There were still a few hours in which to act; and upon that depended the success or failure of the expedition. Mason's report gives a confidential and graphic account of his feelings at this moment: he might run the vessel out of the harbor, and down the narrow channel past the walls of the fort at Port Louis, taking a grave chance of being fired on and sunk. In such an event, his partners would justly hold him or his executors responsible for the loss of their capital in so flagrantly having defied the French laws. Even if he should be successful in evading the authorities, he must sacrifice a joint capital of 1150 pounds Sterling, the balance in the hands of Berard Brothers. It was possible that his partners would hold him

responsible for this entire amount, a large sum in those days.

Then, too, he could give the command of his schooner to someone and remain behind to guard his capital. This was decidedly dangerous, in view of the fact that if his substitute in command of the *Charming Polly* were careless or unlucky enough to be sunk in running out of the harbor, he would be blamed for trusting his ship to an unauthorized person. Morris and Winey could then hold him for the full value of all that was lost.

He could, of course, sit quietly and surrender the vessel. If he did, all of his efforts in behalf of General Washington would come to nothing. He would sacrifice the only hope held before his countrymen. Mason was not of that breed.

He thought over the possible solutions of his problem rapidly. He then conferred with Captain Biddle. He offered the suggestion that if Biddle would sail the *Charming Polly* back to America, he himself would remain in Port l'Orient and execute the commission entrusted to Biddle by the Continental Congress free of charge. This would consist in loading the brig *Chance* with munitions without the knowledge of the French authorities, and sailing her back to America at a later date. Furthermore, as he was more familiar with the channel of the harbor, he would himself take the *Charming Polly* out to sea, and return in a small boat as soon as the danger zone had been passed. Captain Biddle listened to this audacious plan, and, with some hesitation agreed.

There was no time to be lost. Mason made a few hurried preparations, and wrote some letters to his partners regarding the sudden change of plans. These he handed to Biddle, and, in return, received a personal letter from him to be read later. Together they went down to the wharf, and found the wind and tide favorable. It was utterly dark, but Mason was confident of finding his way down the narrow passage. The *Charming Polly* was quietly cast off, and drifted slowly with the tide into midstream. Sail was made rapidly and silently, with every block well greased, and the sailors pattering around in bare feet.

Down the long tortuous channel stole the *Charming Polly*, with Mason at the helm, his eyes glued to the ramparts of the fort for the first flash of a cannoneer's fuse that might be the beginning of a storm of shot from the batteries. They cleared the harbor shortly before dawn; then, when three miles out, Mason bade Biddle farewell, and climbed overside into the long boat of the brig *Chance*, which had been trailing astern with men at the oars ready for any emergency. The *Polly* bent every inch of canvas for her race to America, while her master returned to Port Lorient to await developments.

Charles Biddle was evidently worried over this sudden turn of events. His letter to Thomas Mason is eloquent of his anxiety; yet shows clearly how great was the emergency in America:

Port L'Orient, Oct. 28, 1775.

Dear Sir

I cannot express to you the uneasiness I feel at not being able to comply with the desires of the people by whom I am Employd. However the scheme we have agreed upon I believe will fully Answer the purpose. I put the utmost Confidnce in you, and as Our Country and Everything dear is at Stake I make no doubt but you will do everything that is possible for the Service of it. You'll dispatch the Brig and Schooner as soon as possible, and please to Inclose to me an Acct of the Charges &c that I may be able to Settle with the Gentlemen I am Employ'd by. pray dont neglect Getting all the powder you possible can in the Brig & Schooner.

I am Sir
Your most Obt Servt
C. Biddle.

The French Government was not easily pacified. Mason had committed something of a serious crime by clearing the port without official papers. Moreover, his vessel had eluded seizure, albeit no warrant had actually been served. The Commandant was not foolish enough to believe that the *Charming Polly* would deliver her cargo to Holland, as he had been led to suspect while she was being loaded. He knew now that she was on her way to America. If, by chance, she should be intercepted by a British sloop of war, serious trouble with England might result. He had been tricked by a wily American, and

he was furious. Mason describes the action that followed:

—on my return To Lorient, the Commandant ordered the Guard to take my Body—and had it not Been for the Interposition of a Few Gentlemen, who became Security for my appearance Before him and his Council, I undoubtedly should have been kept in Confinement—when the examination was over & no proff appearing that I Either aided or asisted—I was Released from that Parole.

Mason's mission was, however, only half completed. He had been successful in starting the first shipment of arms on its way to America; but to offset this, he had pledged his word to Captain Biddle to bring back the brig *Chance* equally well loaded. He had incurred the enmity of the Commandant, and the suspicion of all of the authorities of the French government in the port. Whatever move he made now would be watched closely. It would not be unlikely that he would be arrested on some trumped-up charge just to keep him under surveillance. His slightest slip might spell ruin; and might also bring serious charges against Captain Biddle for relinquishing his command of the brig *Chance*.

The strategy employed now by the young adventurer was truly Machiavellian. He retired to his rooms in Lorient, and led the life of the most peace-loving and righteous visitor imaginable. If he appeared upon the streets, he did so openly; if he attended any large gathering, he was careful to avoid being seen in conversation with anyone who had been even remotely connected with the escape of the *Charming Polly*. It was helpful, rather than a hindrance to his plans, that he had incurred the intense hatred of Captain John Craig, now commanding the brig *Chance*, which was idling at anchor empty in the harbor. Biddle had turned over his vessel to Craig; but had stipulated that the orders of Captain Mason were to be followed explicitly in every detail. Craig raved because there were no orders; his men were becoming restless and quarrelsome. If Mason had any plans, Craig was not being told of them. No clearance papers for the *Chance* could be issued without Mason's permission. This suspense was kept up for two long months.

The young mariner was not so idle as it seemed. In his record he says:

—as Berard Brothers was Suspected in asisting to Run the Schooner out of Port—it put a Stop to all our proposed Schemes in their ship—and Necessity Obliged me to Change my Connections to Mr. Gourlade—.

It seems that there was a Dutch vessel in port discharging her cargo. It will be remembered that there was no embargo against the shipment of arms and ammunition to Holland "in any Bottom But American." Mason, knowing this, through the connivance of his new accessory, Mr. Gourlade, quietly chartered this vessel, and loaded her with 109 casks of cannon powder and 36 stands of muskets, ostensibly purchased by the owners of the vessel for shipment to Amsterdam. As soon as the Dutch vessel's clearance papers were made out to her skipper, the shrewd Yankee presented himself at the office of the outraged old Commandant, and told him that since there seemed to be no possibility of the purchase of arms in Lorient, he had been instructed by Captain Biddle to obtain clearance papers for the empty brig *Chance*, and return with her to America. It is even reported that he begged the Commandant to send a detail for the inspection of the brig to see that she was actually empty. He is said to have added, casually, that refusal to grant the clearance papers without due cause being shown would constitute a violation of international law, since the *Chance* was on a special

mission of the American Congress. Whatever misgivings the official may have had that something was in the wind, he had no legal grounds for holding the vessel. He grudingly made out the papers December 28, 1775.

The Dutch vessel, strangely enough, had delayed her departure on a pretext of some sort until Mason's negotiations with the Commandant had been brought to a successful conclusion. She then sailed quietly out to sea. Mason now instructed Captain Craig to be ready to weigh anchor the following morning. What Craig said is not recorded; but it was probably anything but agreeable for him to look forward to a voyage across the Atlantic in an empty brig. However, orders were orders; and, with all his faults, Craig was an able and conscientious man. He did as he was told.

Thomas Mason tells the story of what followed in terse phraseology. Of his overwhelming anxiety for fear something might go wrong at the crucial moment; a sudden storm; an untrustworthy skipper of the Dutch vessel; a misunderstanding of orders; a deliberate act of piracy, perhaps, he says nothing. He relates the facts:

—we dropt our anchors the same day between Bell Isle & the Isle of Groy [Isle de la Croix]—were I received the Cargo, Principally on acct of Congress—the 29th Following being all compleated, we made saile & is the Reason why my receit from Capt. Craig on Acct of Thomas Mason &Co. was dated at Sea—and the 2nd of February 1776 we arrived safe at the Delaware and when I came to Philad. I received the general thanks of Congress for the Integrity of my Transactions & Mr. Morris was the person in a Committee that delivered it.

# THE AMERICAN REVOLUTIONARY ARMY:
## A FRENCH ESTIMATE IN 1777

By Durand Echeverria and Orville T. Murphy*

### PART I

### INTRODUCTION

ON JUNE 17, 1777, a young French ex-army officer landed in Charleston, South Carolina.[1] Unlike Lafayette and his companions on the *Victoire,* who arrived in that city the same day, he had come not to enlist in Washington's army, but merely to satisfy an itch to travel and a lively curiosity by observing firsthand the famous *Insurgents* of whom all Paris was talking. After a stay of nearly a month in Charleston he made his way north by sea and land to Philadelphia, where he remained for six weeks, industriously recording his impressions of American life, both military and civil. At length the approach of General Howe's army in September forced upon him a hurried departure; he journeyed north overland to Boston, whence he sailed for Europe late in October.

After landing in Bilbao he finished writing the record of his observations, which he entitled *Voïage au Continent américain par un françois en 1777. Et Réflexions philosophiques sur ces nouveaux Républicains.*[2] The manuscript was submitted in April, 1778, to the official French censor in Paris, but the strongly liberal and anti-clerical slant of the work made rejection inevitable.

Even though the *Voïage au Continent américain* was not published it occupies a unique position as the first known attempt by a French writer to paint a full-length portrait of American society. To the military historian it is of special interest, for it contains an unusually lengthy and detailed evaluation of the American land forces. This report, translated on the following pages, has the advantage of being the work of an observer who was both professionally competent and at the same time free from the bias which characterized the writings of most of the volunteer European officers, whose views were often prejudiced by frictions with Congress and the American army.

The authorship has been tentatively attributed to Louis de Récicourt de Ganot (1752-?), who served as a cadet and officer in the royal corps of artillery of the French army from 1765 to 1776.[3] Whether the author was De Récicourt or not, it is certain from internal evidence that he was well acquainted with military science. His comments, apart from their interest as eyewitness reports, are of particular value as a sample of professional European opinion of the American military capabilities in the first years of the Revolutionary War.

Since the author, as he himself confessed, recorded his impressions "as he received them," a certain amount of editing seemed advisable, and the following translation is a union of three separate passages.[4] In the in-

*(Echeverria & Murphy) The translators and editors of the original French manuscript teach at Williams College and SUNY, Buffalo, respectively.

[1] For the evidence on the circumstances of the author's arrival in Charleston, as well as for further details on the following document and its authorship, see "The American Character: A French View from Philadelphia, 1777," ed. and trans. Durand Echeverria, *William and Mary Quarterly* (July, 1959). The editors wish to acknowledge with thanks the painstaking and scholarly work of Mrs. Rose Thomasian Antosiewicz, a Brown University research assistant, who prepared the typescript of the original text from microfilm.

[2] Bibliotheque Nationale, FF 14695.

[3] See André Lasseray, *Les Français sous les treize étoiles: 1775-1783* (Màcon, 1935), II, 338.

[4] Ff. 49 verso-72 verso; 96 recto-98 verso; and 101 recto of the original manuscript (of 108 ff.) and of a typescript of the French text have been deposited in the John Hay Library, Brown University, Providence, Rhode Island, and with the Institute for Early American History and Culture, Williamsburg, Virginia. A transcript (not

terest of better organization the editors have grouped De Récicourt's observations under three headings: those having to do with Supply; those dealing with Operations; and finally those containing information about Personnel. The original manuscript contains corrections in another eighteenth century hand by a friend or editor who attempted to clarify the author's somewhat chaotic style, but without materially changing his meaning. Since the emended version was the one originally intended for publication it has been used as the basis of the present translation.

As the document is offered primarily as an example of contemporary French opinion of American military capabilities rather than as a strictly trustworthy historical source, we have called attention in the footnotes only to the more important and interesting errors in fact.

## SUPPLY

The soldiers are of two sorts, the militia and the regulars. The militiamen are farmers, rich or poor as the case may be, who have been snatched from their plows to fight the enemy. They are dressed comfortably if not richly, according to their means, and have no special uniform. For the most part they wear a coat with one or two waistcoats or vests, a pair of cloth breeches, another pair of duck breeches worn over the first, and hats, stockings, and shoes of whatever sort they choose. In addition they carry on their backs a knapsack for their change of clothing, a blanket, and on the end of a cord a small flat canteen like a cartridge pouch, in which they keep

something to drink.[5] I am not including in their dress their military equipment, such as the gun, cartridge pouch, bayonet, and bayonet belt, for which they are paid at the beginning of each campaign and which they buy back by returning the money they have received. Formerly they had to purchase their own food and take care of their other expenses themselves. Now they receive pay, a paltry sum it is true, but about enough to permit them not to be dependent on their families. The tents, cooking pots, etc., are paid for by the government.

The regular soldier presents a quite different appearance, sometimes handsomer and sometimes less so.

When Congress recruited the militia and regular soldiers for only a very short period of service it could not be accused of penny pinching if it did not provide them with clothing, for often a man was discharged before there was time to issue him his enlistment papers and provide him with equipment. Consequently no arrangements were made with suppliers and no warehouses were established, and in short nothing was done to prevent the disadvantages of the unprepossessing apppearance of troops dressed according to the whim of the individual soldier.

As supplies, especially of cloth, began to arrive from Europe, the various provinces provided uniforms for as many soldiers as they could. The wild mixture of colors which resulted made the troops look even worse than they had before, and this would still be the case if the efforts of Congress and continued imports from Europe had not speeded up the change over to a standard uniform for all, which makes a much handsomer show.

wholly accurate) of the first 32 ff. was published by Eugene Griselle, "Un Voyage en Amérique au temps de la Guerre de l'Indépendance," *Revue de dix-huitième siècle*, V (1918), 52-73. The description of Charleston contained in this section has been translated by Elmer D. Johnson, "A Frenchman Visits Charleston in 1777," *South Carolina Historical and Genealogical Magazine*, LII (1951), 88-92. A translation of the portions of the manuscript containing the account of the journey north to Philadelphia and the author's impression of American life in that city is given in "The American Character." (*op. cit.,* n. 1)

[5]*Voiage au Continent américain,* f. 55, recto-verso. Veste longue, avec un ou deux Gillets ou Vestes, une Cullote de Drap, une autre de toile à la matelot par dessus la première . . . un havresac pour leur rechange, une Couverture, et au but d'une Corde suspendue en forme de Gibernes un petit Baril plat ou ils mettent la boisson . . . qu'il leur plaît d'emporter ou faire usage.

The course of the war brought to a halt this luxury. All the regiments having been expanded in order to meet the growth of the enemy forces, it is not now possible to provide each recruit with the complete uniform he is supposed to have, because of lack of cloth or seasonal shortages. This is the reason for the miserable, motley appearance of the American troops, especially of those under General Washington's command, which has provoked so many comments from Frenchmen accustomed to seeing soldiers neat and well-uniformed even though they may be sick and underfed.

Let us consider, however, in a sensible and objective way whether there is any basis for their ridicule and their sarcastic comments. We know that it is generally true that those who are the most ill-clad are the most impoverished part of a population, but it does not necessarily follow that they are the unhealthiest. If this were so the inhabitants of Auvergne and Saintonge would be the sickliest people in France, and this is obviously not the case. If their diet is not inferior, men somewhat less well-clothed may be just as healthy as anyone else. This is true in the case of the American army. Those soldiers who are well clothed are the ones who when they enlisted were lucky enough to be issued new or used uniforms. If such men present a good appearance it is merely because they happened to be among the first to enlist in the regiment or because they got, from men being discharged, uniforms which happened to fit them. One cannot argue that the well-equipped soldier is healthier than the one who is poorly outfitted since both were formerly in want and ill clad and yet were in good physical condition.

It would obviously be wrong if those not issued uniforms were without adequate protection against the weather while others were as well equipped as our French soldiers. It would be inexcusably inhuman to expose to the rigors of winter in a country as cold as this, men on whose support and courage the defense of the nation depends. This, however, is far from the case, as two most convincing facts prove: First, the soldiers in general are all in good health. And, second, in spite of the hardships they seem to be suffering and the good treatment they would get if they deserted and went over to the enemy, the rate of desertion is very low, in contrast to the high rate in all European armies. So there is nothing real about their apparent sufferings. The truth of this assertion was demonstrated last winter at the Battle of Trenton, when it was the soldiers who urged and practically forced their general to attack the enemy. Surely so clear a proof of valor as this could not be produced by suffering and discontent.

It is of course true that soldiers can be in ill health and courageous at the same time. But you need only question anybody who saw the army parade in Philadelphia or at the camp. He will tell you that though they did not have that perfect alignment which you see in troops who are so identical in stature, headgear, dress, and footwear that each man is indistinguishable from all the others, nevertheless the soldiers, ill-clad as they were for the most part, gave an appearance of health and vigor that one would scarcely expect to see in sick and exhausted troops.

Each regiment has its own uniform. I shall not attempt to list all the various colors, but in general the men wear a jacket-coat, that is, a garment halfway between a long waistcoat and a frockcoat, a white cloth waistcoat,[6] a belt around the coat, breeches, stockings, and whatever footgear the individual prefers. Otherwise they are equipped just about the same as the militia, and those who have been issued little or even nothing in the

[6]*Ibid.*, f. 57 verso. Un habit-veste, terme assez moyen entre une Veste longue et un habit, la Veste blanche en drap. . . .

way of clothing are dressed in no way differently from the militia, though we must remember that the militiaman is often a well-to-do farmer. while it has been usually fate, poverty, loose living, or just plain foolishness which has led the regular to enlist.

From the foregoing it is evident that Congress is in no way at fault for having organized the regular army before it found a way to outfit them in uniforms. It is not merely good luck, but good government, good living, and the love of liberty that have made the regulars so healthy and so loyal in spite of the cold and other hardships—sufferings which because of the lack of proper clothing have been far worse than what soldiers normally endure in wartime.

The same circumstances which provided the ships and supplies to organize a naval force gave the material necessary to establish the artillery. When the Royalists were driven out, the Americans seized the forts, arsenals, and all the military stores which the English had been forced to abandon. Thus they turned against the tyrant those arms which he had intended to use against them. The number of cast-iron pieces which they seized was very small, but the wrought-iron guns were numerous enough to arm the frigates in commission and the most important forts, even without the cannon which have been obtained by purchase or from foreign powers since the outbreak of hostilities and the Declaration of Independence. But the captured English guns could not provide the armament for newly constructed forts and for the corps of artillery attached to the various armies. and the astonishing number of guns on privateers. These have been obtained through successful diplomacy and by purchases from European merchants and others.

But guns alone were not enough, and they have been supplemented with so many other military supplies of all sorts, including gunpowder, muskets, bayonets, mortars, bombs,

and cannon balls that if the English had been able to establish a tight blockade such as they are maintaining at present, it is quite certain that the colonies would have been already subdued. Instead, the Americans are now well supplied with everything and are able to offer effective resistance and even to assume the offensive.

The cavalry is a special topic. It was organized in response to patriotic demand in the various provinces, which have furnished the money and equipment. Each province has its own regiment, though it is not absolutely necessary that all the men be natives. Any volunteers are accepted, as is the case with infantry regiments. Completely uniformed, the American cavalry presents a much handsomer appearance than the rest of the army. The men are selected so as to be as nearly as possible of the same stature, the officers come from the wealthy classes, and a special effort has been made to obtain those who have been in the King's service. Their mounts, which are rather tall, would not be the equals of our French cavalry horses, either in endurance or strength to resist the shock of battle. From the small use that is made of the cavalry it appears that it serves only for show.

## Operations

American military tactics are the product partly of the people's way of life, partly of their military traditions, and partly of their inexperience in this cruel art.

The present inhabitants are, as we know, the descendants of the first settlers, the founding fathers who cleared the land and passed it on to their posterity. As the coastal regions became well populated the colonists felt an urge to extend their settlements by occupying new territories. To do so they found it necessary, in addition to clearing the land, to overcome two closely related obstacles. The first was the hostile Indian. Even when there were no Indian wars the Americans had to be continually on their guard. They always kept their guns within reach, and at the first suspicious sound they would crouch behind a tree, ready for any danger. The other obstacle was the wild animals which inhabited the lands to be settled. They had to hunt them to vary their diet and to get pelts, out of which they made clothing warmer than what they could buy and which provided an additional medium of exchange. These conditions forced the first settlers to become hunters, like the Indians, relying on their guns for their daily food. The children of these pioneers, brought up in this sort of life and sharing from childhood its hardships as well as its joys, naturally learned both by the force of example and out of sheer necessity the ways, the agility, and the vigilance of their fathers. So it is not surprising that the present generation, either through necessity or for pleasure, are still attached to this sort of life and are still masters of all the skills which their fathers were forced to learn. This is the reason that American soldiers can fire a fusillade a hundred times more deadly than that of any other troops in the world. Even when they are retreating or pretending to retreat in order to be in a better position to turn back the enemy, they always lose less men than the opposing force, because nearly every shot is taken deliberately and all of them, officers and men, fire only when they have picked out their target, and they rarely miss.

The excellence of their marksmanship, however, would be an even greater advantage if they could discard their prejudices against conventional tactics and abandon their traditional way of fighting. When confronted by an enemy force they always fall back through the woods, pausing to fire when they haw good target. Each man takes shelter in a ditch or behind a tree, fires from cover, and then immediately runs for a different pro-

tected position to wait for a chance for another shot.

These tactics are the result both of their peacetime experience and of their lack of training in the murderous art of war. There is no justification for accusing them of cowardice. How could one expect from such proud and independent men, no matter how much military training they had had, that coolness, that deliberation, that immobility so characteristic of European soldiers? These are valuable military virtues, but they are bought at a high price; for in order to achieve them the European's will, his personality, in fact his very instinct for self-preservation have been stifled and destroyed. In battle he is a mere machine, motionless, without personal feelings, controlled only by hidden springs. Such complete impassiveness constitutes the merit of our soldiers. But if we can forget for a moment our prejudices born of our pride in our past victories, must we not admit that it is far better to command an army of free men fighing for their independence, whose inborn love of liberty is manifested even in their methods of waging war? Such men may be conquered but they will still preserve this spirit of freedom which they have imbibed with their mothers' milk.

This inflexible and independent character, this refusal, so to speak, to surrender to the will of a superior officer, constitutes what might be termed an inevitable disadvantage of the spirit of liberty reigning in America. But there is no reason to consider it, as some have done, a clear or convincing proof of cowardice. For the Americans are still far from being conquered, and if they have lost some battles they have won some hard-fought skirmishes. It is true that they have given ground when faced with the cold steel of disciplined troops, well-trained, advancing in ranks, and that they have indeed sometimes fled from the enemy . Nevertheless, their con-

1 *

duct under fire gives every reason to expect that once they have become accustomed to these unfamiliar tactics and have been tested against them a few times, even under disadvantageous circumstances, their courage, their pride, and especially their newly acquired experience will soon turn them into good soldiers. They will be just as effective as the British troops, who in defeating them will have taught them how to fight, and in the end they will triumph.

We should remember, moreover, a few basic facts: that men are the same everywhere; that Americans are an alert, skillful, hard-working people; that a number of their own native-born officers have demonstrated the ability to conduct successful campaigns; that their army includes officers of all nationalities; that men can always learn from experience and the force of example whenever their own self-interest forces them to do so; that Americans are just as capable as anyone else of perceiving the inadequacies of their present tactics; and finally that they already combine the most fervent patriotism with an incomparable constancy in enduring ice and snow, the lack of the elementary necessities of life, and all the other hardships of war. We shall soon see that there is no reason to accuse them of cowardice for not being able to stand up to an attck by European troops. We shall find that they have learned how to offer effective resistance by adopting sounder tactics and learning how to counter the maneuvers of the enemy. Thus they will force those who have so harshly criticized them to eat their words.

If we merely consider the victories and defeats of the present campaign we shall see the truth of what I have said. The Americans may or may not be as successful as I have ventured to predict. Nevertheless it is impossible not to agree that it is their way of thinking which is the true explanation of their at-

tachment to their own special way of waging war.

The present military successes of the Americans can be ascribed to certain handicaps the English generals have faced: their unfamiliarity with the area of hostilities; their difficulties in obtaining reinforcements and supplies once the armies have advanced inland; the fact that the enemy forces keep steadily increasing, while their own troops are daily depleted;[7] the inevitable exhaustion suffered by soldiers living continually in the forests and without hospitals or recuperation camps where the men might recover from the ill effects suffered from changes in climate and living conditions; the drawn-out, steady fighting in mountainous and unhealthful terrain, where it is necessary to hack out roads even to get at the enemy. To all these difficulties must be added the discontent of foreign troops who have been promised a sure and easy victory and to whom the Americans offer citizenship and good lands if they will desert. It is not surprising if, in spite of the bravery of the Hessian and Royalist troops and the inexperience of the Americans, fortune has favored the Insurgents, for the latter are the more numerous, they are the more effective riflemen, they are fighting in their own land with ample supplies, and they are in a position to encourage desertion among the enemy by offers of rewards and promises of a friendly welcome.

One thing only could forever and completely destroy the hope of an American victory. That would be the capture and dissolu-

[7] The notion that American strength was growing while British strength was diminishing was probably true for the summer of 1777 when the author was in America. John Richard Alden, *The American Revolution: 1775-1783* (New York, 1954), 116. Unfortunately the American strength relative to British strength did not for long maintain such a favorable growth. See *Ibid.*, 198 and note; and Rupert Hughes, *George Washington: The Savior of the States, 1777-1781* (New York, 1930) III, 434-435. This and the following concluding paragraphs are translated from ff. 96 recto-98 verso of the *Voiage au Continent américain*.

tion of Congress. In it alone resides the national power. Formed from representatives of all the provinces, it alone makes the laws, causes the money presses to turn, and gives to the rebels the shadow of legislative authority. Once it were suppressed, before the provinces could be informed, elect new deputies, name a president, agree on a capital, we should soon see. . . . But I prefer to suppress the proofs which I could easily give to convince any doubters. The disaster would be all too real. It would bring about the ruin of so many worthy men that I would rather allow myself to be accused of negligence or presumption in discussing this question than to have to repent having suggested an idea which the English themselves have not thought of, and which it would have been so easy for them to have carried out on the night of September 12 of last year.[8]

The same thing is not true, however, of Philadelphia, the possession of which some have incorrectly believed to be all important on the strategy of the present war. Situated at the confluence of the Delaware and the Schuylkill rivers, this city, which before the war was important because of its foreign trade and was expanding each year in wealth and population, is unprotected on the landside, and the waterfronts are undefended except by the width and depth of the rivers. There is nothing along either river which could stop a victorious army equipped with pontoons and other suitable equipment. The surface of the Schuylkill (which is perhaps once again as wide as the Seine at the Pont Royal at high water) is almost even with the surrounding land, and in all the short and easily fordable course of the stream there is not a single point reasonably well-suited for defense. The Delaware, which is much broader at Philadelphia than the Garonne at Bordeaux, presents a somewhat greater obstacle because of its width. Nevertheless, although its banks are in many places swampy for a long distance inland, there are some spots which would make such good landings and which are so unprotected by high ground that this side of the city likewise can be considered indefensible.

The ease with which Philadelphia can be taken, however, does not prove that its capture is useful or advantageous, for Congress can flee from the city from one side as the enemy enters from the other. It has no arsenals or supply depots of any consequence, and none could easily be established there. Moreover the surrounding bays and rivers, which freeze over in the winter, might make Philadelphia for the Royalists, if they were foolish enough to establish a base there, what the fields of Saratoga were for General Burgoyne. Confined to a restricted and unfortified position from which they could not get out, they would suffer from lack of supplies in the midst of the surrounding plenty, and would soon lose through starvation and shortages the very advantages they had acquired by their bravery and enterprise. So Philadelphia is in no way adapted to serving as a position of strength. The fame that it has had in the present war has come only from the fact that it had been the leading commercial city of the colonies and was chosen by Congress to be the capital of the republic.

Being the handsomest, largest, and richest city on the continent, it won out for these reasons over Boston, Williamsburg, Annapolis, Charleston, etc., though these cities, from the point of view of suitability, defensibility, and magnificence come very close to being able to claim the title of "Mother of the Country," which Philadelphia has been enthusiastically granted in the present crisis.

[8]A reference to the flight of the Continental Congress from Philadelphia before the advancing British army. The correct date, however, was the 19th of September, 1777. Edmund C. Burnett. The Continental Congress (New York, 1941), 246-247.

# THE AMERICAN REVOLUTIONARY ARMY:
## A FRENCH ESTIMATE IN 1777

## Part II — Personnel

THE thirteen provinces, after they had united in a democratic political body, believed they were strong enough to drive out by a sudden, unexpected attack the troops which the British had been maintaining in America for purposes of defense and in well-justified expectation of the revolt which has in fact occurred. It seemed doubtful, however, whether these citizens who had raised the banner of rebellion would be willing to carry through their first efforts at the sacrifice of their own comfort and whether they would continue a prolonged war ruinous to the colonies' agriculture. One special problem was that the soldiers had to return home each year for a few months to take care of the needs of their families. Such fears were prompted by a good understanding of human nature. Men seize blindly upon a new idea that seems to promise desirable rewards, and they recognize the necessary cost and sacrifices only when they are forced to maintain their initial efforts—or when they find they have to begin the task all over again from the beginning. These fears for long kept the provincial assemblies from acting. Even without regular troops they had a reasonable chance, by means of a sudden attack, of driving out the scattered British forces and preventing them from regrouping. But how could they expect to stand up against the troops that would be sent to avenge the initial defeats? The enemy could land without opposition and ravage the country, for there was scarcely a single fort or defensible position capable of stopping them. Moreover, in a land of liberty and equality it was impossible to use the methods of European despotism and force free men to fight against their will for any cause, even one which they believed in. It would have been unjust to have recourse either to a general military service law or to a selective draft by lot in order to compel citizens to serve more than a short period of time and run more than a temporary risk of being killed. There was no justification for inflicting on the people a long and grievous period of military service like that endured by our soldiers, who, once war is declared, even if they are eligible for discharge, must re-enlist and serve for the whole period of hostilities.

According to this reasoning, based on an uncompromising affirmation of complete equality, it was resolved that every man capable of bearing arms would be required to serve for a certain number of days, during which period his fields would be cultivated by the man who was to replace him in the army, or whom he had replaced. Upon the expiration of his term of enlistment he would be under no legal compulsion to re-enlist and he had the right to return to his home after his discharge.

The enactment of this law made it possible to raise a fair-sized army, but it was a poorly trained one and of an impermanent nature. The general never could know exactly how many enlistments were expiring or were about to expire, so that very often when he had counted on a certain number of troops for a battle he found that when the time came to fight he had no soldiers. Yet he could not accuse his men of cowardice, for they were acting according to their contracts with the government. Since they had served out their required enlistments there was no law of equity, reason, or justice which could force them to undergo additional risks or to sign up for a longer period of duty.

The disadvantages of this system of enlistment of the militia, which resulted in General Washington's lack of troops in the winter of 1776-1777 and in the English victories of that year, forced the Continental Congress and the state assemblies to make two changes. First, they extended the period of enlistment for the militia so that every man would serve until the end of the campaign each year or until he had been replaced. Second, they established a certain number of regiments of regular soldiers enlisted for not less than three years or for the duration of hostilities,[1] rather than merely for the period for which the individual volunteered, as had been formerly the practice.

This was the first law of such an oppressive nature to be proposed in the new democracy, and there was considerable difficulty in getting it passed. The measure, however, was supported by a very cogent argument. Regular soldiers had a bad reputation with the general public. The regular regiments were composed entirely of vagabonds and paupers; no enticement or trick could force solid citizens to enlist as regulars, inasmuch as they had to serve as militia anyway. Consequently, it was argued, there could be no danger in making any regulations whatsoever regarding the enlistment of regulars, since a man accepting such an enlistment did so of his own

free will and was presumed to understand the conditions. This reasoning led to the acceptance of the principle that a citizen might obligate himself for a prolonged period of service. In order, however, to alleviate the rigors of the law and to compensate for its unfairness it was stipulated that any soldier who volunteered for service as a regular would receive after his discharge full title to a certain amount of uncleared land from his native state or province, thus becoming the owner of a bit of his own country.[2] This truly Roman reward will serve for a long time to increase in every province the number of volunteers; and these men, once they have served out their enlistments, will at least enjoy a tranquil existence and the assurance of a laborious and modest but secure livelihood.

Thus every province has its militia and also its regular provincial regiments, which are allocated to the forts seized from the English, or to the new ones built to protect the province's approaches and harbors, or to the cities requiring troops as a precaution against a Tory uprising or else to the Continental Armies under Washington, the generalissimo.

Such then is the organization of the militia and the regular army. The make-up of the corps of officers needs to be explained in greater detail, and is as follows:

We have seen that at the outbreak of hostilities King George's forces were in complete control of the forts and military posts on the continent. Although the troops were drafted mercenaries and often foreigners, a number of the officers were American colonists. Since they could serve their king just as well in his colonial regiments as in Europe they were not always required, as in France, to endure foreign duty, the unhappy lot so often of the peacetime soldier. These officers, whether or

---

[1]See the resolutions of the Continental Congress of Monday, September 16, 1776, in *Journals of the Continental Congress: 1774-1784*, ed. Worthington Chauncey Ford (Washington, D. C., 1906), V, 762-763, and of Tuesday, November 12, 1776. *Ibid.*, VI, 944-945.

[2]The bounties of land were granted only to those who enlisted for the duration of the war and not to those who enlisted only for three years. *Ibid.*, VI, 945.

not they had retired from the service, could not help taking sides in their own minds in the quarrel between the royal government and the Americans, since the cause of the latter was their own. The actions of the royalist party, which were aimed at establishing the worst sort of despotism and threatened to wreck the prosperity of the colonies, could not fail to alienate them completely. They loved their native land and were interested in their own welfare. Moreover, they knew they were in disfavor with the Court, and at the same time they were tempted by the rank, dignities, and honors offered by Congress. All these factors contributed to their decision. From such officers came the [Richard] Montgomerys, the [Israel] Putnams, the [George] Washingtons, the De Kassens[3] [sic], the [Horatio] Gates, the [John] Sullivans, the [Benedict] Arnolds,[4] and the others of high rank; and in the lower ranks we find all those formerly in the King's service who found it to their advantage to resign and to join so noble a cause, a cause of which they were to become the heroes and protagonists.

This acceptance by the elite of the nation's officers of the responsibilities and risks of the Revolution influenced the majority of the patriotic American officers on duty in Europe to return to serve and defend their native land. But even with these men there were not enough. Subaltern officers were needed, and they were nominated and elected, regardless of their condition or station, by the people and the assemblies in the same way as the

members of Congress. The people also granted, as was just, to anyone who could do so the right to raise, equip, and name a regiment of his own and to select all the necessary officers, with the approval of Congress or of the commander-in-chief. Lastly, a number of men were promoted from the ranks of the lower grades to commissions as superior or general officers, either through the process of regular advancement or as a reward for meritorious actions. From all these various sources have come the officers of the American Army.[5]

The fact that the soldiers do not show a sense of discipline and respect for their officers when they are not on guard duty or in ranks can be explained by the national character and by the spirit of liberty, independence, and equality which these people possess. Yet whenever insubordination becomes too flagrant it is punished, though never as rigorously as in European armies. The punishments inflicted take into account the fact that except for the difference in military rank the offender is the equal of the man he has offended. Penalties which are light in comparison with those usual in our army are sufficient to keep within strict limits any shirking of duty or insubordination. It is certainly reasonable to obviate the shedding of blood, and to prevent that reciprocal hatred inevitably engendered by a condition of absolute subjection which demands of one man a temporary abnegation often impossible for the best of men or the most tractable spirits— even those most thoroughly disciplined to the caprices, rigidities, and injustices of military law—and which at the same time allows the other man unrestricted, arbitrary, despotic power, often uncontrolled by higher authority.

[3]Probably a reference to Major-General Philemon Dickinson, Commander of the New Jersey militia. Dickinson was never an officer in the Continental Army as were the other officers mentioned.

[4]Only Richard Montgomery and Horatio Gates had served in the British regular army. Putnam, Sullivan, and Arnold had previously served as officers over colonial militia or volunteer troops. Washington had served on General Braddock's staff, but this commission, signed by Governor Dinwiddie and not by the king, was not a regular army commission.

[5]On the selection and election of officers in the colonial militia and the Continental army see Louis Clinton Hatch's The Administration of the American Revolutionary Army (New York,( 1904), 13-14; 35-36.

This same lack of discipline and subordination is to be seen in the officer corps, from the most junior lieutenant right up to the generals, for all are the same sort of men in civilian life. The officers, however, are generally better educated than the enlisted men. Moreover, there does not exist the same sense of inferiority or superiority in the attitude of one officer to another, and their relationships are not so formal and are less governed by regulations. Consequently, it is more rarely necessary to discipline or cashier the officers.

It even happens often that when an officer resigns from a regiment or is discharged because of some minor offense, he may join another regiment, so long as there is no doubt as to his honor, honesty, or loyalty. Or else, if he so requests, he may be reinstated in good standing just as if he had never had any trouble and had never given any cause for dissatisfaction. This leniency, which violates all European military traditions, instead of casting discredit on the Americans in fact does them honor. It is convincing proof of their high moral standards and of their determination to adhere to the laws of reason and humanity. For the officer when reinstated is not ashamed to admit his mistake, and he can accept a generous pardon without thinking his honor or reputation has been besmirched. At the same time the superior who, in accordance with their military regulations, permits such an officer to return to duty does not penalize him for the rest of his life for a single offense or because of some personal disagreement between the two of them in which the junior was quite rightly forced to yield.

Such pardons or reinstatements appear all the more necessary and just, when we imagine what might happen to a zealous Whig who has left his family and the comforts of home to rush to the defense of his country. He might find that because of some mistake, some ridiculous trifle, some slight neglect of his duties, or even merely because of some other officer's prejudice against him, he was forced to return home and live out his days in idleness and disgrace. Certainly, he would not be human if such clear injustice on the part of his compatriots did not destroy his enthusiasm for national independence and turn him into the most ardent of Royalists. These are good laws, then, and good principles which put a man back on his feet and save him from despair and treason. They may be in violent contradiction with the military regulations of all other nations in the world, but they promote the welfare of the country, honor humanity, and are to the eternal glory of the men who have adopted them and who prefer them to all those rules of honor that others defend, tolerate, authorize, and enforce by a system of punishments and rewards. Such a code creates neither better citizens nor better subjects; it only makes men more unjust and more intolerant to one another.

This, then, is that insubordination which has been so violently condemned by French officers who have gone to serve in America. I am not referring to the officers who possess the strength of character befitting their rank and who are self-disciplined, intelligent, fair to their inferiors, and sympathetic to the principle of equality. I mean those who do not understand how an officer should act, who dress up in elaborate uniforms, who cause a lot of trouble—in a word, officers who are a plague to others and no good to their friends. Men of this latter sort are particularly enraged by the fact that they find themselves completely ignored in a country where no consideration is given to birth, name, rank, wealth, or letters of recommendation. For this is a land where honor is paid only to proven merit, and where such tribute is rendered not in words, nor in mere flattery and exaggerated expressions of esteem, but rather in deference and respect for superior merit. It would be well, perhaps, at this point to discuss at some length the French who have gone to America and the motives which took them there.

The French colonies, because they have been the scene of some advantageous marriages for certain officers who have found there opportunities to console widows and old maids weary of celibacy, have long had the reputation of being a good place to make a fortune fast. It has been believed that a man must be singularly lacking in talents if he cannot make a worthwhile match during his tour of duty. But for some time now this attractive myth has been destroyed, and it has finally been recognized that for every one or two officers who have had the luck to make a good marriage in the colonies, a far larger number have been disillusioned and have come back to France to their great chagrin much more unmarried than they expected to be.

Nevertheless many French have conceived these same false ideas about the English colonies. All those who were troubled by poverty and bachelorhood have dashed across the ocean in hopes of putting an end to their complaints. Not one of them, however, has realized his dream. The impoverished have found that, just as in France, making one's fortune by honest means takes a long time. And those who have expected to marry a widow or a rich heiress have found American girls either already engaged or else reserved, retiring, and unapproachable. And the widows, who have turned out to be more sociable but as a rule no less chaste, have avoided them, made fun of their vainglorious talk, laughed at their pretty speeches, and finally snubbed them to their faces by giving their hand to some ordinary American. For they have preferred a man with a background like their own who, combining a simple and honest face with a modest fortune or the reputation of being industrious, was marrying them for themselves and not their money, and who would not make them regret they had said yes so readily. Such has been the fate of those who went to America to make their fortune and "settle down" (this is the word these gentlemen use, though they are incapable of staying put anywhere). They were just as able as anyone else to make a good marriage in France, but they neither could nor should have expected to do so in America so long as they insisted on behaving as though they were still in France.

Disappointed and with their hopes of wealth shattered, they have had to make up their minds either to go back home or else adopt the profession they had claimed they had come to practice. Bred to be proud of their rank and conscious of social distinctions and having lived all their lives in France, they thought, because they found no knights or barons or marquesses in America, that by boasting of their titles they would be able either to obtain commissions at high ranks or at least win a flattering welcome. Most of them, astonished to be received by the members of Congress courteously but without any sort of subservience or deference, began to form of their hosts an unfavorable opinion. They should have stopped to consider that they were 1,500 leagues from home, unknown, without influence, without friends who could recommend them, and in the position of asking for favors. And they should have realized that by the vicissitudes of human affairs values might be different in different countries, and that people might be cordial to someone simply because they liked him and because his presence was useful to the national welfare, but without any intention of doing anything for him. They were incapable, however, of such reflections, for they were not used to thinking on such a high plane. They could not tell the difference between a cool but favorable reception and one which was warm but unfavorable. If we add to all this the fact that it necessarily took a long time to decide on their requests (for Congress, though overwhelmed by business and difficulties, had to vote on the granting of every commission), you will have a good idea of the opinion the typical French officer had of Congress as he received his commission, bonus, and travel expenses. This was the appreciation he felt toward those who had just granted his requests and had taken the risk of rewarding a traitor, a fool, or, as was usually the case, a ne'er-do-well disowned by his family who had fled to America to escape the arm of the law.

Frenchmen, granted commissions of all sorts, and for the most part unable to speak the language of the country, could not be expected to be any happier in the army than they had been in Philadelphia, for they found themselves in the midst of Anglo-Americans who were their equals, their inferiors, and their superiors. No one truckled to them or paid them deference; no one received them with special favors and consideration. In short, they discovered that they could not expect French manners from people who considered themselves all completely equal except for diferences in military rank and who always acted according to this principle.

So they complain loudly and continually that Americans violate all the rules of French etiquette, and they claim that this fact is second only to the quality of American officers and the insubordination of American troops as a cause of their dissatisfaction and the misunderstandings which have arisen.

As we have said, the regular army is composed of volunteers serving for three years and the militia is made up of men drafted for a certain period of time; the junior and senior officers are named by the voters, the provincial assemblies, or the colonels of the various regiments, or else are commissioned because of meritorious actions. So it is not surprising to see officers who come from what appears to French eyes to be the lower social classes—merchants, artisans, and farmers—but who are so well-deserving and worthy that their fellow citizens have thought they were only doing them justice in raising them to a rank above that of the average man. Such citizens who have been distinguished from among their equals by their civic virtures are not likely to bring discredit on the positions to which they have been appointed or to the ranks to which they have been promoted. This fact is obvious to the true philosopher, and it has been recognized by certain French officers of high caliber who have fully understood the circumstances. Indeed, if it were not a valid assumption then the system of popular democratic government, which is regarded both by those enjoying its blessings and by those unable to do so as the only true basis for the happiness of man living in society, would be impossible and self-contradictory.

So the corps of the American officers is composed either of deserving and prosperous artisans or of reputable merchants or of farmers loved and esteemed by their neighbors. These are the equals whom the French officers, friendless drifters who have been commissioned more because of their own high opinion of themselves than because of any real merit, have the audacity to despise, and with whom they say they "have been forced to associate." As if these democratic republicans, kings in their own land, were not, whatever else they might be, better than these immigrants. As if these democrats, recognized by their own fellow citizens and honored by the unanimous consent of the nation, did not have besides this first quality of being republicans the additional advantage of being, whatever their class, the chosen representatives of a free people, who have delegated to them power and authority. This is indeed a noble privilege which does great honor to the recipient both because of what it means and because of the reason for which it was given. The Frenchman may despise a man so honored for his social class and he may regard him as inferior and not fit to associate with, but he can never hope to win such honor in his own country.

This, then, together with the complaints about the lack of discipline, is the source of all the vile satires and contemptible complaints which one hears every day in the mouths of the French. They cannot be sensible enough to put aside their stupid national prejudices; and their unreasonable discontent (which they have no right to feel, since here at least they have a chance to be among equals, which is something they can rarely do at home) is one of the greatest obstacles to their establishing a sane and pleasant relationship with the people among whom they have to live.

This is not to say that there are not a certain number of French officers to whom this mild dose of equalitarianism is a matter of indifference, or even a source of great pleasure. But very seldom does one find a Frenchman sensible enough to conform; and the number of malcontents so great that if the unfavorable reports which they promise to make against the Americans—and which, no doubt, they will make—should be taken as approximate pictures of the truth, then no reasonable man would be willing to support the American cause. For you know well from experience, *Quisque clamat de malo, et susurrat de beneficio.*

Those who happen to hear the complaints and criticisms of these French officers after their return to Europe should consider well the moral character of these accusers and compare them with those whom they condemn. If those in Europe will put aside their political prejudices they will see which is the more reasonable—the man who lives wisely according to the laws of mercy and humanity, or the man who is so full of his own ridiculous national prejudices that he tries to transplant them wherever he goes, who thinks his fondness for his own ways of thinking is quite natural and yet condemns the predilection others may have for their own ideas, who cannot understand the contempt and the indifference his manners inspire, and who, after having revolted common sense and reason, arrives at the verdict that if Americans thought as he does, he would find far less to criticize. The conclusion must be that these French officers have nothing to offer apart from their foibles and their absurd personal and national prejudices, while the Americans, living according to their own principles just as the French live according to theirs, may at least sometimes have justice and reason on their side.

Arguments, it is true, are not facts; but the facts I might present in evidence would be too personal. In order not to offend anyone directly or indirectly, I shall say only this: If Congress has not granted these French officers all they requested, if it has not lived up to all the agreements it made with them regarding their coming to America and their return to Europe, if it has not compensated them for travel and other expenses, if it has not paid them in full for their services, if it has not appointed them to ranks at least a notch higher than those they held in France, if it has discharged them because of protests by native citizens whom they have offended by coming over here and taking ranks to which the Americans had just claims—if any of these allegations are true, then Congress has treated them incorrectly and deserves censure. But the truth is that they have been welcomed as cordially as any stranger could hope to be and that their cases have been handled as quickly as the press of business permitted. Moreover, they have been paid while awaiting their commissions and have been supported and defended against the protests of native citizens.

If under these conditions they seem unable to accustom themselves to the climate and the ways of the people (excepting only those of the fair sex), and to the rudeness and coolness of Americans in general; if their pay, which has proved sufficient for others, is scarcely half enough for them; if they are offended by the lack of discipline in the army and the humble birth of American officers; if the soldiers, not knowing French, cannot execute their orders; and finally, if the fine hopes which brought them have have been dispelled and shown to be physically and morally impossible —if these are their complaints, then Congress is in no way responsible for their discontent. Do they have to cast ridicule on people who are doing all in their power to satisfy them and make them happy, when their unpleasant experiences are entirely their own fault? It is not on the Americans that all the blame should fall. It is up to these French officers to get over their natural instability, pride, and presumption and to be as reasonable as the Dutch, Swiss, Prussian, and German officers serving with the Americans. It is up to them to put aside their pettiness, their vainglory, their absurd prejudices. Then they will see that Americans, just like people everywhere, have agreeable manners and that the men are sociable, their wives virtuous, and their daughters well educated. And they will realize that this country, where at the end of the war they will be given, according to their rank, enough land to support them, this country against whose inhabitants they rail so

freely, is, if not what they first desired, at least a place where they can settle down, live, and enjoy the pleasures of life just as peaceably as anywhere else.

After what I have just said of the childish discontent and complaints of these French officers, I should be unjust to my nation and to the truth if I were not happy to mention certain others whose good conduct corresponds to the high character, integrity, and lofty purposes which impelled them to go to America.

I refer to those who were motivated by ambition for promotion in France or who went to escape the boredom of garrison duty or sought an opportunity to practice their profession as soldiers to the benefit of their own country (for this revolt of the English colonies is most advantageous to France). These men are behaving correctly in their relations with Congress, the army, and the people as a whole. They are dependent only on themselves; they draw no pay from Congress other than what is necessary to meet their daily expenses, and they do not think of that country as a place to make their fortunes, for they have not gone there with any such intention. Consequently they have not brought in their hearts the seeds of discontent, as the others have. Before entering the American service they had clear and well-founded reasons for hating the enemy they came to fight. Their only complaints are the faulty organization of the army, the lack of discipline, and often also the fact that as gentlemen they are not the equals of artisans or laborers holding like ranks. Reasons as flimsy as these ought not to influence officers who give evidence of such good sense. But in any situation men will necessarily reveal their true natures and display some weakness; and unfortunately we French have so many weaknesses and we believe ourselves so perfect that it is not surprising if in America, as anywhere else, we display our own peculiar faults, our prejudices which we alone defend, our absurd foibles to which we alone cling, and our vices which we alone refuse to admit or justify. . . .

I should describe here the reception given to the Marquis de Lafayette, to General Du Coudray, the hero of the Schuylkill,[6] to the brave Armand de la Rouerie,[7] to General Conway,[8] to General La Balle[9] [sic], and to the famous commandant of engineers of the army.[10] But the day will come when the Americans will render sincere and well-deserved eulogies to those who have given loyal service. What I must say, however, after all I have already written about the French who have gone to America, is that no Anglo-American can accuse these men of cowardice, whatever may be their faults. If all the French followed the example of the good behavior and upright conduct of these men whom I have just mentioned, especially La Rouerie and Lafayette, the Anglo-Americans who now hate us for no reason, but merely out of habit, would change their minds. Then they would judge the French not according to their particular faults but rather in relation

to the circumstances of the moment, in which any man, as an individual, is just like anyone-else and should be forgiven whatever faults, real or imaginary, he may appear to have. . . .

It is impossible to give the exact figure of the number of men in the American forces. An estimate, however, of the militia, artillerymen, regulars, and cavalrymen in the four armies which have been operating during this campaign and also in the detached bodies of troops stationed at various points would come to the following figures: 21,000 men in the Northern Army on the fourteenth of October; 14,000 in General Puntnam's army; 10,000 in the army in Rhode Island; 12,000 under General De Kaissen [sic] at Elizabethtown; and 30,000 in General Washington's army.[11] These figures do not include the militia of the states close to the theater of war, who can be called up within twenty-four hours, or the troops which each province needs to guard its ports, roadsteads, passes, and cities. It is clear that the Americans can be conquered only by a major offensive. If they do not win the war the reason will be the superiority of the Hessian troops over undis-

[6]Major-General Tronson du Coudray was drowned September 16, 1777, while crossing the Schuylkill River to join Washington's army. André Lasseray, Les Français sus les treize etoiles: 1775-1783 (Mâcon, 1935) II, 444-454. This paragraph appears in a latter portion of the Voyage au Continent américain, f. 101 recto.

[7]Voyage au Continent américain. Romans de la Roierie. Lieutenant Colonel Armand de la Rouerie commanded his own volunteer corps after June 11, 1777. See John C. Fitzpatrick, The Writings of George Washington: 1745-1799 (Washington, D. C., 1933), VII, 224-225. For Washington's opinion of him see ibid., 90-91.

[8]Thomas Conway, named brigadier general by the Continental Congress May 13, 1777. See Journals of the Continental Congress, VII, 349.

[9]Perhaps a reference to Augustin Mottin de la Balme. See Lasseray, II, 329-336.

[10]Louis le Bèque de Presle Duportail. One of the four engineer officers sent to the United States by the French government. Duportail was appointed commander of engineers July 22, 1777, and was promoted from colonel to brigadier general November 17, 1777. Journals of the Continental Congress, VII, 571; IX, 932. See also Edmund C. Burnett, Letters of Members of the Continental Congress (Washington, D. C., 1932), II, 417.

[11]These figures totaling 87,000 troops operating during the campaign of 1777 represent nearly 50 per cent of the arms-bearing population of all the American colonies. Even if such a number could have been raised it is doubtful that they could have been supplied with arms and provisions. During the summer of 1778, when Washington commanded the "largest body of regular troops ever assembled under the American banner," he had only 16,782 rank and file fit for duty. Douglas Southall Freeman, George Washington: A Biography (New York, 1951), III, 442; Rupert Hughes, George Washington: The Savior of the States, 1777-1781 (New York, 1930), III, 410; Fitzpatrick, Writings of George Washington, XII, 230. The aggregate enrollment for the year 1777, counting all of the militia who served as long as two months, may have reached 68,000, but such a total does not represent effective strength, which was considerably weaker. Hughes, George Washington, III, 434. For more accurate estimates of the American forces mentioned above consult Fitzpatrick, Writings of George Washington, IX, 278; X, 52n., 195; Leonard Lundin, Cockpit of the Revolution (Princeton, 1940), 333-335, and passim; John Richard Alden, The American Revolution: 1775-1783 (New York, 1954), 119-120; and Freeman, George Washington, IV, 520.

ciplined soldiers who have not had sufficient training in the execution of mass maneuvers; it will not be because of any lack of bravery under fire.

In this connection, I hope that the shortcomings of the Americans, for which they have been justly criticized, will no longer be exaggerated by politically-minded censors and by eyewitnesses. Men need only the experience of defeats in order to learn how to defend themselves properly and to acquire the military effectiveness usually necessary in order to inspire respect in the enemy. As soon as the Americans have suffered a few reverses the contempt which certain Frenchmen have had for their bravery will quickly vanish, and we may expect to see no further displays of lack of initiative and inexperience. . . .

# THE AMERICAN REVOLUTIONARY ARMY AND THE CONCEPT OF LEVEE EN MASSE

By Orville T. Murphy*

During the American Revolutionary war there developed in France a popular picture of the American military system which seemed to demonstrate the eighteenth-century belief that Nature was the benevolent source of morals and institutions. One post-war French poet said of the Americans:

In them we still behold the sons of Nature....
By contemplating Her and heeding Her commands,
They have through rightousness made simple all their laws:
Her hand it is that traced throughout their codes sublime
The reasonable bounds to all authority.[1]

The militia system was one of the institutions that appeared to have been formed in conformity with the laws of Nature. Near the end of the American Revolutionary war, one French historian pointed out this fact to his compatriots by reprinting many of the constitutions and declarations of rights of the revolting colonies. "A well regulated militia," the French reader learned, "drawn from the body of the people, and accustomed to arms, is the proper, natural and sure defense of a free state. One must avoid having standing armies in times of peace, because they are dangerous to liberty." The same historian also printed the principles of the Maryland "Declaration of Rights" which advanced a

similar idea: "A well-regulated militia is the suitable and natural defense of a free government."[2] The fact that many Europeans believed that this natural system was unbeatable was indicated by General Lafayette in a letter to Washington in December 1777. After recommending that the militia *not* be called to defend Philadelphia, he said:

Europe has a great idea of our being able to raise when we please an immense army of militia, and it is looked upon as our last but certain resource. If we fall this phantom will fall also and you know that the American interest has always been that since the beginning of this war to let the world believe that we are stronger than we ever expect to be.[3]

A natural way for such an army to form was described in one American's letter, published in a French news sheet. When the British soldiers advanced into the country surrounding Boston "with all their warlike apparel and in order of battle," and "without being provoked" killed several people, "the farmers of the neighborhood assembled suddenly, and repulsed the attack." The contrast between the well-ordered, disciplined British soldier with his "warlike apparel," and the farmer organizing spontaneously to defend his neighbor and himself was significant. It represented the contrast of a people making war naturally as opposed to the machine-like order of the professional or regular troops.[4]

The American farmers fit exactly the

---

*The Author is Professor of History, SUNY, Buffalo.

[1]L. Bourdon, *Voyage d'Amerique: Dialogue en vers entre l'Auteur et l'Abbe* (London and Paris, 1786) p. 20ff.; the translation is by Ramon Guthrie, in Bernard Fay, *The Revolutionary Spirit in France and America* (New York, 1927) p. 236.

[2]Hilliard d'Auberteuil, *Essais historiques et politiques sur les Anglo-Americains* (Bruxelles, 1782) Vol 2, pt. 1, pp. 107 (quoting the "Declaration of Rights of Virginia," Article XV) and 95.

[3]Lafayette *The Letters of Lafayette to Washington: 1777-1779* (New York, 1944) edited by Louis Gottschalk, p. 12.

[4]*Gazette de Leyde*, 10 Aug 1779.

French military theorist, the Comte de Guibert's description of the citizen soldier. His characteristics were:

> . . . terrible when angered, he will carry flame and fire to the enemy. He will terrify, with his vengeance, any people who may be tempted to trouble his repose. And let no one call barbarous these reprisals based on the laws of nature, [though] they may be violations of so-called laws of war. Some one has come to insult this happy and pacific people. He arises, leaves his fireside, he will perish, in the end, if necessary; but he will obtain satisfaction, he will avenge himself, he will assure himself, by the magnificence of this vengeance, of his future tranquillity.

Unlike the mercenary soldier, this citizen warrior was not one who sought out the battlefield as a means of making a living. Indeed, his only recompense, according to Guibert's ideal, was honor. Only when there was no honor involved in fighting did one have to pay soldiers with gold. For this reason the mercenary soldier was held in contempt and could not "count himself among the other orders of citizens."[5]

This distinction between the citizen soldier's honor and the mercenary soldier's reasons for fighting was clearly established in the popular image in France in the period of the American Revolutionary war. According to a letter written by a British officer at New York to a friend in London and printed in the *Gazette de Leyde*, "all America was in flames over tea." The inhabitants of New York, Boston, and Philadelphia were determined that they were not going to permit the unloading of tea in their ports. The reason for this, according to another item in the same issue, was that the "tyrant," the mother country, was threatening the liberties of the colonies. These liberties, the French were told in a later publication, were guaranteed by the charters of the individual colonies and the British Constitution, now so "gravely wounded." The honor of Americans demanded that these abuses be rectified.

Another aspect of the militia type army that distinguished it from a professional army was its lack of rigid class distinctions. Often, the "better classes" were pictured as being the organizers of the militia regiments; but even this distinction did not always hold. The French were informed, for example, that the militia of Duchess County, Virginia, was made up of persons of the "first rank" who did the "duties of the simple soldier" in order to "defend the cause of their country." Another source contained a description of a militia regiment of Connecticut made up of married men who left behind one-hundred and forty-nine children or grandchildren. This regiment chose its own officers and was one of the first to march to the aid of Philadelphia when it was threatened in 1776.

> The example of these respectable citizens proves to what degree Patriotism elevates the hearts here in America, and how difficult it will be to subjugate a people, the very great majority of whom sacrifice their personal relations and most dear interest in order to save the country in danger.

Although these early reports coming from America, usually through British sources, indicated that the Americans were going to attempt first to restore their ancient liberties by the use of boycott and protest, there were indications that perhaps the controversy would go to the point of open war. British soldiers had been ordered to put their muskets in order, and the artillery regiments were told to prepare cartridges.[6] In the fall of 1774 the *Gazette des Deux-Ponts* reported that the Americans seemed determined "to repulse force with force." The Boston militia

---

[5]Comte de Guibert, *Essais General de Tactique* . . . (Liege, 1771) pp. xxii and 9.

[6]*Gazette de Leyde*, 11 Feb and 23 Aug 1774, 10 Aug 1779, and *"Supplement"* 13 May 1777.

had been assembled and the entire province of Massachusetts Bay was confident that if necessary it could raise 119,600 effectives, "all of good will, and prepared to act if they must." To demonstrate that they intended to follow through with their vow, the Boston militiamen had gone through maneuvers in front of the British regulars. The British soldiers, according to the description, were amazed at the precision with which each militiaman fired his *eleven* shots per minute. "They say," continued the correspondent, "that General Gage, who was on the spot and who afterwards made a judgment on what he saw, thought that they would never reduce the Americans to submission without violence. . . ."[7]

In its June twelfth edition of the year 1775, the *Gazette des Deux-Ponts* announced that hostilities had commenced between the Americans and the British. The dispute was now to be settled by the force of arms. The fact that this war was a struggle of a people fighting for liberties against "tyrants" was repeated over and over in the pages of the weekly journals. "All the Anglo-Americans," said the *Gazette de Leyde*, "breathed the same courage, the same desire of defending their rights and their liberties, as men and as Englishmen, to the last individual."[8] Even the Quakers, who from religious principle were opposed to military service, began to set aside their beliefs, take up arms and enroll in the militia. "The American forces augmented themselves day by day," reported a later issue of the *Gazette des Deux-Ponts*, "the fanaticism of liberty attracts everyone to serve under the flag." Even women, if reports were true, were enrolling in the militia.

By August 1775, the colony of New Jersey had already formed two companies of these Amazons who "had taken up arms to second their husbands in the defense of their rights and their privileges. . . ."[9] Later, a French historian added to this report by explaining that the ladies' habit of going hunting had familiarized them with arms.[10] Elsewhere, the women were distributing flags and drums and "exciting the men to the defense of their country."[11]

In 1782 Hilliard d'Auberteuil demonstrated the extent to which this picture of the American citizen army had been accepted in France. In his history of the American Revolution, he described how on all sides Americans prepared for war. Troops were raised in all the provinces by officers who volunteered to direct the military preparations, and then recruited their soldiers by haranguing the local farmers. These officers "inflamed the courage of the people, exercised the militia by detachments, and accustomed them not to fear the regular troops."[12]

One journal reprinted a letter written by a sixteen year old American girl to her brother. She called herself a "Daughter of Liberty" and told her brother that he must come back from the army "victorious, or not come back at all." She informed him that she would much rather look for him among the heaps of cadavers and mutilated, bloody bodies than to hear it said that he was a coward.[13] In Connecticut and New England, the zeal of the citizens was so great that "old men disputed with the young for the glory of defending their homes and serving under

---

[7]*Gazette des Deux-Ponts*, 19 Dec 1774. A well-trained French soldier could fire from two to three shots per minute; See R. Mousnier and E. Labrousse, *Le XVIII Siecle: Revolution Intellectuelle, Technique et Politique* (1715-1815) (Paris, 1953) p. 95.

[8]*Gazette de Leyde*, "Supplement" 4 July 1775.

[9]*Gazette des Deux-Ponts*, 27 July and 24 Aug 1775; see also Hornot, *Anecdotes Americaines ou Histoire Abregee des Principaux Evenement Arrivees dans le Nouveau Monde* . . . (Paris, 1776) p. 734; *Gazette de France*, 25 Aug 1775.

[10]Hornot, p. 734.

[11]*Gazette de France*, 25 Aug 1775.

[12]d'Auberteuil, Vol. 1, pt. 1, p. 117.

[13]*Gazette des Deux-Ponts*, 5 May 1778.

the standard of liberty."[14] Saltpeter for explosives was being manufactured by the people in all of the colonies, and everywhere mills for making gunpowder were being constructed.[15]

This natural way of carrying on war not only brought men to the colors, but it also offered the possibility of solving some of the age-old problems of warfare. One of these problems was supply. One French historian explained that the Americans remained peaceable possessors of all the continent of America. This situation gave them the liberty of cultivating tranquilly their land and procuring for themselves all the things which they needed, either for themselves or their army, while the English army, closely encircled and occupying only a small space of land, which was soon uncultivated because of lack of cultivators, could draw its subsistance only from England.[16]

The fact that the Americans were close to Nature gave them other advantages against the professional armies of England. One French writer noted that if the climate, especially the humidity, of America had made the Americans less robust, it had given them more temerity. Also, "they were less sensitive to wounds than the Europeans and heal more easily."[17] Another writer disagreed with the idea that the Americans were less robust by stating that the American armies were composed "only of strong and robust men, who are accustomed since their infancy to work, and above all to the handling of a rifle."[18] This statement contains two ideas which became central to the image of the

militia: the Americans could endure more because of their everyday contacts with Nature, and they were better soldiers because they were used to handling rifles.

When reports began to appear that indicated that perhaps the Americans were not so well off as had been assumed, the idea still persisted that the insurgent troops, even if without proper clothing and shoes, were well armed and unbelievably efficient soldiers. "There are no soldiers who are harder than they and more accustomed to all the privations imaginable."[19] Lafayette later added to this opinion by judging that "Nobody in the world may have a higher respect than this I entertain for those virtuous men who leaving the plow for the sword . . . brought the Revolution to this glorious period."[20]

While all was in a state of "combustion" among the Americans who were preparing to fight to the death if necessary, the commanders of the British regulars were having difficulties holding together their army. An American citizen army, fired with indignation resulting from the threats to their liberties, was growing; the British army made up of regulars was diminishing as a result of desertions, according to the French newspapers. The Americans were tempting the British troops with land and money. This practice was so successful, if the stories are believed, that Gage had to put sentinels at the exit points of the city of Boston in order to keep his soldiers from leaving. Finally, he had to issue an order that any deserter who would come back to his regiment before a specific date would be pardoned. After that date he could expect no clemency.[21] Thus, before the

[14]d'Auberteuil, Vol. 1, pt. 2, p. 185; see also the *Gazette de France*, 25 Aug 1775.
[15]*Gazette de Leyde*, *"Supplement"* 9 Jan 1776.
[16]Joly de Saint Valier, *Histoire Raisonnee des Operations Militaire et Politique de la Derniere Guerre* (Liege, 1783) Vol. 1, p. 12.
[17]d'Auberteuil, Vol. 1, pt. 2, p. 188.
[18]*Gazette des Deux-Ponts*, 1 July 1776.

[19]*Ibid.*
[20]"Lafayette to Laurens, 23 July, 1778," *South Carolina Historical and Genealogical Magazine* (1908), Vol. 9, pp. 63-64; quoted in Louis Gottschalk., *Lafayette Joins the American Army* (Chicago, 1937) p. 235.
[21]*Gabette de Leyde*, 11 Feb, 9 Sep. and *"Supplement"* 13 Sep, 1774.

war was actually under way, the distinction between the citizen soldiers fighting for their liberties and regular soldiers who considered soldiering a craft, was drawn. The citizen soldier could be depended upon to respond to the call of his nation—or in this case his province—to defend his liberties; the regular soldier responded only to material benefits and hence could be bribed into deserting the cause of the country in whose army he was serving.

After the outbreak of the war, the Whig reports from England, reprinted in the French papers, reinforced this distinction between the professional and citizen soldier by stressing the fact that the British had resorted to the use of German mercenaries to fight the colonists. The Americans, too, made sure that this contrast was clear. "The man who fights generously for the cause of his country, for the defense of his laws, for his liberties," one American preached, "receives the applause of honest hearts." On the other hand, "the man who fights for lucre (a vile mercenary) what is he?" From this initial moral judgment, it was not far to the idea that these undisciplined, inexperienced citizen soldiers were superior to the mercenary troops because of the ardor which motivated them. "No troops could show more intrepidity than these undisciplined and newly raised men. . . ."[22] An army "entirely formed of citizen soldiers, and similar in this respect to the ancient legions of Rome, ought to make any country the master of victory."[23]

Judging from the statistics presented by the French journals and histories, the attempts to raise such citizen soldiers brought overwhelming results. The figures given in the early years of the war varied, but all of them indicated that the American citizen army was going to be a huge one. In April 1776, one gazette quoted a report "they claim is authentic," that the colonists were capable of putting on foot an army of 428,000 men.[24] In the same month another estimate of the Insurgents' military potential totaled 450,000 troops.[25] In July the numbers reported were said to be those actually in arms, not estimates of potential. Washington at the head of a "grand army" of 41,000 citizen soldiers was besieging Boston, according to the *Gazette de France*. This figure was reduced to 20,000 a few months later because large detachments had been sent to aid in the defense of the southern colonies. General Lee, in the South, had raised a huge corps of his own: 15,000 men, one source reported.[26] In August 1777, the tables of the quotas of troops to be furnished by the various colonies were published in the *Gazette de Leyde*. North and South Carolina had been assigned a quota of 6,000 and 8,000 troops respectively, with 2,000 and 4,000 reserves. Virginia had been assigned a quota of 12,000 men, with 6,000 reserves. The correspondent added that the quotas "were already complete or near to being so."[27]

A letter from General Guy Carleton to Lord George Germain was printed in the same newspaper in July 1776. The British General reported that the Americans on the Canadian front had retreated from Quebec, but were reinforcing themselves on the Sorel River. Carlton estimated that at Quebec the Americans attacked with 4,000 men, but after that unsuccessful attempt another thousand had joined them.[28]

In September 1778 a British Whig source, quoted by the French, broke the estimates of the American strength down in terms of

---

22*Ibid.*, 19 Sep 1777, and *"Supplement"* 12 Jan 1776.
23d'Auberteuil, Vol. 1, pt. 2, p. 186.

24*Gazette de Leyde, "Supplement,"* 2 Apr 1776.
25*Gazette des Deux-Ponts,* 8 Apr 1776.
26*Gazette de France,* 12 Feb and 7 Aug 1775.
27*Gazette de Leyde, "Supplement"* 1 Aug 1777.
28*Ibid.,* 5 July 1776.

the types of troops. The Americans, according to this source, had 148 regiments of infantry, forming a corps of 81,380 men, seven regiments of cavalry of 3,315 men, eight regiments of artillery which in all made it possible for the Insurgents to oppose the British with nearly 100,000 effectives.[29] By the spring of 1777 after the reports of the failure of the American army to take Canada and Washington's retreats in New York began to reach France, these estimates were lowered. In fact, one news article came very near to revealing the truth when it contained a statement to the effect that after Cornwallis had entered New Jersey, Washington's army dwindled to 5,000 men. The editors were quick to point out, however, that the source of this news—Scotch—was "justly suspect." In the summer of 1777 it was even reported that 7,000 rebels had deserted the American cause. To this report, too, was added the advice that "it was difficult not to recognize the exaggerated style of this news reporter from New York." By the late summer, the journals were again estimating that Washington had under his command 100,000 men with 47,000 reserves. Only one newspaper version of this report indicated that the authors recognized that this figure represented only a quota that had not yet been filled.[30]

Up to the Franco-American Alliance of 1778, the size of this phantom army in America remained inflated. After discussing the unanimous vote of the Congress in favor of the Alliance, the *Gazette de Leyde* informed its readers that Washington's army was so big that he had countermanded orders to Northern troops marching to join him, and had sent them to join Gates at Kingsbridge. The condition of these troops was similar to that of those described in most of the former reports: "The American forces were better provided with arms, munitions of all types, and with everything that was necessary to them for the campaign."[31]

Once the French entered the affair, however, the Americans appeared to be in the worst state of need. By the fall of 1779 the Insurgent Army was "absolutely without money and nearly without food." A letter from General Rochambeau, published in a journal a year and a half later described the Americans as lacking everything necessary for a soldier to stay in battle. Nevertheless, despite the fact that published letters of the French officers in America added a touch of realism to the estimated size and condition of Washington's army, as late as December 1780, calculations which even the French editors admitted were probably false were printed to the effect that the troops of the United States numbered more than 500,000. But even if this estimate was wrong, argued the journalist, it was known in "all certitude" that the enthusiasm aroused by the arrival of French troops in America had resulted in the enlistment of 10,000 volunteers in Washington's forces.[32]

The precise number of troops actually in the American Revolutionary forces at any one time can only be approximated. Washington's army returns were at best attempts to stabilize on paper numbers which rarely coincided with actuality. This is true especially of the militia forces which never formed or disbanded exactly according to orders or predictions. Indeed, the fluid character of the state militias posed as many problems for Wash-

[29]*Gazette des Deux-Ponts*, 2 Sep 1776; see also *Gazette de France*, 17 and 24 Apr and 10 July 1775 for other exaggerated estimates of the American forces.

[30]*Gazette de Leyde*, 29 July 1777, and *"Supplements"* 11 Feb and 4 July 1777; see also *Gazette des Deux-Ponts*, 7 Aug 1777.

[31]*Gazette de Leyde*, 21 July 1778.

[32]*Gazette des Deux-Ponts*, 21 Sep 1779 and 16 Dec 1780.

ington as state militias posed for the British. Nevertheless, it is certain that the number of soldiers who actually served in the Revolutionary forces was considerably lower than the estimates reported by the French journals. At the high tide of patriotism in 1775 and 1776 Washington probably could have raised an army of 150,000 men,[33] but it would have been impossible to feed that many troops. The returns of the Adjutant-General to the Commander-In Chief during this period reveal that the number of troops under Washington's command ranged from 17,000 to 20,000 counting officers, non-commissioned officers, militia and artillerymen. But these totals are deceptively high since they included the sick, those on furlough and those on detached duty.[34]

In addition to the number of troops under Washington's immediate command were those in the Northern Department under General Richard Montgomery at Montreal and with Benedict Arnold's expedition to Quebec. About 1,100 men set off with Arnold, but only 600 of them arrived at their destination.[35] To this number Montgomery added 300 reinforcements. After the stormy night of December 31, 1775, when Arnold and Montgomery led their men into the catastrophe known as the Battle of Quebec, little more than 600 men were left of the attacking forces. It is doubtful if the troops on the entire Canadian front during 1775-1776 numbered more than 3,000 soldiers, of whom no more than half were fit for duty.[36]

In the South where General Charles Lee took command at Charleston, South Carolina, on June 4, 1776, there were six regiments of provincial troops numbering about 2,000. Three Continental regiments, one from Virginia and two from North Carolina, reinforced these provincial troops after the outbreak of hostilities. If one adds to these figures the militia who volunteered for service, General Charles Lee had under him about 6,500 troops in the defense of Charleston, South Carolina, the 28th of June, 1776.[37]

As the war developed into a long, drawn-out affair, the average number of troops that served each year diminished. On February 20, 1777, for example, Washington reported that his forces numbered only about 4,000 counting militia. By mid-summer this figure had risen to just over 8,000, but fall and winter brought once again the depletion of the ranks. In the Northern Department the armies suffered the same fate.[38]

The total number of troops under Washington during the early months of 1778 are not available, but from July to December the totals including all those in the New England states and in New York never exceeded 20,000.[39] All of these estimates of American strength are, of course, only approximate. The number of Continentals and militia on duty varied, desertion was widespread, and sickness was endemic. Nevertheless, the most optimistic assessment of American strength during the years 1775-1778 would not exceed 30,000, a figure considerably smaller than those reported in the French newspapers.

A comparison of the Adjutant-General's estimates of the size of the American Revolutionary army with those of the French jour-

[33]Lynn Montross, *Rag, Tag and Bobtail* (New York, 1952) p. 71.

[34]Jared Sparks, *The Writings of George Washington* (Boston, 1858) Vol. 3, pp. 493-494.

[35]Christopher Ward, *The War of the Revolution* (New York, 1952) Vol. 1, pp. 163ff.

[36]Peter Force, ed., *American Archives* . . . (Washington, D. C., 1837-46) 4th Series, Vol. 5, pp. 845-846; Douglas Southall Freeman, *George Washington: Leader of the Revolution* (New York, 1951) Vol. 4, pp. 81-82.

[37]Ward, Vol. 1, p. 672.

[38]John C. Fitzpatrick, *The Writings of George Washington* (Washington, 1931-1944) Vol. 7, p. 168 and Vol. 8, p. 99n; Vol. 4, pp. 426, 533-534.

[39]Freeman, *Washington*, Vol. 4, p. 622n.

nals and histories indicates that what the eighteenth-century Frenchman considered to be Washington's troops were figures on paper. They made no attempt to discriminate between estimates and actualities. It seemed logical to the pro-American Frenchman who was somewhat blinded by enthusiasm for the cause, that if the American cause were just, every citizen would want to be a soldier. Thus a people arising *en masse* was a "natural" response to the English attempt to deprive the Americans of their liberties. Patriotism was aroused, vengeance demanded. In this drama there would be only actors, no spectators. Many Frenchmen saw this revolutionary war in the same light they later saw their own: a set of ideals was at stake, and the ideals called for a citizen army aroused to defend the country against a foreign enemy. These fanciful descriptions of the colonists preparing for war against England recall the concept later prevalent in the French Revolution of the people arising *en masse:*

The young men shall go to battle; the married men shall forge arms and transport provisions; the women shall make tents and clothing and shall serve in the hospitals; the children shall turn old linen into lint; the aged shall betake themselves to the public places in order to arouse the courage of the warriors and preach hatred of kings and the unity of the Republic.[40]

The similarity between the French popular image of the American colonists arming themselves against England and the later French idea of the *levée en masse* is striking. While the parallel does not indicate that the French concept came from America, it does mean that this idea of a nation in arms to preserve its liberties had already become an integral part of the paraphernalia of late eighteenth-century thought. It represented the corollary of force, or the military consequence, of ideals which characterized this period of intellectual history. The American Revolutionary army appeared to give substance to a set of abstractions already prevalent.

[40]"Decree for *Levee en Masse*," 23 Aug 1793, from F. M. Anderson, *The Constitutions and Other Select Documents Illustrative of the History of France: 1789-1907* (Minneapolis, 1908) pp. 184-185.

# THE FRENCH PROFESSIONAL SOLDIER'S OPINION OF THE AMERICAN MILITIA IN THE WAR OF THE REVOLUTION

By Orville T. Murphy*

DURING the American Revolutionary War, French journalists, historians, and essayists created a popular picture of the American militia system that was strikingly similar to the later French idea of a nation in arms, or the *levèe en masse*. Quoting American sources, one Frenchman argued that the system was the "proper, natural and sure defense of a free state."[1] The militia army, according to this popular view, arose spontaneously, imposed its own self-discipline, and drew on its natural talents to combat the highly regimented and brutally disciplined professional soldier. To many pro-American Frenchmen the militiaman was without question superior to the mercenary, because he was more "natural," because he was inspired by the ideal of patriotism, and because, some even claimed, he was naturally a harder, tougher soldier.[2] Daily living on the frontier had hardened him, according to the prevailing opinion, to the point where he was able to endure great hardship. The rifleman, for instance, had developed his talents and stamina from his direct experience in the forests of the frontier.

There was a tendency on the part of Europeans to assume that every American was a frontiersman. Few commentators made it clear, if indeed they were aware of the fact, that not all America in the eighteenth century was frontier land. Most seemed to be ignorant of the fact that in the "Tidewater" regions and in eastern New England, civilization as the word was understood in Europe had advanced very far indeed, and that a tour through

Williamsburg or Boston in the latter part of the century would have revealed a level of culture far removed from the frontier.

The origins of the view held in France of the superior fighting qualities of the American militia are not easily traced. Many of the journalists and historians of the time never bothered to reveal their sources; when they did, they usually referred vaguely to British or American informants whose knowledge was "authentic."[3] Nevertheless, there is enough evidence to provide some explanation of how Frenchman formed their notions of the American militia without ever seeing a militiaman.

The long-standing hostility between France and England constituted a sufficient cause for the French government to publicize in France and Europe any news that would embarrass England; and certainly stories of victories of American militiamen over British regulars were embarrassing. Furthermore, the Comte Charles Gravier de Vergennes, the French Secretary of State for Foreign Affairs, was especially sensitive to the value of a public opinion cultivated by a "well-directed administration."[4] As Vergennes began to formulate Louis XVI's policy of intervention in the American Revolutionary War, he was careful to insure that the image of American military power was a favorable one. There is no evidence that Vergennes ever knowingly encouraged the publication of false reports, but he frequently permitted publication in official newspapers of inflated figures of American strength and exaggerated battle reports.[5]

The pro-American attitude which lay behind French acceptance of such reports had

*Dr. Orville Murphy is Professor of History, SUNY, Buffalo.

been prepared long before by the legend of the naturally virtuous and vigorous Americans. The "mirage in the West," as the historian Durand Echeverria calls this legend which was so popular in France in the latter quarter of the eighteenth century, made Americans seem capable of almost any feat.[6] When the playwright Beaumarchais sent from England fantastic stories of the strength of the American militia, Vergennes, with only slight reservations, used them to support his recommendations to Louis XVI. No doubt some of the equally fantastic stories in the official French newspapers came from the same source.[7]

The support given by the French government and Vergennes to the publication of Benjamin Franklin's journal *Affaires de l'Angleterre et de l'Amérique* is another indication of the French government's role in the formation of French opinion. And Franklin's personal propaganda campaign in the aristocratic salons, among the Free Masons, and in the Court was a continuous song in praise of the invincible Americans.

Another important source of the reports about the American militia was England. Time and again the *Gazette de Leyde* and the *Gazette des Deux-Ponts* printed information about the exploits of the rebel militia that were attributed to "British Whig" sources.[8] We never know the names of these "Whigs," but whoever they were and whatever their motives they affected French opinion.

The legend of the invincible militia soldier was not completely false, of course. A segment of the American army—the rifle corps—was the product of the frontier environment. Also, there is no doubt that the Americans who did live on the frontier, or even on a farm, had learned the use of certain tools necessary in warfare. General Charles Lee for example, was of the opinion that Americans were suited for war because of their skills with the musket and because "they were also skillful in the management of instruments necessary for all military works, such as spades, pickaxes, and hatchets."[9]

Yet one great fault in the popular French view of the American militia army was that it often did not include a consideration of the conventional problems of warfare. Somehow the problems of supply, engineering, intelligence were overlooked or assumed to be solved by natural talents or patriotism. Indeed, the necessity for considering these problems seemed slight, since the early reports of the courage and the victories of the militiamen indicated that all was well in this citizen army. If the function of an army is to win battles, then the Americans seemed to be operating at high efficiency. Even the hardships of no shoes and little clothing or food seemed, to the French writers, to intensify the one essential ingredient—patriotism.

More importantly the concept of the American Revolutionary army introduced into France through the journals and books too often overlooked the recruiting problems of a militia force. It was generally recognized that there were a Continental Army and militia armies, and the journals and histories often made a distinction between the two; but the reasons why Washington wanted to segregate a regular army from the militia were only occasionally discussed. The belief prevailed that only a call from Washington to the people was necessary for recruitments and even "in the most rude season of the year, volunteers [would present] themselves for the defense of their country."[10] Sometimes it was the plea of the Continental Congress which "had so amazing an effect on the spirit of this fantastic people that they came in crowds and with the most live ardor to the standard of the Continent. . . ."[11] In the final analysis the motivation of patriotism was considered sufficient to solve all problems of recruiting.

Also, the hard discipline enforced in the regular armies of Europe appeared to be unnecessary. Patriotism again was the magic agent: obedience was given freely out of patriotic love for the country.

On rare occasions information appeared that indicated that perhaps something more than patriotism was needed to hold together an army. For instance, the news of the revolt of the Pennsylvania and New Jersey lines certainly raised some doubts about the efficacy of patriotism as the key to discipline, and the news of Arnold's treason no doubt brought into question the belief that patriotism alone was enough to assure a man's adherence to a cause.[12] But these events, coming after French opinion was largely formed, were apparently considered only exceptions that proved the rule. Europe's belief in the patriotic citizen soldier grew because the American militiamen appeared to give it substance.

The early reports of the battles between militia and regular troops indicated that republican virtues and patriotism were indeed enough to defeat a well-trained regular army. If the accounts were true, it seemed that the abstract theories about citizen soldiers were substantiated by the engagements of Americans against British regulars at Lexington, Concord, and Bunker Hill and in the siege of Boston. Once the prestige of the militiamen had been established by these early encounters, the legend of the militia soldier became an *idée fixe* among the journalists and historians of France.

General George Washington knew how one-sided was such an image of the militiaman. He and his officers discovered that the white heat of enthusiasm soon cooled when the war became a long-term affair requiring enduring support and patience. To Washington the militiaman was a disappointment. But this reconsideration of the value

of the militia soldier was not widely known about in France until long after the alliance of 1778 had been signed, and even when reports arrived in France that were unfavorable to the militia they encountered disbelief and opposition, based on references back to the early episodes of Lexington, Concord, Bunker Hill, or Boston.

Like Washington, the French army officers who came to America looked at the American soldiers with a more sober eye. To them the affair in America was just another armed conflict which raised all of the conventional problems of warfare. They believed in the need for leadership, discipline, experience, supplies, intelligence of the enemy's movements, and a reliable army, to create the conditions for victory. Patriotism played a role in this approach to warfare, but the professional soldier never considered it a magic agent. The same was true with regard to natural ability. While officers like Lafayette admitted that the American soldiers were "harder, more patient than Europeans" and some patriot officers were "enlightened by natural talents," in the last analysis these characteristics were not considered by the professional military man to be sufficient to win battles.

In many cases, of course, the French professional soldier's opinion was biased. Such a bias, for example, colored the judgments of French officers who were disappointed in their hopes for high rank and position in the insurgent army. Furthermore, the contrast between the American military system and the systems prevalent in Europe was enough to shock a military mind accustomed to the traditional forms and practices, and a conservative officer was apt to consider bad what he did not understand. Yet the minds of the French officers were not always tightly closed. For example, some of the officers who disliked the militia came to admire Washington's Continental Regulars. After the Battle of

Yorktown, especially, some of them gave up the notion that the Americans were untrustworthy for assaulting positions with the bayonet.[13] Furthermore many French soldiers admired the endurance and courage of the Continental Regulars, who fought with none of the means considered necessary by European standards. While French popular opinion held that the militia formed the backbone of American military power, French officers usually felt that the Continentals were the more reliable element of the American military forces.

One of the most striking contrasts between the American militia system and that known to the French soldiers was the attitude concerning the occupation of soldiering. The French army officer who came to America was very soon aware of the fact that the Americans did not consider soldiering a legitimate career. The citizen soldier who was by trade a farmer, an artisan, or a frontiersman considered himself only temporarily under arms. Furthermore, even when in the military forces Americans did not observe the rank and class distinctions that characterized European armies. When the Duc de Lauzun arrived in a small town in Rhode Island in the winter of 1780, he was amused by one of the good villagers who very innocently asked him what trade his father followed in France.[14] Claude Robin, in his description of the Americans and the war, also noted this attitude toward war and soldiering. His explanation is the interesting one that American society was closer to nature than that of Europe: "These people, still in the Happy century where distinctions of birth and of rank are unknown, see no difference between the soldier and the officer, and they often ask the latter what was his trade in his country, not realizing that that of warrior could be a fixed and permanent one."[15]

In the early part of the war it was the substantial farmers, married men, and artisans who filled the ranks of the American armies. While some of these men were veterans of the French and Indian War, undoubtedly most of them considered their return to war as only a temporary, though possibly exciting, suspension of their normal functions in the community. In many respects they were what Lafayette described as "only armed peasants who have sometimes fought."[16] George Washington explained to General Rochambeau, rather apologetically, that "service in the militia was preferred by the people [of America] to that of the regular troops, because it paid considerably more, there was less duty and the discipline was more relaxed."[17] The relaxed discipline in the militia appealed to the American because he did not consider it necessary to be bound by the codes of the professional soldier. If asked to explain his attitude, he undoubtedly would have responded that it was not duty or discipline, but rightness of cause and patriotism that formed men into victorious armies.

The French officer, too, came to consider the American militiaman not bound by the customs of professional armies. When Rochambeau in Rhode Island learned that English troops were embarking in New York to aid by land the British ships standing off Rhode Island, he was authorized by Washington to call out the militia of Boston and Rhode Island to assist in the preparation of defenses. Rochambeau noted in his memoirs that these troops fulfilled their mission with "quite patriotic zeal," but he also remembered that he kept only two thousand of the "four or five thousand" militiamen raised and sent the "remainder back to their harvest, which they had been kind enough to leave to come to our assistance."

A characteristic of these militia soldiers which most frustrated the French officers was their slowness in assembling. Lafayette's impression of them was that "even in their diligence" they were characterized by a "slowness which makes them always arrive too late."[18] DeFleury was of the same opinion: ". . . The arrival of the militia still expected is so uncertain."[19] Axel Fersen judged the militiamen even more harshly: ". . . [They] assemble only when the danger is imminent; and flee when it becomes great."[20] The Comte d'Estaing apparently agreed with these gentlemen, for he wrote back to M. de Sartine, the Secretary of State for the Navy, that General Sullivan, who was to give him aid in Rhode Island, was the "creator of what he [Sullivan] called an army, [but] all the soldiers were still at home."[21]

After assembly, the commanders had to keep the militia together, and often this proved as difficult a task as raising it. Lafayette's frantic letter to General Weedon during the Virginia campaign in May 1781 puts into words this problem: ". . . There is more militia going off than there is militia coming in. What we have, is, however, called the Army, and that is expected from us which an Army could perform."[22] To Washington, Lafayette said in effect the same thing: "It has been a great secret that our army was not superior and was most generally inferior to the enemy's numbers, our returns were swelled up as generally militia returns are but we had very few under arms particularly lately."[23] . . . "The fluctuation of the American army," another French officer reported, "sometimes 8,000 often less, and composed of a lot of curious people counted for soldiers, still makes their force and projects vary."[24]

The recognition that the American force fluctuated in size brought to light one of the most serious deficiencies of the militia army—its unreliability. Enlistments often expired before long-range plans could be carried out. Projects were upset by variations in the size of the forces available to the Amer-

ican officers in the field, and despite the fact that militiamen were successful in the Lexington and Bunker Hill affairs and in other battles they were not always dependable. They were, according to one French officer, "without any instruction," and sometimes, another French observer recorded, ". . . after the first discharge, they picked up their feet and went home; not one of them stopping until he was well within his home."[25] Lafayette warned the Comte d'Estaing in August, 1778, that as long as the Americans had only the militia, "we will have, I fear, some bad affairs."[26] Lafayette's evaluation of the militiamen is indicated also in the fact that he never counted them among his casualties.[27] Robin considered the militiamen as only "undisciplined troops,"[28] and the Comte d'Estaing even refused to give them the name of soldiers. Speaking of Lafayette's forces in Rhode Island, he said Lafayette had ". . . announced soldiers, and raised only militiamen."[29] The Duc de Lauzun revealed the soldier's contempt for the coward when he said of the militiamen who were used as sappers in an attack on Gloucester in 1781, "At the first shot, the half of them threw down their hatchets and their guns in order to run faster."[30] Undoubtedly the French officers would have agreed with Lafayette when he wrote to d'Estaing that the militia at Rhode Island would "be useful only to show [to the enemy], to make noise, and frighten," while "the French did the fighting."[31]

The French officers were not unaware that the militiamen had won some laurels in battle. For instance, they knew about the militia's role at the Battle of Saratoga, and the opinion was widespread that Morgan's victory at Cowpens was a case of "peasants" defeating "regular and superior" troops.[32] While this generalization is not altogether accurate, since Morgan did have some Continentals under his command at

Cowpens who were veterans as experienced as any of the British Regulars, nevertheless the militia did give a good showing in this battle. Robin gave the Pennsylvania and Virginia militias their due credit for Washington's success at Trenton, and Rochambeau opined that though the Boston militia were without provisions they did have "a lot of courage."[33] Another favorable estimate of the American militiamen was written by an unidentified French officer who visited America in 1777. This observer, probably an artillery officer by the name of de Récicourt, felt that once the Americans had experience they would be "just as effective as British troops."[34]

There are other instances in which French officers gave the militia credit for bravery or patience. But these cases the officers sometimes considered notable because they were exceptions. Furthermore, for these professional soldiers, the value of the militiamen was not to be judged simply by whether they had sometimes performed exceptional feats of bravery, but whether they could be consistently depended upon to be available when needed, to execute orders, and to stand firm when under fire. The Frenchmen observed that the militiamen often played a brilliant role in the war but they could not be depended upon to give a good performance of the work-a-day, non-heroic sort.

Ironically enough, the French professional soldiers felt that the militia's role should be the least exciting of all. The militiamen were considered to be of excellent use in preparing defenses against an attack, but as Axel Fersen asked, when the shooting starts, "What dependence can one place on such troops . . . ?"[35] "For the defensive," Lafayette wrote to Washington, "they are useless to us, nay they were hurtfull. . . ."[36] To Rochambeau, Lafayette suggested in July, 1780, that perhaps the militia "as workers, or light troops, or behind the en-trenchments could be employed with advantage."[37] Lafayette no doubt agreed with Washington, who suggested to the Marquis that if the militia were mixed with the regulars, the regulars might "inspire Confidence" in them. In any case they would "probably act better than if they were alone."[38]

When the militia were used as workers they seemed to fulfill all expectations. In Rhode Island in 1780, when the militia was called out to help Rochambeau prepare his defenses against a possible British attack, their enthusiasm created such a sensation that a French colonel called his officers together and advised them to make use of the good example given to the French soldiers by the American militiamen. Nevertheless, perhaps in order to avoid future disillusionment, Lafayette did not neglect letting Rochambeau know that the "militia have done more for their allies [the French] than they would have done for the security of their own Continental troops in a similar occasion."[39] Again during the siege of Yorktown the militiamen gave a good account of themselves as workers. Robin praised their action of 1 October 1781, when during the night the American militia began constructing two redoubts. The enemy directed his fire at the men working, but, despite the fact that some of them were killed, "their companions did not show the least fright, and continued their work with no less ardor." Robin felt called upon, however, to point out that this kind of behavior on the part of the militiaman was a "spectacle . . . absolutely new."[40]

The basic difference between the French officer's opinion of the American militia and the image presented in the contemporary French newspapers and histories is more than a question of firsthand experience in contrast to hearsay or legend. At bottom the French professional soldier did not believe that patriotism was a sufficient motivating agent in warfare, nor that "nature" was really a sufficient training ground for the citizen soldier. The professional soldier, in other words, did not see the American Revolutionary war as a facet of an ideological movement, or an *esprit révolutionnaire,* as it was later called. To him the Revolution was to be considered in terms of the factors that had traditionally constituted warfare. Instead of looking for the correct ideological responses in the army, they looked for discipline, training, and dependability. Rochambeau saw Washington's army in May, 1781, not as a symbol sacrificing itself for an ideology but as a multitude which "lacked everything at the same time,"[41] and was therefore incapable of performing the functions of an army. The Duc de Lauzun considered affairs in America in 1780 critical not because the Americans lacked the right attitude but because the American army "lacked men, money, food and clothing. . . ."[42]

It was Axel Fersen who, after observing the state of affairs in the American army, recognized the crux of the problem. In a letter to his father he concluded that in the formation of armies "one could only raise and sustain them by force of money. The spirit of patriotism resides only with the chief and principle people of the country, who make the very great sacrifices, the others, who make the majority, think only of their personal interests. Money is the prime mover of all their actions. . . ."[43] Even Lafayette, who often praised patriotism as a moral virtue, recognized its inadequacy when it came to the practical problems of carrying on a long war.[44]

The exaggeration that built up the popular legend of the American militia at the beginning of the war may account for some of the French officers' disappointment in the militia. Perhaps they had been led to expect too much from the patriots. Or perhaps the professional soldier assumed something that non-military observers did not: that if the patriot army was indeed succeeding, then many of the practical problems characteristic of eighteenth-century warfare had been solved. When the officers saw the militiamen, they learned that such an assumption was false and concluded that the militia system was a very poor solution for most of the conventional problems of warfare.

Thus, while many French civilians and officials placed great confidence in the American militia soldier, the French professional officers formed a dissenting minority. From a military point of view their opinion is significant, because it is additional evidence for the hypothesis that in France the arguments *pro* and *con* concerning the capabilities of the citizen soldier had their spokesmen long before the French Revolution. The notion of the citizen soldier was not, in other words, a creation of that Revolution.

Diplomatically, the French officers' opinions are important because they raise the interesting question of what might have been French diplomatic policy if they had been widely known. Fortunately for the American cause, the French army officers' judgments of the American militia were not generally known in France until after the conclusion of the Franco-American treaty of 1778, or even until after the war, when the officers found time to write their memoirs. If the Comte de Vergennes, the French Secretary of State for Foreign Affairs, had received his intelligence of the capacity of the American forces from the professional soldiers, his support for the American alliance would no doubt have been less enthusiastic; and certainly those who opposed his policies would have had at their disposal information that could have seriously undermined Vergennes' claim that the Americans would prove to be militarily dependable allies.

# REFERENCES

1. Hilliard d'Auberteuil, *Essais historiques et politiques sur les Anglo-Américains* (Bruxelles, 1782), II, Part 1, 107.

2. See the author's "The American Revolutionary Army and the Concept of Levée en masse," *Military Affairs*, XXIII (1959), 13-20.

3. See *Gazette de Leyde*, "Supplement," 2 April 1776.

4. "Mémoire de M. de Vergennes à Louis XVI sur la situation politique de la France rélativement aux differentes puissances," 1774, *Archives Nationales*, K 164, No. 22.

5. For example, see *Gazette de France*, 12 February and 7 August 1775.

6. Durand Echeverria, *Mirage in the West* (Princeton, 1957), pp. 39ff.

7. John Durand, *New Materials for the History of the American Revolutionary War* (New York, 1889), p. 49; *Archives des affaires étrangères: Correspondance politique*, Vol. DXV, Fol. 14.

8. See for example, *Gazette de Leyde*, 19 September 1777, and "Supplement," 12 January 1776; *Gazette des Deux-Ponts*, 2 September 1776.

9. *Lee Papers*, Collection of the New York Historical Society (New York, 1872-73), I, 162.

10. *Gazette de Leyde*, "Supplement," 18 April 1777; see also *Ibid.*, 4 April 1777, and *Gazette des Deux-Ponts*, 7 August 1777.

11. *Gazette de Leyde*, "Supplement," 6 June 1777; 11 April 1777.

12. See *Gazette des Deux-Ponts*, 28 November 1780, 19 December 1780, 6 March 1781, 10 March 1781.

13. Letter of Marquis de Lafayette to Samuel Cooper, 26 October 1781, printed in *American Historical Review*, VIII (1902-1903), 90; Report of Vioménil to Rochambeau, 16 October 1781, printed in *Magazine of American History*, VI (1881), 47-48.

14. Comte de Rochambeau, *Memoirs of the Marshal Count de Rochambeau Relative to the War of Independence of the United States*, ed. and transl. by M. W. E. Wright (Paris, 1838), p. 28.

15. Claude C. Robin, *Nouveau Voyage dans l'Amérique Septentional en l'année 1781 en compagne de l'armée de M. le Comte de Rochambeau* (Philadelphia and Paris, 1782). (Translation by the author.)

16. Marquis de Lafayette, *Mémoires, correspondances et manuscrits* (Bruxelles, 1837), I, 397.

17. "Washington to Rochambeau, 7 April 1781," in John Clement Fitzpatrick (ed.), *Writings of George Washington from the Original Manuscript Sources, 1745-1799* (Washington, D.C., 1937), XXI, 426.

18. "Lafayette to d'Estaing, 6 September 1778," in H. Doniol, *Correspondance inédite de Lafayette* (Paris, 1892), p. 42.

19. "DeFleury to d'Estaing, 5 August 1778," in H. Doniol, *Histoire de la participation de la France a l'établissement des États-Unis d'Amérique* (Paris, 1886-92), III, 373-74.

20. F. U. Wrangel (ed.), *Lettres d'Axel Fersen à son père pendant la Guerre d'Indépendance d'Amérique* (Paris, 1929), Letter dated 9 January 1781.

21. "Report of the Comte d'Estaing to the Secretary of State for the Navy, 5 November 1778," in Doniol, *Histoire*, III, 456.

22. Louis Gottschalk, *Lafayette and the Close of the American Revolution* (Chicago, 1942), p. 228.

23. Louis Gottschalk (ed.), *The Letters of Lafayette to Washington* (New York, 1944), Letter dated 8 July 1781, p. 204.

24. Doniol, *Histoire*, III, 456.

25. Claude Blanchard, *Guerre d'Amérique: 1780-1783, Journal de Compagne* (Paris, 1881), p. 115; Wrangel, *Lettres d'Axel Fersen*, p. 109.

26. "Lafayette to d'Estaing, 24 August 1778," in Doniol, *Correspondance de Lafayette*, p. 30.

27. Gottschalk, *Lafayette and the Close of the American Revolution*, p. 266.

28. Robin, *Nouveau Voyage*, p. 65.

29. Doniol, *Histoire*, III, 450.

30. *Mémoire de Duc de Lauzun*, ed. by M. F. Barrière and M. de Lescure (Paris, 1882), p. 355.

31. "Lafayette to d'Estaing, 5 August 1778," in Doniol, *Correspondance de Lafayette*, p. 28.

32. Blanchard, *Guerre d'Amérique*, p. 65.

33. Robin, *Nouveau Voyage*, p. 78; "Rochambeau to La Luzerne, 4 August 1780," in Doniol, *Histoire*, V, 353.

34. Durand Echeverria and Orville T. Murphy, "The American Revolutionary Army: A French Estimate in 1777," *Military Affairs*, XXVII (1963), 6.

35. Wrangel, *Lettres d'Axel Fersen*, p. 78.

36. Gottschalk, *Letters of Lafayette to Washington*, pp. 100-101.

37. "Lafayette to Rochambeau, 9 July 1780," in Doniol, *Histoire*, V, 359.

38. Lafayette, *Mémoires*, I, 186-87.

39. Gottschalk, *Letters of Lafayette to Washington*, p. 103.

40. Robin, *Nouveau Voyage*, pp. 104, 104n.

41. "Rochambeau to de Grasse, 28 May 1781," in General de Cugnac, *Yorktown, 1781: trois mois d'opérations combinées sur mer dans une guerre de coalition* (Nancy, Paris, Strasbourg, 1931).

42. Lauzun, *Mémoire*, p. 330.

43. Wrangel, *Lettres d'Axel Fersen*, p. 98.

44. Gottschalk, *Letters of Lafayette to Washington*, p. 27.

# IN CONCLUSION

# PENOBSCOT ASSAULT—1779

By Henry I. Shaw, Jr.*

A MERICAN military history is not a dry collection of statistics and battle outlines, nor is it the story of a continuous parade of victories. It is a living record of human successes and failures, a record that should be seriously studied by every professional soldier. Weapons and tactics may change with the passage of time, but the essential elements in the military picture, men and the art of leading them, remain basically the same. And if, as has been said often, men learn from their mistakes, then nowhere is that truism more evident than on the battlefield.

Although many times defeat is a better teacher than victory, the full story of our military failures has often missed the pages of patriotic histories. For example, the largest American amphibious operation of the Revolution is virtually unknown, given at best only a few paragraphs in the most comprehensive histories. Yet the Penobscot Bay Expedition furnishes a demonstration of amphibious warfare as its fumbling worst, small enough to be grasped in its totality with each mistake a glaring error, each delay a clear path to disaster. In these days, when corps and armies make up the landing forces,

the scope of amphibious warfare is so vast that even serious mistakes are countered by the weight of power with the assaulting forces. The passage of 174 years then has not lessened the value of examining an operation once characterized as "bad in conception, bad in preparation, bad in execution."[1] The principles of war violated then are as evident today as they were in 1779.

In the spring of that year the British commander-in-chief in North America, Gen. Sir Henry Clinton, directed that a strong outpost be established on the coast of Maine. Troops were to seize Bagaduce Peninsula in the bay of the Penobscot River and set up a fort guarding the harbor.[2] (See Map 1) From this new base British sloops could strike swiftly to stop the damaging raids of New England privateers. The forests of Maine, long the prime source of ship timbers and masts for New England yards, would be denied to the Americans. Finally, the loyalists who had been driven from their homes by the patriotic fervor of their neighbors would find a haven from persecution under the protection of the king's guns. In short, the British contemplated a move to hit Yankee purse and pride, a situation fraught with explosive possibilities.

---

*Mr. Shaw is with the Historical Section, Headquarters, US Marine Corps.
[1]Clowes, W. L., et al., The Royal Navy, 7 vols. (London, 1897-1903), IV, 28-9.

[2]Moore, J. C., The Life of Lieutenant General Sir John Moore (London, 1834), 19; Batchelder, S. F., John Nutting, Cambridge Loyalist (Cambridge, 1912), 78.

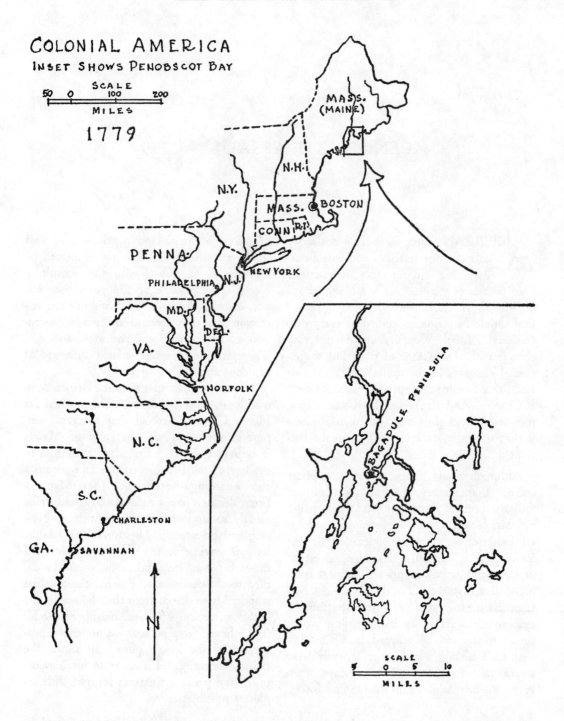

COLONIAL AMERICA
INSET SHOWS PENOBSCOT BAY
SCALE
50   0   100   200
MILES
1779

Clinton selected a veteran officer, Brig.Gen. Francis McLean, military commander of Nova Scotia, to lead the expedition.[3] McLean in turn drew his men from the Halifax garrison—450 Scotsmen from the 74th Foot (the Argyle Highlanders) and 200 Englishmen from the 82d Foot (the Hamilton Regiment). These detachments, plus engineers and artillerymen, brought the force total to about 700 men.[4] Neither regiment had been blooded as yet and few of the officers and fewer still of the rank and file could boast battle experience.[5]

Exercising tactical command of the 82d was Lt. Col. Sir William Erskine in lieu of Gen. McLean, who held the largely honorary post of regimental colonel.[6] The 74th was literally commanded by the Campbell clan, since 24 of its 43 officers, including the commander, Lt. Col. John Campbell, both majors, and seven of the eight captains, bore that name.[7] Although these units were newly raised (1777) and not battle tested, they were regulars, well disciplined, and thoroughly trained in the tactics of the day.

The target of the expedition, Bagaduce Peninsula, is located about 20 miles from the mouth of Penobscot Bay along the wildly irregular eastern shore. Roughly triangular in shape, the peninsula extends a mile and a half on an east-west axis and is a little less than three quarters of a mile wide at its broadest part where a narrow isthmus joins it to the mainland. A protected harbor is formed by the peninsula's southern shore, nearby Banks Island, and a jutting headland which faces Bagaduce across 800-1000 yards of open water. In the late 1700's most of the region was heavily wooded, although farmers had cleared a good portion of the shoreline in the vicinity of the harbor. The British intended to erect their post, Fort George, on a narrow plateau that neatly bisected the peninsula. With cannon emplaced there, they could easily sweep the harbor. (See Map 2)

McLean sent his force aboard ship early in June intent on taking advantage of the full summer for work on fortifications. After an uneventful voyage, the troop convoy reached Bagaduce on 17 June and commenced landing men and supplies.[8]

Word soon reached Boston of the enemy's presence in Massachusetts' territory. The reaction, as could be expected, was immediate and violent. The State Board of War began assembling ships, men, and munitions for an expedition designed to oust the unexpected and unwelcome visitors. The watchword of the preparations was speed, for the intent was to strike before the British could erect too formidable fortifications. By 26 June the land force commander had been chosen, the groundwork laid for collecting the largest flotilla of American ships seen during the war, and requisitions sent out for the troops who would make the assault.

But the budding expedition met with unforseen difficulties. Neither Washington nor Gates could spare any of their veteran troops, at least not enough to meet the Massachusetts timetable. Therefore, the burden of supplying the troops fell on the state. Draft quotas of 600 militiamen were assigned to Cumberland and Lincoln Counties while 300 were to be drawn from York County.[9] In all, barely enough men were called to give the attackers a two to one superiority.

---

[3]*Moore, op. cit.,* 19-20.

[4]Calef, J., "The Siege of Penobscot by the Rebels, Containing a Journal of the Proceedings, etc., 1783," *The Magazine of History,* III, 1910, 15; hereinafter cited as *Calef Journal.*

[5]Curtis, E. E., *The Organization of the British Army in the American Revolution* (New Haven, 1926), 72-3.

[6]*Calef Journal,* 15.

[7]Gt. Brit., War Office, *Army List* (London, 1779).

[8]*Calef Journal,* 15.

[9]"Proceedings of the General Assembly and of the State of Massachusetts-Bay Relating to the Penobscot Expedition—1780," *The Magazine of History,* XXV, 1923, 44-5, hereinafter cited as *Proceedings.*

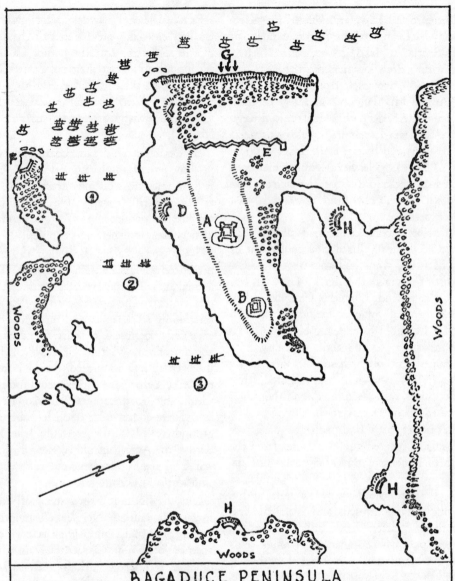

BAGADUCE PENINSULA

Adapted From a Sketch Map Of The Area Done In 1779

KEY

A - Fort George
B - Naval Redoubt
C - Battery Taken by Marines
    on July 28
D - Battery Surprised July 31
E - American Siege Lines

F - Battery on Banks Island Taken
    By Marines on July 26
G - Landing Area July 28
H - American Batteries (only center
    one finished)
①②③ Successive Positions of British
    Ships.

SCALE
200    0        800

YARDS

The naval situation was somewhat better. The whole of the state navy, three small brigs—*Active* (16 guns), *Hazard* (14), and *Tyrannicide* (14) — was ordered to accompany the expedition. The services of three ships of the Continental Navy, the frigate *Warren* (32), brig *Diligent* (16), and sloop of war *Provident* (12), then lying in Boston harbor, were obtained through Congress' Eastern District Navy Board,[10] after such influential citizens as Samuel Adams threw their weight behind the project. In addition, 12 privateers, most of them mounting 18 to 20 guns, were taken into the state service. For logistical purposes, 19 transports and provision ships were added to the total to move the landing force.[11] Patriotism prompted most private ship owners to volunteer their ships, but some had to be impressed into state service: privateering was a very profitable business. All shipowners made sure, however, that their vessels were insured by the state, covering themselves in the event the expedition should run amiss.[12]

Aboard the vessels of the Continental and Massachusetts navies were slightly over 300 marines. These men, some of them veterans of sea battles of the infant republic, formed a welcome addition to the meager landing force. The senior marine officer of the fleet, Capt. John Welsh of the *Warren*, took command of the sea soldier contingent.[13]

Assigned to lead the expedition's ground forces was Brig. Gen. Solomon Lovell,[14] a militia officer of considerable reputation with-

in the state, little if any of it gained as a combat commander. His second-in-command, Brig. Gen. Peleg Wadsworth, State Adjutant General,[15] was a man of admirable personal qualities but little battle experience. The force artillery was given to Lt. Col. Paul Revere,[16] night rider at Lexington and Concord, who completed a triumvirate of earnest but inexperienced leaders.

Afloat, Lovell's opposite number was Capt. Dudley Saltonstall of the *Warren*, who was appointed commodore of the growing fleet. This stolid and overly cautious officer was enjoined by the Board of War "to take every measure and use your utmost Endevours to Captivate, kill or destroy the Enemies whole Force both by Sea and Land and the more effectively to answer that purpose, you are to Consult measures and preserve the greatest harmony with the Commander of the Land Forces, that the navy and the army may Cooperate and assist each other."[17]

Gen. Lovell's instructions were in much the same vein, but neither leader was given command responsibility for the success of the entire enterprise.[18] Once the flotilla left Boston, the unifying force of the Board of War would be lost, and the expedition would continue with a divided command.

On 19 July, less than a month after news of the British occupation, the American fleet cleared Boston harbor. Due in part to the haste of departure, less than two-thirds of the expected 1500 militiamen were aboard.[19] In addition, many privateer crews were under-

[10]*Ibid.*, 46.

[11]Gould, E. K., *Storming the Heights* (Rockland, Me., 1932), 10-12; Wheeler, G. A., *History of Castine, Penobscot, and Brooksville, Maine* (Bangor, Me., 1875), 38; *Calef Journal*, 30-32.

[12]*Proceedings*, 50-51.

[13]McClellan, Maj. E. N., *History of the Marine Corps* (Washington, 1925), Vol. I, Chap. VI, 1ff. This copiously footnoted, unpublished typescript, available at the USMC Historical Branch archives and the Library of Congress, is probably the most scholarly and valuable of all works dealing with early Marine history.

[14]*Proceedings*, 45.

[15]Gould, *op. cit.*, 8.

[16]*Proceedings*, 45; Goss, E. H., *The Life of Colonel Paul Revere*, 2 vols. (Boston, 1891), contains the diary kept by Revere during the expedition, hereinafter cited as *Revere Diary*.

[17]*Massachusetts Revolutionary Archives*, CXLV, 39, quoted in Allen, G. W., *A Naval History of the American Revolution*, 2 vols. (Boston, 1913), II, 424.

[18]*Proceedings*, 48-9.

[19]Gould, *op. cit.*, 29. This work contains the journal kept by Brig. Gen. Lovell during the expedition, hereinafter cited as *Lovell Journal*.

manned, since there seemed little profit and much risk involved in this venture.[20] On 21 July, the ships dropped anchor off Townsend in Boothbay Harbor, Maine, where additional privateers from Salem and Portsmouth joined. Lovell got his first good look at his troops the following afternoon when they assembled for a review. The sight was not reassuring. The adjutant general of the expedition recorded that "some were old men, some boys, and some invalids; if they belonged to the Train Band, or Alarm List, they were soldiers, whether they could carry a gun, walk a mile without crutches, or were only *compos mentis* sufficient to keep themselves out of fire and water."[21]

Following this disheartening review, Lovell and Saltonstall met with the ships' captains and the field officers of the militia. This was the first of many councils of war where every frustrated Clausewitz and Mahan had his say. The upshot of the meeting was a decision to leave the initial conduct of the campaign to the two top commanders.[22] Despite the obvious defects of the militia and the patchwork semblance of a navy, the general feeling was one of optimism. The Americans were sure their 328 ships' guns[23] would more than compensate for lack of manpower and experience. The expedition left Townsend on the 24th bound for Penobscot. All along the coastline trails of smoke from alarm fires traced the passage.[24] The British were not sleeping.

Actually loyalists had brought McLean his first news of the expedition on 18 July and thereafter kept him well informed of the convoy's location. Fort George was still in its beginning stages, even though all troops had put in a solid month's work clearing ground, laying foundations, and erecting outworks. McLean now stepped up the pace, abandoning all frills and concentrating on gun platforms, abbattis, and essential protective cover. One hundred loyalist volunteers swung axe and shovel alongside the soldiers to clear fire lanes and build up walls.[25]

Most of the ships that had convoyed McLean's command to Bagaduce had already departed, leaving only three sloops of war, *North* (20), *Nautilus* (18), and *Albany* (18), to see the fort in operation. Both the *North* and *Nautilus* were due to depart when news came of the American advance.[26] The senior naval officer, Capt. Henry Mowat of the *Albany*, immediately countermanded the departure orders and ordered the three ships "into the best possible situation to defend the harbour, annoy the Enemy and co-operate with the land forces."[27] He sent 180 of his sailors and marines ashore to assist in the construction work at the fort. The warships were anchored broadside to the harbor entrance with decks cleared for action. Four small transports, the only other vessels present, were brought up close behind this line of battle, prepared to slip their cables and ram should the Americans penetrate the harbor.[28]

Small guard boats stationed well down toward the mouth of the bay reported the unwelcome news at 1600 on 24 July that the American fleet, "40 sail," had dropped anchor about nine miles from Bagaduce. The two bastions of the fort facing the harbor were as yet unfinished and the rest of the breastworks in perhaps worse state. One wag among the troops observed "he could jump over them [the walls] with a musket in each

[20]*Proceedings*, 51-2.
[21]Quoted in a footnote to a copy of Lovell's journal published in *The Weymouth Historical Society Proceedings for 1879-80*.
[22]*Revere Diary*, II, 363-4.
[23]See footnote 11.

[24]*Lovell Journal*, 30.
[25]*Calef Journal*, 15-6.
[26]Mowat, Capt. H., "A relation of the services in which Capt. Henry Mowat was engaged in America from 1759 to the end of the American War in 1783," *The Journal of History*, III, 1910, 48-50.
[27]*Calef Journal*, 15.
[28]*Ibid.*, 17; Mowat, *op. cit.*, 51.

hand."[29] The approach of the Americans successfully halted construction work; ships' crews hastened aboard as recall flags were flown, and soldiers saw to the placing of shot and powder by their poorly protected cannon.[30] Afloat and ashore, the meager preparations were made; night passed all too rapidly for those who faced what looked to be an overwhelming armada.

The sun was well up when the first American mast was sighted. About noon the whole of the fleet was visible sailing slowly upriver. The fighting ships hove to off the harbor mouth, well out of cannon range, while the transports proceeded about a half mile up river and anchored. Shortly afterwards, the American ships' captains reported aboard the *Warren* for final instructions. To the gunners standing with glowing matches aboard the British men of war, the outcome of that conference was soon apparent.[31]

Nine ships, led by the 32-gun *Warren*, formed line of battle and stood toward the British sloops. A brisk cannonade started with the three King's ships giving as good as they got, which truthfully wasn't much. Two hours of firing at maximum range resulted in rigging damage only. The British were amazed at the "random and irregular fires" and confused maneuvering of this impressive force.[32] This was to be only the first of many indications of the inability of the hodge-podge navy to operate effectively. Capping the day's operations was an abortive attempt to land militia on Bagaduce. A strong wind disorganized the boats of the first units off the ships and Lovell signalled recall, although not before a good shot among the men of

the 82d guarding the peninsula head managed to kill an Indian scout in one of the boats.[33] In light of the day's events it was small wonder that the British soldiers manned their outworks and exchanged lusty cheers with the seamen.[34]

The calm of the next morning was jarred by a two and a half hour cannon duel between Saltonstall's and Mowat's ships but the results showed only more rigging damage.[35] Shortly thereafter the war council held aboard the *Warren* hatched one of its few good ideas: namely, to capture Banks Island, which dominated the positions of the British ships. Orders were issued "that the Marines under Captain Welsh should land and take possession of the island . . . covered by armed vessels."[36] Militia under Gen. Wadsworth would feint another landing on Bagaduce to cover the attempt on Banks.[37]

At sunset two 14-gun brigs and the Continental sloop of war *Providence* moved close inshore off Banks, protecting 200 marines loaded in whaleboats.[38] The landing party quickly covered the distance to the beach, grounded, leaped ashore, and charged through the thick brush seeking the enemy. Discretion being the better part of valor, their opponents on this occasion, 20 Royal Marines, precipitously abandoned their four small field pieces and high-tailed it over the hump of the island to the harbor side.[39] Artillerymen from Revere's command, with the help of seamen and marines, brought two 18-pounders, a 12-pounder, and a howitzer ashore.[40] The night was spent in erecting a breastwork on the highest point of the island and emplacing the cannon.

At dawn on 27 July the new battery

---

[29]Quoted in "The Narrative of William Hutchings," a native of the Penobscot area who worked on the defenses of Fort George, and included in Wheeler, *op. cit.*, 323.
[30]*Calef Journal*, 17-8.
[31]*Ibid.*, 18.
[32]*Ibid.*
[33]*Lovell Journal*, 30; *Revere Diary*, II, 364.
[34]*Calef Journal*, 19.

[35]*Ibid.*
[36]*Massachusetts Revolutionary Archives*, CXLV, 246, quoted in McCellan, *op. cit.*, 21.
[37]*Revere Diary*, II, 365.
[38]McClellan, *op. cit.*, 21.
[39]*Calef Journal*, 19.
[40]*Revere Diary*, II, 365.

opened up, drawing a smart return fire from the British men-of-war. The superior position of the Americans soon began to tell, however, as solid shot hulled the sloops. Three hours of this unequal exchange were enough to convince Capt. Mowat that his position was untenable. The three ships slipped anchor and moved farther into the harbor.[41] The battery on Banks, having cleared the harbor mouth, was now free to engage the British outworks on Bagaduce. Both sides kept up a desultory fire throughout the day, each seeking, ineffectively, to silence the other's guns.

The main business of the expedition was now at hand. With the British ships cleared from their stations near the head of the peninsula, the way was clear for an assault. At the war council on the *Warren* Saltonstall added 227 marines, reembarked after their success at Banks Island, to the land forces under Lovell.[42] The decision was made to put every available man ashore; even Revere's cannoneers were given muskets and drafted as the infantry reserve. The landing force was split into three divisions: marines on the right under Welsh, militia in the center and on the left under Wadsworth.[43] A narrow, easily defended isthmus on one side of Bagaduce and the aggressive British ships on the other limited the choice of landing beaches to the narrow strip of sand at the foot of the steep and heavily forested bluff on the peninsula's western face. Ships' fire arching overhead would cover the boats on their way to shore but the tangled foliage concealed most targets. Bayonet and ball would have to clear the path.

Shortly after midnight of the 28th, the militiamen, seamen, and marines began manning whaleboats from the transports and warships for the landing. Saltonstall's orders "to begin fire into the Woods with an intent to scower them of the Enemy"[44] were answered at 0300, when two ships and three brigs commenced firing on the landing area. Just before dawn the last boats were filled, divisions formed, and the sailors bent to their oars.

The covering ships now moved in closer, raising their tempo of fire to protect the troops in the open boats. Atop the bluff men from the 82d Foot were seeking protection among the trees from the plunging cannon shot and crashing branches. Word was passed to hold fire until the Americans touched shore.[45] Ships' cannon ceased fire as the leading elements of the landing force, 200 marines and 200 militiamen, hit the beach. Men scrambled out of the boats as the first scattered shots found targets. The militiamen in the center, unable to climb the steep slopes to their front, began firing to cover the flank assault groups. These men, grasping the shrubbery to keep from sliding back, fought their way up the bluff face.[46] The green men of the Hamilton regiment, getting their first taste of battle, let loose one volley which caught the struggling climbers and then withdrew through the woods toward the fort.[47]

On the left of the British line, determined resistance was offered by a small detachment of 20 men guarding the rear of the harbor battery. The attacking marines attempting to flank this outpost were temporarily held up despite musket volleys loosed as close as 30 yards, which cut down 7 of the 20 defenders.[48] Numbers soon began to tell, however, and these last defenders soon fell back

[41]*Calef Journal,* 19.
[42]McClellan, *op. cit.,* 21.
[43]*Revere Diary,* II, 367.
[44]*Revolutionary Rolls,* XXXIX, 113, quoted in Allen, *op. cit.,* II, 426.
[45]Letter from Lt. John Moore to his father quoted in Moore, *op. cit.,* 22, hereinafter cited as *Moore Letter.*

[46]Letter from Peleg Wadsworth to William D. Williamson, January 1, 1828, contained in Goold, N., *History of Colonel Jonathan Mitchell's Cumberland County Regiment of the Bagaduce Expedition* (Portland, Me., 1899), 19-22.
[47]*Moore Letter,* 22.
[48]*Ibid.,* 23.

through the trees. In the short space of 20 minutes, at the cost of 14 dead (including the senior marine officer, Capt. Welsh) and 20 wounded, the Americans had gained a toehold on the peninsula. The Hamilton regiment as it withdrew toward the guns of Ft. George left behind 15 dead and 8 stragglers, mostly wounded.[49]

The Americans took advantage of their initial successes and before the sun was fairly up the entire landing force was ashore and following the British through the woods. Lovell halted the advance, however, 600 yards from the low walls of the fort and sent orders to Revere to bring in his cannon.[50] Soon the flush of victory faded in the confusion of orders and aimless marching and countermarching as the Americans retired to assembly points out of reach of enemy guns.

Troops manning the makeshift walls of Ft. George expected momentarily to see the Americans break from the cover of the woods and charge to overwhelm their defenses. McLean, who thought till the end that he was opposed by a force of 300 men, stood by the halyards of the garrison's flag. As he wrote later, "I was in no situation to defend myself, I meant only to give them one or two guns, so as not to be called a coward, and then to have struck my colours, which I stood by for some time to do, as I did not wish to throw away the lives of my men for nothing."[51] It soon became apparent, however, that both troops and commander were needlessly apprehensive. Their opponents did not attack; in fact they gave every evidence of attempting to conduct a classical siege operation in the rugged woods of Maine.[52]

It was not long before another abortive naval attack was added to the day's lost opportunities. Saltonstall in the *Warren*, leading three of the heaviest gunned ships, again attempted to break Capt. Mowat's line. During a sharp half-hour exchange the American flagship was hit twice in the mainmast, once each in the bowspit and forestay, and nearly rammed ashore. The *Warren* retired to repair the damage, leading her ineffective flotilla out of the range of the sharpshooting British sloops.[53] The battery on Banks Island took up the fight, forcing Mowat to retire farther up the river that night. After an auspicious beginning, the Americans had again bogged down through lack of aggressive leadership. McLean put his men to work strengthening defenses and Mowat anchored his ships to protect the fort's flank.[54]

The Americans spent the next two days cutting a road from the beach to a position where artillery could pound the rapidly growing British defenses.[55] Late in the afternoon of 30 July the new battery, two 18-pounders, one 12 and a howitzer, opened fire. The British, meanwhile, had sunk three of their transports and added the cannon and crews to the fort's garrison. Mowat contributed more cannon from the offside batteries of the sloops and sent his Marines and 140 seamen ashore to augment McLean's command and assist in constructing the fort's defenses.[56] Both sides spent the 31st in "the usual sport of cannonading at each other."[57]

A heavy fog that night provided concealment for a force of 300 men under Gen. Wadsworth, composed of marines, sailors from the men-of-war, and militiamen, who moved through the woods guided by Indians and surrounded an outlying battery guarding the approaches to the fort from the harbor.

[49] *Lovell Journal*, 32.
[50] *Revere Diary*, II, 368.
[51] Statement of Col. Brewer of the Maine militia in the *Bangor Whig and Courier*, August 13, 1846, quoted in Wheeler, *op. cit.*, 332.
[52] *Moore Letter*, 25.

[53] *Calef Journal*, 20.
[54] *Ibid.*, 21.
[55] *Revere Diary*, II, 369.
[56] *Calef Journal*, 22, 29.
[57] Journal of Orderly Sergeant Lawrence of the Royal Artillery contained in Wheeler, *op. cit.*, 316, hereinafter cited as *Lawrence Journal*.

The battery picquet, seamen and marines from Mowat's ships, was driven in by heavy fire from the attackers who overran the position. At daylight 50 men of the 82d sortied from the fort, caught the recent victors unawares and succeeded in recapturing the lost guns, which they then removed to the main defenses.[58] This fruitless exchange cost both sides about 20 men killed, wounded, and prisoners,[59] and was typical of the actions of the following days.

During the next week the Americans watched the bastions and walls of Fort George grow stronger despite the fire of their cannon. Battery positions were begun by the attackers on the mainland in an attempt to ring the peninsula and cut off the effective cooperation of ships and fort.[60] The British retaliated by erecting a redoubt on the eastern end of Bagaduce, manned by seamen and guns from Mowat's sloops, which protected the line of communication.[61] By day the cannon of both sides exchanged shot, killing and wounding an occasional man. At night the guardboats of both fleets ranged the waters of the harbor entrance repeating the exchange of fire. Raiding parties from both sides clashed in the woods as the siege wore on, but the strain was beginning to tell on the poorly disciplined militiamen and privateer seamen far more than on the regulars of McLean's and Mowat's forces.

Morale on board the ships of the American fleet had nosedived after the successful landing when it became increasingly clear that Mowat's sloops refused to recognize that they were outnumbered and outgunned and continued to offer effective resistance. Privateer captains, knowing the temper of their men and anxious for the safety of their valuable commerce raiders, seconded the cautious Saltonstall when he demanded that Fort George be taken before he ventured into the harbor again. Until the landing force silenced the fort's cannon on his flank, he said, "I am not going to risk my shipping in that damned hole."[62]

Ashore, militia commanders were equally adamant that the British ships must be taken before their men could storm the fort. It was feared that a crossfire from the harbor and the fort would be too much for the green troops. Already the constant cannonading, the probing attacks of McLean's men, and the deep gloom of the woods in which they encamped had taken its toll. The war council of 11 August concluded "that on an alarm on any special occasion, nearly one fourth part of the army skulked out of the way and concealed."[63] By 7 August, a poll of field officers showed only one who felt that he could hold his men in the open field against the enemy, the rest being uncertain of the results of a pitched battle.[64]

This lack of confidence was reflected in the war councils where progressively stronger sentiment was recorded for raising the siege. In this division of opinion, Saltonstall was consistently for abandoning the undertaking,[65] while Lovell felt the fort could be taken.[66] The general's optimism was shaken more than a little, however, on 11 August, when a party of 200 militiamen maneuvering in the opening to the south of the fort fled in "utmost disorder"[67] when fired upon by a scouting party of 50 men from the 82d.[68]

It finally took the Naval Board of the Eastern District sitting in Boston to resolve

[58]*Calef Journal*, 23.
[59]*Ibid.; Lovell Journal*, 32.
[60]*Revere Diary*, II, 370.
[61]*Calef Journal*, 26.

[62]Quoted in Brewer statement, see footnote 51.
[63]Proceedings of a council of war held at Lovell's headquarters, 11 August 1779, quoted in Goss, *op. cit.*, II, 331.
[64]*Revere Diary*, II, 329-30.
[65]*Ibid.*, II, 371-3; *Proceedings*, 67.
[66]*Lovell Journal*, 34; Captured letter from Lovell to Saltonstall appended to *Calef Journal*, 40-41; *Proceedings*, 67.
[67]*Revere Diary*, II, 372.
[68]*Lawrence Journal*, 318.

the impasse between the fleet and the army. A dispatch boat arrived on 12 August bearing orders to Saltonstall to press the attack on the British ships.[69] Preparations were made for a concerted assault on the 13th.

Deserters and prisoners had kept McLean and Mowat informed of the state of their opponents.[70] In contrast to the Americans, the British spirits were high. One artillery sergeant summed up the garrison's feeling in those tense days when he wrote, "We were always in expectation of their coming to storm us, and we were as ready to receive them at the point of our bayonets."[71] In the face of impending American attack the British commanders made their last preparations. Boarding pikes and cutlasses were issued to the seamen ashore in the garrison and ships were stripped of guns, powder, and shot to the limit of safety to reinforce the fort and its outworks.[72]

One factor underlying the attitude of both sides towards the coming battle was the knowledge that the Royal Navy controlled the seas.[73] Should the American fleet be caught in the restricted waters of the Penobscot by the king's ships, the results could be disastrous. On the other hand, should a relief expedition fail to arrive in time, the weight of the American ships' guns, if handled aggressively, would certainly decide the issue.

A heavy fog during most of 13 August screened Lovell as he personally led 400 men through the sparse woods to the southeast of the fort and took position in its rear ready for the planned assault.[74] The same fog blanket covered Saltonstall as he maneuvered five of the most powerful American ships, doubly manned with picked seamen and marines, to

enter the harbor.[75] The British, afloat and ashore, double-shotted their guns, passed orders to hold station, and awaited the two-pronged assault. In late afternoon the fog lifted, and lookouts from both sides spotted five sail far down the bay.[76] The Americans had waited too long to make their move.

Scout boats soon confirmed the sighting and identified the strangers, seven British ships led by the 64-gun *Raisonable,* flagship of Adm. Sir George Collier.[77] Fortunately, a heavy, driving rain began to fall at dusk, covering the withdrawal of the Americans. Revere and his men, aided by militiamen and sailors, worked feverishly to get off the cannon ashore on Bagaduce. All else was abandoned in precipitous haste. By daylight the expedition's troops were again aboard ship hoping for a miracle to enable them to break through the blocking force downstream.[78]

The Americans got underway at 0700, but the tide was against them so that most of the slower ships and transports fled up the Penobscot River. The fighting ships formed line of battle, but evidently lost their desire to engage when the van of the British fleet came steadily onward. It soon was every ship for itself as they fled in all directions. Lovell, from his post on the deck of a transport, observed the rout and later wrote that an "attempt to give a description to this terrible day is out of my Power, it would be a fit subject for some masterly hand to describe in its true colours, to see four ships pursuing seventeen sail of Armed Vessels, nine of which were stout ships, Transports on fire, Men of War blowing up . . ."[79]

For this was the end result of the day's action. Not a ship escaped, all were either run ashore and burned by their crews, blown up to escape capture, or taken by the British

[69]*Proceedings,* 65.
[70]*Calef Journal,* 28.
[71]*Lawrence Journal,* 316.
[72]*Calef Journal,* 29.
[73]*Lovell Journal,* 34.
[74]*Ibid.,* 36; *Revere Diary,* II, 373.

[75]*Calef Journal,* 29.
[76]*Ibid.; Lovell Journal,* 36.
[77]*Calef Journal,* 29.
[78]*Revere Diary,* II, 374.
[79]*Lovell Journal,* 36.

fleet.[80] The American seamen, militiamen and marines left their burning ships and retreated through the woods to Boston.[81] Before the last stragglers were in, charge and countercharge of cowardice began to fly. Saltonstall was courtmartialed and cashiered for his conduct at the siege, and others very nearly received the same treatment.[82] Massachusetts learned to its sorrow that the expedition had cost them 1,739,174 pounds (about $8,500,000), a sum which discouraged the state's appetite for any retaliatory forays.[83] So the British retained their hold on Fort George until January 1784, when the garrison evacuated this last fort to be held in New England territory.[84] Seldom has there been such a complete defeat in our military history. And seldom have the reasons for that defeat been so overwhelmingly obvious.

An amphibious attack is at best a hazardous undertaking and perhaps requires more careful, detailed planning than any other type of military operation. Over the span of years, from British landings during the Napoleonic Wars to American assaults in Korea, this principle has been repeatedly proven. And it has followed logically that veteran troops, or in lieu of them thoroughly trained and well-disciplined new levies, should be used in this type of operation.

It is axiomatic that a divided house must fall, and by the same token two men cannot concurrently exercise command over an operation without precipitating serious problems that have no place in a successfully conducted assault. Even if an attack force does have a smoothly functioning chain of command, leaders at all levels must be just that—leaders. An amphibious assault requires swift and decisive action by commanders, whether in contact with the enemy or in support of attacking troops.

The Penobscot Bay Expedition was unsuccessful because it violated in large part most of the foregoing principles. When the expedition left Boston, the groundwork had already been laid for its defeat. There was no overall commander, and the fleet was a jerry-rigged organization thrown together at the last moment to transport and support a landing force wholly inadequate for the task assigned.

Despite these grave defects, victory was within the Americans' grasp at one point, the Bagaduce landing, but slipped out again because of a definite lack of aggressive leadership on both land and sea. This, then, might be the outstanding lesson to be learned from the Penobscot Bay fiasco, as, indeed, it is in most military operations — the precept that vigilant, aggressive, and intelligent leadership is the keystone to military success.

[80]*Calef Journal*, 30-33; Admiralty Captains Log No. 118 of HMS *Blonde*, quoted in Allen, *op. cit.*, II, 433-4.
[81]See the journal of Drummer Moody of Col. Mitchell's Regiment in Goold, *op. cit.*, 30-34.
[82]Goss, *op. cit.*, II, 317-79.
[83]Introduction to copy of Calef journal in *The Magazine of History*, III, 1910, 296.
[84]Goss, *op. cit.*, II, 374.